Relativism

'It's all relative.' In a world of increasing cultural diversity, it can seem that everything is indeed relative. But should we concede that there is no such thing as right and wrong, and no objective truth?

Relativism surveys the different varieties of relativism and the arguments for and against them, and examines why relativism has survived for two thousand years despite all the criticisms levelled against it. Beginning with a historical overview, from Protagoras in ancient Greece to Derrida and postmodernism, Maria Baghramian explores the resurgence of relativism throughout the history of philosophy. She then turns to the arguments for and against the many subdivisions of relativism, including Kuhn and Feyerabend's ideas of relativism in science, Rorty's views on truth, and the conceptual relativism of Quine and Putnam. Baghramian questions whether moral relativism leads to moral indifference or even nihilism, and whether feminist epistemology's concerns about the very notion of objectivity can be considered a form of relativism. She concludes the relativism debate by assessing the recent criticisms such as Davidson's claim that even the motivations behind relativism are unintelligible. Finding these criticisms lacking, Baghramian proposes a moderate form of pluralism which addresses the legitimate worries that give rise to relativism without incurring charges of nihilism or anarchy.

Relativism is essential reading for anyone interested in contemporary philosophy, sociology and politics.

Maria Baghramian is Senior Lecturer in Philosophy at University College Dublin. She is editor of *Modern Philosophy of Language* (1998) and co-editor of *Pluralism: The Philosophy and Politics of Diversity* (Routledge 2002). She also edits the *International Journal of Philosophical Studies*.

The Problems of Philosophy

Editors: Tim Crane and Jonathan Wolff
University College London

This series addresses the central problems of philosophy. Each book gives a fresh account of a particular philosophical theme by offering two perspectives on the subject: the historical context and the author's own distinctive and original contribution. The books are written to be accessible to students of philosophy and related disciplines, while taking the debate to a new level.

Recently published:

Relativism

Maria Baghramian

Routledge
Taylor & Francis Group

LONDON AND NEW YORK

First published 2004
by Routledge
2 Park Square, Milton Park, Abingdon, Oxfordshire, OX14 4RN

Simultaneously published in the USA and Canada
by Routledge
270 Madison Avenue, New York, NY 10016

Routledge is an imprint of the Taylor & Francis Group

© 2004 Maria Baghramian

Typeset in Times by The Running Head Limited, Cambridge
Printed and bound in Great Britain by
TJ International Ltd, Padstow, Cornwall

British Library Cataloguing in Publication Data
A catalogue record for this book is available from the British Library

Library of Congress Cataloging in Publication Data
Baghramian, Maria
Relativism / Maria Baghramian
p. cm. — (The problems of philosophy)
Includes bibliographical references and index
1. Relativism. I. Title. II. Series: Problems of philosophy (Routledge (Firm))
BD221.B34 2004
149—dc222004000297

ISBN 0–415–16149–5 (hbk)
ISBN 0–415–16150–9 (pbk)

*For my mother, Gohar Baghramian, and
in memory of my father, Gregor Baghramian*

A spectre haunts human thought: relativism. If truth has many faces, then not one of them deserves trust or respect.

(Ernest Gellner 1982: 181)

Relativism, like scepticism, is one of those doctrines that have by now been refuted a number of times too often. Nothing is perhaps a surer sign that a doctrine embodies some not-to-be-neglected truth than that in the course of the history of philosophy it should have been refuted again and again. Genuinely refutable doctrines only need to be refuted once.

(Alasdair MacIntyre 1985: 22)

§661: Where two principles really do meet which cannot be reconciled with one another, then each man declares the other a fool and heretic.

(Ludwig Wittgenstein 1968: 81e)

Forms of life differ. Ends, moral principles, are many. But not infinitely many: they must be within the human horizon. If they are not, then they are outside the human sphere.

(Isaiah Berlin 1991: 11)

Contents

Contents

Acknowledgements

Many people have encouraged me to pursue this project and helped me along the way. The late and greatly missed John Blacking in his provocative undergraduate lectures on social anthropology was the first person to show me the shape of the intellectual debate surrounding this topic. Colleagues in University College Dublin and elsewhere have given helpful comments on various aspects of the book. Special thanks to Dermot Moran, Richard Kearney, Attracta Ingram, Rowland Stout, Iseult Honohan, Jim O'Shea, Brian O'Connor, Tim Mooney, Jack Ritchie, Máire O'Neill, Eoin Ryan, Vasilis Politis, Jim Levine, Tim Williamson, Philip Pettit, and Patrick Honohan who have been generous with their support and advice. Hilary Putnam's influence permeates much of this book. I am grateful to him for his kindness and generosity.

Mary Boland and Gayle Kenny have helped me with the preparation of the manuscript and have given me valuable assistance. The students in my MA classes and my research students have contributed more than they might realise. Mary Buckley, Margaret Brady and Máire Doyle in their unfailingly capable ways have made for pleasant working conditions in the Department and the Faculty. Our current head of Department, Gerard Casey, has provided an atmosphere conducive to research.

Some of the ideas in this book were presented at conferences in Ireland, England, Germany, the USA, and the Czech Republic. I thank the participants for their helpful comments. A President's Research Fellowship enabled me to complete this work, and I am very grateful for having received it. A grant from University College Dublin Publications Fund covered the cost of indexing. I am grateful for it too. I am also grateful to three anonymous referees who offered invaluable criticisms and suggestions. The series editors, Tim Crane and Jonathan Wolff, have been valued advisers and friends. Working with Tony

Acknowledgements

Bruce at Routledge over the past many years has been enormously rewarding. His editorial insight and unfailing optimism and calm were great sources of help. My friends in Ireland have given me loyalty and support in ways I had not experienced before; my life and work would be much poorer without them. My greatest debt of gratitude goes to my family. Without the constant support, encouragement and prodding of my husband, Hormoz Farhat, this book would never have been finished. Our son Robert gives meaning to everything I do. My mother Gohar Baghramian and my late father Gregor Baghramian in their outlooks to life exemplified some of the diversity that motivates the ideas behind this book. I lovingly dedicate it to them.

Introduction

The many faces of relativism

This book was written out of the conviction that the cluster of views falling under the heading of 'relativism', despite many problematic features, captures important insights. As a member of three distinct cultural and linguistic groupings (Armenian–Iranian–Irish) and as I attempt to negotiate their at times conflicting social and ethical outlooks, I remain convinced of the fact of diversity and the significance of intellectual and political efforts to comprehend and accommodate it. The idea of relativism arises out of an acknowledgement of the existence of deep differences in attitudes and beliefs. In the wake of political ideologies with global and universal aspirations, relativism has come to occupy a prominent place in the intellectual ethos of our time. It has become a constant theme in the theoretical orientation of various fields – including the social sciences, literary theory and cultural studies – and is often treated as a credo by undergraduate students in humanities. At its most basic, relativism is the view that cognitive, moral or aesthetic norms and values are dependent on the social or conceptual systems that underpin them, and consequently a neutral standpoint for evaluating them is not available to us. This simple definition, however, ultimately proves unsatisfactory since the single label 'relativism' has been used for a great variety of doctrines and positions. In analytic philosophical circles relativism is either dismissed readily as an incoherent position or is identified with irrationalism and cognitive anarchy. For instance, Popper argues:

> One of the more disturbing aspects of the intellectual life of our time is the way in which irrationalism is so widely advocated, and the way in which irrationalist doctrines are taken for granted. One of the components of modern irrationalism is relativism (the doctrine that truth is relative to our intellectual background).
>
> (Popper 1994: 33)

1

Such a dismissive attitude has not had much impact on the popularity of the doctrine outside the confines of analytic philosophical circles. Philosophical arguments against relativism have failed partly because its opponents have ignored the variety of doctrines coming under that title, and partly for the lack of due attention to the reasons that have made it into an attractive philosophical position for many thinkers over the past two thousand years. In addition, opponents of relativism have a tendency to conflate the arguments against the various strands of relativism and consequently miss their target. This book attempts to understand the allure of relativism by looking at the family of doctrines that fall under its general heading, and to critically evaluate some key versions of it.

WHAT IS RELATIVISM?

Relativism is frequently defined negatively, in terms of the doctrines it denies, as well as positively, in terms of what it affirms (see, for instance, Harré and Krausz 1996: 24). Defined negatively, relativism amounts to the denial of a cluster of interconnected philosophical positions that are traditionally contrasted with it; in this sense negative relativism is 'anti-anti-relativism'[1] for it provides legitimacy for relativism by denying:

(a) the thesis of universalism or the position that there could and should be universal agreement on matters of truth, goodness, beauty, meaningfulness, etc.;
(b) the thesis of objectivism or the position that cognitive, ethical and aesthetic values such as truth, goodness and beauty are mind-independent, 'capable of being presented from a point of view that is independent of the point of view of any human being in particular and of human kind in general' (see ibid.);
(c) the thesis of absolutism or the view that truth, goodness, beauty, etc. are timeless, unchanging and immutable;
(d) monism or the view that, in any given area or on any given topic, there can be no more than one correct opinion, judgement, or norm. Relativism is compatible with local but not universal monism, for a relativist may accept that in any given culture or society there can be no more than one correct view on any topic but deny that one single correct norm or belief can apply cross-culturally.[2]

A number of philosophers who, despite their protestations, are

2

frequently accused of being relativists – Hilary Putnam, Nelson Goodman, Richard Rorty, and maybe even Jacques Derrida – can be seen as negative relativists in so far as they tend to deny a–d, but do not accept straightforward attempts to relativise epistemic and moral values to social or historical contexts.[3]

It is more difficult to define the positive claim of relativism. We can begin by distinguishing between relative and non-relative (or absolute) properties. A property is non-relative if its ascription depends only on the subject to which it is being attributed. For instance, 'three-dimensional' is a non-relative property because whether an object can be rightly described as possessing three dimensions depends only on the spatial features of the object under consideration. A property is relative, on the other hand, if its correct ascription depends on additional background factors. Robert Nozick gives the example of the probability of a statement or an event as an instance of something relative – the probability of a statement varies with different evidence and is not detachable from the evidence available (Nozick 2001: 17). Some properties can be construed both in absolute and relative terms – poverty is a case in point. Absolute poverty is usually defined in terms of not possessing or being able to obtain the bare necessities of life. Poverty is seen as a relative property when its ascription involves a comparison to the standards of life prevailing in a society or a given historic period. (Someone with a monthly income equivalent to €300 would be considered poor in Ireland but not in Chad.) Relativised properties often only implicitly involve a reference to background factors (such as social or cultural background); however, we cannot determine whether the property in question is present or not if these non-explicit background factors are not specified.[4] The background factors to be brought into consideration may be construed in two distinct ways. We can, at least in principle, distinguish between (a) relativisation to the circumstances or the contexts in which an ascription or an evaluation takes place (agent or speaker relativism) and (b) relativisation to the context or background of the objects of ascription or evaluation. For instance, in moral philosophy the truth of a statement such as 'slavery is wrong' may be relativised to the society in which the sentence is uttered or to the society about which the sentence is uttered.[5] In cases where the speaker and object of evaluation belong to the same society (e.g., Aristotle speaking about slavery in ancient Greece) the judgement 'slavery is wrong' will receive the same valuation whichever mode of relativisation we adopt. In cases where the evaluator belongs to a different society or background than the object of evaluation, today's Ireland for

3

instance, there will be a discrepancy between the outcomes of the evaluations.

Relative properties should be distinguished from what I call 'relational properties'. Relational properties, such as being colder or taller, are dyadic properties predicated in contexts where two or more subjects are being compared, contrasted or otherwise connected. The difference between relative and relational properties can be expressed in terms of the distinction between one-place and many-place (meaning two or more) predicates. One-place predicates have only one subject place, as in 'John is tall'. Two-term predicates, such as 'John is taller than George', involve two, not necessarily distinct, subject terms. Similarly for three-place relational predicates, such as 'between', and many place predicates (e.g., 'tallest' among the ten boys in his class). Relative properties have the appearance of being monadic properties. They can be, and often are, expressed by one-place predicates, but they are elliptical for two- or many-place predicates. For instance, 'John is poor', where 'poor' is used as a relative predicate, has the grammatical form of a one-place predicate, but is elliptical for 'John is poor in relation to (i.e., in comparison with) other members of his society'. Relativists propose that predicates such as 'is true', 'is right', 'is rational' have the apparent logical form of one-place predicates, but that a correct analysis or understanding of them would show that they are in fact elliptical for two-place predicates such as 'is true relative to', 'is right according to', etc. In general then, according to the relativist, a statement of the form 'A is P', within a given domain (e.g., science, ethics, metaphysics), is elliptical for the statement 'A is P in relation to C', where A stands for an assertion, belief, judgement or action, P stands for (normative) predicates such as 'is true', 'is beautiful, 'is right', 'is rational' 'is logical', 'is known', etc., and C stands for a specific culture, framework, language, belief-system, etc.[6] The framework or culture may be that of the person engaged in evaluation or the culture to which the object of evaluation belongs. The relativity clause 'in relation to C' is often not stated explicitly but is thought to be inherent in the statement of 'A is P'. Relational properties can also be relativised. For example, the relational (dyadic) judgement 'child-abuse is a more heinous crime than murder', according to a relativist, is elliptical for 'child-abuse is a more heinous crime than murder according to the standards of culture C'. In this sense, relative predicates cut across the distinction between relational and non-relational (monadic) predicates.

It is also commonplace to distinguish between the class of judgements whose truth and falsity depend on their context (time, place, location, setting, etc.), e.g., 'I have been sitting here since this morning', and those whose truth and falsity obtains independently of context and indexical attributes, e.g., Maria Baghramian was sitting at the desk, in room D503, Department of Philosophy, University College Dublin, 8:30 a.m. to 12:30 p.m. on Friday, 13 October 2002. Relativists argue that, contrary to common assumption, all judgements are context-dependent. For instance, a statement or a judgement such as 'murder is wrong' cannot be deemed true or false (*tout court*), rather, it should be understood as 'murder is wrong according to . . .', or 'in the context of the cultural, historical, social norms of culture x murder is wrong'. The relativist, in effect, is claiming that she is uncovering the correct logical form of a class of statements that have been misunderstood and misapplied by non-relativists.

The relativist claim, then, is that the presence or absence of properties such as truth, rationality, goodness, etc., and the correct ascription of predicates such as 'is true', 'is rational', 'is ethical', etc., depend not only on the objects to which the ascription is being made but also on factors such as social and cultural norms, cognitive frameworks, historical epochs, etc.[7] Furthermore, it is assumed that it is impossible to rank judgements of truth or falsity, etc. or to privilege one over another, for all cultures, historical epochs or cognitive frameworks that give rise to such judgements have equal standing. As Robert Nozick puts it, 'relativism is egalitarian' (Nozick 2001: 19).

VARIETIES OF RELATIVISM

Relativism takes many shapes and forms and their conflation has made an intricate problem even more difficult. One difficulty facing discussions of relativism is the absence of a consensus on how to classify its various forms. A plethora of issues common to relativisms of different hues makes the task of classification quite difficult. A useful way of approaching the issue is by posing the dual questions:

What is being relativised? Or what are the objects of relativisation? and
What is the object of relativisation being relativised to? Or what is the context of relativisation?

Susan Haack (1996: 5), in attempting to answer these questions, has proposed an identikit picture of various types of relativism, which has been used by other writers on the subject (see, for instance, O'Grady 2002). According to Haack:

(1) Meaning is relative to (a) language.
(2) Reference is relative to (b) conceptual schemes.
(3) Truth is relative to (c) theory.
(4) Metaphysical commitment is relative to (d) scientific paradigm.
(5) Ontology is relative to (e) version, depiction, description.
(6) Reality is relative to (f) culture.
(7) Epistemic values are relative to (g) community.
(8) Moral values are relative to (h) individuals.
(9) Aesthetic values are relative to (i) historical periods.

Haack's identikit tends to over-complicate the task of classification, and yet does not fully capture the various permutations of the relativistic claims. To take a few examples, moral and epistemic values, as well as truth, as we shall see, are often relativised to cultures, communities and individuals; frequently no clear distinction is drawn between language, theory and conceptual schemes (see, for instance, the discussion of Quine in chapter 7); the distinction between reality, ontology, and metaphysical commitment is unclear, and even if a case can be made for distinguishing between them, the distinction is not observed by those engaged in debates on these issues.

The following is a more economical way of classifying different types of relativism: Depending on whether cognitive, moral or aesthetic norms are being considered we can distinguish between the broad categories of cognitive, moral and aesthetic relativism. Cognitive relativism is the view that what is true or false, rational or irrational, valid or invalid can vary from one society, culture or historical epoch to another and that we have no trans-cultural or ahistorical method or standard for adjudicating between the conflicting cognitive norms and practices. Within the broad category of cognitive relativism we can make finer-grained distinctions between: relativism about truth (or alethic relativism); relativism about rationality, norms of reasoning and justification; relativism about knowledge-claims (or what in this book I call 'epistemic relativism'); and relativism about ontology or theories of what there is (or conceptual relativism). Relativism about truth and relativism about logic are the strongest forms of cognitive relativism and, as we shall see, they can entail both epistemic relativism and relativism about rationality. However, it is possible to defend a relativistic position regarding rationality and knowledge without espousing either of these stronger claims.

Moral relativists claim that the truth or falsity, the appropriateness or inappropriateness of an ethical belief, is relative to its socio-historical background and that moral beliefs cannot be assessed independently of their social framework. They point to the existence of diverse moral systems and maintain that moral values are grounded on societal conventions, historical conditions, metaphysical beliefs, etc., which vary from one society or social grouping to another, and argue that there are no neutral standards available to adjudicate between these competing claims. Aesthetic relativism rehearses the arguments put forward by the moral relativists, with the difference that it is values such as beauty, originality, creativity (in other words, aesthetic rather than moral values) that are relativised.

The question of what the cognitive, moral and aesthetic values are being relativised to carves up relativism in a slightly different way and allows us to distinguish between subjective relativism (or subjectivism[8]), social (cultural and historical) relativism, and conceptual relativism. Subjectivists or subjective relativists maintain that the truth and falsity of judgements, the right and wrong of actions, and the acceptability of ethical and aesthetic evaluations, are all in a non-trivial sense dependent on the beliefs and opinions of individual thinkers and actors – they are expressions of the private psychological states of agents.

Social relativism is the claim that the truth and falsity of beliefs, the justification for knowledge-claims and the right or wrong of actions, depend on and are relative to prevailing social and cultural conditions. According to this type of relativism, we are in a position to distinguish between true and false beliefs and right and wrong actions and judgements, but only within the parameters of socially given norms and conventions. Cultural relativism, inspired by the work of social anthropologists who conducted fieldwork among tribal people, is one of the most influential forms of social relativism where it is argued that there can be no such thing as a culturally neutral criterion for adjudicating between conflicting claims arising from different cultural contexts. Historicism, another subspecies of social relativism, is the view that all thought, knowledge and evaluation are constrained by their historical conditions and bear the imprints of their time and place. Historicism in its more extreme form is distinguishable from cultural relativism only in its emphasis on the diachronic rather than the synchronic dimensions of the determinants of thought and action.[9]

Conceptual relativism relativises ontology, or our theory of what there is, to conceptual schemes, scientific paradigms, world versions, categorial schemes or frameworks. Conceptual relativists argue that the world does not present itself to us ready-made or ready-carved, rather we supply the different ways of categorising and conceptualising it. Our knowledge of the world is mediated through a language, a theory or scheme and there is a plurality of such mediatory schemes. Conceptual relativism, when appropriately specified, can entail cognitive relativism, for it could be argued that acts of cognition are shaped, if not determined, by the conceptual scheme or framework within which they take place. Conceptual relativism would be co-extensive with cultural relativism if it were further assumed that conceptual frameworks are products of specific cultures. However, frequently the arguments adduced in favour of conceptual relativism are based on a priori reasoning about the relationship between the mind and the world rather than empirical observations about cultural and linguistic diversity. Moreover, many conceptual relativists, such as Hilary Putnam and Nelson Goodman, emphatically disassociate themselves from cultural relativism.

The classification I am suggesting can be presented in the following table.

Objects	*Contexts*
α Cognitive norms: truth, rationality, logic, epistemic standards (cognitive relativism, epistemic relativism)	I Individuals (subjectivism)
β Moral values (moral relativism)	II Historical epochs (historicism)
γ Aesthetic values (aesthetic relativism)	III Cultures, social groupings (cultural relativism, social relativism)
δ Knowledge claims, worldviews,[10] ontologies, systems of belief (cognitive, conceptual, and epistemic relativism)	IV Conceptual schemes: languages, theories, frameworks (conceptual relativism)

The important point to note is that each of α–δ may be relativised to either I, II, III or IV.[11] We can now see how Haack's identikit fits into this scheme; focusing on Haack's list a–i allows us to distinguish broadly between subjectivism (h) social (cultural and historical) relativism (f, g, i) and conceptual relativism (a–e). On the other hand, 1–9 fit into the categories of cognitive relativism (3–7), conceptual relativism (1, 2, 4, 5, 6), moral relativism (8) and aesthetic relativism (9).[12]

More detailed distinctions can be made between different types of relativism by focusing on the scope rather than the content of relativistic claims. Philosophers have distinguished between restricted (first-order) and total (second-order) relativism (e.g., Putnam, 1981;

Hankinson, 1995). First-order relativism is the claim that specific judgements, for instance moral, cognitive and aesthetic judgements, are relative to social and cultural norms. Second-order or total relativism claims that all judgements – including this one – are relative. In addition to making the distinctions introduced above, I shall differentiate between strong and moderate (or restricted) relativism. Strong relativism is the claim that *all* cognitive and moral values (epistemic, aesthetic or ethical norms) are relative to a cultural/historical/individual outlook. Moderate (or restricted) relativism allows for the existence of some universal (non-relative) truths and norms either by restricting the relativistic claim to specific domains, e.g., the domain of ethical or aesthetic, or by conceding that even within a given domain, such as the ethical, there are some very general universal truths. The term 'relativism' has been qualified in numerous other ways and has been used in a variety of contexts. In the course of this book we will come across some of them.

Relativism should be distinguished from pluralism. Pluralism, as discussed in this book, is the claim that for many questions in the domains of metaphysics, aesthetics, ethics, and even science, there could be more than one appropriate or correct answer. The pluralist, like the relativist, rejects absolutism and monism but does not accept the relativists' claim that issues of truth, right and wrong, etc., can be arbitrated only relative to and in the context of their cultural or conceptual background. For the pluralists, in many domains and situations, there can be more than one correct *context-independent* evaluation and description.

WHY RELATIVISM?

A variety of not always compatible philosophical considerations and intellectual currents motivate the arguments for different types of relativism. This further complicates debates on the subject. Some of the main philosophical impulses motivating relativism are:

Context-dependence

Many of our judgements and assertions are expressed through sentences and expressions that refer to events that happen at a particular time and place and to particular persons. Such sentences seem to be true only at the time, place or context of their utterance. This is particularly true of sentences containing indexical expressions such as 'I', 'here', 'now', etc., whose reference varies with their context of utterance.

For instance, the sentence 'It's raining here now' is true at the time of writing this sentence but may be false when uttered at a different time or place. This feature of our judgements has led some to argue that the truth of all our judgements depends on, and in this sense is relative to, their time, place and context. This argument for relativism as it stands is not convincing. The context of utterances containing indexical expressions such as 'this', 'here', 'now', 'I', etc. can be made explicit in such a way that their truth or falsity would arise from specifiable events occurring at a particular time, place or context. For instance, in 'It's raining here now' 'here' and 'now' refer to Dublin and 12 September at 5:45 local time, 2002. And the sentence 'It's raining in Dublin on 12 September at 5:45 local time, 2002' is either true or false depending on the weather conditions in Dublin on that day.

Arguments for the context-dependence of human beliefs and judgements take other, philosophically more interesting, forms. For instance, it is often argued that all our judgements and beliefs are context-sensitive in that they always take place within a social and cultural framework and a background of both personal and collective assumptions, interests and values, and if not wholly determined, they are at least influenced by them. Beliefs are also situational, i.e., they are formed and held under specific physical and material conditions. Therefore, it is argued, evaluations of judgements should include a reference to their context and background conditions. But then such evaluations themselves would be influenced by their specific historical, cultural and psychological conditions, and hence no neutral ground for surveying beliefs and judgements is available.

Mind-dependence

Philosophers, opposing the realist claim that we can have knowledge of how things are in reality, have argued that all our judgements and beliefs, including those about the physical world, are irredeemably mind-dependent. A God's-eye view or a view from nowhere is not available to us. The suggestion is that 'It simply does not make sense to think of reality as it is in itself, apart from human judgements' (Miller 2002: 14). Such anti-realism should not be equated with relativism; however, as we shall see (in chapters 4 and 7 in particular), the arguments for mind-dependence and opposition to realism are often the starting point for various relativistic stands.

Perspectivalism

All reports of our experiences and judgements are made from a perspective or a point of view. We cannot get out of our skin, so to speak, or our language, culture and socio-historical conditions to survey reality, as it is, from a neutral standpoint. Perspectivalism goes beyond the mere context-dependence of our judgements in that even a seemingly context-independent judgement – for instance, 'there are nine planets in the solar system' – is a statement made from a human perspective and is informed by human perceptions and conceptions. Perspectivalism also implies that judgements are selective and constrained by the position we occupy in time and space as well as our interests and background knowledge. Relativism ensues if it is also assumed, explicitly or implicitly, that the different perspectives are non-convergent, and that what is true or right from one perspective may not be so from a different one, and that consequently, different perspectives may render incompatible judgements. The truth of such judgements, then, is relative to the perspective or point of view we adopt.

Considerations arising from the perspectival nature of human judgements also apply to arguments for conceptual relativism. It is argued that we are not in a position to decide which, if any, of the various conceptual perspectives available is correct or superior, since such a judgement would presuppose that there is something outside all perspectives to which they could be compared, or by the standards of which they could be judged. And since, per hypothesis, all thinking and judging is done from within a conceptual perspective, there can be no such neutral vantage point available to the would-be surveyor of the various schemes. We shall examine this view in detail in chapters 7, 8 and 10.

Philosophical Manichaeism

Arguments for relativism often assume the truth of various philosophical dichotomies – in particular the dichotomies of subjective vs. objective, the mind vs. the world, and the factual vs. the evaluative. Modern philosophy, from Descartes to Kant to the Logical Positivists, has bequeathed a number of dualisms which, despite their absolutist overtones, have contributed greatly to the development of relativistic tendencies in contemporary thought. For instance, the fact–value dichotomy has cleared the way for moral relativism; the distinction between the subjective and the objective has resulted in subjectivism and subjective relativism (see chapters 4 and 9); and the postulation of a strong divide between the mind and the world has led to conceptual relativism (chapters 7 and 10). I suggest that one way to bypass some pernicious forms of relativism is to overcome the philosophical Manichaeism inspiring them.

Underdetermination of empirical theory by data

The thesis of underdetermination states that more than one theory can successfully explain a given body of data, hence our selection of any one theory among a range of possibly incompatible theories will not be determined purely by the available evidence. The thesis plays a crucial role in W. V. O. Quine's ontological relativity (see chapter 7); it has also been instrumental in the development of relativistic views in science (see chapter 6) and has been used to defend both relativism and pluralism in ethics.

In addition to the above philosophical considerations, a number of intellectual currents have provided a ready ground for the development of relativistic views over the last century:

The collapse of old certainties

The disappearance of old certainties in the religious, political and scientific arenas has been instrumental in the popularity of relativism in recent times. The collapse of a religiously motivated cosmology, which fixed the position of individual human beings within a larger and immutable framework and provided firm foundations for their ethical outlook, helped to create a climate that was conducive to relativistic views. In science, the discovery of the possibility of non-Euclidean geometries, followed by developments of the early twentieth century, particularly Einstein's theory of relativity and the discoveries in quantum physics, eroded the confidence once placed in what was considered unassailable. The disillusionment with utopian political ideologies that espoused global aspirations, and the dismay experienced at the intractability of ethical and political problems also added to the attraction of relativism. As there seems to be neither a decision procedure for solving ideological conflicts nor a neutral ground to adjudicate between incompatible moral viewpoints, the only alternatives appear to be either to impose our worldview on others or to grant each person or culture full and incorrigible authority over the truth and justification of her beliefs and convictions.

Cultural diversity

Increasing awareness of the extent of the diversity of beliefs, practices and customs of different cultures and historical epochs has had a decisive impact on our ethical thinking. Reports by anthropologists about remote peoples have led to the suggestion that all normative judgements, whether cognitive or ethical, may have only a limited or local authority. Opponents of relativism, on the other hand, argue that the extent and scope of diversity between different cultures and individuals are often exaggerated. Beyond the apparent dissimilarities, they argue, there are many core similarities which unify all human cultures and systems of beliefs.

The prominence of social-scientific explanations

The nineteenth century saw the advent of the social sciences in their modern form. A variety of thinkers, e.g., Karl Marx, Max Weber and Wilhelm Dilthey, introduced the idea that genuine understanding of human beliefs and actions would inevitably include a reference to their social and economic background and historical context and that such contexts often determine the content of beliefs. Their ideas gained further prominence through the work of social anthropologists (e.g., Ruth Benedict, Margaret Mead), sociologists (e.g., Émile Durkheim, Talcott Parsons) and hermeneutic philosophers (e.g., Hans-Georg Gadamer), who in turn were central to the development of a relativistic orientation in twentieth-century thought.

The imperative of tolerance

The most common justifications offered on behalf of relativism have an ethical dimension. The social and political profile of those most sympathetic towards relativism often comprises those who feel marginalised, excluded or alienated from the dominant political (and intellectual) powers – the young, racial minorities, feminists, the political left, etc. Relativism is not only egalitarian but also liberating. It not only acknowledges our equal role and voice in constructing 'reality', 'facts', 'truths' and 'rights and wrongs', but it also liberates us from the shackles of the dominant paradigm. For many, relativism is a doctrine of tolerance and open-mindedness. Those sympathetic towards relativism argue that Western ethnocentrism and the intellectual legacy of the Enlightenment prevent us from appreciating or even seeing the uniqueness of different cultures and modes of thought and respecting the legitimacy of their epistemic and ethical claims. Allan Bloom, one of the most vocal opponents of relativism in recent years, has argued that:

> Openness – and the relativism that makes it the only plausi-ble stance in the face of various claims to truth and various ways of life and kinds of human beings – is [treated as] the great insight of our times . . .
>
> The study of history and of culture [according to this view] teaches that all the world was mad in the past; men always thought they were right, and that led to wars, persecutions, slavery, xenophobia, racism, and chauvinism. The point is not to correct the mistakes and really be right; rather it is not to think you are right at all.
>
> (Bloom 1987: 25–6)

Bloom pours scorn over the relativistic ethos of American universities but fails to appreciate the strength of the intellectual currents that have given rise to this ethos.

THE STRUCTURE

The books falls into two parts. Part I (chapters 1–3) provides a histor-ical examination of the idea of relativism in its many forms, from ancient Greece to the present. Part II critically examines a variety of relativistic doctrines in different domains.

According to the *Oxford English Dictionary*, the first use of the term 'relativism' can be traced to J. Grote's *Exploratio Philosophica* (1865):

> The notion of the mask over the face of nature is . . . *what I have called 'relativism'*. If 'the face of nature' is reality, then the mask over it, which is what theory gives us, is so much deception, and that is what relativism really comes to.
>
> (Grote 1865: I.xi: 229; emphasis added)

Grote in this passage seems to be discussing a version of what, in this book, I call 'conceptual relativism' (see chapter 7). However, the idea of relativism has a much longer and quite complicated history. I examine the history of relativism by discussing not only some of the main claims made on its behalf, but also key philosophical theories which have influenced the development of various forms of relativism.

Chapter 1. The beginnings: relativism in classical philosophy. The earliest documented source of relativism in the Western intellectual tradition is Plato's account of the Sophist philosopher Protagoras and his famous dictum, 'Man is the measure of all things' (Plato 1997g: *Theaet.* 152a1–3). Plato's charge of self-refutation against Protagoras has become the model for frequent attempts to show that relativism is incoherent. I discuss some possible interpretations of the Protagorean doctrine and assess Plato's criticisms. Aristotle also argued that relativism is an unintelligible doctrine as it contravenes the law of non-contradiction – which is presupposed by all thought. Subsequently, relativism was subsumed under scepticism by the Pyrrhonian sceptics who gave a new life to Protagoras' doctrine. I examine these developments in turn.

Chapter 2. Relativism in modern philosophy traces the development of a variety of philosophical positions linked to relativism over the past three centuries. The disparate strands of contemporary relativism, I argue, have their sources in various philosophical currents of the eighteenth and nineteenth centuries. We begin with Michel de Montaigne, who was greatly influenced by Pyrrhonian scepticism, and is the precursor of both relativism and scepticism in modern thought. The chapter also examines the influences of the French Enlightenment, Kant's introduction of the distinction between conceptual schemes and sensory content, the romanticism and anti-rationalism of the Counter-Enlightenment, the post-Hegelian historicism of Engels and Dilthey, and Nietzsche's perspectivism, on the development of relativistic views.

Chapter 3. Contemporary sources of relativism. A variety of contemporary intellectual currents has contributed to the resurgence of interest in relativism. The theoretical and empirical observations of social anthropologists on the diversity of cultural practices have led directly to cultural relativism. Ludwig Wittgenstein's ideas on the role of language and forms of life in shaping thought and action have been used, by philosophers and anthropologists alike, to draw relativistic conclusions about rationality and logic. The intellectual climate created by the writings of postmodernist philosophers and literary theorists has fostered relativism and has had a decisive impact on its popularity.

Part II (chapters 4–9) is devoted to a critical discussion of a variety of relativistic positions.

Chapter 4. Relativism about truth. Relativism about truth (alethic relativism) is the claim that the truth of an assertion is relative to the beliefs, attitudes and other psychological idiosyncrasies of individuals or, more generally, to their social and cultural background.

Relativism about truth is central to many relativistic positions since the arguments for various subdivisions of cognitive relativism, and even ethical relativism, can be recast as a question about the truth of judgements in those particular domains. Since Plato it has been frequently argued that relativism about truth is incoherent because of the dubious status of the claim that 'truth is relative'; for if 'truth is relative' is itself true unconditionally, then there is at least one truth, which is not relative, and hence relativism is not true. The chapter examines the force of this famous argument. The self-refutation argument, often seen as the most decisive argument against relativism, is directed at the most extreme form of alethic relativism. Several philosophers have argued in favour of more restricted forms of relativism about truth. One such view has been proposed by Richard Rorty, who problematises traditional accounts of truth. In the final part of the chapter, I examine his influential views on truth and find them unconvincing.

Chapter 5. Relativism and rationality. The relativist about rationality argues that various societies or cultures have different standards of rationality and that we are not in a position to choose between them; the search for universal standards of rationality is futile, she argues, because rationality consists of conforming to the prevalent cognitive norms and different societies may subscribe to different norms. Rationality can be seen as the requirement of having good reasons and justifications for one's beliefs and actions. Adherence to universal rules of logic has often been seen as a prerequisite of rationality. However, it has been argued that laws of logic are defined by and hence are relative to their social context. In this chapter, I examine and reject relativism about logic. But this rejection does not completely rule out moderate forms of relativism about rationality. Stephen Stich has argued that empirical studies support the view that human beings in their day-to-day reasoning do not adhere to standard norms of rationality. Alasdair MacIntyre, on the other hand, argues that norms of rationality are, to a large extent, products of specific cultural and historic conditions. I examine these views in turn.

Chapter 6. Epistemic relativism. Philosophers of science Thomas Kuhn and Paul Feyerabend have emphasised the role of different modes of reasoning at various historical periods in shaping our conceptions of scientific knowledge. According to them, scientific theories belonging to different paradigms are incommensurable, and the co-evaluation of different cognitive frameworks (and even cultures and ways of life) is impossible. I shall argue that the connection between incommensurability and relativism is more complex than the participants in the debate about relativism in science have led us to believe. In doing so, I distinguish between different forms of incommensurability and suggest ways of overcoming them.

Feminist philosophers have questioned the very notion of objectivity that underpins the ideal of science, and the possibility of giving a universal account of knowledge without taking into account the specific social and political contexts which give rise to them. Their questioning of the theory and practice of science has, at times, assumed a relativistic tone. I shall argue that the legitimate concerns of feminist epistemologists need not lead to relativism.

Chapter 7. Conceptual relativism. The roots of conceptual relativism rest with Kant's distinction between the data of our sense experiences and the principles of organisation or categories we use to organise them. Once the distinction between a conceptual scheme and its content was introduced, it became easy to accept that there may be more than one system or scheme of organisation, and the idea of conceptual relativism was born. In this chapter I discuss the views of some prominent defenders of different strands of conceptual relativism – a group of philosophers I call Harvard relativists. Harvard relativism can be traced back to the pragmatist philosophers, William James and C. I. Lewis in particular. The most influential version of this view was proposed by W. V. O. Quine, according to whom to be able to talk about the world and cope with our stream of sensory experiences, we must impose upon them a conceptual or linguistic scheme or theory. However, it is possible to envisage a plurality of conceptual or theoretical frameworks all of which explain and predict our experiences of the world equally well. Quine's so-called 'ontological relativity' influenced his colleagues, Nelson Goodman and Hilary Putnam, who have proposed very sophisticated forms of conceptual relativism. This chapter critically assesses their contributions to this topic.

Chapter 8. Relativism, interpretation and charity examines some of the recent influential criticisms levelled against various forms of relativism. Critics of relativism question the intelligibility of the claim that one and the same statement may be true for one linguistic community and false for another. A correct understanding of the beliefs and other propositional attitudes of a person, they argue, leads to the conclusion that speakers of other languages, members of other cultures, must have beliefs and cognitive practices very similar to ours. Arguments for relativism often rely on the premise that there are fundamental cultural and conceptual differences between human beings. If this assumption is incoherent or untenable, then so is relativism. In this chapter I examine the arguments offered by Quine, Donald Davidson and Richard Grandy against, respectively, relativism about logic, truth and rationality. In the process I also examine, in some detail, Davidson's arguments against the key presupposition of conceptual relativism – the dualism of scheme and content – and find them wanting.

Chapter 9. Moral relativism. Moral or ethical relativism is probably the most popular relativistic doctrine. It is the claim that there exist diverse and incompatible answers to questions on ethics, and that there is no overarching criterion for deciding between the various replies. Ethical relativism can be embraced independently of cognitive relativism. Many ethical relativists argue that convergence between different worldviews and theoretical frameworks is possible in the natural sciences but not in the realm of ethics. According to this view, moral precepts and judgements are not part of the natural furniture of the universe; they are man-made and would not exist independently of human actions, beliefs and customs; hence, there exists a fundamental difference between scientific investigations and moral enquiry. In addressing these issues, I critically discuss naïve moral relativism, normative moral relativism, metaethical claims arising from naturalism (Mackie and Gilbert Harman) and the limits of commensurability (Bernard Williams). In conclusion, I defend a form of pluralism (inspired by Isaiah Berlin) that rejects the absolutist conceptions of moral value without accepting the relativist conclusion that moral evaluations are the expressions of social and cultural conventions.

Chapter 10. Conclusion: relativism, pluralism and diversity. In discussing issues relating to epistemic, conceptual and moral relativism I propose a form of pluralism that may satisfy some of the intellectual concerns that give rise to the various strands of relativism, without plunging us into the anarchy of 'anything goes' or the intellectual paralysis that comes with the inability to reject or condemn any worldview as false or wrong. In the concluding section I use the metaphor of map making to accommodate pluralism without succumbing to relativism. Pluralism, as construed in this book, allows for diversity and multiplicity of 'right' worldviews, belief-systems, ethical orientations and cognitive frameworks, but is curtailed by the imperatives of our shared physical world and biology. Our conceptions of the world are varied and diverse, I maintain, and yet they are answerable to the natural world. There are many, and at times incompatible, right conceptions, but their rightness, although context-sensitive, is not in any sense relative.

PART I

The history of an idea

1

The beginnings

Relativism in classical philosophy

1.1 INTRODUCTION

The first known statement of a relativist position in Western philosophy is the famous dictum 'man is the measure of all things' by the Sophist, Protagoras (*c*. 490–420 BC). However, intimations of relativism were present in Greek thought even earlier. Increasing contact between the Greeks and other civilisations – the Persians, Babylonians, Egyptians, Scythians, Thracians and Indians – through both war and trade brought with it the realisation that societies arrange their social and political institutions and moral customs in radically different ways.[1] The Persian Wars (490–480 BC), in particular, and the political turmoil that ensued, cast doubt over the old certainties and introduced the idea that social and ethical rules which had been construed as unchanging, universal or of divine origin were in fact merely transitory and local. The historian Herodotus (*c*. 485–430 BC) cites a vast array of practices and customs which by Greek standards would be seen as abnormal and unacceptable. For instance, marriage between a brother and sister was considered natural among the Egyptians and was even prescribed by their religion, while to the Greeks it appeared disgusting and reprehensible. He contends that if any man was asked to name the best laws and customs, he would name his own; as the following story illustrates:

> Darius, after he had got the kingdom, called into his presence certain Greeks who were at hand, and asked – 'what he should pay them to eat the bodies of their fathers when they died?' To which they answered, that there was no sum that would tempt them to do such a thing. He then sent for certain Indians, of the race called Callatians, men who eat their fathers, and asked them, while the Greeks stood by, and knew by the help of an interpreter all that was said – 'What

he should give them to burn the bodies of their fathers at their decease?' The Indians exclaimed aloud, and bade him forbear such language. Such is men's wont herein; and Pindar was right, in my judgement, when he said that law [*nomos*] is the king over all.

(Herodotus 1988: Book III, Chapter 38)

And the dramatist Euripides (*c.* 485–*c.* 406 BC), who was deeply involved in the intellectual currents of his time, noted that incest was practised among the non-Greeks and no law forbids it, and shocked his audiences when one of his characters stated that no behaviour is shameful if it does not appear so to those who practise it (Guthrie 1971: 16).

In addition to the impact of the encounter with diverse cultures and customs, several intellectual and social currents contributed to the emergence of relativistic tendencies in Greek thought. Unresolved tensions within and between various intellectual currents gave support to both relativistic and sceptical conclusions. The first generation of Presocratic philosophers aimed to give all-encompassing metaphysical-cum-scientific explanations of the ultimate constituents and principles of the universe. The various systematic proto-scientific explanatory schemes, however, were in conflict with each other, and no single theory emerged as a paradigm for scientific/philosophical explanation of the world. Irresolvable disagreement among the natural scientists on the constitutive elements and origins of the universe led to disillusionment with the idea of there being a single unifying account. The grand system-building of the Presocratics which led to the multiplication of theories on the nature of reality, where no method was available to adjudicate between them, gave rise to the hypothesis that there may be a variety of non-convergent explanatory systems or worldviews on each subject. The diversity of opinions in debates on political and social matters in the Assembly and the law courts cast further doubts on the possibility of finding a unique framework for solving all ethical or political disputes. The Sophistic approach, as a whole, was an antithesis of the totalising tendencies of its precursors, and Protagorean relativism may, in part, be seen as a reaction to the prevailing disagreements.

Glimpses of relativistic thinking are evident in the fragments left by a number of Presocratic philosophers. Xenophanes (*c.* 570–475 BC), for instance, pointed out that different people have different conceptions of God: 'Ethiopians say that their gods are black and snub-nosed, while the Thracians say that theirs are blue-eyed and red-haired.' Indeed, 'if cows, horses, and lions had hands, and were able to draw with their hands and do the work men do, horses would draw images of gods like horses and cattle like cattle' (Clement of Alexandria, *Stromateis*, 7 22 1 and 5 109 3 in Hankinson 1995: 31–2). According to Xenophanes, human knowledge of the divine is relative while the divine and its knowledge are absolute. Heraclitus (*c.* 540–*c.* 480 BC) is regarded by Plato, Aristotle and Sextus Empiricus as a direct influence on Protagoras. His doctrine of the unity of opposites and his theory of flux are seen as the ontological backbone of the Protagorean thesis. Some of the extant Heraclitean fragments give us a glimpse of why this is so. For instance, 'Sea water is the most pure and the most polluted, drinkable and life-preserving for fish, un-drinkable and destructive for men' (in Hippolytus, *Refutation of Heretics*, 9.105 in Hankinson 1995: 41), from which it follows that sea water is life-preserving (for fish, or relative to the needs of fish) and destructive (for man, relative to his needs). Sextus Empiricus sees the theory of flux as the metaphysical underpinning of Protagoras' relativism. According to him, Protagoras, following Heraclitus, 'holds the belief about matter being in flux and about the presence in it of the reasons for all apparent things. But these things are unclear and we [the Pyrrhonian sceptics] suspend judgement about them' (Sextus Empiricus 1994: 1, xxxii, 219). He argues that since matter is in flux and cannot be said to have a definite nature, it follows that man is the only measure or criterion for deciding what is real and what is not.

Heraclitus also advocated the doctrine of the unity of opposites. The extant fragment, 'God is day and night, winter and summer, war and peace, satiety and hunger' (in Hippolytus, *Refutation of Heretics*, 9 10 8 in Hankinson 1995: 41), seems to highlight the possibility of attribution of contrary, and even contradictory, properties to one and the same object, which in turn suggests the denial of the law of non-contradiction. As we shall see, Plato and Aristotle see Protagoras' relativism at one with the denial of this law. Various fragments of writings by earlier Sophists also seem to herald relativism; for instance, Anaxagoras (*c.* 500–*c.* 428 BC), according to Aristotle, held that 'existent things would be for them such as they take them to be' (Aristotle 1908: *Met.* Γ, 1009b). But it is in Protagoras, the most respected and influential Sophist, that relativism finds its first official champion.

1.2 THE PROTAGOREAN DOCTRINE

Protagoras of Abdera, the best known of the Sophists, was called 'the wisest man alive' by Plato (Plato 1997e: *Protagoras* 309d). The Sophists were a diverse group of travelling teachers who taught rhetoric, oratory, political theory, law, literature and science to the political elite in return for substantial fees; Plato rather disparagingly called them 'hired hunters of rich young men' (Plato 1997f: *Sophist* 231d). The Sophistic movement flourished in the Periclean democracy in Athens and reflected and responded to the perceived need for well-trained participants in the more open political arena of the time. The Greek word '*sophistēs*', meaning 'wise man' or 'expert', referred to poets and orators and it was only much later, under Plato's influence, that it acquired the negative connotations of empty rhetoric that it has today. Although the Sophists did not constitute a homogeneous philosophical school, they shared a common framework of beliefs and practices, which made them distinct from the members of other philosophical movements of ancient Greece. They 'were the first to voice the rationalism and humanism of the age, a strong confidence in man's autonomy and his capacity to understand and give new shape to the civilization he himself had created'. To the Sophists, 'man's worth – and success – depended on knowledge and "education", not on birth or privilege' (Johansen 1998: 99). They believed that progress is achieved through technological and political developments, and that education, the acquisition of political skills and the art of oratory, in particular, were consequently of great public value.

Almost all our knowledge of Protagoras comes to us indirectly through the works of Plato, Aristotle and the later Hellenistic philosophers, as there are only eleven extant fragments of his work. Protagoras came to Athens in the middle of the fifth century BC from Abdera, an outpost of Ionic culture, and is characterised as a 'foreigner' and not a 'citizen' by Plato (Plato 1997e: *Protagoras* 309c). In that, he seems to fit the profile of many latter-day relativists who are culturally the perennial outsider–insiders.[2] In 444 BC, he was given the task of drawing up a constitution for the colony of Thurii in Sicily by Pericles. Diogenes Laertius claims, in his *Lives of the Philosophers*, that Protagoras was indicted for blasphemy because of his book on the gods, and was condemned for impiety. He managed to escape from the city before his trial but was drowned on the crossing to Sicily. However, some of Plato's comments cast doubt on this story, for according to Plato, Protagoras 'was nearly seventy when he died and had practiced his craft for forty years. During all that time to this very day his reputation has stood high' (Plato 1997d: *Meno* 91e).

According to Diogenes Laertius, Protagoras was the first philosopher to maintain 'that there are two sides to every question, opposed to each other' (Diogenes Laertius 1925: IX.51), and he used the maxim 'on every topic there are two arguments contrary to each other' as the starting point in all his teachings. Aristotle claims that by this method Protagoras was able to make the weaker argument seem stronger and either side of any debate seem the winner (Aristotle 1924: *Rhet.* B.24.1402a23). He is reputed to have taught his pupils to praise and blame the same things and to find support for the weaker arguments and to undermine the stronger ones.

Protagoras' relativism is expressed in the famous dictum 'man is the measure [*metron*] of all things [*chrēmata*]: of the things which are that they are, and of the things which are not, that they are not' (Plato 1997g: *Theaet.* 152a1–3), believed to be the opening passage of one of his treatises, *Truth*. Plato reports the passage in the *Theaetetus*, when Socrates, Theaetetus and Theodorus are debating the question of knowledge. Theaetetus claims that knowledge is the same as perception and Plato responds that this was also Protagoras' view and that by it Protagoras meant: 'Each thing appears [*phainesthai*] to me, so it is for me, and as it appears to you, so it is for you – you and I each being a man' (ibid. 152a6–8).[3] Plato uses the example of the same wind feeling cold to one person and hot to another and asks: 'are we going to say the wind itself, by itself, is cold or not cold? Or shall we listen to Protagoras, and say it is cold for the one who feels cold, and for the other, not cold?' (ibid., 152b7), and concludes (152c1–3):

> The appearance [*phantaisa*] of things, then, is the same as perception, in the case of hot and things like that. So it results, apparently, that things are for the individual such as he perceives them.

The question how to interpret Protagorean relativism is particularly difficult, especially since so little of his writing has reached us. The early commentators on Protagoras, Plato, Aristotle and the Stoics, are the only direct sources available and they tend to give differing accounts of what Protagoras had in mind. The text, or what little we have of it, and the early interpretations suggest a number of alternative readings. We can distinguish between the individualistic (subjectivist), ontological, logical, alethic and cultural interpretations of the famous dictum.

Some preliminary points: It seems that 'man' in Protagoras' dictum refers to the individual person, and that Protagoras' thesis has more in common with modern subjectivist views than with relativism. This is particularly evident in passages where Plato addresses the imaginary Protagoras through Theodorus, one of his two interlocutors in the dialogue:

> Now, Protagoras, 'Man is the measure of all things' as you people say – of white and heavy and light and all that kind of thing without exception. He has the criterion of these things within himself; so when he thinks that they are as he experiences them, he thinks what is true and what really is for him.
> (Ibid., 178b)

'Man' in this passage seems to be the individual agent who has direct knowledge of and authority over what he believes to be true or false. Plato, however, extends the scope of the claim to include both the state and mass opinion, where he argues:

> Then consider political questions. Some of these are questions of what may or may not fittingly be done, of just and unjust, of what is sanctioned by religion and what is not; and here the theory may be prepared to maintain that whatever view a city takes on these matters and establishes as its law or convention, is truth and fact for that city. In such matters neither any individual nor any city can claim superior wisdom.
> (Ibid., 172a2–6)

This emphasis on the social and political scope of relativisation brings Protagoras' views more in line with modern understanding of the doctrine when Plato attributes to him the view that 'whatever in any city is regarded as just and admirable *is* just and admirable in that city for as long as that convention maintains itself' (ibid., 167c4–6). Protagoras' relativism probably was also influenced by his agnosticism. He is said to have written: 'As to the gods, I have no means of knowing either that they exist or that they do not exist. For many are the obstacles that impede knowledge, both the obscurity of the question and the shortness of human life' (Diogenes Laertius 1925: IX.51). In this case, as in many others, there are two sides to the issue: some people believe in God and others do not and there can be strong arguments for either view. Given the 'man is the measure' dictum,

God exists for some and does not for others. However, faced with this paradox, agnosticism becomes a plausible choice.

There is further uncertainty over the range of what is being relativised. How widely do we interpret the word 'thing'? Is Protagoras limiting his theory only to subjects of experience and the content of sensory experiences or does he wish to claim that nothing (no objects) can exist independently of man's judgement? Plato, as we saw, gives us the Heraclitean example of the wind feeling cold to one person and not cold to another. The Heraclitean background seems to make the objects of sense-perception the focus of Protagorean relativism, and give us a rather bland version of perceptual relativism, whereby all reports of first-person perceptual experiences are incorrigibly true for the person avowing them. A given gust of wind is not hot or cold *per se*, but hot for the person who feels it hot and cold for those who experience it so. This reading, particularly when coupled with the individualistic reading of 'man', gives an air of subjectivism to Protagoras' dictum, where the truth of certain statements, in this instance statements about the content of perceptual states, is relativised to individuals. On such a reading, Protagoras, at most, is advocating individualistic relativism, rather than the social or cultural relativism that is usually ascribed to him. Sextus Empiricus, in fact, at times interprets Protagoras' dictum as a subjectivist thesis in the sense that 'every appearance whatsoever is true' (Burnyeat 1976a: 172).

Alternatively, we can understand the passage as saying that the wind is both warm and cold and different people perceive one or other of these properties, which would amount to a strong and highly implausible ontological relativism concerning how things *are* in the world.[4] This ontological reading of the dictum is also present in the conclusion Plato draws – that, for Protagoras, nothing is a single non-relative entity; rather things are continually undergoing generation, destruction and change. According to Plato, this is Protagoras' 'secret doctrine', a version of the Heracleitean doctrine of flux, not expressed in his *Truth*, but revealed to his pupils (Plato 1997g: *Theaet.* 152c). Plato explains:

> the theory that there is nothing which in itself is just one thing: nothing which you could rightly call anything or any kind of thing. If you call a thing large, it will reveal itself as small, and if you call it heavy, it is liable to appear as light, and so on with everything, because nothing is one or anything or any kind of thing. What is really true, is this: the things of which we naturally say that they 'are', are in process

of coming to be, as the result of movement and change and blending with one another. We are wrong when we say they 'are', since nothing ever is, but everything is coming to be.[5]

(Ibid., 152d–e)

Sextus Empiricus also, as we saw, ascribes a version of the flux theory to Protagoras and reports that Protagoras 'says that matter is in a state of flux, and as it flows, additions continuously replace the effluxes' (Sextus Empiricus 1994: PH 1 217). The ontological dimension of Protagoras' relativism commits him to the view that 'what appears to each individual is the only reality and therefore the real world differs for each' (Guthrie 1971: 171). That is, the qualities of things may be relative, private, and possibly unique to each agent, and consequently there is no common shared reality. What is real or exists depends on the judgement of men, nothing is constant, things are continually undergoing change, therefore everything *is* as it appears to the perceiver.

The logical reading of the doctrine is supported by Plato's report that Protagoras rejected the principle of non-contradiction. In the *Euthydemus*, Socrates tells us that the followers of Protagoras 'and even earlier thinkers' believed that it is impossible to contradict, which, according to Socrates, is tantamount to the claim that 'there is no such thing as false speaking' (Plato 1997: *Euthyd.* 286c). Whatever the world may be like, in itself, Protagoras seems to have been arguing, we can only experience it, and hence talk of it, as being thus and so in relation to us and therefore statements such as 'the wind is hot' and 'the wind is cold', in this non-relativised form, would not contradict each other. The problem with this interpretation is that once the relativising clause 'for . . .' is added we can get an outright contradiction between statements 'the wind is hot for x (at time t1)' and 'the wind is not hot for x (at time t1)' and it becomes difficult to see why Protagoras should have thought that contradictions are impossible. What Protagoras may have had in mind, however, is that, contrary to common assumption, disputants in arguments do not contradict each other, for 'a is F (for me)' does not contradict 'a is not F (for you)'. And this is a doctrine that Plato is at pains to reject. Ordinarily, we take any statement, such as 'the sky is blue', to be contradicted by its negation, 'the sky is not blue'. For the Protagorean relativist, however, no contradiction would arise for 'the sky is blue for me' does not contradict 'the sky is not blue for you'. All statements, and their negation, can be true relative to some person (or time-slice of a person) or another. The logical interpretation is also favoured by Aristotle who argued that for Protagoras 'contradictory statements about the same thing are simultaneously true' and that 'it is possible either to assert or deny something of every subject' (Aristotle 1908: *Met.* Γ 1007b). The ontological and the logical theses are fundamentally at one, for if the world is such that contradictory properties may simultaneously be ascribed to the same object, then the law of non-contradiction would be refuted by empirical means. Conversely, if the law of non-contradiction is denied, then at least in principle it is possible to ascribe contradictory properties to the same object.

Most significantly, at least in so far as the history of the problem of relativism is concerned, Plato attributes a thesis of alethic relativism, or relativism abut truth, to Protagoras, to the effect that if somebody believes or judges P, then P is true for that person. This interpretation of the dictum is particularly evident in the famous passages where Plato offers his self-refutation argument (see 1.3 below). If we accept that Plato saw the Protagorean doctrine primarily as a defence of alethic relativism, then we can interpret the ontological and logical arguments as mere supporting planks. For the concept of truth is intimately related to the principle of non-contradiction, and what we take to be true is not easily separable from what we assume to exist.

Plato also adds a social dimension to the thesis by extending the discussion, as we saw above, beyond the individual man, to the public sphere, and suggests that a Protagorean should maintain that the kinds of behaviour which each community sanctions are right or acceptable for that society. This is the interpretation that resonates most closely with today's more popular versions of cultural relativism and is supported by passages where Plato also seems to think that ethics is the prime instance of Protagorean relativism. In the *Theaetetus*, for instance, he argues: 'It is in those other questions that I am talking about – just and unjust, religious and irreligious – that men are ready to insist that no one of these things has by nature any being of its own; in respect of these, they say, what seems to people collectively to be so is true, at the time when it seems that way and for just as long as it so seems' (Plato 1997g: *Theaet.* 172b).

This multiplicity of interpretations is also mooted in Aristotle's discussion of the 'man is the measure' doctrine (see 1.4 below). Whatever the preferred interpretation of Protagorean relativism, it is a mark of the great anxieties caused by Protagoras' arguments that both Plato's Theory of Forms and Aristotle's formulation of the categories, which included the category of 'the relatives', were, in part, attempts to neutralise the threat posed by it (Barnes 1988–90).

1.3 PLATO'S REFUTATION OF PROTAGORAS

Plato's argument against Protagoras, known as *'peritropē'* (turning about or reversal argument), is the first of numerous attempts throughout the history of philosophy to show that relativism is self-refuting. Socrates argues against Protagoras thus:

> Suppose you come to a decision in your own mind and then express a judgement about something to me. Let us assume with Protagoras that your judgement is true for *you*. But isn't it possible that the rest of us may criticise your verdict? Do we always agree that your judgement is true? Or does there rise up against you, every time, a vast army of persons who think the opposite, who hold that your decisions and your thoughts are false? . . . Do you want us to say that you are then judging what is true for yourself, but false for the tens of thousands? . . . And what of Protagoras himself? Must he not say this, that supposing he did not believe that man is the measure, any more than the majority of people (who indeed do not believe it), then this *Truth* of his which he wrote is true for no one? On the other hand, suppose he believed it himself, but the majority of men do not agree with him; then you see – to begin with – the more those to whom it does not seem to be the truth outnumber those to whom it does, so much the more it isn't than it is?
>
> (Plato 1997g: *Theaet.* 170d–171a)

Plato offers three interlinked arguments to refute Protagoras:[6]

(a)
(1a) According to the Protagorean doctrine, for all belief P if, for any person A, A believes P, then P is true for A.
(2a) And if, for any other person B, B believes P false, then P is false for B.
(3a) Then in such an event P is true for A and false for B.

(b)
(1b) Protagoras' doctrine is true for Protagoras.
(2b) Protagoras' doctrine is false for others.
(3b) Protagoras' doctrine is false in proportion to the number of people who believe it to be false.

Then comes the main thrust of the argument, in a well-known and much disputed passage of the *Theaetetus*, which is worth repeating in its entirety, Plato argues:

> Secondly, it [Protagoras' doctrine] has this most exquisite feature: Protagoras admits, I presume, that the contrary opinion about his own opinion (namely, that it is false) must be true, seeing he agrees that all men judge what it is . . . And in conceding the truth of the opinion of those who think him wrong, he is really admitting the falsity of his own opinion . . . But for their part the others do not admit that they are wrong . . . But Protagoras again admits *this* judgement to be true, according to his written doctrine . . . It will be disputed, then, by everyone, beginning with Protagoras – or rather, it will be admitted by him, when he grants to the person who contradicts him that he judges truly – when he does that, even Protagoras himself will be granting that neither a dog nor the 'man in the street' is the measure of anything at all which he has not learned . . . Then since it is disputed by everyone, the *Truth* of Protagoras is not true for anyone at all, not even for himself.
>
> (Plato 1997g: *Theaet.* 171a–c)

So Plato seems to be arguing:

(c)
(1c) Protagoras' doctrine is believed to be false by others, for most people do not believe that 'man is the measure of all things'.
(2c) Protagoras' doctrine is believed to be true by Protagoras, otherwise he would not have proposed it.
(3c) Protagoras must then believe that his opponents' view is true, i.e., that the 'man is the measure' doctrine is mistaken.
(4c) Therefore, Protagoras must believe that his own doctrine is false.

(c) is not a good argument as it stands. As has frequently been noted,[7] Plato's argument can undermine relativism only when the qualifier 'for them' is dropped from step 3c (as Plato does). Plato, however, is not entitled to do this, at least not without some further arguments. What Plato should have said is:

(1c′) Protagoras' doctrine is believed to be false by others, for most people do not believe that 'man is the measure of all things'.

(2c′) Protagoras' doctrine is believed to be true by Protagoras, and hence is true (for him).

(3c′) Protagoras must then believe that his opponents' view is true (for them).

(4c′) Therefore, Protagoras must believe that his own doctrine is false (for others).

It would be uncharitable to interpret the omission of the relativising clause simply as a crass philosophical oversight or, even worse, a wilful lapse. Two more charitable interpretations suggest themselves. Plato's refutation may hinge on his understanding of the conceptual properties of the predicate 'is true'. He seems to hold that Protagoras' doctrine is incorrect because if Protagoras is committed to the truth of the 'man is the measure' doctrine, then he is committed to its truth for everyone. By the same token, if someone is committed to the falsehood of the doctrine then that person is committed to its falsehood for everyone. In which case, Protagoras is committed to both the truth and falsehood of the doctrine. Furthermore, Protagoras, as a consequence of his relativism, is committed to the view that no one ever is mistaken and hence the majority of people, who disagree with Protagoras, cannot be mistaken either. Therefore, Protagoras' doctrine does not allow the possibility of false belief, and similarly for true beliefs, and hence fails to provide a satisfactory account of truth and of what it means to make an intelligible assertion. The predicate 'is true' cannot be understood unless it can rule out some false propositions. Relativistic conceptions of truth either fail to do this, and hence cease to be a conception of truth, or implicitly assume it, in which case they become incoherent. More specifically, in order for relativism to be an intelligible doctrine, it should exclude non-relativistic doctrines, but to do so would be tantamount to the denial of the truth of relativism.

This is the interpretation currently favoured by several commentators. Myles Burnyeat, for instance, suggests that Plato's argument assumes that 'Protagoras puts forward his doctrine as a valid theory of truth for everyone's judgements and beliefs. It is meant to be true of those judgements and beliefs; what it asserts of them it asserts, implicitly at least, to be true (period)' (Burnyeat 1976a: 190). The relativist makes the implicit and illicit assumption that there is at least one absolute truth, namely the truth of his own doctrine.[8] Similarly, Hilary Putnam has argued that Plato was the first philosopher to discover that to be a consistent relativist then you have also to be a 'total relativist'. A 'total relativist would have to say that whether or not X is true relative to P is itself relative. At this point our grasp on what the position even means begins to wobble' (Putnam 1981: 123). Putnam's argument hinges on the distinction between restricted and total relativism.[9] Restricted relativism relativises first-order beliefs and judgements only, while total relativism relativises the second-order judgements about those first-order judgements as well. Thus not only for any assertion P, P is true relative to A, but also 'P is true relative to A' itself is true only relative to a belief-system, a culture, a person or what have you. The only way to avoid the self-refutation argument is to accept that restricted relativism collapses into total relativism. But then the question is whether Burnyeat and Putnam, among others, are right to believe that total relativism is also incoherent. We will return to this topic, in chapter 4, where the charge of self-refutation will receive a further airing.

There is, however, a difficulty with Burnyeat's defence of Plato. It can be argued that Plato has begged the question against Protagoras by assuming a non-relativist conception of truth, that is, while debating the question of the relativity of truth, Plato was implicitly presupposing the very conception of truth that was being attacked by Protagoras in the 'man is the measure' doctrine. The point is that Protagoras and Plato were working with two different conceptions of truth, and to accuse Protagoras of inconsistency by saddling him with a conception of truth that he is at pains to reject is to beg the very question at stake. Plato and his defenders of course assume that there is only one correct conception of truth, namely the objectivist and absolutist view, and that any intelligible assertion implicitly or explicitly presupposes it. But the very point of Protagoras' thesis is to call into question the absolutist views of truth. Protagoras, I shall propose presently, may have had a proto-pragmatist, rather than a realist, conception of truth, in which case the charge of self-refutation would be more difficult to sustain.

Alternatively, Plato may have believed that Protagoras faces a genuine dilemma. He either leaves in the relativising clause 'for me' and ends up advocating a view that is believed only by him, with no weapons available in his dialectical armoury to convince others of its truth, or he leaves out the relativising clause and becomes susceptible to the charge of self-refutation. Relativism denies the possibility of disagreement: 'X is true for me' does not contradict 'X is false for you'. Without the possibility of disagreement no debate can take place. If we accept the relativist conception of truth, then we are depriving ourselves of the means for arguing for the superiority of our view in comparison to alternative conceptions of truth. Any conception of truth becomes as good as any other, so it is a puzzle why

anyone should take the trouble to offer arguments in favour of relativism. Relativism inevitably leads to quietism, so even if relativism
is not formally self-refuting, it still leads to a performative contradiction, for a relativist is not in a position to defend his views against his
opponents.

Protagoras, however, may have had the conceptual resources to
overcome the charge of quietism. To see this we have to return to an
earlier passage where Plato offers a defence of Protagoras by arguing
on his behalf that although all beliefs may be equally true, they are not
all equally good or valuable. Protagoras' reply as reconstructed by
Plato is:

> There are countless differences between men for just this very
> reason, that different things both are and appear [*phainomai*]
> to be to different subjects. I certainly do not deny the exis-
> tence of both wisdom and wise men: far from it. But the man
> whom I call wise is the man who can change the appearances
> – the man who in any case where bad [*kaka*] things both
> appear and are for one of us, works [*metaballei*] a change and
> makes good [*agatha*] things appear and be for him.
>
> (Plato 1997g: *Theaet.* 166d7)

Plato thinks that this position also leads to a paradox, for how could
two men's beliefs on the goodness or badness of something be equally
true and not equally valuable? Or as Plato argues elsewhere, 'if
wisdom exists and foolishness likewise, then Protagoras cannot be
telling the truth. After all, if what each person believes to be true is
true for him, no one can truly be wiser than anyone else' (Plato 1997b:
Cratylus 386c). The answer is to reappraise the connection between
'the true' and 'the valuable'. A judgement is true, according to Protagoras, if it meets the criterion of truth used by the individual or
society subscribing to it. The value of a belief, on the other hand, is
judged according to its consequences relative to specific situations and
circumstances. Not every judgement is equally appropriate, fruitful or
expedient.

There is textual evidence in support of this view provided by Plato
himself. Protagoras, in Plato's reconstruction of his defence, argues:

> [T]o the sick man the things he eats both appear and are
> bitter, while to the healthy man they both appear and are the
> opposite. Now what we have to do is not to make one of these
> the wiser than the other – that is not even a possibility – nor is

it our business to make accusations, calling the sick man ignorant for judging as he does, and the healthy man wise, because he judges differently. What we have to do is to make a change from the one to the other, because the other state is better. In education, too, what we have to do is to change a worse state into a better state . . . This, in my opinion, is what really happens: when a man's soul is in a pernicious state, he judges things akin to it, but giving him a sound state of the soul causes him to think different things, things that are good. In the latter event, the things which appear to him are what some people, who are still at a primitive stage, call 'true'; my position, however, is that the one kind are better than the others, but in no way *truer*.

(Plato 1997g: *Theaet.* 166e4–167b7)

The Protagorean position sounds remarkably similar to the pragmatist argument that we can cash in our conceptions of the truth and falsity of beliefs only in terms of their value to us.[10] Protagoras seems to reason that:

The expert can persuade you that his view is more expedient than that of others, and hence he can make his judgement true for the person he persuades – the physician is in this sense an expert on health and sickness, the farmer on the tilling of his soil, and the wise man, 'the Sophist', can persuade you that his view of justice and morals in the long run will be profitable to the individual and society.

(Johansen 1998: 105)

Interpreted in this light, Protagoras will have justification for advocating his theory of truth in preference to other theories, since this is a more expedient and fruitful view than the absolutist conception he tries to overcome.

It has also been argued that the main problem with Protagorean relativism is that a relativist cannot distinguish between what is right and what one thinks is right. Hilary Putnam maintains that the relativist cannot make sense of the distinction between being right and thinking that he is right (because whatever seems right to him is right). However, the distinction between being right and thinking that one is right is essential to our ability to distinguish between asserting and making noises. What the relativist fails to see, and what Plato presumably did see, is that 'it is a presupposition of thought itself that some kind of objective rightness exists' (Putnam 1981: 124) and to think otherwise is 'to commit a sort of mental suicide' (ibid.: 122).[11]

The objection loses its bite once we substitute 'better' for 'right'. The relativist is not in a position to allow the vocabulary of 'being right' into his language, if 'being right' is defined in terms of speaking truly, or saying how things really are. Protagoras, however, seems to think that he can distinguish between better and worse beliefs, a distinction that is only contextually and situationally available and, unlike the predicate 'is true', is apt to be used in comparative forms. Thus the relativist doctrine, Protagoras might argue, is better than Plato's absolutist doctrine of truth but is in no sense more true. It may be objected that for Protagoras' argument to go through he will require an absolutist conception of 'better' as a contrast to seeming better, and he is not in a position to offer such a distinction. Protagoras, however, does offer situational comparisons and discriminations between better and worse states; for instance, he argues that a sick man would come to prefer to be healthy, once he has had an experience of both states. We do not need to know what the absolute good is in order to be able to distinguish between better and worse states. The point is that Protagoras and Plato, as reconstructed by Burnyeat and Putnam, seem to have different conceptions of truth. Plato's self-refutation argument might work with the assumption of the very conception of truth that Protagoras is at pains to reject; but it is not effective against the alternative, pragmatically inclined, conception of truth that Protagoras is offering.

1.4 ARISTOTLE'S ANTI-RELATIVISM

According to Aristotle, Protagorean relativism is tantamount to the denial of the principle of non-contradiction. Aristotle assigns two philosophical motivations to the doctrine.[12] First, he cites the views of the natural philosophers such as Democritus and Anaxagoras who believed that nothing comes from non-being and argues that Protagoras' position is at root the same as that of Democritus who argued that 'things must both be and not be'. Aristotle reasons that if something manages to take on the characteristics opposite to those it originally possessed, for instance becomes non-white after having been completely white, then you have to conclude either that it was generated from nothing or that it originally existed as both white and non-white. Since nothing can be generated from non-being, then it follows that it must have possessed contrary or even contradictory qualities. The second source of Protagorean relativism, for Aristotle, is the fact that not all men have the same knowledge about the same things; a given thing appears one way (pleasant, sweet, warm, etc.) to some and the contrary to others (Aristotle 1908: *Met.*, book Γ, 10062 15–30). Aristotle includes Protagoras among the philosophers who believe that

> the truth should not be determined by the large or small number of those who hold a belief, and that the same thing is thought sweet by some when they taste it, and bitter by others, so that if all were ill or all were mad, and only two or three were well or sane, these would be thought ill and mad, and not the others.
>
> (Ibid., book Γ, 1009b1–10)

Aristotle's explanation of the origins of Protagoras' dictum demonstrates some of the difficulties in tracing the history of a philosophical problem in a two thousand year time-span. Protagoras' philosophical motivations for adopting relativism do not seem to coincide fully with present-day ones. Interpretations of Protagoras, as we saw, are ambiguous between individual (subjective) and social (cultural) relativism, and Aristotle seems to be attacking both views simultaneously. Relativism, under one of Aristotle's construals, stems from the differences in the ways individuals experience the world, rather than from cultural differences. As Burnyeat puts it:

> in Aristotle, Sextus Empiricus, and the later sources generally, Protagoras is understood . . . not as a relativist but as a subjectivist whose view is that every judgement is true *simpliciter* – true absolutely, not merely true for the person whose judgement it is. To illustrate the difference: the subjectivist version of the Measure doctrine is in clear violation of the law of contradiction, since it allows one person's judgement that something is so, and another person's judgement that it is not so, both to be true together whereas the relativist version can plead that there is no contradiction in something being so for one person and not so for another.
>
> (Burnyeat 1976b: 46)

Certainly, Aristotle seems to interpret the 'man is the measure' dictum as a subjectivist doctrine, to the effect that what a thing is thought to be by each man is precisely what the thing is. For instance, when he argues that 'a thing often appears to be beautiful to some but the contrary to other people, and that which appears to each man is the measure' (Aristotle 1908: *Met.* book Γ, 10062 15–30), he seems to be concentrating on the sensible experiences of individuals at a purely subjective level. Interpreted in this way, Protagoras seems to be arguing that truth is in fact absolute, but that there are as many absolute truths as there are arbiters of truths and falsity. But as Burnyeat acknowledges in a footnote, Aristotle seems also to be attributing a relativist position to Protagoras (Burnyeat 1976b: 46), where he says: 'they are compelled to say that everything is *relative to opinion* and sensation, so that nothing has occurred and nothing will be unless someone has first formed an opinion about it' (Aristotle 1908: *Met.*, book Γ, 1001b5). This is closer to the subjective relativism also present in Plato's interpretation of Protagoras in the *Theaetetus*. Aristotle also gestures towards an ethical dimension in the Protagorean view, when he argues:

> The saying of Protagoras is like the views we have mentioned; he said that man is the measure of all things, meaning simply that that which seems to each man also assuredly is. If this is so, it follows that the same thing both is and is not, and is bad and good, and that the contents of all other opposite statements are true, because often a particular thing appears beautiful to some and the contrary of beautiful to others, and that which appears to each man is the measure.[13]
>
> (Ibid.: book K, 1062b15)

The key point in Aristotle's discussion of Protagoras is the insistence that the opposing views in any disagreement cannot all be right. Take the example of sensations, Aristotle argues: something does not appear sweet to one person and the contrary to another unless the olfactory senses of one of them have been damaged or are defective; in such cases the healthy, and not the injured or the defective, person would be the measure. The argument applies to other judgements, such as the good and the bad, the beautiful and the ugly, as well.

The main problem with Protagorean relativism is that it contravenes the law of non-contradiction by ascribing contradictory or contrary properties to the same subject. If man is the measure of all things, then given that different people may assign the value true or false to the same assertion, it follows that the same assertion is both true and false and hence 'the same thing must both be and not be'. Aristotle says

> There are some who, as we said, both themselves assert that it is possible for the same thing to be and not to be, and say

that people can judge this to be the case. And among others many writers about nature use this language. But we have now posited that it is impossible for anything at the same time to be and not to be, and by this means have shown that this is the most indisputable of all principles. Some indeed demand that even this shall be demonstrated, but this they do through want of education, for not to know of what things one should demand demonstration, and of what one should not, argues want of education.

(Ibid., book Γ, 1006a)

Aristotle argues that the principle of non-contradiction is the most certain of all basic principles, for even though the principle cannot be demonstrated it cannot be denied either, because all thought and speech presuppose it. Contradictory assertions cannot be true at the same time, and contrary predicates cannot be applied to the same thing. 'Since it is impossible for contradictories to be truly said of the same object at the same time, it is evident that neither can contraries belong to the same object at the same time' (ibid., book Γ, 1011b).

Aristotle's arguments have been aired from time to time as a *reductio* of relativism. The scholastics, for instance, used it against the resurgence of scepticism and relativism in the sixteenth century. The argument, taken at face value, is singularly unconvincing because of the illegitimate move from the statements

> P is true for A
> P is false for B
> to
> P is true and false.

The contradiction P & –P is achieved by dropping the crucial relativising clause 'for A' and 'for B'. The correct inference that 'P is true for A and P is false for B', of course, does not involve us in a contradiction in any obvious way. However, as in the case of Plato, Aristotle probably had something deeper in mind. His argument, like Plato's, may hinge on the ramifications of what he saw as the correct understanding of the predicate 'is true' and the conditions for the intelligibility of beliefs. If it can be shown that no sense can be made of the suggestion that one and the same proposition may be true for one person and false for another, then the Aristotelian worries about the incoherence of relativism will be legitimised.

In book Γ of *Metaphysics*, Aristotle argues that Protagoras' doctrine implies that contradictory judgements are true at the same time about the same thing because

> Again, if all contradictory statements are true of the same subject at the same time, evidently all things will be one. For the same thing will be a trireme, a wall, and a man, if of everything it is possible either to affirm or to deny anything (and this premise must be accepted by those who share the views of Protagoras). For if any one thinks that the man is not a trireme, evidently he is not a trireme; so that he also is a trireme, if, as they say, contradictory statements are both true. And we thus get the doctrine of Anaxagoras that all things are mixed together; so that nothing really exists.
>
> (Ibid., book Γ, 1007b21)

In other words, if all assertions are equally true and false then there is no such thing as meaningful speech, or belief or thought. The point is that a contradictory statement does not make an intelligible assertion.[14] For any assertion to have content and to be informative, it must exclude certain possibilities. Contradictions fail to do that and hence a contradictory statement fails to have content. If, by asserting P, the speaker does not exclude its negation –P, then he is not excluding anything (see also 5.4). The relativist assumes that every utterance and its negation is true, so long as it is deemed to be so by the measure of the utterer. Therefore, the relativist is unable to make a meaningful statement, and even the very expression of relativism as a position is meaningless since it does not exclude its denial. Furthermore, if all statements, and their negations, can turn out to be both true and false then we face the following paradox: if all statements are false, to say that 'all statements are false' will be a false statement, and if all statements are true, to say that 'all statement are false' will not be a false statement. The converse of this point also applies. The relativist, then, by attaching the relativising clause to all statements makes contradictions in principle impossible, and by doing so devoids all discourse of content. If relativism is true, and if relativism involves flouting the law of non-contradiction, then every theory, including those denying relativism, would come out true or rationally acceptable and no one would be rationally obliged to give up any of her beliefs, no matter what the evidence against it.

However, Protagorean relativism may be constructed in such a way that it does not lead to the denial of the law of non-contradiction and avoids the charge that it makes all statements equally true, or false. As suggested in the last section, Protagoras may by urging us to reform our concept of truth and to employ pragmatic and epistemic values such as usefulness, fruitfulness, etc., rather than truth and falsity. This pragmatic approach would allow Protagoras to rank various beliefs and to exclude those that are not appropriate for the purposes at hand. For instance, he may use a criterion for rational acceptability, which might include norms such as effectiveness, simplicity, problem-solving abilities, practical usefulness, etc. In this way the relativist can make comparisons between the merits of different beliefs, within a continuum of pragmatic values, even though she has to eschew the traditional distinction between truth and falsity.

We shall return to the question of whether an objectivist conception of truth is a prerequisite of making intelligible assertions or whether a pragmatist approach is adequate in chapter 4. However, it is important to note that, unlike a number of contemporary philosophers who claim that relativism can be dismissed simply by a one-line self-refutation argument, both Aristotle and Plato acknowledge the genuine philosophical worries surrounding the issue and attempt to overcome them by introducing complex philosophical theories.[15]

1.5 RELATIVISM AND PYRRHONIAN SCEPTICISM

Pyrrhonian sceptics used the Protagorean arguments for relativism to justify sceptical conclusions about the very possibility of knowledge. Pyrrhonism receives its name from Pyrrho of Elis (*c.* 360–270 BC) who had acquired a legendary reputation for his 'philosophical imperturbability'. Pyrrho, like Socrates, wrote nothing and most of our information about him and Pyrrhonian scepticism comes through the writings of Sextus Empiricus (second to third century AD), who compiled a systematic survey of Hellenistic sceptical doctrines in his *Outlines of Pyrrhonism*. According to Sextus, the goal of the sceptical attitude is *ataraxia*, or the state of tranquillity, and this is achieved by the power to produce oppositions (*antitheseis*) and the suspension of judgement or *epochē* on the question of the real nature of things. The Pyrrhonian sceptics use argument schematas, or patterns of argument known as Modes (*tropos*) of scepticism, in order to establish the need for suspension of judgements. The strategy is to adduce arguments from various sources to show that for every judgement and assertion there is an equally convincing counter-assertion or contrary judgement and thus they cast doubt on claims to truth and certainty. The approach, as we saw, was also favoured by Protagoras and other

Sophists, except that Protagoras drew relativistic rather than sceptical conclusions. In fact, in Aenesidemus' (first- century AD) version of the Modes of scepticism, which appears in Diogenes Laertius' *Lives of Philosophers* and Philo of Alexandria's *Essay on Drunkenness*, we see arguments closely paralleling those frequently used in both ancient and modern philosophy in support of relativism. For instance:

> Fifth is the mode depending on lifestyles, laws, belief in myth, conventions due to custom and dogmatic suppositions. This includes questions about what is fine and base, true and false, good and bad, about gods, about the production and destruction of all the things that are apparent. For instance, the same behaviour is just for some and unjust for others, to some good and to others bad. Thus Persians do not regard it as strange to have sex with their daughters, while Greeks regard it as prohibited. The Messegetae, according to Eudoxus in Book 1 of his *Journey round the World*, have their wives in common; Greeks do not. The Cilicians used to take pride in being pirates; but not the Greeks. Different people believe in different gods; some believe in divine providence and others do not. The Egyptians dispose of their dead by embalming, the Romans by cremation, the Paeonians by throwing them into lakes. Hence the suspension of judgement as to what is true.
>
> (Diogenes, in Annas and Barnes 1985: 154)

Although the conclusion drawn is that we should suspend judgement on such matters, the relativistic overtones of the examples given resonate with the contemporary readers.

The Pyrrhonists frequently discussed relativism in a slightly different context from that used by Protagoras. In an anonymous commentary on Plato's *Theaetetus*, probably dating back to the first century BC, we find the following:

> The Pyrrhonists say that everything is relative, inasmuch as nothing exists in its own right but everything relative to other things. Neither shapes nor sounds nor objects of taste or smell or touch nor any other object of perception has a character of its own . . . Nor do our sense-organs possess a substance of their own; for otherwise animals would not be affected differently – as goats take pleasure in the vine-shoots and pigs in mud while humans object to both. From the

objects of perception they move to reason, urging that this
too is relative; for different people assent in different ways,
and the same people change and do not stand by it.[16]

(Anon., in Annas and Barnes 1985: 97)

The commentary highlights a crucial ambiguity in discussions of relativism, both in classical philosophy and later in the writings of
medieval philosophers, namely a conflation of relativism and relativity.
Most Greek philosophers discuss relativity (*tapros ti*) or 'things relative to something' but give different characterisations of it. To say that
something is relative can mean that it is what it is in relation to other
things, that it has no *sui generis* properties. In this sense, discussions of
tapros ti may be equated with relational properties (see introduction).
Statements about relational properties, however, assert an absolute
truth about the properties of things in the world and therefore should
not be equated with relativistic claims. Relativism is the claim that
what is true and false is relative to cultures, belief-systems or the psychological make-up of different people; it is the denial of absolute
truths.[17] This conflation of the two meanings is particularly evident in
the third of the Five Modes of scepticism introduced by Agrippa
(sometime between the first century BC and the second century AD),
the Pyrrhonist philosopher of whom very little is known, except that
he probably was the inventor of the Modes. Agrippa's third Mode is
specifically called 'the Mode of relativity' and states:

In the mode deriving from relativity . . . the existing object
appears to be such-and-such relative to the subject judging
and to the things observed together with it, but we suspend
judgement on what it is like in its nature.

(Annas and Barnes 1985: 182)

Despite its name, this Mode has little in common with relativism as
understood in contemporary philosophy. Agrippa seems to be talking
about the relational nature of all claims to knowledge. We cannot
know how things are in themselves; rather we can only apprehend
them in relation to the person making the judgement and the circumstances within which the judgement is made. The claim, then, is that
all judgement is observer-dependent and hence we cannot know the
nature of anything.

In later Pyrrhonism, the Ten Modes of Sextus share a common
form that generalises Agrippa's Five Modes. The generic argument
schema, which Sextus calls the 'relativity mode' has the form:

(1) X appears F relative to a.
(2) X appears F* relative to b.
(3) At most one of the appearances of 1 and 2 can be true.
(4) No decision procedure tells decisively either for 1 or 2.
     So
(5) We should suspend judgement as to what X is like in its
     real nature.

(Hankinson 1995: 156)

In addition, Sextus specifically introduces Mode eight, or the Relativity Mode, according to which 'we conclude that since everything is relative, we shall suspend judgement as to what things are independently and on their own in nature' (Sextus Empiricus 1994: PH I 135). He argues that everything is relative in two senses: firstly, relative to the person who makes the judgement and, secondly, relative to the context and object being observed. The example he gives is that of the right and left which can be established only in relation to other objects. The conclusion Sextus derives, like Agrippa, is

> So, since we have established in this way that everything is relative [*pros ti*], it is clear then that we shall not be able to say what each existing object is like in its own nature and purely, but only what it appears to be like relative to something. It follows that we must suspend judgement about the nature of objects.

(Ibid.: 140)

The argument from relativity once more shows the conflation of relativism and relativity. Sextus gives the impression that he is talking about the relational nature of predicates such as 'is right' and 'is left'. However, there is a suggestion that he is also considering subjective relativism, when he argues that everything is relative to the person who makes judgements.

The tenth Mode of Sextus bears greater similarities to the modern understanding of relativism. It runs parallel to the fifth Mode of Agrippa's version and concerns social and ethical matters.

> [W]e oppose custom to the others – for example to law, when we say that in Persia homosexual acts are customary, while in Rome they are forbidden by law; that among us adultery is forbidden, while among the Massagetae it is accepted by custom as indifferent . . .; that among us it is forbidden to

44

have sex with your mother, while in Persia it is the custom to favour such marriages; and in Egypt they marry their sisters, which among us is forbidden by law.

(Ibid.: PH I 152–3)

After listing many more such examples Sextus goes on to argue:

Thus, since so much anomaly has been shown in objects by this mode too, we shall not be able to say what each existing object is like in its nature, but only how it appears relative to a given persuasion or law or custom and so on. Because of this mode too, therefore, it is necessary for us to suspend judgement on the nature of external existing objects.

(Ibid.: PH I 163)

He also compares the different customs people have regarding their dead and concludes: 'None of these things is thus and so by nature: all are matters of convention and relative' (Ibid.: PH III 232). Although the empirical data presented may seem to support relativism, the conclusion Sextus drew is sceptical rather than relativistic. This opens up the important question of the similarities and differences between relativism and scepticism. On the difference between the two, Sextus writes:

Protagoras has it that human beings are measure of all things, of those that are that they are, and of those that are not that they are not. By 'measure' he means the standard, and by 'things' objects; so he is implicitly saying that human beings are the standard for all objects, of those that are that they are and of those that are not that they are not. For this reason he posits only what is apparent to each person, and thus introduces relativity. Hence he is thought to have something in common with the Pyrrhonists.

(Ibid.: PH I 216–17)

However, he argues that Protagoras was not a Pyrrhonian, because he does commit himself to the nature of unclear things while the Pyrrhonians would not. Protagoras' philosophy, despite its affinities with scepticism, he argues, differs from it in at least one fundamental point: Protagoras adhered to Heraclitanism and therefore held one non-relative belief, namely that all matter is fluid. Sextus interprets Protagoras as a subjectivist and proposes the following refutation of his view:

> One cannot say that every appearance is true, because of its
> self-refutation, as Democritus and Plato urged against Pro-
> tagoras; for if every appearance is true, it will be true also,
> being in accordance with an appearance, that not every
> appearance is true, and thus it will become a falsehood that
> every appearance is true.
>
> (Sextus Empiricus, in Burnyeat 1976b: 47)

The argument was seen by Sextus as a version of the *peritropē* argument that Plato had used against Protagoras.

Despite this refutation of Protagorean relativism, both Sextus and
later commentators on Pyrrhonian scepticism have often conflated
relativism and scepticism. Seneca, for instance, attributes to Protagoras the view that it is 'possible to dispute with equal validity on either
side of every question, including the question whether it is possible to
dispute with equal validity on either side of every question' (Seneca,
Epistles 88, 43 quoted in Burnyeat 1976b: 60–1) and turns Protagoras
into an early Pyrrhonian sceptic. Burnyeat argues that it is difficult
to reconcile this attribution with the relativism of the historical Protagoras, but that it is reconcilable with subjectivist interpretations of
Protagoras: 'the idea that there are two equally valid sides to every
question is a consequence of that subjectivism. In this sense it was fair
to claim that Protagoras said first what the Skeptics said later' (Burnyeat 1976b: 61).

Conversely, ancient commentators on Sextus have characterised his
views as relativistic. Aulus Gellius (*c.* AD 130–80), the author of *Attic
Nights*, seems to attribute a perceptual relativism to Pyrrhonists and
reports that:

> absolutely everything that reflects the human senses is rela-
> tive. That means that there is nothing at all which exists in its
> own right or which has its own power and nature: everything
> is referred to something else and appears such as its appear-
> ance is while it is appearing, i.e., such as it is made in our
> sense to which it has arrived and not such as it is in itself
> from which it has set out (*Attic Nights* XIV 7–8).
>
> (Annas and Barnes 1985: 96–7)

Similar points are made by the anonymous ancient commentary on
Plato's *Theaetetus* cited above.

It can be argued the absence of a clear demarcation between
relativism and scepticism is the main reason for the relativistic inter-

pretations of Pyrrhonism. Jonathan Barnes sees this as a philosophical failure on the part of Sextus and argues that Sextus should have
made it clear that

> relativism itself is not a sort of scepticism, and the relativist is
> not the sceptic's ally. For where the sceptic suspends judge-
> ment, there the relativist claims knowledge. The nature of
> things, which is opaque to the sceptic, is lucidity itself to the
> relativist.
>
> (Barnes 1988–90: 5)

Undeniably, there are important and interesting differences between
scepticism and relativism, even though the two topics have often been
conjoined without any clear distinction between them. Scepticism,
like relativism, can be construed in several ways. In its strongest
sense, (global) scepticism is the denial of the possibility of all knowledge. Descartes' anti-sceptical arguments are aimed at sceptics of
this hue. Global scepticism is in conflict with relativism since the relativist is happy to accept local knowledge-claims. A weaker type of
scepticism can be detected in the work of various philosophers
throughout the history of Western philosophy, who have questioned
the possibility of infallible knowledge in any domain. This type of
sceptic may accept some provisional knowledge-claims but would
deny the possibility of certainty or knowledge of absolute truths
in all areas. Relativism shares some common ground with weaker
scepticism in that both doctrines deny the possibility of infallible
knowledge or knowledge of absolute, immutable and universal
truths. The sceptic and the relativist, then, are united in their opposition to absolutist and universalist conceptions of knowledge, and, in
this sense, the weaker type of scepticism is a necessary condition for
the doctrine of relativism. However, the relativist draws a positive
conclusion from this negative starting point in arguing for the possibility of a context-dependent or conditional (relative) knowledge,
while the sceptic ends up denying the possibility of knowledge. What
scepticism and relativism have in common is their opposition to a
particular view of knowledge. Their shared cause is the denial of the
possibility of universal and absolute knowledge; thereafter they part
company. The sceptic believes that knowledge is impossible and truth
unattainable, even though she might grant the possibility that there
are absolute truths. The relativist, on the other hand, claims that
there are as many truths as there are context-relative claims to knowledge, but talk of absolute truth is misguided. Burnyeat has argued

that scepticism and Protagorean relativism are equally inimical to the idea of reason, and that renunciation is at the heart of the self-refutation argument (Burnyeat 1976b: 61). Burnyeat is right in that scepticism and relativism deny a certain conception of reason and truth. Whether this denial leads to incoherence and whether this is enough for undermining the case for relativism will be discussed in subsequent chapters.

1.6 CONCLUSION

Our discussion of ancient relativism throws light on the difficulties in giving a univocal account of a doctrine that has always had many facets. It highlights one of the reasons why relativism has had to be refuted so frequently in its two thousand year history of doctrinal existence. There are many relativisms, motivated by different, but also overlapping, philosophical preoccupations and questions. No single argument can be used to defeat or rescue this many-headed hydra.

One obstacle in tracing the history of relativism is that ancient philosophers define its scope more widely than many modern philosophers do. According to Sextus, for instance, not only the 'objects of perception are relative to those who are sensing them but even the objects of thought are relative, because they are expressed relative to the one thinking about them' (Sextus Empiricus 1994: HP I 176). This generalised notion of relativity is most evident where he talks about instances of relativity; in addition to beliefs and sense experiences, signs and causes are seen by Sextus as examples of the relative things and he argues that 'we shall not be able to say what each object is like in its nature, but only how it appears relative to a given persuasion or law or custom and so on' (ibid.: HP I 163).

Nevertheless, we also see similarities with contemporary views of relativism, for instance, when Sextus argues 'there is nothing good or bad by nature, for if good and bad exist by nature, then it must have the same effect for everyone. But there is nothing which is equally good or bad for everyone, therefore, there is nothing good or bad by nature' (ibid.: HP III 179). In particular the arguments adduced in the fifth Mode of scepticism, which echoes more ancient writings, parallel the modern argument proposed for cultural relativism concerning ethics and value judgements. The Greek philosophers introduced a framework for discussing relativism that has remained in place for more than two thousand years, as Plato's self-refutation argument, for many, remains the strongest weapon against relativism.

The discovery of Pyrrhonian scepticism was instrumental in shaping the beginnings of modern philosophy through the work of Michel de Montaigne (1533–92). With the publication in 1562 of a Latin edition of the *Outlines of Scepticism* by the French scholar Henri Éstienne, the problem of scepticism and relativism, which had been ignored for almost fifteen centuries, once more became a live philosophical issue.

2

Relativism in modern philosophy

2.1 INTRODUCTION

The diverse strands of contemporary relativism originate in philosophical developments of the eighteenth and nineteenth centuries. In what follows, I shall examine the links between various forms of relativism and some of the major historical currents in modern philosophy.

Philosophy in the Middle Ages was marked by a background of Christian faith, its concomitant theology, and preoccupations with metaphysical and moral questions arising out of theological concerns. The cultural milieu of the period, as well as the philosophical influence of figures such as Thomas Aquinas (1224/6–74), militated against the development of relativistic currents of thought.[1] Discussions of the 'relative', or the relational nature of predicates such as 'tall', 'short', etc. took place in the context of debates about the Aristotelian categories, but these were largely devoid of the connotations of cultural relativism that were present in Protagorean and Pyrrhonian relativism.

The breakdown of the intellectual and social frameworks of medieval society prepared the ground for a resurgence of interest in scepticism and relativism. The religious ferment that culminated in the Reformation had the effect of raising troubling questions about the criteria of truth and knowledge. The Reformation's challenge to the dominance of the Catholic Church contained within it the seeds of a more fundamental doubt; doubt about the very possibility of knowledge – not only in matters of faith but also increasingly in all other areas of belief. With the renewal of interest in the problem of scepticism in the sixteenth century and the attendant quest for certainty, the problem of relativism was once more brought into focus.

The encounter with 'exotic' cultures in newly discovered lands

50

became the occasion, if not the cause, of much of the debate about universalism, relativism and what in today's debates is known as 'ethnocentrism'. Amerigo Vespucci's letter *Mundus Novus* (1503) became a dominant model for the depiction and understanding of the 'other' – the primitive and uncivilised non-Westerner – who was treated as a point of comparison with existing Western cultures:

> They have no cloth, of either wool, flax, or cotton, because they have no need for it; nor have they any private property, everything being in common. They live amongst themselves without a king or rule, each man being his own master, and having as many wives as they please. The children cohabit with the mothers, the brothers with the sisters, the male cousin with the female, and each one with the first he meets. They have no temples and no laws, nor are they idolaters. What more can I say! They live according to nature.
>
> (Vespucci, in Todorov 1993: 267)

Similar sentiments are expressed by the French historian André Thevet who in 1558 writes: 'America today is inhabited by marvellously strange and savage peoples . . . living like irrational beasts *just as nature has produced them*' (Sale 1990: 202). In Montaigne's scepticism, in Thomas More's vision of Utopia and in Rousseau's idealisation of the noble savage, the image of the natural man became a point of departure for highlighting the ills of society. These first stirrings of awareness of cultural diversity also prepared the ground for relativistic currents in early modern philosophy.

2.2 RELATIVISM IN EARLY MODERN PHILOSOPHY

The most notable proponent of both scepticism and relativism in the early modern period is Michel de Montaigne (1533–92)[2] and although, like his precursors, he often fails to distinguish clearly between relativism and scepticism, he anticipates some of the key contemporary debates and acts as a central link between the relativism of the ancients and the various relativistic doctrines developed by modern philosophers.[3]

Montaigne's sceptical and relativistic outlook was influenced by a variety of intellectual currents. The rediscovery of Pyrrhonian scepticism had a profound impact on the formation of modern philosophical sensibilities. Montaigne deploys the argument made familiar by the Pyrrhonian sceptics, that our judgements change because of our bodily and emotional conditions in such a way that one and the same judgement may seem true to us on one occasion and false on another. He also cites evidence from the ongoing scientific revolution to support relativism. He argues that since there is tremendous diversity of opinion on scientific matters – the Ptolemaic astronomers disagree with Cleanthes or Nicetas as well as with the much more recent Copernican claims that the Earth moves – then we are not in a position to make a well-grounded choice between these varying claims. How do we know that, a millennium hence, another theory will not be offered which would replace the existing ones? Even geometry, the allegedly certain science, he argues, can be doubted, since alternative systems (such as Zeno's) can be sketched (Popkin 2003: 53).[4]

The discovery of the New World was a further impetus for Montaigne's arguments in favour of cultural relativism and against the view that there is an immutable human nature. He relies on the evidence based on hitherto unknown cultures and ways of life in the New World to argue that there are no universal laws of human behaviour and human nature. For instance, in discussing the habits of cannibals, he proclaims that he finds nothing 'savage or barbarous about those peoples, but that every man calls barbarous anything he is not accustomed to; it is indeed the case that we have no other criterion of truth or right-reason than the example and form of the opinion and customs of our own country' (Montaigne 1991c: 82). Montaigne connects this last point to the tenth Mode of Sextus (see chapter 1) and concludes that, given the diversity of moral, legal and religious behaviour, ethical relativism is the only possible position. Thus, as Richard Popkin claims, 'Armed with evidence about the savages of America, the cases in Ancient Literature, and the mores of contemporary Europe, Montaigne drove home the message of ethical relativism' (Popkin 2003: 53).

Such a tolerant attitude was in sharp contrast with the justifications offered by the conquerors of the New World and their spiritual and intellectual defenders. Two examples will show the great contrast. Here is the Dominican monk, Tomás Ortiz, writing to the Spanish Council of the Indies in the mid-sixteenth century:

> They are stupid and silly. They have no respect for truth, save when it is to their advantage. They are unstable. They have no knowledge of what foresight means. They are ungrateful and changeable. . . . They are brutal.
>
> (Sale 1990: 202)

And the humanist and nationalist Juan Ginés de Sepúlveda in 1550 compares the prudence, genius, magnanimity, temperance, humanity and religion of the Spanish with the Indians 'in whom you scarcely find even vestiges of humanity', and concludes that no one 'can doubt that these people – so uncivilized, so barbaric, contaminated with so many impieties and obscenities – have justly been conquered' (ibid.).

In contrast with the bigotry surrounding him, Montaigne's relativism is tolerant and open-minded. The argument he uses to deny the existence of a single universal human nature is empiricist in its orientation and relies on the diversity of human experience – both at the individual and social levels. The empirical fact of diversity demonstrates that there cannot be a natural law for humankind. According to him, if there was such a thing as natural law, then there would also be consensus on customs, laws and ethics. But 'Nothing in all the world has greater variety than law and custom' (Montaigne 1987: 163). He concludes that human laws are based on opinions and traditions and not on any natural truths, but what is more, even when it comes to matters of truth and falsehood, 'it seems we have no other test of truth and reason than the example and pattern of the opinions and customs of the country we live in' (Montaigne 1991c: 82).

Montaigne's own ethical and political position was one of 'conservatism in one's own affairs, tolerance towards others' (Todorov 1993: 37). He, like many latter-day relativists, couples the moral imperative of tolerance with the empirical observations of diversity of cultures. Using a line of argument that is commonplace nowadays, he remarks: 'I do not loathe ideas which go against my own', 'I am . . . far from shying away when others' judgements clash with mine'. He is not 'unsympathetic to the companionship of men because they hold to other notions or parties', he maintains, because 'the most general style followed by Nature is variety' and in 'the whole world there has never been two identical opinions' for their 'most universal characteristic is diversity [and discordance]' (Montaigne 1991b: 231).

He does, however, condemn the behaviour of conquerors of the New World towards the natives, and argues that instead of creating 'a brotherly fellowship and understanding', we

> took advantage of their ignorance and lack of experience to pervert them more easily toward treachery, debauchery and cupidity, toward every kind of cruelty and inhumanity, by the example and model of our own manners. Whosoever else has ever rated trade and commerce at such a price? So many cities

razed to the ground, so many nations wiped out, so many millions of individuals put to the sword and the most beautiful and the richest part of the world shattered, on behalf of the pears-and-pepper business. Tradesmen's victories!

(Montaigne 1991a: 344)

The concurrence of relativism and tolerance has been one of the main attractions of the doctrine to all those who condemn bigotry and closed-mindedness, and Montaigne's writings are one of the earliest expressions of the openness that contemporary cultural and moral relativists advocate (see chapter 9). However, not all expressions of tolerance should be equated with relativism. A case in point is the work of Pierre Bayle (1647–1706), one of the most influential figures in the early Enlightenment. In his *Commentaire philosophique*, Bayle defends tolerance for all religious views, even those of the heretics, and maintains that 'those who adhere to heretical doctrines sincerely, and according to their conscience, are just as much worthy servants of the Lord as those who adhere to true Christian teaching' (Israel 2001: 326). However, Bayle also believes that the light of natural reason enables us to separate truth from falsehood, a view that sets him apart from both the sceptic and the relativist.

2.3 THE CARTESIAN IMPACT

Modern philosophy is usually traced from René Descartes (1596–1650). Cartesian rationalism, with its project of securing unwavering foundations for knowledge and a universal conception of reason, did not leave much room for relativism.[5] Once reason and rationality were accepted as universal methods and avenues for the discovery of truth, then relativism could hold no appeal. The scientific revolution, initiated through the discoveries of Copernicus, Galileo, Kepler and Descartes, imposed a new framework on our understanding of the universe, a framework that displayed faith in our ability to discover objective mind-independent truths using the invariant and universal procedures of the scientific method. Knowledge is gained by discoveries of facts that are independent of us. The Cartesian framework presented a picture of the world divided between the 'inner' and the 'outer', the subjective and the objective. The mind, i.e., the inner, has the function of representing the outer – the mind-independent world. The thinking subject, by using his faculty of reason, achieves knowledge in various fields; in particular he can rely on knowledge attained by introspection. The Cartesian ego is the source of our subjective descriptions of the world and, in so far as it is a rational faculty, these descriptions represent the objective world as it is. The Cartesian framework opened up the possibility of subjective, first-person, epistemic authority. In Descartes this subjective authority was mediated and legitimised by the light of reason. But once the possibility of the authority of the subjective views of individuals was accepted, and given that the threat of scepticism loomed large, the way was open for subjectivism to become the only credible justification for claims to knowledge. The full impact and the consequences of this division become clear only with the emergence of romanticism in the nineteenth century. In the romantic movement, which had its roots in some of the excesses of the Enlightenment and the ensuing Counter-Enlightenment, the Cartesian divide between the subjective and the objective was turned on its head and reason was made subservient to the imaginative, creative and personal aspects of the human mind. And, as we saw in the Introduction, the boundaries between subjectivism and relativism are not always very firmly drawn.[6] The Cartesian approach, therefore, is one aspect of the philosophical Manichaeism that, at least in part, motivates relativistic views.

2.4 RELATIVISM AND EMPIRICISM

Empiricism's formative idea is that all our knowledge is derived from sense experiences. In its Lockean version, the human mind is a *tabula rasa* on which information is imprinted. John Locke (1632–1704), following Galileo, Boyle and Descartes, distinguished between two sources of knowledge acquired through sense experiences: the primary and secondary qualities. Primary qualities, such as shape, extension and solidity, are characteristics that objects actually possess; they are features of the natural world as it exists itself, independently of human perceptions and conceptions. Secondary qualities, such as colour, smell, or taste – what later became known as 'sense-data'– are on the other hand not properties of objects; they 'are nothing in . . . objects themselves but powers to produce various sensations in us' (Locke, 1959: ii.viii.10). Objects do actually have the shape or weight that we attribute to them, but the colour, taste and smell are not inherent in the object, rather they are a function of the impact objects have on the sense-organs of the individual perceivers. Locke's distinction between primary and secondary qualities introduces the possibility of relativising the truth of assertions about secondary qualities to the experiential and mental states of individual perceivers.

Locke also discusses the variability of ethical outlooks in different societies and historical epochs. In *An Essay Concerning Human Understanding*, he writes:

> He that will carefully peruse the History of Mankind, and look abroad into several Tribes of Men, and with indifferency survey their Actions, will be able to satisfy himself, That there is scarce that Principle of Morality to be named, or *Rule of Vertue* to be thought on (those only excepted, that are absolutely necessary to hold Society together, which commonly too are neglected betwixt distinct Societies) which is not, somewhere or other, *slighted* and condemned by the general Fashion of the *whole Societies of* Men, governed by practical Opinions, and Rules of living quite opposite to others.
>
> (Locke 1959: Book 1, Ch. III, §10)

However, Locke did not draw any relativistic conclusions from observations of human diversity; rather, he argued that we need institutions which would regulate the moral and civic conduct of the members of various societies.

David Hume (1711–76) also discussed the issue of diversity in moral opinion, but even though he was sceptical about the possibility of rational foundations to morality, he believed that there were shared common starting points for ethics. For Hume, sentiments, rather than reason, were the universal source of morality. He argues: 'The sentiments which arise from humanity are not only the same in all human creatures, and produce the same approbation or censure, but they also comprehend all human creatures, etc.'(Hume 1972: 362). But there is scope for diversity despite a background of commonality. He observes:

> The customs of some nations shut up the women from all social commerce: Those of others make them so essential a part of society and conversation that, except where business is transacted, the male-sex alone are supposed almost wholly incapable of mutual discourse and entertainments. As this difference is the most material that can happen in private life, it must also produce the greatest variation in our moral sentiments.
>
> (Ibid.: 364)

However, such diversity can be explained as local variations on the application of the same moral principles, for 'the principles upon which men reason in morals are always the same; though the conclusions which they draw are often very different' (ibid.: 361). Diversity in custom and practice is acknowledged but it does not readily lead to relativism, for underlying such diversity there is constancy of human sentiments, such as sympathy, mutual attachment, fidelity and friendship. However, as we shall see in chapter 9, Hume's most famous contribution to ethical thought, his argument for an unbridgeable gap between facts and value judgements, has had a formative impact on the development of moral relativism and has been yet one more influential plank of the Manichaeism of modern philosophy (see 9.4).

Empiricist assumptions motivated some of the relativist positions taken by eighteenth-century philosophers. Montaigne already foreshadows this tendency, but a more obvious example can be found in the work of the French philosopher Claude-Adrien Helvétius (1715–71). Helvétius was a self-confessed Lockean empiricist, and, unlike Locke, a materialist, who rejected the possibility of the existence of anything beyond that of concrete matter, the knowledge of which comes to us through our sense experiences. His radical materialism rejects even abstract general ideas. According to Helvétius, moral philosophers belong either to the absolutist or to the relativist camp. The absolutist camp, headed by Plato, argues 'virtue is always one and the same' (Helvétius 1758; Todorov 1993: 45). The relativists, headed by Montaigne, hold the position that 'every nation forms a different idea of [virtue]' (Todorov 1993: 45). The first position is dismissed by Helvétius as a simple illusion. Montaigne's relativism is accepted in principle, but criticised for its lack of rigour and rational justification. According to Helvétius, all abstract ideas, including that of humanity, are fictitious. In engaging in the study of ethics, our unit of study should be the individual alone. Individual human beings seek pleasure and avoid pain, and what is pleasurable is identical with what is good. The judgement of individual human beings, and their aggregates, i.e., societies, are based on a hedonistic motivation of self-interest. It is an empirical fact, Helvétius goes on to argue, that individuals and groups of people differ greatly in what they consider pleasurable or to their interest. The empirical fact of diversity of preferences, coupled with a hedonistic definition of the good, establishes relativism (ibid.: 46–7).

Helvétius's relativism has a rather limited scope, for he allows that there can be individuals who are not subject to the same self-regarding hedonism as the general population, rather they are concerned with the higher issues of truth and justice. Helvétius himself is among this select few, so his own views have universal truth and are exempt from relativisation. His position is one instance of the dilemma confronting the defenders of relativism. Faced with the empirical fact of diversity, and in the absence of a philosophical justification for belief in a uniform human nature or natural law, relativism might seem the most plausible position. However, it is not possible, consistently, to make universal judgements from within the relativist framework and still maintain the truth of relativism. This is the paradox that haunts all relativists from Protagoras to the present.

2.5 RELATIVISM AND THE FRENCH ENLIGHTENMENT

The wide-ranging intellectual movement that falls under the umbrella title of 'the Enlightenment' heralded the emergence of a new scientific outlook, a secular humanist ideology and new and very different certainties. The Enlightenment emphasised the universal traits of human nature – reason and rationality in particular – together with ideas of progress towards a common point of perfection and the brotherhood of man. On the face of it, the emphasis on a universal human essence and trans-cultural norms of rationality did not leave much conceptual space for relativism. However, certain strands of this so-called 'Enlightenment Project' (MacIntyre 1988, 1990), paradoxically, facilitated the emergence of relativistic views. Chief among these was the advocacy of tolerance for other creeds and ways of life, conjoined with a strong interest in distant cultures which had been cultivated since the discovery of the New World. The result of all this was Exoticism (Todorov 1993) or the valorisation of alien cultures and peoples – an intellectual practice which, if not directly leading to relativism, certainly was conducive to the development of a relativistic ethos in cross-cultural evaluations.

One aspect of this paradox can be gleaned from the writings of French Enlightenment figures such as Voltaire (1694–1778), Diderot (1713–84) and Montesquieu (1689–1755) who were influenced, both directly and indirectly, by Montaigne's humanism. These authors were the first to explore the idea of viewing one's culture as an outsider might. The abundance of still-fresh accounts of travellers charting unknown territories and peoples led to idealised versions of the purportedly exotic practices they had discovered. These accounts, in turn, were presented as a means of criticising local customs and norms.[7] For instance, Diderot, in his 'Supplement to Bougainville's "Voyage"' (Diderot 1956: 183–239), outlines the by now all too familiar idealised image of the noble savage. The Tahitian is mild, innocent and happy, he claims, while civilised people are corrupt, vile and wretched. The natives live according to customs and rules that vary greatly from the familiar Western ones. They do not possess private property, operate their affairs based on egalitarian principles, and exercise sexual freedom not accepted in 'civilised societies' (Todorov 1993: 276). Diderot is opposed to the European mission of civilising the natives, who, by this account, are already superior to Europeans. He poses the particularly modern question of how to arrive at acceptable moral norms in the face of the plurality of incompatible ethical outlooks. Ultimately, he thinks that human nature can give us the foundation for establishing a trans-cultural method. But, simultaneously, he acknowledges that the only sensible advice is to 'be monks in France and savages in Tahiti. Put on the costume of the country you visit, but keep the suit of clothes you will need to go home in' (Todorov 1993: 238, 13).

Montesquieu's *Persian Letters* presents a further instance of the thinking about questions of diversity and relativism in the French Enlightenment. The book consists of the correspondence between two Persian visitors to Europe and their friends and family and staff in Persia. It explores 'the eternal contrast between real things . . . and the strange ways in which those things are perceived' (Montesquieu [1821] in Shklar 1987: 30). Usbek, the Persian visitor, assesses European culture and society perceptively and offers a rational analysis of its ills, but, at least initially, fails to see the limitations of his own society and point of view. Although the book is a trenchant criticism of European customs and religious beliefs, the encounter with the unfamiliar also leads to self-questioning by the visitors, so much so that the more gentle traveller, Rica, decides not to return to his homeland, and even the harsher and more despotic Usbek starts to wonder where his ideas about religious beliefs come from. In the end, both Muslim and Christian zeal and dogmatism seem absurd to him, and the way is opened for tolerance and mutual understanding.

A central concern of the book is the question of the natural versus the cultural. The French ask Rica, 'how can anyone be a Persian?' (Montesquieu [1821] 1964: XXX 55), the underlying assumption, obviously, being that there is something unnatural about being a non-European. For Montesquieu, the 'natural' is nothing but our acquired beliefs and practices, i.e., our customs. Our established practices and habits constitute the world and reality for each of us and lull us into believing that what is alien, different or 'other' is unnatural. In letter lix Rica writes to Usbek: 'it seems to me, Usbek, that we judge things only by applying them secretly to ourselves. I am not surprised that Negroes paint the devil in dazzling white and their gods in carbon black' (Montesquieu [1821] 1964: lix 100) and concludes 'if triangles were to create a god, they would describe him with three sides' (ibid.). Montesquieu's message resonates with liberals and multi-culturalists today: plurality of religions should be encouraged and a spirit of tolerance should accompany such pluralism.

Similarly, on political matters, Usbek argues,

> I have often asked what kind of government most conformed to reason. It has seemed to me that the most perfect is that which attains its goal with the least friction; thus that government is most perfect which leads men along paths most agreeable to their interests and inclinations.
>
> (Montesquieu [1821] 1964: lxxx 136)

The best political system is the one that satisfies the inclinations and goals of a given people, but since these inclinations may vary according to their social and natural backgrounds, any judgement of the merits or demerits of political systems can be made only relative to, and in the context of, such goals and inclinations.[8] Montesquieu's social/geographical relativism is also evident in his other writings. In *Spirit of the Laws*, he argues that laws must be regarded as 'relative' to the climate in which they are produced. Heat and cold, the terrain, the modes of subsistence, as well as the religion, customs and manners of a people, determine the nature of the laws fashioned for and by them, and should be studied and evaluated according to their context. Each climate dictates the lifestyle appropriate to it. For instance, liberty will not be produced by all climates (Shklar 1987: 93–110). This leads to a type of relativism whereby, in Europe, Catholicism is suited to the south and Protestantism to the north; while as far as foreign parts are concerned, Montesquieu argues, Montezuma would know better than the Spaniards what religion would suit his own people. Even a custom which may seem aberrant or repulsive to us, such as polygamy, cannot be condemned or even judged once we appreciate that it is part of a social order and appropriate to the society in which it has been produced. The view is relativistic in so far as it judges the appropriateness of religious and political ideologies and practices only in the context of the climatic and social order of particular societies and eschews universal verdicts on the rights and wrongs of such matters.

There is a tension between the avowed universalist aspirations of the Enlightenment, espoused by Montesquieu as well as other major figures in the movement, and the relativistic tone of his views. Montesquieu's work is one of the prime examples of what Todorov has labelled the attempt to 'conceptualise the diversity of peoples and the unity of the human race at one and the same time' (Todorov 1993: 353). Montesquieu attempts to solve the tension in his article on taste in the *Encyclopédie*. He argues that the soul has two kinds of passion: inherent and acquired. Among the inherent passions are desire for knowledge and curiosity, which arise out of the fact that human beings are primarily thinking beings. However, the effect of physical and bodily influences on these inherent traits should not be underestimated; we also possess acquired sentiments that are bequeathed to us from the society in which we live. Consequently, the values that arise from our inherent human traits are universal, while the ones that are dependent on local conditions such as climate and prevailing social conditions are local, particular and relative. The spirit of the individual, in so far as it is shaped by its local setting, is relative to her social and natural environment, he concludes.

The tension between universalism and particularism is apparent, albeit to a lesser degree, in the writings of other major Enlightenment figures. Even Voltaire does not think that there is unwavering uniformity among mankind. On the contrary, he believes that 'Men's inclinations and natures differ as much as their climates and their governments' (Voltaire [1771] 1994: 85). However, he argues:

> Even though that which in one region is called virtue, is precisely that which in another is called vice, even though most rules regarding . . . good . . . are as variable as the languages one speaks and the clothing one wears; yet it seems to me, nevertheless, certain that there are natural laws with respect to which human beings in all parts of the world must agree . . . [God] endowed man with certain inalienable feelings and these are the external bonds and the first law of human society.
>
> (Ibid.: 65)

Voltaire's expression of faith in universal constraints on human action is thus accompanied by a strong awareness of diversity and contingency.

Recent philosophical expressions of discontent with the Enlightenment have focused on the perceived universalising and totalising tendencies of the 'Enlightenment Project'. Postmodernist philosophers have cast doubt on notions of objectivity and rationality and the valorisation of universal reason, which they see as part of the unwelcome intellectual inheritance we have acquired from the

Enlightenment. Instead, they advocate, often only implicitly, a relativist position, not only on ethico-political questions but also in cognitive domains. Among English-language philosophers, Alasdair MacIntyre and John Gray, under the influence of Isaiah Berlin, have focused on the consequences of the Enlightenment for our moral and political outlook. They maintain that the Enlightenment Project was based on the unrealisable hope that 'human beings will shed their traditional allegiances and their local identities and unite in a universal civilisation grounded in generic humanity and a rational morality' (Gray 1995b: 2). The core project of the Enlightenment, Gray argues, was to replace local, customary or traditional moralities, and all forms of transcendental faith, with a critical or rational morality, which was projected for the creation of a future universal civilisation. The philosophical anthropology of the Enlightenment, Gray argues, amounted to the view that the 'diverse and often rivalrous cultural identities manifest throughout human history are not expressive of any primordial human disposition to cultural difference' (ibid.: 125). He believes that this failed discourse should be replaced by a recognition of the pluralist nature of our moral lives.

The same type of sentiments are expressed by MacIntyre, even though he arrives at very different conclusions. The Enlightenment Project, he argues, was the attempt to give an independent rational justification of morality. The breakdown of this project is responsible for the distinctively modern and contemporary standpoint that 'envisages moral debate in terms of a confrontation between incompatible and incommensurable moral premises and moral commitment as the expression of a criterionless choice between such premises, a type of choice for which no rational justification can be given' (MacIntyre 1984: 39). For MacIntyre, relativism is a consequence of the breakdown of the aspirations of the Enlightenment.

The postmodern critique of the legacy of the Enlightenment, and the criticisms by Gray and MacIntyre, despite their differing motivations, are similar in so far as they see the Enlightenment as the antithesis of pluralism, relativism and subjectivism. However, contrary to these critiques, I believe that a closer inspection of the work of individual figures of the French Enlightenment shows that their attitudes towards ethics, cultural relativism and universalism are more complex and multifaceted than may at first appear. Depending on which features of the Enlightenment we choose to valorise, we can find different connecting threads between relativism, monism and universalism. The writings of some thinkers of the French Enlightenment show their preoccupation with issues that form the basis of contemporary debates on relativism. In particular, at least two of the premises on which arguments for cultural relativism often rely found expression within the Enlightenment. The descriptive starting point for social and cultural relativism is the empirical observation that there exist a multiplicity of incompatible and irreconcilable world-views and value-systems. The normative premise of relativism is the liberal affirmation of the value and the desirability of tolerance and respect for other worldviews. The idea of tolerance, conjoined with an interest in distant cultures which had been cultivated since the discovery of the New World, informed the writings of several major and minor Enlightenment figures and led to discussions that are reminiscent of contemporary cultural relativism.

The core intellectual elements of relativism were present in the Enlightenment Project from its inception. The empirical observation of diversity, together with the humanist principle of respect and tolerance for other human beings, shaped the intellectual climate that fosters cultural (particularly moral) relativism. Most Enlightenment figures were unwilling to embrace outright relativism and, as critics of the Enlightenment have pointed out, they hoped that by recourse to the inherent universal traits of human nature they could find a solution to the dilemmas arising from their Exoticism and belief in the value of tolerance. However, as Montesquieu's work shows, even the core idea of universal human nature was rendered problematic once it was conjoined with awareness of diversity and difference.

2.6 KANT AND THE CHANGING ASPECT OF RELATIVISM

The writings of Montaigne in particular, and to a lesser extent those of some Enlightenment figures, both foreshadowed and influenced the development of cultural relativism in later periods. A number of philosophical developments in the eighteenth and nineteenth centuries facilitated the emergence of other strands of relativism.

The tension between relativistic tendencies and universalism inherent in the Enlightenment is also present in the work of Immanuel Kant (1724–1804). Kant, more than any other philosopher, is responsible for making explicit what was already implicit in Locke and Berkeley – that there are ineliminable conceptual contributions in all knowledge-claims and that a view from nowhere is not available to the human thinker. Kant expresses this point through the distinction between a noumenal and a phenomenal world. The noumenal world, the world of the 'thing in itself', has to exist in order for thought to be possible, but cannot be grasped directly by human thought. 'What objects may be in themselves, and apart from all this receptivity of our sensibility, remains completely unknown to us' (Kant 1929: A26/B42). The phenomenal world – the knowable world – is grasped by our senses, but this grasping is mediated through conceptual schemes or categorial frameworks. The raw data we acquire through our sensory experiences are organised, and made intelligible, by the 'forms of intuition' or the 'categories' that are the necessary elements of all knowledge. Concepts or the forms of intuition such as space and time, and the categories of understanding such as cause, unity and substance are the necessary forms of all actual and possible experience. Without them we would have no experiences, for all our experiences of the world, and their descriptions, are subject to the laws of these a priori categories.

Kant saw the introduction of scheme and content dualism as a necessary corrective measure to Leibniz's rationalist account of sensations and Locke's purely empiricist account of concepts, and a crucial step towards establishing a comprehensive story about how objective and universal knowledge is possible. According to Kant:

> though all our knowledge begins with experience, it does not follow that it all arises out of experience. For it may well be that even our empirical knowledge is made up of what we receive through impressions and of what our own faculty of knowledge (sensible impressions serving merely as the occasion) supplies from itself.
>
> (Kant 1929: B1)

For Kant there could be only one set of categories, which would form all experiences; hence, understanding and knowledge have an irredeemably universal character. The categories are not accidental features of individual human thought, or products of social and cultural forces; rather they are universal, necessary preconditions of thought.[9] They constitute the framework within which the very act of thinking becomes possible. However, Kant's own absolutism notwithstanding, the distinction between the data of experience and the conceptual principle for organising and conceptualising them allowed for the possibility that there may be more than one system or scheme of organisation. In the nineteenth century, Kant's transcendental categories were reinterpreted as contingent descriptions of actual human thinking practices. This psychologistic interpretation of Kant contributed to the relativistic interpretations of the scheme–content distinction and Kant's grand scheme was thus turned on its head for

> The study of the Kantian a priori sources of human cogni-
> tion was now taken to be an enquiry into what is psychologi-
> cally or physiologically prior to whatever humans obtain as
> material knowledge, and thus a topic for the physiologists
> (like von Helmholtz) or the psychologists (like Wundt). This
> philosophical naturalism reached its peak in the attempt to
> treat logic in a psychological way.
>
> (Kusch 1995: 2)

The conclusion drawn was that the laws of logic are an empirical
generalisation about human thinking and hence their scope and
authority may be limited to the human species only. For instance,
the early neo-Kantian Friedrich Albert Lange (1828–75) advanced a
biological and psychological interpretation of the a priori elements of
Kant's scheme–content dualism. He argued that the categories and
the forms of intuition and perception are ultimately grounded in
human biology (see Kusch 1995).

The view was criticised strongly by both Gottlob Frege (1848–1925)
and Edmund Husserl (1859–1938), the founders of contemporary
analytic philosophy and phenomenology respectively, who identified
psychologism with relativism – and relativism with subjectivism.
Husserl following his teacher Carl Stumpf saw psychologism in the
hands of neo-Kantians such as Jonas Cohn and Wilhelm Windelband
as the attempt to reduce all philosophical problems – epistemology in
particular but even logic – to psychology. In Chapter 7 of the *Prolegomena to the Logical Investigations*, Husserl uses arguments similar
to the one used by Plato against Protagoras (see 1.3) to claim that relativism is inconsistent and absurd, and that since relativism is a species
of psychologism, then psychologism is also inconsistent and absurd.
He defines relativism as: 'The measure of all truth is the individual
person. What is true for a person is what appears to him to be true;
one thing to one person, the opposite to another, if it so appears
to him' (Husserl [1900] 1970: P A/B 14). What is true or false then,
according to the relativist, depends on and varies with the subjective –
psychological – make-up of individual human beings (subjectivism),
or the collective make-up of different species (species-relativism or
anthropologism). Both views amount to a non-objective or psycho-
logist view of truth and logic. Husserl argues that truth, as well as the
laws of logic, is necessarily objective (and hence non-psychological).
According to him: 'It is not possible to relativise truth and yet maintain the objectivity of being. Clearly the relativisation of truth
presupposes an objective being as a point of reference, and therein lies

relativism's inconsistency' (ibid.: P A/B 132). We will return to the charge of self-refutation in chapter 4; the interesting point here is that in tracing the development of Kant's originally non-relativistic distinction between the noumenal and phenomenal world, and the contributions of conceptual categories in the construction of the latter, we arrive at discussions of relativism in one of its most ancient and traditional forms. Husserl assigns the fault to Kant's emphasis on the role of the subjective faculties in determining the supposedly a priori and objective categories of thought. There is nothing in Kant, he maintains, that can prevent us from arguing that the Kantian table of Categories could vary in different species or even individuals. The theoretical orientation of neo-Kantian psychologists and anthropologists, with their attendant relativism, he thinks, is rightly to be blamed on Kant.

A second way in which Kant's work has contributed to discussions of relativism can be seen in the development of twentieth-century views on conceptual relativism. As we shall see in chapter 7, Kantian dualism of scheme and content has paved the way for relativising ontology, or our accounts of what there is, to conceptual schemes.

2.7 RELATIVISM AND THE COUNTER-ENLIGHTENMENT

More direct intellectual forebears of twentieth-century relativism are thinkers of the Counter-Enlightenment of the eighteenth century, and the ensuing romantic movement in Germany. Giambattista Vico (1668–1744), Johann Georg Hamann (1730–88), Johann Gottfried Herder (1744–1803) and Wilhelm von Humboldt (1767–1835) introduced the idea that an understanding of cultural outlooks and norms is possible only in the context of the historical framework in which they originate. They rejected the Enlightenment's belief in the universal traits of human nature by emphasising the uniqueness of spirit (*Geist*) of individual nations or peoples (*Volk*). The Enlightenment thinkers were interested in human progress, while their opponents concentrated on the particular destinies of nations (Kuper 1999: 7). These authors thus opened the way for a historicised and situational interpretation of cognitive and moral systems, which in turn has strong connections with modern relativism (Berlin 2000: 255).

Giambattista Vico was an outspoken anti-Cartesian who criticised the primacy attached to rationality and emphasised the role of imagination in thinking and understanding. He proclaimed, against

Descartes, that 'knowing clearly and distinctly is a vice rather than a virtue of human understanding' (Vico [1774] 1984: 142).

Vico's most important contribution to Western intellectual history is, says Berlin, 'the proclamation of the autonomy of historical studies and of their superiority over those of nature' (Berlin 2000: 47). This doctrine is encapsulated in a famous passage in Vico's *New Science*, where he argues:

> But, in this dense night of darkness that hides the earliest antiquity, so remote from ourselves, there shines the eternal and never failing light of a truth beyond all doubt: that the world of civil society has certainly been made by men, and that its principles are therefore to be found within the modifications of our own human mind. Whoever reflects on this cannot but wonder that the philosophers should seriously have sought to attain *scienza* of the natural world, of which, since God made it, God alone has *scienza*; and that they should have neglected to meditate on the world of nations, or the civil world, of which since men had made it, men could attain *scienza*.
>
> (Vico [1774] 1984: §331)

Vico expresses a view that has shaped much of later debates on the status of the social sciences; the position that there is a fundamental difference between the human and the natural sciences and that we cannot understand social institutions, value-systems and our lives without placing them within their socio-historical contexts. As we shall see in chapter 3, this formative idea shaped the thinking of the social anthropologists in the twentieth century who have been instrumental in popularising cultural relativism.

Johann Georg Hamann was the father of the *Sturm und Drang* movement – an intellectual movement in Germany developed in the 1770s and characterised by its anti-Enlightenment sentiments.[10] His influence on romanticism is beyond dispute. The core of his philosophical thesis is opposition to the rationalist tendencies in all of Western philosophy – from the Greeks to his contemporaries – the French *philosophes*, which was shaped by a mystical experience in London in 1758. Berlin has called him the 'most passionate, consistent, extreme and implacable enemy of the Enlightenment and, in particular, of all forms of rationalism of his time . . . His influence, direct and indirect, upon the romantic revolt against universalism and scientific method in any guise was considerable and perhaps crucial'

(Berlin 2000: 250). Hamann's attack on rationalism in philosophy was directed against reliance on science, reason and analysis, the application of mathematical calculation and methodology, abstractions, a priori reasoning and deductive inferences, all of which he believed to be the main sources of the intellectual malaise of Western thought. 'He argued that reason is not autonomous, but governed by the subconscious; that it cannot grasp the particular or explain life; that it is inseparable from language, whose only foundation is custom and use; and that it is not universal but relative to a culture' (Beiser 1987: 18).

He may be seen as a precursor of modern relativism in two senses. First, he initiated what Berlin calls 'the great romantic revolt, the denial that there was an objective order, a *rerum natura*, whether factual or normative, from which all knowledge and all values stemmed, and by which all action could be tested' (Berlin 2000: 354). This romantic revolt in turn became the inspiration of those who have argued against the universalising tendencies of Western metaphysics, starting from Nietzsche down to contemporary postmodernist thinkers. Second, Hamann's views on language are reminiscent of contemporary epistemic and linguistic relativism.[11] He argued against the Kantian views on the primacy of reason and maintained that

> the purism of reason is a fallacy . . . because reason exists only in particular activities. There is no special faculty of reason, there are only rational ways of thinking and acting. To identify reason, we must refer to the ways people think and act; and that means, more specifically, how they act, write and speak in their language and in their cultures . . . reason is only a function, a specific way of thinking and acting in specific cultural and linguistic contexts.
>
> (Beiser 1987: 39)

Most significantly, Hamann maintained that language is both the instrument of reason and the source of all the confusions and fallacies of reason (Hamann 1967). Furthermore, the rules of rationality are embedded within languages whose only authority is tradition and use (ibid.). Not unlike some twentieth-century philosophers,[12] Hamann also believes that languages express a way of life. A way of life, he maintains, is based on patterns of experience which are not subject to criticism, for we cannot find an Archimedean point from which to conduct such critical examination (Berlin 2000: 359–60). Hamann's analysis of language and meaning foreshadows the arguments of contemporary relativists who deny the possibility of access to an external point of view from which to compare and criticise different worldviews and value-systems and who emphasise the need for criteria internal to a language or way of life for understanding and evaluating various belief-systems.

Similar arguments can be found in the work of Wilhelm von Humboldt who believed that language is the medium through which the collective spirit of a people manifests itself. According to him, 'language is, as it were, the outer appearance of the spirit of a people, the language is their spirit and the spirit their language; we can never think of them sufficiently as identical' (Humboldt [1835] 1999). Every language, Humboldt believed, has an inner linguistic form and 'there resides in every language a characteristic *worldview*' (ibid.: 60). Moreover, from 'every language . . . we can infer backwards to the national character' (ibid.: 154) of its speakers. Language is not just a means of communication or a way of labelling the world; rather, it provides a conceptual framework or a way of thinking for its users. And since different linguistic communities partake in their own particular 'linguistic form' then there is a multiplicity of such frameworks, each with its own ontological and metaphysical commitments.

Hamann directly influenced Herder, another major figure in the Counter-Enlightenment, who 'revered Hamann as a man of genius, looked upon him as the greatest of his teachers, and after his death venerated his ashes as the remains of a prophet' (Berlin 2000: 256). For Herder, as for many of the figures discussed in this section, 'the defining enemy was rational, scientific, universal civilization: the Enlightenment itself' (Kuper 1999: 7) – a view that is shared by many postmodernist thinkers today. Herder's views, in at least some of his writings, can be seen as a species of relativism, for he argues that in questions of moral, prudential and aesthetic values different historic periods demonstrate different tastes and preferences and we are not in a position to rank them or objectively choose between them. He asks:

> Could it be that what a nation at one time considers good, fair, useful, pleasant, true, it considers at another time bad, ugly, useless, unpleasant, false? – And yet this happens! . . . one observes . . . that ruling customs, that favorite concepts of honor, of merit, of what is useful can blind an age with a magical light, that a taste in these and those sciences can constitute the tone of a century, and yet all this dies with the century.
>
> (Herder 2002: 256)

Herder's views on the fundamental differences between the beliefs, concepts and values held at different historical periods negate the universalism of the philosophers of the Enlightenment such as Voltaire and Hume. In his most influential work, *Ideas about the Philosophy of History of Mankind*, he introduces the idea that to understand a belief or a value we should view and assess it as it is viewed, valued and assessed within the particular culture or tradition to which it belongs. 'Each nation', he argues, 'must be considered solely in its place with everything that it is and has – arbitrary separatings, slingings into a confused jumble, of individual traits and customs yields no history' (ibid.: 395).

Herder has also been credited by Berlin as one the first thinkers to realise that there is not only a multiplicity, but also an incommensurability in values of different cultures and societies (Berlin 2000: 176), and since incommensurability and incompatibility of equally valid value-systems are often seen as cornerstones of relativism, Herder then may be seen as a proto-relativist. Herder complains that 'The general, philosophical, philanthropic temper of our age seeks to extend "our own ideal" of virtue and happiness to each distant nation even to the remotest ages in history' (quoted in Berlin 2000: 216). The correct historical understanding of the human condition shows that there are 'many ways of life and many truths – to believe that everything is either true or false is a wretched general illusion of our progressive age' (ibid.). The French *Encyclopédistes*, for instance Voltaire, had made the mistake of assuming that man is the same at all times and places, or that morality is the same among 'all civilized peoples'.[13] According to Herder, diversity is the defining feature of human existence: 'Every group has a right to be happy in its own way. It is terrible arrogance to affirm that, to be happy, everyone should become European' (ibid.: 223). We should avoid the temptation to rank nations and cultures.

> The nature-investigator presupposes no *order of rank* among the creatures that he observes; all are equally dear and valuable to him. Likewise the nature-investigator of humanity. The Negro has as much right to consider the white man a degenerate, a born albino freak, as when the white man considers him a beast, a black animal.
>
> (Herder 2002: 394–5)

A unifying theme running through the work of many Enlightenment thinkers was the belief that humankind has a uniform nature, which can give rise to similar universal goals such as justice, happiness and the rule of wisdom. These universal goals, however, might be affected variously by the needs and desires of different people, depending on the circumstances and the environment in which they are formed. Herder's key insight, on the other hand, is

> that one must not judge one culture by the criteria of another; that differing civilisations are different growths, pursue different goals, embody different ways of living, are dominated by different attitudes to life; so that to understand them one must perform an imaginative act of 'empathy' into their essence, understand them 'from within' as far as possible and see the world through their eyes.
>
> (Berlin 2000: 236)

This is because, according to Herder, historical writing and understanding is an art form rather than a science. He believes that 'one is more likely to find exemplars of history rather than rules for a historical art' and each example cannot be understood or appreciated unless 'situated in its historical moment'. No one example could be used for explaining the history of all nations and all times. (Zammito 2002: 335). This stance greatly influenced German romanticism as well as important philosophers such as Hegel, Nietzsche and Dilthey.[14]

2.8 RELATIVISM AND NINETEENTH-CENTURY HISTORICISM

The towering philosophical figure of the nineteenth century was Georg Wilhelm Friedrich Hegel (1770–1831). The Hegelian contribution to the development of relativism in modern thought, like that of Kant, came about in a circuitous manner for, like Kant, Hegel cannot in any sense be seen as a relativist. There is, however, a palpable tension between two aspects of Hegel's theory of rationality. On the one hand, he emphasises the all-encompassing and absolute nature of reason which has 'infinite power' and 'rules the world' and hence ensures that 'world history has been rational in its course' (Hegel 1975: 28). On the other, he highlights the historical dimensions of human reason and understanding. Once it is allowed that reason and knowledge have a strong historical dimension, then the possibility arises that different histories, rather than the transcendental absolute idea of history, shape understanding and knowledge in different ways. In a unique way Hegel has managed to combine absolutism and relativism in his philosophical orientation. This paradoxical feature of his work has been noted by several philosophers in recent years. Hilary Putnam, for instance, has pointed out:

> Hegel, who introduced the idea that Reason itself changes in history, operated with two notions of rationality: there is a sense in which what is rational is measured by the level to which Spirit has developed in the historical process at a given time . . . And there is the limit notion of rationality in Hegel's system; the notion of that which is destined to be stable, the final self-awareness of Spirit which will not itself be transcended.
>
> (Putnam 1981: 158)

Karl Popper has expressed somewhat similar views in much stronger, and rather oversimplified, terms. He argues:

> Hegel was both a relativist and an absolutist . . . According to [him], truth itself was both relative and absolute. It was relative to each historical and cultural framework: there could thus be no rational discussion between such frameworks since each of them had a different standard of truth. But Hegel held his own doctrine that truth was relative to the various frameworks to be absolutely true, since it was part of his own relativistic philosophy.
>
> (Popper 1994: 47)

Many thinkers since Hegel have emphasised only the historical dimensions of rationality and thought, neglecting Hegel's transcendental conception of rationality, and thus have embraced historicism or the view that cognitive norms, such as rationality, truth and justification, as well as ethical values, are both particular and relative to their specific historical and social conditions. The Hegelian influence on the development of social relativism in general and historicism in particular can be traced through two distinct routes.

The first is Marxist and neo-Marxist historicist views. The most forceful statement of Marxist historicism can be found in a famous passage by Karl Marx (1818–83) and Friedrich Engels (1820–95):

> The ideas of the ruling class are in every epoch the ruling ideas . . . The ruling ideas are nothing more than the ideal expression of the dominant material relationships.
>
> (Marx and Engels 1963: 39)

The view, as later developed by Marxist intellectuals, leads to histori-cal relativism. For instance Michel Foucault, whose views and their relativistic implications will be discussed in chapter 3, has argued that 'the concept of liberty is "an invention of the ruling classes" and not fundamental to man's nature' (Foucault 1977: 141).

The original statement of Marxist relativism is found in Engels' *Anti-Dühring* where he argues against Eugen Dühring's (1833–71) universalistic view of ethics. According to Engels, the ethical domain does not deal with unassailable universal principles, for truth and fal-sity have absolute validity only within an extremely limited sphere, and even logic cannot give us conclusive truths. Knowledge-claims, particularly those concerning the historical or human sciences, Engels argues, are essentially relative and are 'limited to an apprehension of the pattern and the effects of certain forms of society and of the state that exist only at a particular time and for a particular people and that are by their very nature transitory' (Engels [1886] 1985: 18). The effects of societal and historical forces are even clearer in the ethical domain. 'Notions of good and evil have varied so much from society to society and from one time to another that they often directly contradict one another' (ibid.: 22). Social systems and group-ings can be individuated on the basis of their modes of production, and each of them – the feudal aristocracy, the bourgeoisie and the proletariat, for instance – has its own particular ethical beliefs and practices. The economic base–structure, the class relationship and the practical conditions operating in each of these social systems deter-mine the values according to which people lead their lives. No ethical system possesses absolute truth or finality, but Engels hopes that proletarian ethics – to become dominant in the future communist world – will have the most enduring principles, but unlike Lenin, he does not think that even these will have absolute truth (Ladd 1985).

The influence of Hegelian historicism is also evident in the work of one of the leading figures in continental philosophy – existentialism and hermeneutics in particular – Wilhelm Dilthey (1833–1911). In a manner reminiscent of Herder and Vico, Dilthey argues that each nation is a self-contained unit with its own 'horizon', i.e., a character-istic conception of reality and system of values. He also believes that the Hegelian 'objective *Geist*', or collective spirit, manifests itself through texts and other uses of language, and so is available for study, but only by way of subjective, intuitive empathetic understanding. The methods of the natural sciences are completely inappropriate for such purposes (Kuper 1999: 35).

Dilthey's historicism leads to what he calls 'historical relativism'.

According to him, by making historical comparisons we discover the relativity and contingency of all historical convictions; in particular we realise that all values and belief-systems that have emerged in the course of history bear the mark of their historical conditions and consciousness. Different historical epochs have produced different values or norms – each presenting itself as unconditional and universal. This is because 'The concept of value arises from life [and] . . . the norm for every judgement, etc., are given in the relative conceptions of meaning, value and purpose of nations and ages' (Dilthey 1961: 167). By acquiring historical consciousness we become aware of the conflicts between these supposedly unconditional and hence absolute values and discover their historical contingency. However, Dilthey believes that relativism does not lead to a free-for-all cognitive anarchy, because:

> The historical consciousness of the finitude of every histori-
> cal phenomenon . . . and of the relativity of every kind of
> faith, is the last step toward the liberation of man. With it,
> man achieves the sovereignty to enjoy every experience to the
> full and surrender himself to it unencumbered, as if there
> were no system of philosophy or faith to tie him down . . .
> the mind becomes sovereign over the cobwebs of dogmatic
> thought . . . And in contrast to relativity, the continuity of
> creative forces asserts itself as the central historical fact.
>
> (Ibid.)

Dilthey then confronts the dilemma facing all relativists by bravely exempting his own theory from the scope of historical relativism. He argues that some 'life-experiences' are truly historical, in the sense that only an immersion in the 'objective mind' of the society in which they were produced can make them intelligible. Philosophical propositions as well as mathematical theories are not historically situated, for we can understand them without having to know anything about their historical context.[15] Although some metaphysical systems are historically relative, historical relativism is not, and the discovery of this truth leads to liberation from dogmatism and ensures continuous creativity.

Dilthey's hermeneutics also influenced Max Weber and his sociologist heirs. Weber radicalised the Hegelian standpoint by introducing a 'perspectival' view of historical understanding, according to which there is a plurality of rationalities for different spheres of life such as music, religion, law, etc. The perspectival sociological approach, as well as Marxist views on the dependence of superstructural phenomena, such as ethical or aesthetic values, on historical and economic foundations, provided some of the theoretical bases for cultural relativism, a topic for the next chapter.

2.9 NIETZSCHE'S PERSPECTIVISM

Weber's doctrine of perspectivalism has its roots not only in Hegelian historicism but also in Nietzsche's devastating critique of both Kant and Hegel. Given Nietzsche's very personal aphoristic style of writing and unconventional lines of thought, it is difficult to assess the extent to which he subscribed to relativism; however, his role in the rise of relativism in the twentieth century cannot be doubted. Even where no direct line of influence can be found, Nietzsche foreshadows many of the key ideas of twentieth-century philosophy. His anti-metaphysical diatribe is echoed in the work of the logical positivists; his view of philosophy as a therapeutic activity, where traditional philosophical problems are to be dissolved rather than resolved, and his conviction that we are misled by the grammar of our language, are echoed in the writings of the later Wittgenstein (see chapter 3). His advocacy of a pragmatic view of truth and his rejection of the correspondence theory of truth have parallels in the works of the American pragmatists and neo-pragmatists (see chapters 4 and 7).[16] Postmodernist thinkers, both in their critical standpoint towards the intellectual ideals of the Enlightenment and in their relativistic tendencies, often take their lead directly from Nietzsche (see chapter 3).

One prominent feature of Nietzsche's work is his revolt against metaphysical system-building in general, and Kant's legacy to philosophy in particular. Kant, as we saw, maintained that we are incapable of unmediated knowledge of the world or the 'thing in itself', since we gain knowledge of the world only under the forms of our perception. Nietzsche to some extent agrees with this diagnosis, but goes much further by claiming that we not only construct the world in which we live but also can construct it in different ways. This radicalisation of the Kantian position arises out of Nietzsche's rejection of the very distinction between the noumenal and the phenomenal world. There are no means available to the human mind for drawing such a distinction, because the distinction presupposes what Kant ruled out – the possibility of a 'view from nowhere', i.e., the possibility of separating what the mind contributes to the world and what is in the world. All reports of so-called 'facts' are statements of interpretation which could always be supplemented or replaced by other interpretations.

The thing in itself is devoid of significance; it is an empty category.

> The value of the world lies in our interpretation . . . previous
> interpretations have been perspective valuations by virtue of
> which we can survive in life . . . The world with which we are
> concerned is false, i.e., it is not a fact but a fable and approxi-
> mation on the basis of a meagre sum of observations; it is 'in
> flux' as something in a state of becoming, as a falsehood
> always changing but never getting near the truth: for – there
> is no 'truth'.
>
> (Nietzsche 1968: §616)

Language is not simply a means of describing what there is; rather, it
imposes a framework of interpretation on our thoughts. All the categories invented by metaphysicians, including the Kantian categories,
such as cause, identity, unity, substance, etc., arise out of language
and are imposed on our thinking by language. Language, according
to Nietzsche, far from giving us a true account of things as they are in
the world, inflicts a false metaphysics on our thinking. These considerations apply not only to the everyday common-sense world, but also
to sophisticated scientific theories. 'It is perhaps just dawning on five
or six minds that physics, too is only an interpretation and arrange-
ment of the world (according to our own requirements, if I may say
so!) – and not an explanation of the world' (Nietzsche [1886] 1996:
§14). Scientists are not capable of saying how the world is because
even 'The atom which [the scientists] posit, is inferred in accordance
with the logic of consciousness–perspectivism – and is thus itself a fiction' (Nietzsche 1968: III 339). Common sense constitutes one
perspective among many and it, no less than the others, seeks to
impose itself where it can: this is the metaphysics of the masses or, as
Nietzsche will say, 'of the herd'.

What of the reality that we take for granted? 'What we now call the
world is the result of errors and fantasies, which in the total development of organic being, gradually emerged and interbred with one
another, and have been bequeathed to us as the accumulated treasury
of the entire past' (Nietzsche [1878] 1984: 16), he argues. 'We cannot
by any possible means get at the truth, since that would mean getting
at the bare uninterpreted facts, or objects with real being, But we
know there are no such things despite our temptation to follow language into a belief in them. Therefore the word "true" becomes
meaningless, and we must learn to do without it"' (Warnock 1978:
42). There is nothing true, or good for that matter, in the objective or

absolutist sense of the word – for 'there are many kinds of eyes, even the sphinx eyes – and consequently there are many kinds of "truths", and consequently there is no truth' (Nietzsche 1994: III §12). In his most iconoclastic moments he proclaims:

> What, then, is truth? A mobile army of metaphors, meto-nymies, anthropomorphisms, in short a sum of human rela-tions which have been subjected to poetic and rhetorical intensification, translation, and decoration, and which, after they have been in use for a long time, strike a people as firmly established, canonical, and binding; truths are illusions of which we have forgotten that they are illusions, metaphors which have become worn by frequent use and have lost all sensuous vigour, coins which, having lost their stamp, are now regarded as metal and no longer as coins.
>
> (Nietzsche 1999: 146)

We should put aside our prejudices regarding the antithesis between truth and falsity, he advises, 'Indeed, what compels us to assume there exists an essential antithesis between "true" and "false"? Is it not enough to suppose grades of appearances and, as it were, lighter and darker shades and tones of appearance – different *valeurs*, to speak in the language of painters?' (Nietzsche [1886] 1996: 65 §34). Although he does not proclaim relativism about truth in any simple or direct manner, the claim that 'truth', in some sense, is both a product and expression of human relations does allow for relativistic understand-ing of truth-claims.

Nietzsche's comments on ethics also frequently have a strong rela-tivistic flavour. In *Human all too Human* he contends:

> The hierarchy of the good . . . is not fixed and identical at all times. If someone prefers revenge to justice, he is moral by the standard of an earlier culture, yet by the standard of the present culture he is immoral.
>
> (Nietzsche [1878] 1984: 45 §42)

And in *Beyond Good and Evil* he tells us

> The diversity of men is revealed not only in the diversity of their tables of what they find good, that is to say in the fact that they regard diverse goods worth striving for and also differ as to what is more or less valuable, as to the order of

rank of the goods they all recognize – it is revealed even more in what they regard as actually *having* and *possessing* what they find good.

(Nietzsche [1886] 1996: 116–17)

The attempt by philosophers to find universal and objective moral precepts is based on illusion, for

What philosophers called 'the rational ground of morality' and sought to furnish was, viewed in the proper light, only a scholarly form of faith in the prevailing morality, a new way of expressing it, and thus itself a fact within a certain morality.

(Ibid.: 109)

The important point to realise is that all descriptions of reality and all claims of knowledge, including moral knowledge, are inevitably made from a certain standpoint or perspective and hence cannot be representations of what is really out there. 'There is only a perspective seeing, only a perspective knowing' (Nietzsche 1994: III 12). Our perceptions as well as our understanding of the world are perspectival and hence partial in three different senses. We can only see the world, both literally and metaphorically, from a particular angle and furthermore our perceptions and conceptions are coloured by our values and desires. In addition, they are informed by our particular historical and social circumstances. To fail to realise this, to believe that all metaphysical and philosophical systems can be anything other than projective or perspectival representations of reality, is to fall into the trap of dogmatism, and paradoxically a certain kind of naïve nihilism, or belief in nothing.

Unsurprisingly, Nietzsche often uses visual metaphors to explain the idea of perspectives, thus giving the impression that a perspective is something akin to a visual standpoint. But a Nietzschean perspective is better understood as a means of interpreting and coping with our experiences. It has the elements of a worldview and in that sense the visual metaphors are apt. In fact Nietzsche believes that human consciousness can grasp the world only at the level of signs and this constitutes 'the essence of phenomenalism and perspectivism' (Nietzsche [1882/1887] 1974: 354). His perspectivism is one aspect of his holistic view of knowledge and beliefs. According to him, 'the *observed* cannot but be seen partially since everything in the world ... is ultimately "bound to and conditioned" by everything else' (May [1999] 2002: 141).

We cannot speak of a perspective without relating it to the person(s) whose perspective it is. Perspectives do not have a *sui generis* existence, they always depend on the subject of the experience. The question then arises, 'what is it that we interpret?' or, 'what is it that we have different perspectives of?' But these questions, despite their air of legitimacy, are nonsensical. Ordinarily we speak of many perspectives of the same object, but for Nietzsche there cannot be any meaningful talk of 'same object', other than through a perspective. Furthermore, no one perspective can occupy a privileged position; there are no true perspectives, only perspectives that prevail at any given time in history, and Nietzsche does not allow for convergence of different perspectives. It is in this sense that his perspectivism becomes tantamount to relativism. Since we cannot appeal to any facts or criteria independently of their relation to the perspectives we have, we can do little more than insist on the legitimacy of our own perspective, and try to impose it on other people.

According to Nietzsche then, 'There are no facts, only interpretations' (quoted in Danto 1980). What is more, we are not in a position to contrast these interpretations with the world out there because there would be no world left over once we subtract our interpretation from it. 'We see all things by means of our human head, and cannot chop it off, though it remains to wonder what would be left of the world if indeed it had been cut off' (Nietzsche [1878] 1984: 9). Consequently, 'There are no eternal facts, no absolute truths' (ibid.: 20). Even logic and reason are not immune from this perspectivism. 'Rational thought is interpretation according to a scheme that we cannot throw off. The world seems logical to us because we have made it logical' (Nietzsche 1968: III, 521). Logic and reason are the means of arranging the world for our own use. The universe, then, is rational only to the extent that we have made it so. We have made the mistake of seeing logic and reason as touchstones of truth, and of positing our 'anthropocentric idiosyncrasy as the measure of Things, as a guide to the "real" and the "unreal"' (ibid. III, 584). Every description of 'objective facts', whether proposed by scientists or by our common sense is coloured and informed by the needs dictated to us by the historical conditions in which we find ourselves and by our physical limitations. The only legitimate use of the concepts of truth and good is a pragmatic one: truth is that which furthers our survival. The falseness of a judgement, Nietzsche claims, 'is to us not necessarily an objection to a judgement: it is here that our new language perhaps sounds strangest. The question is to what extent it is life-advancing, life-preserving, species-preserving, perhaps even species-breeding' (Nietzsche [1886] 1996: 35). However, 'there would be no life at all if not on the basis of perspective evaluations and appearances' (Nietzsche [1878] 1984: 34), and 'The world that we have not reduced to terms of our own being, our own logic, our Psychological prejudices and presupposition, does not exist as a world at all' (Nietzsche 1968: III, 568). We cannot set aside our perspective because it contains errors necessary for life. 'Without measuring reality against the purely invented world of the unconditional and self-identical, without a continual falsification of the world by means of numbers, mankind could not live – to renounce false judgements would be to renounce life, would be to deny life' (Nietzsche [1886] 1996: 35§4). But we should keep in mind that 'a belief, however, necessary it may be for the preservation of a species, has nothing to do with truth' (Nietzsche 1968: III, 487).[17]

There are strong connections between perspectivism and relativism. A belief or statement may be legitimate, acceptable or even true from one perspective and not so from another, and since we cannot rank perspectives or even compare them, relativism ensues. But this is a precarious philosophical position. As Richard Rorty points out:

> As long as he is busy relativizing and historicizing his predecessors, Nietzsche is happy to redescribe them as webs of relations to historical events, social conditions, their own predecessors, and so on. At these moments he is faithful to his own conviction that the self is not a substance, and that we should drop the whole idea of 'substance' or something that cannot be perspectivalized because it has a real essence, a privileged perspective on itself. But at other moments . . . he is interested in finding a perspective from which to look back on the perspectives he inherited, in order to see a beautiful pattern.
>
> (Rorty 1990: 106)

Perspectivism, like relativism, can lead to the paradox of self-referentiality, which seems to be the trap ahead of all relativists who wish to make a totalising statement about the human condition. The dilemma Nietzsche faces is whether his own thesis is made from a perspective. For if it is, then there may be perspectives in which the thesis is not true. If, on the other hand, the doctrine of perspectivism is not itself perspectival, then there is at least one truth that is not perspectival.[18]

A variety of solutions to this paradox have been suggested. Some commentators have argued that, since Nietzsche denies the force of logic, he would be happy to embrace the paradoxical nature of his doctrine. Albert Cinelli, for instance, has argued that to attribute to Nietzsche a consistent and unitary theory of truth is to be, to some extent, 'anti-Nietzschean' for Nietzsche is 'the philosopher of the dangerous maybe' (Cinelli 1993: 43). Others have tried to tame Nietzsche by attributing to him some variants of traditional theories of truth, albeit in a weakened and modified form. Maudemarie Clark, for instance, has argued that Nietzsche rejects a strong or metaphysical version of the correspondence theory of truth and replaces it with a minimalist correspondence theory, which is consistent with perspectivism (Clark 1990: 31–40). Steven D. Hales and Rex Welshon, on the other hand, have distinguished between weak and strong forms of perspectivism. Strong perspectivism is the thesis that 'for every statement, there is some perspective in which it is true, and some perspective in which it is untrue' (Hales and Welshon 2000: 31). Weak perspectivism, on the other hand, is the thesis that 'there is at least one statement such that there is some perspective in which it is true, and some perspective in which it is untrue . . . it is consistent with weak perspectivism that some statements have the same truth value in all perspectives, that is one can maintain that very many, nearly all statements have their truth value perspectivally, and yet hold that some statements have their truth value absolutely' (ibid.).

The tone of Nietzsche's writings often indicates that he regards his thesis as true without qualification, that he indeed believes that the thesis of perspectivism is true across all possible perspectives. However, it is possible for there to be truths that are invariant across all perspectives, and therefore universal, but still perspectival. Simon May, for instance, argues that 'there are some items that, according to Nietzsche, would be seen (as true or existing) from any perspective' (May [1999] 2002: 17). Understood in this light, Nietzsche does not seem to succumb to the charge of self-refutation levelled against relativists, for there is no formal conflict in the claims that all statements are perspectival and that some statements are true from all perspectives. However, we are still justified in feeling at least some unease about the claim that we are all limited or imprisoned by our 'all too human' perspectives, unable to see 'around our corner', except for Nietzsche, who has the capacity to overcome these limitations and see a truth which is invariant across all perspectives.

2.10 CONCLUSION

Relativism, unlike various other philosophical theses or problems, does not constitute a unified doctrine with a more or less discrete linear history and intellectual genealogy. As the discussions in this chapter have demonstrated, different strands of relativism were developed and shaped in response to a wide variety of philosophical concerns. A number of recent cultural and intellectual currents have contributed to the resurgence of interest in relativism over the past hundred years. In the next chapter, we shall look at some of these.

3

Contemporary sources of relativism

3.1 INTRODUCTION

Relativism has shaped the intellectual ethos of our times. As early as in the 1950s it had found its way into the more popular debates on the scope and requirements of morality when 'absolute relativity' was seen as 'hip', and traditional views of moral duty were deemed to be 'square'. Norman Mailer in 1957 wrote:

> Character . . . enters then into an absolute relativity where there are no truths other than the isolated truths of what each observer feels at each instant of his existence . . . What is consequent therefore is the divorce of man from his values, the liberation of the self from the Super-ego of society. The only Hip morality . . . is to do what one feels whenever and wherever it is possible, and – this is how the war of the Hip and the Square begins – to engage in one primal battle: to open the limits of the possible for oneself, for oneself alone because that is one's need.
>
> (Mailer, quoted in Cook 1999: 41)

The resurgence of interest in relativism in the last few decades has a variety of sources. This chapter examines some of the more prominent cultural and intellectual currents that have helped to make relativism such a prominent feature of our intellectual life.

3.2 EROSION OF OLD CERTAINTIES

The process of secularisation that had begun in Europe with the Enlightenment gathered momentum in the nineteenth century. Advances in science, Darwin's theory of evolution in particular, further weakened faith in the biblical account of the universe and man's place therein. T. H. Huxley, a fervent proselytiser on behalf of Darwin's revolutionary ideas, coined the term 'agnosticism', thus capturing an intellectual sentiment that became common in the twentieth century. At the turn of the twentieth century, an increasing number of intellectuals, following Nietzsche, proclaimed the end of the Christian era and the death of God. With the waning of religious belief, there was also a sharp decline in moral confidence; if God is dead, then indeed everything may be possible, or at least thinkable.

In the nineteenth century the discovery of the possibility of non-Euclidean, 'alternative', geometries delivered a further blow to some of the old epistemological certainties. Euclid's *Elements* had often been seen as a perfect model of how, given some intuitively plausible assumptions, together with logical deductions, we can arrive at a priori and necessary knowledge. Kant famously saw Euclid's geometry as proof that our intuitions of space are a priori. Of all the assumptions made in the *Elements*, the fifth or the 'parallel postulate, which states that 'through any given point there is one and only one parallel to a given straight line (which does not go through the given point), i.e., one straight line which lies in the same plane with the first and does not intersect it' (Reichenbach 1957: 2) had proven to be the most troublesome, since it depended on the presupposition that space is infinite. Nicolai Lobachevsky (1792–1856) in Russia and János Bolyai (1802–60) in Hungary independently announced the discovery of a new geometry of space where more than one parallel could be accepted and the three angles of a triangle could add up to less than 180 degrees. Their work led to Riemannian geometry (Bernhard Riemann 1826–66), according to which space is not flat as Euclid had postulated, but intrinsically curved, and can have more than three dimensions. Riemann's work in turn made Einstein's general theory of relativity possible. Euclidean geometry lost its status as an a priori science, and Kant's grand scheme of the distinction between a priori and a posteriori knowledge began to crumble. It is an indication of the enormity of this discovery that Frege steadfastly resisted the possibility of non-Euclidean geometry because it would have undermined his own project of finding univocal foundations for another necessary and a priori field of knowledge – mathematics.

With the discovery of non-Euclidean geometries it became possible to ask whether geometry was simply an empirical science and, if so, whether other exemplars of necessary truths, such as logic, may not also turn out to be contingent and empirical. The developments of formal 'alternative' logical systems, particularly Łukasiewicz's many-valued logics, which had philosophical import as well as technical merit, gave further ammunition to those who were no longer inclined to accept the absolute authority of purportedly univocal, necessary and a priori truths. It was felt that if the most secure of traditional areas of knowledge is open to such radical revision then nothing is immune from doubt.

The scientific developments at the beginning of the twentieth century further eroded the old certainties. Einstein's general and special theories of relativity, which made descriptions of space and time dependent on or *relative to* the motion of observer and observed, not only cast doubt on Newtonian physics, depriving it of the unassailable status it had enjoyed in the previous two centuries, but it also popularised and conferred scientific respectability on the slogan 'everything is relative'. This confluence of relativity theory with relativism became a strong contributory factor in the increasing prominence of relativism: social theorists and even philosophers frequently cited the findings of Einstein in support of their theses. For instance, as we shall see later in this chapter, Benjamin Lee Whorf acknowledges his debt to Einstein in developing his theory of linguistic relativity. Even some contemporary philosophers see a ready conceptual ground for relativism in the special theory of relativity, hence Chris Swoyer:

> Earlier in this century, the special theory of relativity was sometimes taken as a model for relativism, though because of misunderstandings of the theory this often led only to confusion. Nevertheless, there is something to be said for the paradigm. On Einstein's view such qualities as mass and velocity, once believed to be invariant or absolute, are now seen to be relative to inertial frameworks. To say that such qualities are relative is to say that they call for one more argument place or parameter than was formerly thought to be needed, and as a first approximation we may view relativism as the thesis that some concept Φ requires relativization to some parameter π.
>
> (Swoyer 1982: 85)

The influence of the theory of relativity on discussion of relativism is also apparent indirectly though analogies and examples used in this area. For instance, Gilbert Harman draws the following analogy between Einstein's relativistic conception of mass and his own relativistic conception of morality:

Einstein's relativistic conception of mass involves the following claim about the truth conditions of judgements of mass.

(1) For the purposes of assigning truth conditions, a judge-
    ment of the form, the *mass of X is M*, has to be
    understood as elliptical for a judgement of the form, *in
    relation to spatio-temporal framework F the mass of X is
    M* ... [Similarly] ... Moral relativism makes the follow-
    ing claim about moral judgements.
(2) For *the* purposes of assigning truth conditions, a judge-
    ment of the form, it would be morally wrong of P to D,
    has to be understood as elliptical for a judgement of the
    form, *in relation to moral framework M, it would be
    morally wrong of P to D. Similarly for other moral judge-
    ments.*

(Harman 1996: 4)

Further discoveries in theoretical physics undermined traditional
views of science and conceptions of the world. Heisenberg's uncertainty principle in particular lends itself to the belief that even in the
realm of natural sciences invariant and absolute laws may be hard to
find. According to the uncertainty principle, it is impossible to measure accurately both the velocity and the position of a fundamental
particle, or to determine whether particles have retained their original
character after colliding with each other. The principle casts doubt on
the operation of normal causal laws at the level of elementary particles and further undermines the certainties of the Newtonian
mechanistic worldview. Heisenberg writes:

> we can no longer consider 'in themselves' those building
> stones of matter which we originally held to be the last objec-
> tive reality. This is so because they defy all forms of objective
> location in space and time, and since basically it is always our
> knowledge of these particles alone which we can make the
> object of science. Thus the aim of research is no longer an
> understanding of atoms and their movements 'in themselves'
> ... From the very start we are involved in the argument
> between nature and man in which science plays only a part,
> so that the common division of the world into subject and
> object, inner world and outer world, body and soul, is no
> longer adequate and leads us into difficulties. Thus even in
> science *the object of research is no longer nature in itself, but*

man's investigation of nature. Here again, man confronts himself alone.

(Heisenberg [1958] 1959: 24, emphasis added)

By casting doubt on the idea of objectivity, Heisenberg introduces an
intellectual perspective that is ultimately conducive to relativism. The
connection between a rejection of traditional conceptions of objectivity and acceptance of relativism is even more explicit in Robert
Nozick's views on relativism. Nozick argues:

> Quantum mechanics is our most fundamental theory of the
> microlevel, so if, according to it, all definite facts (involving
> conjugate variables) are definite only relative to states of
> measuring systems, then we are well on our way to holding
> that all facts (or at any rate, all the physical facts that are
> reducible to quantum mechanics) are relative.
>
> (Nozick 2001: 33)

Developments in science influenced relativistic thinking in philosophy
in quite subtle ways. As we saw in chapter 2, Kant's grand epistemological project was to provide a priori foundations for intelligible
empirical descriptions of science. However, with the advent of alternative logics and geometries the status of a priori first principles itself
has come under scrutiny. As Michael Friedman points out:

> [the] a priori has indeed lost its fixed or absolute status: it can
> change and develop with the progress of science, and it varies
> from the context of one scientific theory to another (Euclid-
> ean geometry is a priori in the context of Newtonian physics,
> but Riemannian geometry is a priori in the context of gen-
> eral theory of relativity). As Reichenbach put it in his *Theory
> of Relativity and a priori Knowledge* of 1920, we must distin-
> guish two meanings of the Kantian a priori: the first involves
> unrevisability and the idea of absolute fixity for all time; the
> second means 'constitutive of the concept of the object of
> knowledge'. In acknowledging the profound philosophical
> importance of Einstein's theory of relativity, we do not aban-
> don the Kantian a priori altogether. We simply discard the
> first meaning while continuing to emphasize the crucial
> scientific role of the second. What relativity shows us, in fact,
> is that the notion of apriority must itself be relativized.
>
> (Friedman 1993: 50)

In more recent years, disillusionment with Marxism and other utopian political doctrines also contributed to the development of an intellectual climate where scepticism about the existence of any objective standards of truth or what is right and wrong seemed the only viable alternative. However, as we have seen, scepticism is not to be confused with relativism. The denial that there is one truth or objective account of the truth or the right does not by itself lead to the espousal of the doctrine that any view may be true or right relative to its social or conceptual background. To see how the denial of objectivism and absolutism has led to relativism we need to look at another significant intellectual development in the twentieth century: the advent of social anthropology.

3.3 CULTURAL RELATIVISM

One of the most influential currents to shape contemporary relativism can be found in the work of social anthropologists. Ethnographic data, gathered by social anthropologists, are often cited to establish that there are substantial differences in the beliefs, practices and worldviews of different cultures. These empirical observations in turn have been used to support what has become known as 'cultural relativism'. Cultural relativism is defined by one of its strongest proponents, the anthropologist M. J. Herskovits, as:

> an approach to the question of the nature and role of values in culture. It represents a scientific, inductive attack on an age-old philosophical problem, using fresh, cross-cultural data, hitherto not available to scholars, gained from the study of the underlying value-systems of societies having the most diverse customs. The principle of cultural relativism, briefly stated, is as follows: Judgments are based on experience, and experience is interpreted by each individual in terms of his own enculturation . . . Even the facts of the physical world are discerned through the enculturative screen, so that the perception of time, distance, weight, size, and other 'realities' is mediated by the conventions of any given group.
>
> (Herskovits 1960: 61)

The arguments for cultural relativism ordinarily rely on the following assumptions:

The descriptive assumption: empirical observations show that there exists a multiplicity of incompatible and irreconcilable worldviews and value-systems.

The epistemic assumption: there is no single criterion or reliable method for adjudicating between contrasting or incommensurable worldviews and value-systems.

The normative assumption: tolerance and respect for other worldviews is more desirable than attempting to impose our views on others.

The roots of cultural relativism can be traced back to Herodotus (see 1.1), and we also see a tendency towards it, at the inception of modern philosophy, in the work of Montaigne and the French Enlightenment (2.2 and 2.4). The philosophical groundings of contemporary cultural relativism are traceable directly to Dilthey (2.7). Franz Boas, arguably the founder of cultural anthropology as we know it today, attended Dilthey's lectures in Berlin, and Ruth Benedict, who popularised cultural relativism, cites Dilthey in her *Patterns of Culture* (1934). Boas saw cultural relativism as a counterpoint to the then prevailing evolutionary theories of culture advocated by E. B. Taylor and J. G. Frazer, who saw tribal cultures as early stages of the development of human civilisation, where Western societies occupy the higher echelons of a progressive continuum. Boas believed the evolutionary account to be ethnocentric and not conducive to fruitful understanding of individual cultures. He also argued against racial explanations of cultural differences. Instead, the explanation of our patterns of action and thought is to be found in the culture to which we belong and not our nature or biological make-up. Our personality traits, our habits and manners are all due to a particular cultural background. Even race, age and sex are cultural constructs. According to him, 'The data of ethnology prove that not only our knowledge but also our emotions are the result of the form of our social life and of the history of the people to whom we belong' (Boas 1940: 636). For these reasons Boas has often been seen as the key figure in the development of cultural relativism in anthropology.[1]

Anthropologists frequently distinguish between descriptive, prescriptive and philosophical cultural relativism (see, e.g., Herskovits 1960, 1972). Descriptive cultural relativism is an empirical thesis to the effect that different societies have different systems of belief and value; and it is claimed to be supported by observations of cultural diversity. Herskovits, for instance, says 'The principle of cultural relativism derives from a vast array of factual data gained from the application of techniques in field study that have permitted us to penetrate the underlying value-systems of societies having divers customs' (Herskovits 1972: 63). Alfred Kroeber and Clyde Kluck-hohn also believe that 'sincere comparison of cultures leads quickly to recognition of their "relativity"' (Kroeber and Kluckhohn 1952: 174 in Cook 1999: 8). To take a few examples, the Yoruba claim that they carry their souls in boxes covered with cowrie shells which they treat with special regard; the Nuer believe that twins are birds; the Trobriand Islanders claim that women are impregnated by the ghosts of their ancestors, rather than by their husbands; the Azande[2] believe in and practise witchcraft and magic. These are the types of ethno-graphic data used to support the descriptive relativist thesis. Anthro-pological descriptions of allegedly irresolvable cross-cultural ethical conflicts are also plentiful: socially sanctioned cannibalism, genital mutilation and patricide, are some of the examples often cited. For instance, L. T. Hobhouse, after commenting on the anomaly of the contrast between, on the one hand, the customs of hospitality, cour-teousness and brotherly kindness of the Dyaks of Borneo and, on the other, the ferocity of their practice of head-hunting, concludes, 'the Dyaks have a morality of their own, for many purposes as good as ours, but limited by the conditions of their life and coloured by their ideas of the supernatural' (Hobhouse 1951: 25).

Ethnographic data are cited not only as evidence for the diversity of human belief or the empirical doctrine of descriptive cultural rela-tivism, but also as supporting evidence for the adoption of prescriptive cultural relativism. Prescriptive cultural relativism enjoins the practis-ing anthropologist to refrain from taking judgemental positions towards the people under study, in order to attain a greater degree of objectivity. This is a methodological principle to be used in contexts of anthropological fieldwork. In this, the least ideological or doctrinaire form of relativism, methodological cultural relativism is simply 'a commitment by the anthropologists to suspending moral judgment until an attempt can be made to understand another culture's beliefs and practices in their full cultural, material, and historical contexts' (Turner 1997: 118). It is also a warning against provincialism – 'the danger that our perceptions will be dulled, our intellects constricted, and our sympathies narrowed by the overlearned and overvalued acceptances of our own society' (Geertz 1989: 15).

The philosophical doctrine of cultural relativism presupposes the truth of descriptive relativism; it is based on the assumption that there are fundamental, i.e., irresolvable, differences in ethical and cognitive belief-systems across cultures. The differences between cultures, it is argued, are not simply superficial disagreements on where the facts lie, but are indicative of a fundamental divide between Western and non-Western thinking about values, reason, logic and the nature of rationality itself. The upshot is the denial of the possibility of objective cross-cultural judgements or comparisons of diverse belief-systems (the epistemic assumption).[3]

The practical consequence of cultural relativism is respect for other cultures and value-systems – which can manifest itself as an adherence to multi-culturalism and avoidance of 'ethnocentrism'. Kroeber defines ethnocentrism as the 'tendency . . . to see one's in-group as always right and all out-groups as wrong wherever they differ' (Kroeber 1948: 266). According to him, relativism is an antidote to ethnocentrism, as it leads to tolerance and respect. Cultural relativism is based on the assumption of descriptive relativism, but it is also motivated by the rejection of the imperialist and colonialist attitudes of the early anthropologists towards the peoples they were studying. In the work of nineteenth-century anthropologists – such as E. B. Tylor in *Primitive Culture* (1871) – their cultural evolutionism 'typically implied that non-Western ways of life were worthy of respect just to the extent that they did not differ very much from supposedly "higher" ways of life familiar to European anthropologists' (Moody-Adams 1997: 24). Liberal anthropologists, following Franz Boas, Ruth Benedict and Margaret Mead, on the other hand, have seen cultural relativism as a way of counteracting the imperialist tendency to impose Western values on other cultures and societies.

A further stimulus for the adoption of cultural relativism has come from the study of languages of non-Western people. The work of Benjamin Whorf is the *locus classicus* of the approach known as 'linguistic relativity'. Whorf believed that the most direct and fruitful way of understanding human thinking is through the study of language, for such study would show that

> the forms of a person's thoughts are controlled by inexorable laws of patterns of which he is unconscious. These patterns are the unperceived intricate systematizations of his own language – shown readily enough by a candid comparison and contrast with other languages, especially those of a different linguistic family.
>
> (Whorf 1956: 252)

Whorf's study of American Indian languages, such as that of the Hopi, led him to argue, in a much cited passage, that:

we dissect nature along lines laid down by our native languages. The categories and types that we isolate from the world of phenomena we do not find there because they stare every observer in the face; on the contrary, the world is presented in a kaleidoscopic flux of impressions which has to be organised by our minds – and this means largely by the linguistic systems in our minds. We cut nature up, organise it into concepts, and ascribe significances as we do, largely because we are parties to an agreement to organise in this way – an agreement that holds throughout our speech community and is codified in the patterns of our language.

(Ibid.: 213)

A linguistic system, according to Whorf, is not merely an instrument for reproducing and voicing ideas; rather it moulds our worldview. Different grammars can shape to varying degrees of difference our process of forming ideas about the world. For instance, according to Whorf, the Hopi articulate, and hence perceive, the world in terms of events rather than objects, and see time not in terms of duration as English speakers do, but as relations between events. In the Hopi language, Whorf tells us, 'lightning', 'wave', 'flame', 'meteor', 'puff of smoke', 'pulsation' are all verbs, events of necessarily brief duration, and cannot be anything but verbs. He also claims that the Hopi, unlike speakers of Indo-European languages, describe the universe without recourse to a dimensional time. Whorf thus proposes 'a new principle of relativity, which holds that all observers are not led by the same physical evidence to the same picture of the universe, unless their linguistic backgrounds are similar, or can in some way be calibrated' (ibid.: 214). This principle of linguistic relativity, which receives its name and inspiration from Einstein's work, leads to the conclusion that users of radically different languages live in different worlds. Whorf argues:

[U]sers of markedly different grammars are pointed by their grammars toward different types of observations and different evaluations of externally similar acts of observation, and hence are not equivalent as observers but must arrive at some different views of the world.

(Ibid.: 221)

Edward Sapir, a student of Whorf's, went even further, and argued:

the real world is to a large extent unconsciously built upon the language habits of the group. No two languages are ever sufficiently similar to be considered as representing the same social reality. The worlds in which different societies live are distinct worlds, not merely the same world with different labels attached. We see and hear and otherwise experience very largely as we do because the language habits of our community predispose certain choices of interpretation.

(Sapir [1949] 1985: 162)

Whorf's work, and the so-called Sapir–Whorf hypothesis, has inspired various relativistic conclusions in contemporary philosophy. For instance, Paul Feyerabend (see chapter 6) uses Whorf's notion of covert classification to explain the possibility of incommensurability between languages or theoretical frameworks. Whorf's thesis also has been seen as a species of conceptual relativism and has been criticised by Donald Davidson (see chapter 8). Whorf, however, did not believe that his linguistic relativity would lead to incommensurability or untranslatability.[4] He argues that although no scientist is free to describe nature with absolute impartiality, for we are all constrained to certain modes of interpretation because of our linguistic background, a linguist familiar with widely differing linguistic systems will be able to adopt a more detached view. Awareness of linguistic relativity will have the practical consequence of making us more humble in our claims about the universality of our science and worldview, but would not lead to failure of communication.[5]

There are several empirical and conceptual problems with the arguments in favour of cultural relativism as developed by social anthropologists. Firstly, there are doubts concerning the reliability and the interpretation of the data gathered by social anthropologists. For instance, as we saw, Whorf had said that the Hopi have 'no words, grammatical forms, or constructions or expressions that refer directly to what we call "time", or to past or future, or enduring or lasting' (Whorf 1956 in Pinker 1994: 63). They did not possess the Western notion of time as a flowing continuum nor did they see time as countable – capable of being placed in exact sequences – or have calendars and chronology. The anthropologist Ekkehart Malotki casts doubt on the reliability of the linguistic data used by Whorf. According to Malotki, the Hopi language makes use of units of time, such as days, weeks, months and seasons, as well as terminology for yesterday and tomorrow, as shown in the following translation: 'Then indeed, the following day, quite early in the morning at the hour when people pray to the sun, around that time then he woke up the girl again'. Furthermore, they did make use of solar calendars, and other time-keeping devices and dated with precision various events such as ceremonial days (Malotki 1983 in Pinker 1994: 63). The issue here is one of correct translation of the Hopi utterances. Was Whorf ignoring or mistranslating certain Hopi locutions concerning time?[6]

Furthermore, dissenting voices within anthropology have argued that cultural relativists, in their eagerness to show the exoticism – or, to use more fashionable terminology the 'otherness'– of the subjects of their study, have exaggerated the differences between cultures and societies and have underestimated the extent of commonality that exists at both a biological and social level between all human beings. For instance, Donald E. Brown (1991), based on his extensive study of ethnographic data gathered by anthropologists, has argued that a large number of cultural values and practices are common to societies studied by anthropologists. They include:

(1) At the linguistic level the practice of gossip, lying, misleading humorous insult, engaging in story telling, narrative, poetry and rhetoric and use of metaphors are universal. All human languages seem to have words for days, months, seasons, years, past, present, future, body parts, emotion, thoughts, sensations, behavioural dispositions, flora, fauna, weathers, tools, space, motion, speed, location, spatial dimensions, giving, lending, affecting things and people, numbers and counting (at the very least 'one', 'two' and 'more than two'), proper names, possession.

(2) Elements common to human reasoning include the use of logical and abstract relations such as negation (not), conjunction (and), identity and equivalence. Binary opposites such as general versus particular, part versus whole, male and female, black and white, natural and cultural, good and bad are also found in all cultures studies.

(3) At the behavioural level, human beings from all cultural backgrounds use the smile as a friendly greeting and cries and squeals as means of non-linguistic vocal communication. They shed tears and display affection. They also use and are adept at interpreting facial expressions of happiness, sadness, anger, fear, surprise, disgust and contempt.

(4) At the psychological level, they distinguish between a sense of self versus other, and of voluntary versus involuntary actions. They are also aware of responsibility, intention, private or inner life, normal versus abnormal mental states, empathy, sexual

attraction, jealousy and envy. Childhood fears, such as fear of loud noises and of strangers (at the end of the first year) are universally present.

(5) At the social level, human beings tend to live in groups, form societies and have a sense of being a distinct people. Other common patterns of social behaviour include: recognised and institutionalised right of sexual access; organisation of family relations revolving around a mother and child (with one or more men); standard pattern and time for weaning and toilet training of children; the avoidance of incest between mother and son; and an awareness of kinship relations and preference for closer kin.

(6) At the normative level, human beings distinguish between right and wrong and recognise the rule of law and the existence of rights and duties. Murder, rape, violence and conflict are condemned and there are standard punishments for wrongdoers as well as means of seeking redress for wrongs. There is also great interest in the topic of sex, but sexual acts are usually performed in private and there are some standards of sexual modesty. All the societies studied acknowledge rules of etiquette and hospitality. Feasting is also a common practice.

(7) Members of all societies manufacture and use tools, use fire for cooking food, and make use of drugs for medicinal and recreational purposes.

(8) At the political and economic levels, all societies have procedures for making binding decisions on public affairs. There is acknowledgement of hierarchy, prestige and status usually on the basis of age, sex or kinship. A degree of economic inequality is also present. All societies have a division of labour where women do more child-care and men are assigned more aggressive and violent roles (hunters, warriors, etc.) and men are more dominant in political spheres.

(9) Supernatural beliefs are present in all the societies studied. Theories of fortune and misfortune, explanations of disease and death, rituals (including rites of passage), mourning the dead, magic to sustain and increase life and to attract the opposite sex, interpretations of dreams, and food taboos are also common to all cultures.[7]

1–9 indicate the presence of a rather large number of universal, cultural and biological, traits in all human societies. Relativists, on the other hand, tend to acknowledge the existence of some universal traits but argue that the enormous variation in how they are inter-preted, enacted and elaborated upon undermines the universalist claim. The strength of the relativist's case rests in the details of the human canvas rather than its broad brushstrokes.

Finally, cultural relativism is based on a number of questionable theoretical assumptions about the unity of cultures, on the one hand, and the relationship between cultures, seen as integrated wholes, and their individual members, on the other. Ruth Benedict, one of the most influential figures in popularising relativistic ideas in the United States in the 1950s, has argued that cultures have collective personali-ties. For instance, she claims, the Dobuans were paranoid and the Kwakiturl were megalomaniacs. For each human being,

> From the moment of his birth, the customs into which he
> is born shape his experience and behaviour. By the time
> he can talk, he is the little creature of his culture, and by
> the time he is . . . able to take part in its activities, its habits
> are his habits, its beliefs his beliefs, its impossibilities his
> impossibilities.
>
> (Benedict 1934b: 2–3)

The assumption shared by all the social anthropologists under dis-cussion is that culture is a variable system of symbols, which can shape its members in radically different ways. In the words of Mar-garet Mead, the so-called 'high-priestess' of cultural relativism, the social anthropologist has knowledge of 'the determinism of culture [and] the plasticity of human beings' (Mead [1928] 1978: 12). The conclusions drawn from this hypothesis were not just empirical but also normative. The malleability of human nature and our know-ledge of cultural diversity would allow us to teach future generations that:

> many ways are open to them, no one sanctioned above its
> alternative, and that upon them and upon them alone lies the
> burden of choice. Unhampered by prejudices, unvexed by
> too early conditioning to any one standard, they must come
> clear-eyed to the choices which lie before them.
>
> (Ibid.: 196)

Cultural relativism follows from empirical observation of cultural diversity conjoined with Benedict's characterisation of cultural learn-ing as the primary source of beliefs and actions. Herskovits also claims that cultural relativism developed because of the facts of differences in moral and cultural outlooks among diverse peoples in addition to the newfound anthropological understanding of the mechanisms of cultural learning.

This deterministic model of socialisation and cultural learning is seriously flawed for several reasons. As Moody-Adams (1997), among others, has argued, the assumption that cultures are integrated wholes, with self-contained sets of practices and beliefs, is open to criticism. Almost all cultures have porous and fluid boundaries; cultures seldom are self-sustaining and isolated islands. It is also unlikely that any society would operate as a fully integrated unit, for we can always find voices of dissent and opposition within any given social unit. The accounts given by those marginalised from centres of power – for instance women, children, the infirm – would often be very different from the accounts of those who occupy positions of authority. Furthermore, the relationship between culture and individual beliefs cannot be wholly deterministic; for were it so then it would be difficult to explain either the occurrence of dissent and change within particular cultures, or changes of allegiance by members of one culture to the norms and values of another. Finally, the model of enculturation used by cultural anthropologists does not take into account the role of our genetic endowment and our innate propensities.

The cultural relativism of the earlier generations of American social anthropologists was replaced by the relativism of 'difference' in the 1980s. A new generation of social anthropologists influenced by trends in postmodernism took up the banner of relativism once again. James Clifford, one of the most influential figures in this movement, writes:

> A conceptual shift, 'tectonic' in its implications, has taken place. We ground things, now, on a moving earth. There is no longer any place of overview (mountaintop) from which to map humans' ways of life, no Archimedean point from which to represent the world. Mountains are in constant motion. So are islands: for one cannot occupy, unambiguously, a bounded cultural world from which to journey out and analyse other cultures. Human ways of life increasingly influence, dominate, parody, translate, and subvert one another. Cultural analysis is always enmeshed in global movements of difference and power.
>
> (Clifford and Marcus 1986: 19 in Kuper 1999: 209)

Many social anthropologists have come to believe that it is no longer possible to construct objective accounts of other ways of life. They also proclaim that there is a moral obligation to celebrate cultural difference (Kuper 1999: 218). The denial of the very idea of objectivity and the celebration of 'difference' (in ethnic identity, cultural practices, gender, sexual orientation) are conceptual tools that social anthropologists, like writers in other areas of humanities, are borrowing from post-structuralist and deconstructionist continental philosophers. Anthropology, then, has become not only the intellectual progenitor of cultural relativism but also an active player in the intellectual trend known as 'postmodernism'. In the phantastic world of postmodernism, which social anthropologists helped to create, all aspects of our intellectual life – from the most abstract theories of physics to mundane descriptions of our everydayness – are self-consciously redefined as 'texts' or social constructs ready to be deconstructed.[8] I shall return to the topic of postmodernism below, but before that I would like to discuss the views of a philosopher whose work has had a marked impact on many areas of contemporary thought, including developments in social anthropology and postmodernism.

3.4 WITTGENSTEIN'S INFLUENCE

The Austrian philosopher Ludwig Wittgenstein (1889–1951) has been a seminal figure in the development of major trends in twentieth-century philosophy, from logical positivism to ordinary language philosophy, from philosophy of mind to philosophy of religion. He has also been frequently credited (or discredited, as the case may be) with contributing to the development of a relativist ethos in philosophy. Peter Winch, Jean-François Lyotard, Barry Barnes and David Bloor are some of the philosophers who draw upon Wittgenstein's work in support of their particular versions of relativism.[9]

In his second philosophical reincarnation, Wittgenstein famously came to repudiate the philosophical outlook he had so elegantly formulated in the *Tractatus Logico-Philosophicus* (1921). The young Wittgenstein was a realist who aimed to give a unitary account of linguistic meaning in terms of a relationship of picturing between language and the world. By the end of the 1920s, Wittgenstein had come to doubt the conception of language that underlined the *Tractatus*. To think that language has a formal unity, he argued, is to fall into a philosophical trap set by a failure to pay attention to how language actually works, how words are used in lived, social contexts.

Wittgenstein's revisionary conception of language and meaning is encapsulated in his remark 'For a large class of cases – though not for all – in which we employ the word "meaning" it can be defined thus: the meaning of a word is its use in the language' (Wittgenstein 1958: §43). Instead of looking for abstract relations between language and the world, Wittgenstein exhorts us to pay attention to the context in which language is used. Linguistic communication is a rule-governed social activity that takes place in the context of a whole host of other purposive social behaviour or what he calls a 'language-game'. All human life, including our conceptual life, is played out in a cultural, social and biological context, or a 'form of life'. Language cannot be understood in isolation from the goals and needs of the participants of specific language-games and the background of their form of life. At all times we should remember that 'What has to be accepted, the given, is – so one could say – *forms of life*' (ibid.: 226e).

The meaning of most words, including those of particular importance to philosophers, such as 'truth', 'rationality' and 'validity', is conditioned by our way of life, by our native history and by some facts of nature. Furthermore, any description of reality is mediated through our common stock of concepts, which we inherit through the language we use. The idea of reality existing somehow independently of these descriptions, as something that these descriptions can be compared to, does not make sense. We can never get outside our form of life and the particular language-games we play to compare our 'form of life' with an uninterpreted reality. The philosopher's quest for Truth, in its reified sense, is misguided because it presumes access to an objective reality, independent of any and all language-games.

Wittgenstein is unwilling to exempt even areas that may seem foundational to the very possibility of thought. Even the acts of thinking and reasoning, according to him, are bounded by the role they play in a form of life. The form of life in which various modes of reasoning are practised is the background from which all concepts – even those of logic, such as 'necessity', 'certainty', 'proposition' or 'following a rule' – take their meaning and significance. Not to see that logic is grounded in a form of life is to fall into the trap of seeing logic as something 'sublime', 'pure' and 'crystalline', a trap that Wittgenstein accuses himself of having fallen into when he wrote the *Tractatus*.

Several lines of thought in Wittgenstein's approach to language and meaning are conducive to relativism. The emphasis he places on the role of the communal, shared nature of the form of life that informs all conceptual activities finds a sympathetic ear among the cultural relativists. The ensuing contextualisation of meaning and significance also has relativistic overtones. All judgements can meaningfully arise only from within the context of a form of life, and there is no possibility of standing outside all forms of life in the hope of making objective, external, comparisons or offering criticisms of the comparative merits of various belief-systems.

Roger Trigg, one of a number of philosophers[10] to accuse Wittgenstein of being a relativist, says that the upshot of Wittgenstein's arguments is a complete onslaught on the very possibility of rationality, objectivity, truth and knowledge. For we 'can never get outside all language-games and talk rationally, just as it is never possible to reason properly beyond the limits of language' (Trigg 1991: 218). Wittgenstein's views, as developed by followers such as Peter Winch, it is argued, lead to relativism and even nihilism, where there is no role for social sciences as a source of knowledge, no possibility of comparison between different societies and no possibility of criticism of an alien society. According to Trigg:

> the implicit attack on the possibility of unprejudiced reason, the removal of the possibility of truth as a standard – all this adds up to a direct onslaught on the very possibility of rationality. It is not surprising that the application of Wittgenstein's ideas in the field of social anthropology has seemed to result in a paralysing relativism. The issue is not just that an anthropologist cannot make any distinction between rational and irrational behaviour. Anthropology itself can no longer claim truth, or even the right to be heard, since it too merely gains its meaning from particular practices (presumably those of twentieth-century academics in the Western World).
>
> (Ibid.: 218–19)

A further line of thought in Wittgenstein's later writings that lends itself to the charge of relativism is the suggestion that there could be alternative language-games or *forms* of life (see Wittgenstein 1958: 226e above), not compatible with ours, which embody concepts and conceptions very different from the ones we find familiar. For instance, he envisages communities with different approaches to measuring length or quantity (e.g., using rubber rulers that expand and contract), or ones with alternative ways of counting (e.g., counting the same object twice) or people who calculate the amount of wood in different-sized piles by measuring only the areas these piles cover. In the same way, he suggests, there could be forms of life which use rules of logic and processes of reasoning substantially different from the ones we take for granted. Similar views are expressed in his controversial discussion of the notion of rule-following. In the *Remarks on the Foundations of Mathematics*, Wittgenstein suggests that it is we, or rather our interpretation of the rules, that determines when an inference or step of reasoning is in accord with a rule (Wittgenstein 1978: 17). He argues:

> Then according to you everybody could continue the series as he likes, and so infer anyhow! In that case we shan't call it 'continuing the series' and also presumably not 'inference'. And thinking and inferring (like counting) is of course bounded for us, not by an arbitrary definition, but by natural limits corresponding to the body of what can be called the role of thinking and inferring in our life.
>
> (Ibid.: 20)

Wittgenstein is denying that rules can exist outside the actual practices which involve their application, or be understood independently of these applications. No rules, including rules of logic, exist independently of the occasions of using them. In language, as in reasoning, 'in the beginning was the deed' (Wittgenstein 1980: 31). He also argues that there are numerous, maybe even infinitely many possible interpretations for any given rule. This does not mean that we will be correct in following rules according to our individual interpretation, because rules, like games and language, are institutions and hence have a social character. However, different forms of life can have different standards of agreement and practices, and consequently there could be alternative, incompatible ways of constructing rules of mathematics and logic. Rules of logic and standards of reasoning, he seems to suggest, are relative to the form of life from which they emanate and in which they are embedded. Even the law of non-contradiction, the most fundamental law of logic, does not seem to be immune from change. He writes:

> Indeed, even at this stage I predict a time when there will be mathematical investigations of calculi containing contradictions, and people will actually be proud of having emancipated themselves even from consistency.
>
> (Wittgenstein 1975: 332)

Wittgenstein's line of argument, if interpreted as a defence of the possibility of relativism about logic, is quite unconvincing. In the first place, it is not clear whether the analogy between the rules of logic and the rules of measurement is apt. For one thing, rules of logic are prior or antecedent to the game of measurement, in the sense that they are presupposed by it. No one can engage in measurements or calculations of any sort without also engaging in some simple logical inferences. Furthermore, in Wittgenstein's examples the alternative modes of measurement provide us with inaccurate or imprecise information about what is being measured. It is not clear what the parallel with the rules of logic would be; maybe a set of rules that provide us with arguments, which only approximate to the truth, such as those used in fuzzy logic. Perhaps Wittgenstein would object that this type of criticism is misguided since it presupposes exactly what he is at pains to deny. That is, it assigns a unitary function to logic, namely, achieving truth. However, if the rules of logic are not there to help us to move from true premises to true conclusions, then it is not clear what their function is. It might be objected that the above line of thought presupposes that the act of measurement in any society would necessarily have the same function as in ours, when all that is required is that it would have a loose family resemblance to our acts of measurement. But, would we be able to identify an alien activity as an instance of measurement if it did not involve a certain amount of calculation? We shall return to the question of relativism about logic in chapter 5. The question facing us is whether we should treat Wittgenstein's imaginative explorations of the limits of the use of certain concepts, such as counting, inferring, etc., as an indication of his relativism.

A number of passages in *On Certainty*, and elsewhere, make the relativistic interpretations seem even more plausible. In §§602–8, he ponders the questions of the status of physics and what is involved in believing in physics or thinking that it provides good grounds for one's actions. He continues

§609 Supposing we met people who did not regard that as a telling reason. Now, how do we imagine this? Instead of the physicist, they consult an oracle. (And for that we consider them primitive.) Is it wrong for them to consult an oracle and be guided by it? – If we call this 'wrong' aren't we using our language-game as a basis from which to *combat* theirs?

§610 And are we right or wrong to combat it? Of course there are all sorts of slogans which will be used to support our proceeding.

§611 Where two principles really do meet which cannot be reconciled with one another, then each man declares the other a fool and heretic.

§612 I said I would 'combat' the other man – but wouldn't I give him *reasons*? Certainly; but how far do they go? At the end of reasons comes *persuasion*. (Think what happens when missionaries convert natives.)
(Wittgenstein 1968: 80–1)

One natural reading of the above is that he is urging us to adopt a relativistic position in our encounters with radically alien forms of life. When faced with a tribe who use oracles rather than physics to guide their action, all *we can* ultimately resort to, he argues, is the criterion of what counts as a good ground for action or thought *in our language-game*, which may not be applicable to their language-game.[11] In the *Philosophical Investigations* he asks:

'So you are saying that human agreement decides what is true and what is false?' – it is what human beings *say* that is true and false; and they agree in the *language* they use. That is not agreement in opinions but in form of life.
(Wittgenstein 1958: §241)

The implication seems to be that what is true and false, in some sense, is decided by a shared form of life, and in that sense it is relative to it. And in *Zettle* he tells us: 'I want to say: an education quite different from ours might also be the foundation for quite different concepts. For here life would run on differently' (Wittgenstein 1967: 387).

Despite the evidence of the above passages, it is not clear whether Wittgenstein's emphasis on the social character of thought should be taken as an indication of his relativism. In numerous passages, Wittgenstein signals clearly that he has a naturalistic, in addition to a sociological, interpretation of what a form of life is. In *On Certainty*, for instance, he claims that a man cannot make a mistake unless he already judges in conformity with mankind (Wittgenstein 1968: §156), a statement that seems to emphasise the universal features of human judgement. The form of life we have is a background to all our activities of speech and thought, but that form of life is constituted by our physical nature as well as socio-linguistic conventions. In the *Philosophical Investigations* Wittgenstein had argued, 'If language is to be a means of communication there must be agreement not only in definitions but also (queer as this may sound) in judgements' (Wittgenstein

1958: §242). These points of agreement include not only cultural posits but also the natural, biological, inheritance of the human species.

How much relativism follows from the observations about the rule-governed character of our linguistic and other social activities is open to debate, but what is beyond doubt is that Wittgenstein introduced a view of language where all criteria of meaningfulness and significance are internal to our practices. This internalist view, in turn, furthered relativistic thinking in a number of intellectual circles, including in the social sciences and religion (see, e.g., Lewis 1995). Even if we do not take Wittgenstein to be a relativist, the fact remains that his work has been a source of inspiration for many latter-day relativists and post-modernists.

3.5 POSTMODERNISM

The topic of relativism has gained greater prominence in recent years because of its associations with the postmodernist movement in the humanities. The term 'postmodern' was first used by the architect Joseph Hudnut, in the title of his 1945 article 'the post-modern house'. The term became popular in the late 1970s, after the publication of 'The Rise of Post-Modern Architecture' by Charles Jencks who defines it as 'Double coding: the combination of Modern techniques with something else (usually traditional building) in order for architecture to communicate with the public' (Jencks 1986: 14). It gained currency in the arts, literature, political theory and in philosophy in the 1980s. Postmodernists in various fields are often reluctant to discuss their position in any systematic manner; its opponents, on the other hand, often characterise it so broadly that it no longer serves any useful purpose. Anthony Appiah, for instance, defines post-modernism in philosophy thus:

> postmodernism is the rejection of the mainstream consensus from Descartes through Kant to logical positivism on foundationalism (there is one route to knowledge, which is exclusivism in epistemology) and of metaphysical realism (there is one truth, which is exclusivism in ontology), each underwritten by a unitary notion of reason; it thus celebrates such figures as Nietzsche (no metaphysical realist) and Dewey (no foundationalist). The modernity that is opposed here can thus be Cartesian (in France), Kantian (in Germany), and logical positivist (in America).
>
> (Appiah 1992: 142)

The definition, although it reflects some of the main features of post-modern thought, is so general that it can be applied to any number of contemporary philosophers, including Hilary Putnam and Nelson Goodman (see chapter 7) who have disassociated themselves from postmodernism. Furthermore, it ignores the subversive aims and methods of the movement. Postmodernist philosophers do not simply reject traditional philosophical doctrines such as realism or foundationalism; rather, they attempt to show that all systematic thought and metaphysical system-building involves hierarchical presuppositions, which once laid bare, undermine themselves or deconstruct.

It has become a truism among many analytic philosophers that postmodernism is nothing but a jumble of incoherent, self-refuting relativistic claims. As we shall see, however, not all postmodernists accept the charge of relativism. But even if postmodernist philosophers do not explicitly adopt relativism as a doctrine, or state it as a thesis, their approach to questions of truth, objectivity and reason makes their position often indistinguishable from some forms of relativism. The postmodernists cast doubt, through aphorisms and metaphors rather than traditional philosophical argumentation, on the presuppositions of non-relativistic positions. They aim to 'emancipate [Western culture] from the whole philosophical vocabulary clustering around reason, truth, and knowledge' (Rorty 1998: 24). They problematise the notions of objectivity, truth, logic, reason and knowledge and aim to free us from their oppressive shackles through therapeutic deconstruction. Hence the relativistic tone of postmodernism is a consequence of the rejection of the very possibility of objective cognitive norms – truth, reason, justification – and their role as arbiters between various conflicting claims and theories. In this sense, postmodernists are at least anti-anti-relativists (see Introduction), however, as we shall see, many embrace more overt forms of relativism.

The label 'postmodernism' covers a wide spectrum of views and approaches, so the following brief account inevitably will leave much out. However, we can single out some main philosophical currents that contributed to the establishment of a relativistic ethos in the humanities in the past twenty years. The key ideas of postmodernism were propagated by a number of post-structuralist French philosophers in the 1970s, prominent among them Michel Foucault, Jacques Derrida, and Jean-François Lyotard. The postmodernists trace their intellectual genealogy to Marx, Heidegger, Saussure and, above all, Nietzsche. Nietzsche's iconoclastic approach to questions of truth and objectivity, conjoined with his perspectivism (see chapter 2), has probably been the greatest source of inspiration to postmodern theorists. The linguistic theories of Ferdinand de Saussure were a further important source of postmodern relativism (see Putnam, 1992a: 125). According to Saussure, meaning in a language is given only by way of contrast to other meanings in the same language; 'in language there are only differences' (Saussure 1974: 120). Language, he tells us, should be understood and analysed in terms of sets of binary oppositions (man/woman, up/down, large/small, etc.) and he uses binary oppositions such as signifier and signified and language and parole to explain the workings of language itself. Different languages, however, do not necessarily have the same set of oppositions or contrasts and therefore they will not express the same meanings. The structuralist anthropologist Claude Lévi-Strauss extended the scope of Saussure's claim beyond language and applied it to the study of human societies. Postmodernist philosophers and cultural theorists expanded the scope of the original Saussurian idea even further, applying it to all discourses, worldviews, and truth-claims, which on this account turn out to be both non-convergent and incommensurable.[12]

In its rejection of the role of reason and its mistrust of claims of objectivity, postmodernism has strong parallels with romantic irrationalism and the Counter-Enlightenment, which were also developed in reaction to the ascendancy of scientific and technological modes of thought and belief in a universal human nature[13] (see 2.6). Steve Fuller, a sympathetic commentator on postmodernism, for instance, tells us

> Postmodernism emerged in the late 1970s to capture the changed character of the sciences in the 20th century, which called into question the idea that the organised pursuit of knowledge has a unique and natural course of development that, in turn, can provide the basis for the general improvement of humanity, typically in the form of rational statecraft ... The term 'enlightenment' is increasingly used for the tendency in the history of Western thought that postmodernism is said to have undermined.
>
> (Fuller 2000: 3)

Postmodernism scorns the quest for universal values, cognitive and moral, as a manifestation of the will to power masquerading as objectivity. The Enlightenment is seen as a monolithic, authoritarian movement closely allied with Western imperialism and colonialism, while postmodernism is an ally in the fight for emancipation from tyrannies of all sorts. Catherine Belsey is eloquent in voicing this point:

> the Enlightenment commitment to truth and reason, we can now see, has meant historically a single truth and a single rationality, which have conspired in practice to legitimate the subordination of black people, the non-Western world, women . . . None of these groups has any political interest in clinging to the values which have consistently undervalued them. The plurality of the postmodern, by contrast, discredits supremacism on the part of any single group. It celebrates differences of all kinds, but divorces difference from power. Postmodernism is in all these senses the ally of feminism.
>
> (Belsey quoted in Norris 1993: 287)

A further common theme running through postmodernism is the emphasis on 'text' (understood in the broadest sense possible) or language, over and above the claims of the author (or the reader) who, from a modernist perspective, was deemed to have authority over the interpretation of her own text. The examination of the meaning of a text should not centre on its author, it is argued, for interpretation is an open-ended procedure where no single reading or understanding can be seen to have priority or ultimate authority. This move from author to text was the harbinger of the new 'anti-humanism' and the proclamation of the 'death of the man' or the 'death of the author' which has become one of the battle-cries of postmodernist literary criticism.

We can now briefly examine the views of the philosophical triumvirate most responsible for postmodernism. For Michel Foucault, the rejection of the role of the author's intention and responsibility is bound up with his influential thesis that all knowledge-claims are disguised power relationships. Foucault denies the role of truth as an objective and neutral criterion for interpretation of texts. Truth is always located in particular social relations; in this he is following Nietzsche's lead in questioning the value of truth and its problematic link with power. According to him, Nietzsche is the philosopher to uncover the essential connections between power and philosophical discourse. In passages directly citing and echoing Nietzsche, he argues:

> It is now impossible to believe that 'in the rending of the veil, truth remains truthful; we have lived long enough not to be

taken in' (Nietzsche *Contra Wagner*: 99). Truth is undoubtedly the sort of error that cannot be refuted because it was
hardened into an unalterable form in the long baking process
of history.

(Foucault 1977: 143)

The will to truth is always bound up with particular political (social,
cultural, economic) hegemonies, and philosophers discussing traditional ideas of truth inevitably share the presuppositions of such
power structures.

Each society has its regime of truth, its 'general politics' of
truth: that is, the types of discourse which it accepts and
makes function as true; the mechanism and instances which
enable one to distinguish true and false statements, the
means by which each is sanctioned; the techniques and procedures accorded value in the acquisition of truth; the status
of those who are charged with saying what counts as true.

(Foucault 2001: 14)

Reason and rationality are one aspect of the attempt to dominate.
The historical analysis of reason and knowledge shows that 'all
knowledge rests upon injustice (that there is no right, not even in the
act of knowing, to truth or a foundation for truth) and that the
instinct for knowledge is malicious' (Foucault 1977: 160). In different
historical and political periods the claims to power, and hence to
knowledge and truth, take different forms. Each society or locus of
power generates its own truths and moral imperatives. Foucault
singles out the Renaissance, the Classical Age (seventeenth and eighteenth centuries) and the Modern Age (nineteenth and twentieth
centuries) as three key historical periods when distinct conceptions of
knowledge or 'epistemes' were produced. These conceptions, in turn,
were based on implicit but distinct views on how 'the order' or the
relationship between things is construed. For example, the Renaissance emphasised the relationship of resemblance, while the Classical
Age prioritised the relationship of identity. Conceptions of truth
would vary according to 'the order of things' or the historically
constituted epistemes (see Foucault 1970). Foucault's views may,
properly speaking, be seen as historicist (see Introduction) as he relativises knowledge and truth to historical epochs.

Foucault is a severe critic of the Enlightenment project of prioritising reason and rationality and of the subsequent emphasis on the

scientific method as the most secure way of attaining objective knowledge. The Enlightenment is seen as a source of the ills of modern
rational-liberal cultures. In *Discipline and Punish* (1975) Foucault
argues that modern science, particularly in the form of social sciences,
is an instrument of social control to such an extent that its very constitution is inseparable from the exercise of social and political power.
Thus the revolt against the ideas of objectivity, truth, reason, or the
ideals of the Enlightenment becomes a revolutionary political act
rather than simply an intellectual exercise.

Derrida has launched a full-scale attack on Western metaphysics
or 'the metaphysics of presence'. His favourite terminological innova-
tions, '*différance*', 'trace', 'logocentrism', 'phonologism', 'supplementarity' have become signposts in the postmodernist rejection of the
Enlightenment ideas of the authority of reason and the possibility of
context-transcendence. A crucial step in the denunciation of metaphysics is Derrida's rejection of classical logic, which, by emphasising
binary thinking and the law of excluded middle, he claims, excludes
difference and privileges one set of values over another. The uncritical
reliance on accounts that privilege thinking within binary oppositions
gives the illusion that there are hierarchies of moral and epistemic
values, and that such hierarchies reflect foundational or metaphysical
truths. The privileging of speech over writing (phonologism) and
of absence over presence are examples of such logocentric thought.
The laws of binary logic, the principle of identity ($P = P$), the laws
of non-contradiction $-(P \ \& \ -P)$ and excluded middle ($P \ v \ -P$)
suppress 'the logic of supplementarity', where 'supplementarity',
he claims, 'is nothing, neither a presence nor an absence, is neither a
substance nor an essence of man' (Derrida [1967] 1997: 244). And
'we designate the impossibility of formulating the movement of supplementarity within the classical logic, within the logic of identity'
(ibid.: 94). Similarly, it seems to be a virtue of the concept of trace
that it 'is in fact contradictory and not acceptable within the logic of
identity' (ibid.: 61).[14] It is difficult to know what to make of these, and
other similar, statements. Derrida, like many other French philosophers, seems to take pleasure in paradoxical and extreme formulations *pour épater la bourgeoisie*, and yet he frequently qualifies his
more extreme pronouncements to such an extent that he renders them
almost trivial.[15]

In this, as in many other places, Derrida draws directly from Nietzsche, who believed that language and the 'prejudices' of traditional
metaphysical thinking emphasise 'faith in opposite values', good and
evil, truth and falsehood, being and becoming – and privilege the first

of these opposites.[16] Nietzsche's influence is most obvious in Derrida's earlier work (up to 1980) where

> Derrida speaks regularly to Nietzsche in his own attempt to deconstruct the logocentric tendencies of metaphysical thinking. More specifically, Nietzsche often appears in the Derridean text as an alternative to the nostalgic longing for full presence that Derrida locates at the core of Western Metaphysics. In fact, 'Nietzsche' comes to serve a talismanic function as a proper name for the very possibility of thinking otherwise, a shorthand marker for the *other* of logocentrism.
>
> (Schrift 1995: 10)

Derrida, infamously, announces that there is nothing outside the text, by which he seems to mean that we are not able to access reality directly without language and the context within which it is embedded. Within language, no one vocabulary is privileged; we are not in a position to prefer one set of interpretations over another, because we have no grounds for such a decision (Hekman 1986: 19). Language is infinite 'play', and meaning is created afresh in the act of reading a text. The meaning of a text is at least partly fashioned by the reader and is dependent on the context of reading. There is then no room left for the idea of an ultimately correct or legitimate interpretation.

Derrida has objected to what he sees as misunderstandings arising from careless readings of such remarks. For instance, he complains that the idea of undecidability as complete freeplay was used by American literary theorists in ways that did not reflect his original use of the word '*jeu*' (Derrida 1988: 115). He complains that his remark 'there is nothing outside the text' is singularly misused. He says:

> The phrase, which for some has become a sort of slogan, in general so badly understood, of deconstruction ('there is nothing outside the text'), means nothing else: there is nothing outside context. In this form, which says exactly the same thing, the formula would doubtless have been less shocking. I am not certain that it would have provided more to think about . . . What I call 'text' implies all the structures called 'real', 'economic', 'historical', 'socio-institutional', in short: all possible references. Another way of recalling once again that 'there is nothing outside the text'. That does not mean that references are suspended, denied, or enclosed in a book, as people have claimed, or have been naïve enough to believe

and to have accused me of believing. But it does mean that every referent, all reality has the structure of a defférantial trace, and that one cannot refer to this 'real' except in an interpretative experience.

(Ibid.: 136, 148)[17]

The explanation Derrida provides does not alter the impression that he is ultimately proposing a relativistic thesis. The passage quoted above seems to involve Derrida in relativism in two senses. First, he seems to be advancing a version of anti-realism or the claim that we cannot have access to a mind-independent reality and that all our descriptions of 'what there is' bear the mark of our conceptual schemes and interpretative frameworks coupled with conceptual relativism arising from the belief that there exist a multiplicity of such networks (see chapter 7 for a discussion of conceptual relativism). Second, he seems to be emphasising the context-dependence of all our judgements and the absence of a context-neutral criterion for adjudicating between them – a claim which, as we saw in the Introduction, is a formative idea of relativism.

Derrida, however, has insisted in several places that it is a 'radical' misunderstanding to see him as a relativist. In response to my direct question about his relativism, he responded:[18]

I am shocked by the debate around this question of relativism. What is relativism? Are you a relativist simply because you say, for instance, the other is the other, and that every other is other than the other? I want to pay attention to the singularity of the other, the singularity of the situation, the singularity of language, is that relativism? . . . relativism is a doctrine, which has its own history in which there are only points of view with no absolute necessity, or no references to absolutes. That is the opposite to what I have to say. Relativism is, in classical philosophy, a way of referring to the absolute and denying it; it states that there are only cultures and that there is no pure science of truth. I have never said such a thing. Neither have I ever used the word relativism.

(Derrida 1999: 78)

Furthermore, he has emphasised that in order to give an account of the logocentric and phonocentric tradition, expressions like 'epoch' and 'historical genealogy' must be removed 'from all relativism' (Derrida [1967] 1997: 14) and has supported Husserl's criticism of relativism and historicism, arguing: 'the critique of historicism in all its forms seems to me indispensable' (Derrida [1972] 1981: 104–5 n. 32). Despite these disclaimers, the feeling remains that Derrida cannot and should not disassociate himself so readily from the relativistic implications and interpretations of his work. In discussing the Nazi use or misuse of Nietzsche's work, Derrida argues that at least some of the blame for the misreadings rests with Nietzsche himself; that something in Nietzsche's texts must have lent itself to the spectacular perversions of his views (Derrida 1988: 28–31). The same can be said of Derrida's own writing. Derrida at times wishes to disassociate himself not just from relativism but also from the postmodernist movement (Derrida [1972] 1981: 24–8). However, he is answerable to the question why he is considered the leading voice and champion of both by so many. How do we account for such 'radical' misunderstandings?

The third major figure in this postmodernist triumvirate is Jean-François Lyotard whose book *The Postmodern Condition* (1984) made the term 'postmodern'– which, as we saw, originally was applied to a new architectural trend – a common currency of intellectual debate. Lyotard has railed against what he calls 'Grand Narratives', or the ideology of 'Total Theory', particularly the Enlightenment accounts of a universal human nature and historical progress. He defines '*postmodern*' as 'incredulity toward metanarratives' which he believes is 'the condition of knowledge in the most highly developed societies' (Lyotard 1984: xxiii f.). The *modern* legitimates itself by appealing to a metadiscourse, a grand narrative such as that of the Enlightenment. It is unwarranted metaphysical hubris, however, to think that theories or narratives refer to an independent reality. Rather, their referent is simply other narratives or theories. All grand narratives or meta-discourses – Marxist, Kantian, Hegelian, Enlightenment – which were presented as self-validating and universal perspectives and which were the defining features of *the modern*, have been shown to be perspectival and culture-bound. Instead, the emphasis should be on the multiplicity of irreducible texts, discourses, practices and interpretations. Borrowing Wittgenstein's key idea of multiplicity of language-games, he maintains that different narratives are not amenable to reduction into a single overarching system of meaning, for language-games are 'heteromorphous, subject to heterogeneous sets of pragmatic rules' (Lyotard 1984: 66). The value placed on the idea of consensus within various language-games is also suspect and outmoded. The recognition of the heteromorphous nature of language-games leads to the conclusion that: 'Any consensus on the rules defining a game and the "moves" playable within it *must* be local, in other words, agreed on by the present players and subject to eventual cancellation' (ibid.: 66–7). Moral ideals, such as justice, should be defined provisionally and locally in the context of the rules specific to the game at hand. There is no neutral standpoint to assess the varied and conflicting claims made by this multiplicity of viewpoints.

Christopher Norris clarifies Lyotard's position in the following terms:

> As the idea gains ground that all theory is a species of subli-mated narrative, so doubts emerge about the very possibility of knowledge as distinct from the various forms of narrative gratification . . . The 'postmodern condition' – as Lyotard interprets it – . . . rests . . . on the idea that prejudice is so deeply built into our traditions of thought that no amount of rational criticism can hope to dislodge it. Any serious think-ing about culture and society will have to acknowledge the fact that such enquiries have meaning only within the context of a certain informing tradition.
>
> (Norris 1985: 23–4)

As readers and interpreters of texts and participants in various con-flicting narratives, all we can do is to avoid any attempt to override the specific interests, motives or criteria of judgements inherent within that particular narrative. In other words, no one is ever in a position to act as an objective independent arbiter of the truth or reasonableness of a claim.

Ironically, in the light of what has been claimed, there is a good deal of disagreement over the 'correct' interpretation of these seminal postmodern writers. Not least because of the frequently wilful obscu-rity of their styles and their unwillingness to explain or expand their views in terms other than the neologisms coined by them. However, what is beyond doubt is the impact of the work of French post-structuralists on relativistic currents of thinking in the humanities in English-speaking countries. For instance, Barbara Herrnstein Smith, one of the main exponents of postmodernism in American academia, proclaims: 'the credibility of all beliefs, including those currently regarded as true, reasonable, self-evident, and so forth, is equally contingent: equally the product, in other words, of condi-tions (experiential, contextual, institutional, and so forth) that are fundamentally variable and always to some extent unpredictable and uncontrollable' (Smith 1997: xvi–xvii). Hence, no judgement is or could be objective in a context-independent or subject-transcendent sense. (ibid.: 6). The relativistic implications of deconstruction are also evident in the writings of historiographers such as Hayden White who has claimed that 'There is an inexpungeable relativity in every representation of historical phenomena. The relativity of representation is a function of the language used to describe and thereby constitute past events as possible objects of explanation and understanding' (White 1977: 392).

Postmodernist writers deny the distinction between fictive, poetic and imaginary styles of writing, on the one hand, and scientific, historical, theoretic and sociological claims, on the other, and consequently leave no room for assessing truth-claims on the basis of such considerations as evidence or logical consistency (Norris 1993: 225). Furthermore, by linking the idea of truth and objectivity with relationships of power, domination and control, they obliterate the traditional distinction between reason and coercion, and simultaneously assign an emancipatory role to their approach that in liberal circles has made their message difficult to resist. Postmodernism has proven particularly recalcitrant to arguments by analytic philosophers for the very presuppositions of rational argument – objectivity, truth, consistency, logic, etc. – are questioned by them. To echo a point made by Hilary Putnam, to argue against postmodernists is somewhat like entering into a boxing match with the fog. But the exercise can prove beneficial. Recent debates about truth and objectivity between Richard Rorty and his critics, for instance, have sharpened our grasp of what is involved in traditional views of truth and knowledge (see 4.6). As Robert Nozick argues, 'Even someone who rejects postmodernist theories can welcome their existence, for they force us to look anew at some fundamental notions – a quintessential philosophical task' (Nozick 2001: 55)

Recently the intellectual and political consequences of postmodernism, and its attendant relativism, have come to the attention of a wider public for two very different reasons. The first occasion was the publication of a hoax article by the theoretical physicist Alan Sokal in *Social Text*, a prominent postmodernist journal of cultural studies (see Sokal 1998). The article, which was nothing but a string of nonsequiturs couched in postmodern jargon, purported to show how theoretical physics in the twentieth century reaffirmed the insights of postmodernism on the instability of the notions of truth and objectivity. The long and heated debate that followed has implications for discussions of relativism. For instance, Paul Boghossian, in a much-cited article in the *Times Literary Supplement*, claims that one of the important lessons to be learned from the Sokal affair is that 'dubiously coherent relativistic views about the concepts of truth and evidence really have gained wide acceptance within the contemporary academy, just as it has often seemed' (Boghossian 1996: 14–16). Boghossian proceeds to argue that relativism is self-refuting and hence incoherent,[19] but since logic is seen as an instrument of political oppression an argument presupposing it could not have much impact on committed postmodernists. Nevertheless, the Sokal Hoax and the subsequent debate and publications effectively demonstrated the intellectual instability inherent in the postmodern approach, particularly when it relies on poorly understood scientific ideas to cast doubt on truth and objectivity (see Sokal and Bricmont 1998).

The second event to bring postmodern ideas and the question of relativism to a wider audience was the very public cultural and political backlash against postmodernism and its relativistic implications following the tragedy of 11 September 2001. Stanley Fish, in 'Don't Blame Relativism', lists the attacks in the media on postmodernism and relativism which ranged from the claim that postmodernism was now dead or proven to be wrong (since no one can deny the reality of an aeroplane hitting a building) to the accusation that relativism was responsible for weakening the national resolve which, in turn, had allowed the enemy in. The response Fish gives sheds interesting light on the postmodern understanding of relativism. He tells us:

> if by relativism one means the practice of putting yourself in your adversary's shoes, not in order to wear them as your own but in order to have some understanding (far short of approval) of why someone else – in our view, a deluded someone – might want to wear them, then relativism will not and should not end because it is simply another name for serious thought.
>
> (Fish 2002: 27–31)

If Fish's argument is to be taken as representative of the postmodernist view of relativism, then the distance between postmodernism and traditional accounts of relativism as a philosophical doctrine is far greater than one might have imagined. Fish's definition of relativism turns a heady and radical doctrine into a variant of the fairminded but commonplace injunction to adopt an unbiased approach to interpreting other people's beliefs and actions or to be fallibilists. If this is relativism, then we are all relativists or ought to be.

In the light of recent events, postmodernism may prove to be a transitory intellectual fad, but it would be a mistake to think that with the demise of postmodernism relativism will also disappear from the intellectual scene. As we shall see, relativism is a varied and multi-faceted doctrine which is not dependent for its motivation and justification on the arguments adduced for postmodernism by con-temporary philosophers and cultural theorists. A full discussion of the merits, or lack thereof, of postmodernism is well beyond the scope of this book. However, I shall end this section by making some brief comments on some conceptual and normative issues arising from it.

At the conceptual level, postmodernist philosophers seem to be claiming, implicitly or explicitly, that since all our judgements are made within, and influenced by, historical, social and cultural con-ditions, there is no possibility of finding an ahistorical, culturally neutral criterion for arbitrating between conflicting truth-claims. They seem to base this on the more abstract philosophical position that thought (beliefs, judgements, reasoning) is not only mediated by language, but is also an essentially linguistic act. There is no neutral location outside language for us to step into and assess our beliefs and judgements. The argument is singularly unconvincing. Even if we grant that all judgements are, in the relevant sense, context-sensitive or context-dependent, the relativistic implications drawn by most postmodern thinkers do not follow. From the fact (if it is indeed a fact) that all our ideas, discoveries and judgements bear the imprint of their time and place, it does not follow that they are all equally good or true. We may not shed all our historical baggage in the judge-ments we make, but it does not mean that we cannot shed any of it. If human beings were indeed unable to step outside the conceptual boundaries of their time and place, then it would be impossible to explain the phenomenon of intellectual dissent and innovation. In particular, it would be impossible to explain the status of postmod-ernism as a critique of the objectivist views of truth. Furthermore, the deterministic view of knowledge implicit in postmodernism calls into question the very status of postmodernism and its critique of mod-ernism. Why should we give preference to the postmodern views of truth as opposed to the Enlightenment position?

One answer given by postmodernists is to emphasise the politically progressive nature of their views, but the normative conclusions drawn by them are not borne out by the evidence available. Histori-cally, the intellectual heroes of postmodernism – Nietzsche and Heidegger, and not Voltaire and Diderot – have been associated with and celebrated by the Nazis and other right-wing groups. The post-modern suspicion of science and reason has much in common with the views expressed by reactionary neo-romantic thinkers such as Oswald Spengler (1880–1936) who had claimed that every truth, including self-evident truths such as those of mathematics, is entirely culture-bound and that 'Nothing whatever is really "true" in a deeper sense' (Norman Smith 2001: 159). Also, the postmodernist discourse of celebrating difference and denying universal human rights and other Enlightenment values has frequently been appropriated by reactionary forces, from China to the Islamic Republic of Iran, who use it to justify their abuses of human rights in the name of 'difference'. Probably the best argument against identifying relativism with progressive political views comes, indirectly, from Benito Mussolini. He argues:

> Everything I have said and done in these last years is relativism by intuition . . . If relativism signifies contempt for fixed categories and men who claim to be the bearers of an objective, immortal truth . . . then there is nothing more relativistic than Fascist attitudes and activity . . . From the fact that all ideologies are of equal value, that all ideologies are mere fiction, the modern relativism infers that everybody has the right to create for himself his own ideology and to attempt to enforce it with all the energy of which he is capable.
>
> (Mussolini, quoted in Cook 1999: 17)

3.6 CONCLUSION

The intellectual currents discussed in this chapter have contributed to a variety of interpretations of relativism. In the next section of the book we will examine, in some detail, the different forms of contemporary arguments for relativism and, in the process, attempt to understand the appeal of relativism.

PART II

Varieties of relativism

4

Relativism about truth

4.1 INTRODUCTION

Relativism about truth (alethic relativism) is the claim that views and standards of truth and falsity may vary across cultures, social groups, historical periods or even individuals, and every effort to adjudicate them is bound to be futile. The truth of beliefs, it is argued, is relative to a personal viewpoint, to the attitudes and other psychological idiosyncrasies of individuals, or more generally to the conceptual, historical or cultural background of the believers. Truth-claims are inexorably bound up with the personal, cultural and historical contexts which give rise to them and hence their assessments should also be context-dependent. Alethic relativism is at once the most radical and most general of all relativistic positions, for other varieties of cognitive relativism, and even moral relativism, are reducible to it. For instance, relativism about rationality can be restated as the claim that there are no true (universal) standards of rationality; relativism about logic as the contention that logical truths are relative to specific cultures or cognitive schemes and not universal in their scope and application; and moral relativism as the view that the truth of ethical judgements is relative to their context or the cultural background.

Alethic relativism is often contrasted, in an undifferentiated way, with a host of views on truth, including objectivism, absolutism, universalism and realism. We shall examine these in turn. A judgement is objective if its truth or falsity depends on how things are in the world, rather than what individuals think or feel. Objectivism is contrasted with subjectivism, the view that truth or falsity, right and wrong, etc., are expressions of individuals' psychological states. A judgement or statement is objective if its truth and falsity can obtain independently of our thoughts and beliefs; it is subjective if its truth and falsity depend on the beliefs and other psychological states of the person making that judgement. A feature of the world (a property, object) is mind-dependent if it is not possible (conceivable) for that feature to obtain in the absence of minds and cognitive activities (beliefs, judgements, experiences, interests, etc.). A feature of the world (a property, object) is mind-independent if it is possible (conceivable) for that feature (property, object) to obtain in the absence of all minded creatures and independently of their beliefs, judgements, experiences, etc. All subjective judgements are mind-dependent, but the converse does not hold – i.e., not all mind-dependent judgements are subjective – for judgements may also be true intersubjectively. A judgement is intersubjective if its truth and falsity depend on the agreement between persons making that judgement. Intersubjectivity allows for the convergence of different perspectives; it leads to a shared point of view. A judgement or a statement is perspectival if its truth and falsity depend on occupying a point of view or a position and the question of its truth and falsity cannot be settled without reference to that point of view or position. To have a view from nowhere is to see the world from outside all perspectives, or to have what Putnam has called 'A God's-eye view'. Objective judgements strive to be independent of particular points of view or perspectives. However, despite its popularity, the metaphor of viewing or seeing is not very helpful in formulating the idea of objectivity because all seeing is inevitably perspectival, while this is not obviously the case with cognition. It may be easier to allow for the idea of conceiving from nowhere or a-perspectival conceptions of the world rather than a view from nowhere.

Relativism is also contrasted with absolutism and universalism about truth. A judgement is absolute if it is not perspectival, it is not from a point of view, and if its truth is immutable. It is sometimes argued that a truth has absolute authority if there are no circumstances under which it can be doubted. However, the denial of such an extreme claim should not be confused with alethic relativism. To deny that we can have access to absolute truths, to accept that all our opinions are open to revision, is an indicator of rationality and does not entail relativism.[1] A judgement is universal if it is either absolute or it holds from every point of view. The relativist, unlike the sceptic, does not doubt or deny the existence of truth or the possibility of our having access to it; rather, she casts doubt on the suggestion that truth is univocal, that propositions are true for all times, places, and thinkers.

Traditionally, the major debates on the question of truth have been conducted along the realist and anti-realist divide. Alethic relativism is often contrasted with realist conceptions of truth and consequently conflated with other anti-realist theories of truth. Realism explains truth in terms of a relationship between beliefs – expressed by sentences or statements and abstracted into propositions – and the world. The truth and falsity of propositions (sentences, statements), according to this view, depend on how things are in the world; truth is mind-independent, universal and objective. The correspondence theory of truth, stating that propositions are true if they correspond to or picture facts, is one of the ways that realists explain truth. However, in recent decades realist philosophers tend to prefer more deflationary or minimalist accounts of truth.[2] Anti-realist philosophers deny the coherence of the suggestion that we can have access to wholly mind-independent facts and truths. Many idealist philosophers advocate a coherence theory of truth, according to which the truth or falsity of beliefs depends on their location within a network of beliefs and on their relationship with the other beliefs in the network. Epistemic theories of truth, proposed by verificationist philosophers for instance, emphasise the role of warrant and justification in establishing the truth and falsity of a belief. According to this brand of anti-realism, the idea that there can be truths which are in principle unknowable is incoherent, for such a truth would also be in principle, inconceivable. Realists believe in the existence of mind-independent facts and truths, and in so far as relativists deny the existence of 'a view from nowhere' or a 'God's-eye view', their position is incompatible with realism. In addition, the presumed objectivity of truth and its mind-independence imply that truth is both universal and absolute – for a realist, if a judgement is true then it is true across different cultures, times and places. The denial of realism, however, does not necessarily lead to relativism, for in addition to the negative doctrine of what truth is not, the alethic relativist puts forward a positive claim to the effect that all truth is necessarily context-dependent. Epistemic views of truth, because they link truth with conditions of epistemic evaluations, such as warrant or assertability, *prima facie*, seem more hospitable to relativism as it can be argued that what counts as warrant for asserting a sentence varies from culture to culture and that there is no overarching decision-procedure for adjudicating between these diverse accounts. Similarly for the coherence theory, for there could be more than one non-convergent, internally coherent, system of beliefs and the truth or falsity of a given belief would depend on, and hence be relative to, the system of belief of which it forms a part. Very few philosophers subscribing to either of these views take a straightforwardly relativistic position, but some have defended weaker versions of alethic relativism.[3] In general, we can distinguish between four major relativistic positions on truth:

(1) Subjectivism or subjective relativism
(2) Strong alethic relativism
(3) Restricted (moderate) alethic relativism
(4) Questioning truth.

4.2 SUBJECTIVISM

Subjectivism or subjective relativism is the claim that the truth and falsity of judgements are relative to the beliefs, opinions and points of view of individuals – that truth-claims are, in effect, nothing but expressions of our most cherished personal beliefs and likes and dislikes. The view seems to be quite popular outside of professional philosophical circles; and certainly for most undergraduate students it is the starting point, and for some also the end point of their thinking about truth. The arguments offered on behalf of subjective relativism are similar to those used in defence of other forms of relativism. The subjectivists point to the diversity of human beliefs and argue that in many domains – ethics, politics and aesthetics in particular – there is a marked absence of agreement on what is true or false. Different people have different views, occupy different positions and seem equally convinced of their veracity. Since many of these differences have proven to be intractable, then the only reasonable stance is to accept that truth is only a question of personal opinion. The subjectivist adopts a sceptical attitude towards truth by claiming that questions of truth and falsity cannot be resolved at the public and objective level, and then, rather than denying the possibility of attaining truth, as the sceptic does, claims that what is true or false depends on an individual's perspective, point of view, taste, etc. As a result, the subjectivist attains the kind of certainty that is denied to the objectivist. If truth is co-extensive with what I believe, then I am immune from the sceptical challenge, the evil demon cannot 'really' touch me. The cost, however, is the denial of the distinction between knowledge and strongly held beliefs, between 'P is true' and 'P is believed to be true [by x]'. Thus, the subjectivist faces the type of objections levelled against Protagorean relativism in chapter 1.

The most common form of stating alethic relativism is through the expression 'true for'. The claim is that what is true *for* one person or society or culture may not be true *for* another. The subjectivist understands any occurrence of the predicate 'is true' as a truncated version of the longer statement 'true for person x at time t'. There are different ways of understanding the locution 'true for'.[4] Frequently a sentence such as 'it is true for John that abortion is wrong' simply means that John believes (strongly) that abortion is wrong (or feels certain that it is wrong); similarly, 'it is true for Muslims that pork is unclean' is used as an equivalent for 'Muslims believe that pork is unclean'. Since 'A believes that P' is equivalent to 'A believes that P is true', the substitution of 'true for' for 'believes', although somewhat unfortunate because of the misunderstanding it can create, makes some sense. Such a claim however, taken at face value, would make the relativist doctrine either trivial or absurd: trivial if we take the suggestion to be that for any belief P and believer X, 'X believes P if and only if P is true for X', and absurd if it is claimed that 'if X believes P then P is true'. The former is trivially true because believing a proposition is logically equivalent to holding it true. The latter is absurd because it implies that there is no distinction between true and untrue beliefs, between being right and being wrong. It renders disagreement and change of belief either inexplicable or attributable to capricious shifts in taste and preferences.

Subjective relativism, however, comes very close to embracing this absurd position. Subjectivism rules out the possibility of disagreement and the very distinction between correct and incorrect judgements, for it turns all our judgements, as long as we believe in them, into correct or true ones. As Aristotle pointed out more than two thousand years ago (see 1.4), subjective relativism contravenes the most fundamental of all the laws of logic, the law of non-contradiction. According to this law, for any proposition P, not both P and its negation –P can be true. No rational agent, it is argued, can hold both P and its negation true, because it is constitutive of the very meaning of the predicate 'true' that the truth of a proposition or sentence rules out its falsity.[5] A subjectivist S who, for instance, believes that (I) 'the invasion of Iraq is politically misguided' is not ruling out the truth of the contrary belief (–I), 'the invasion of Iraq is not politically misguided'. For according to her, I is true for S but false for those who believe –I. For the subjectivist, then, public disagreement is impossible, but without disagreement there can be no agreement either; subjectivism renders all our judgements true; but if all our beliefs are correct or true, then the very distinction between correct and incorrect judgements becomes superfluous, and the idea of holding a belief or making a judgement loses intelligibility. On the plus side, the subjectivist manages to dissolve the problem of disagreement in political, ethical and even scientific arenas. All sides of a dispute can be right, if the truth of their respective beliefs is relativised to their personal view-point, likes and dislikes or taste. However, this dissolution carries a high cost, for to accept that opposing beliefs can be true is to relinquish the distinction between being right and wrong. As Davidson has argued, 'Someone cannot have a belief unless he understands the possibility of being mistaken, and this requires grasping the contrast between truth and error – true belief and false beliefs' (Davidson 2001: 170). In other words, to have a belief is to accept that there is such a thing as truth, that there is a distinction between how things are and how they seem to us.

The subjectivist may argue that she can, in fact, distinguish between truth and falsity, for by asserting that a belief P is true (for her) she is ruling out the falsity of that belief (for her), and in this way she is not contravening the law of non-contradiction, for at no point does she assent to the contradictory assertion 'P & –P (for S at time T)'. What the subjectivist is reluctant to do is to impose her private criterion of right and wrong, truth and falsity, on others. In all her judgements she relies on a private and personal standard of truth and falsity, right and wrong, for she believes that no more can be achieved by anyone, and that those who think otherwise suffer from a lamentable intellectual hubris.

The question then is, could there be a purely private criterion for distinguishing between right and wrong, and what form would such a criterion take? Ordinarily we use information gathered from observations of our environment as well as the testimony of others to distinguish between truth, illusions and mistakes. We check our beliefs against those held by others, or what we learn from other people's testimonies, as well as basing them on information we receive directly from the natural world. The first of these means of distinguishing between truth and falsehood, or being right and simply thinking that one is right, is not available to the subjectivists. They cannot appeal to intersubjectively available criteria of truth and falsity, for by definition they deny the provenance of such criteria. Any judgements as to the reliability of the testimony of others will also be grounded on subjective criteria and thus encounter the initial difficulty. The appeal to 'how things are in the world' is more complex. The subjectivist may argue that she accepts or rejects a given belief depending on how it fits in with her other beliefs, including what may be called 'evidential beliefs', or beliefs on how she thinks the world is. But then the same question arises at the level of evidential beliefs: how can the subjectivist distinguish between beliefs that are true and those that merely seem to be true to her? Without recourse to publicly available standards or procedures, the subjectivist is trapped within her private web of belief, unable to distinguish between what is true and what she believes to be true. The pragmatist solution canvassed on behalf of Protagoras in chapter 1 is not available to the subjectivist either, because the distinction between being better and seeming better also relies on publicly available standards of right and wrong.

The subjectivist may accept the force of these arguments, but retort that we all face the same predicament. The objectivist, like the subjective relativist, can only believe what she thinks to be true, use evidence that she thinks to be convincing and distinguish between truth and falsity based on criteria that ultimately she finds convincing. There is no meaningful distinction between being true and simply appearing true. All claims to truth are claims about 'appearing true' and it is only a sign of cognitive arrogance or naïvety to think otherwise. This reply neglects, or at least underestimates, the role that the natural world and other people play in shaping and reshaping our beliefs; subjectivism, when fully developed, is ultimately indistinguishable from solipsism. The subjectivist, like the solipsist, ignores at her peril the role of the world and the evidence it provides for or against beliefs and judgements. To paraphrase W. V. O. Quine, by privatising the criterion of right and wrong, by reducing truth and falsity to what the individual likes or believes, a convinced subjectivist embraces the prospect of her own quick but timely demise. To enable our survival, our beliefs about the world we inhabit, at least at the most mundane level, have to be minimally true or accurate, and provide us with correct predictions about the world. A child who does not learn to distinguish between the edible and non-edible, the lethal and non-lethal, etc., will not live long enough to become a subjectivist.

Arguments against the coherence of subjectivism can also be found in Wittgenstein who in his private language argument questioned the very possibility of there being such a thing as a private language, a language that can be used by an isolated individual to record his or her private (subjective) states of mind. According to Wittgenstein, a prerequisite of being able to speak a language is the ability to make a distinction between being right and seeming to be right, or truth and falsehood. Without this ability, a language would not be a medium of expression and thought. A person who uses a private language would not have the resources to determine the difference between veridical and non-veridical statements about her personal subjective experiences. An isolated user of a putative private language would not be able to distinguish between how things are and how things seem to her. In order for language to operate as a medium for recording or expressing any beliefs about the world you need at least two people.[6]

For these reasons, subjective alethic relativism does not have much currency in contemporary debates and is repudiated, in no uncertain terms, by all the philosophers who are classified as relativists in this book. For instance, Ian Hacking, whose defence of one form of relativism is discussed in 6.5, dismisses subjectivism as the absurd position that by thinking we might make something true or false (Hacking 1982: 49). Other forms of alethic relativism are compatible with the denial of subjectivism and it is to these views that we now turn.

4.3 STRONG ALETHIC RELATIVISM

Strong alethic relativism is the claim that the truth or falsity of judgements or beliefs cannot obtain independently of the context or background in which these judgements are made. It is argued, by Jack Meiland for instance (see below), that contrary to common assumption, 'true' is a three-place rather than a two-place predicate in that truth-claims not only involve a relation between an assertion and either the world or other assertions, but also an irreducible, but often implicit, reference to a third thing. This third thing is variously construed as a culture, worldview, tradition, belief-system, etc., but in almost all its constructions the emphasis is on the role the human mind plays in 'making' its world rather than simply describing it. Any truth-claim, e.g., 'It is true that dinosaurs roamed the Earth before mankind had evolved', according to this view, should be reinterpreted as, 'It is true relative (or according to) our cultural beliefs, our conceptual frameworks, our historical understanding, our present scientific paradigm, etc., that dinosaurs roamed the Earth before mankind had evolved'.[7] Strong alethic relativism accepts that there is a distinction between truth and falsity, appearance and reality, being right and thinking that one is right, but insists that all such distinctions take their meaning and content from the cultural, linguistic, historical background and context which give rise to and shape our beliefs. Thus, we cannot make any claims about the truth or falsity of 'dinosaurs existed on this planet', or any other statements for that matter, that do not implicitly involve a reference to a prevailing paradigm, cultural precept, etc.

There are two distinct steps involved in arguments for strong alethic relativism: first, the belief that truth is not independent of context/background/culture; second, that there are significant variations among the contexts, the backgrounds and cultures within which truth-claims are made. This second premise is used to argue against universalism or uniqueness of truth, for truth could be both context-dependent and universal if there were only a single context that gave rise to all truth-claims.

Meiland is one of the few philosophers who have been willing to defend strong alethic relativism. According to him, truth is a three-term relation between statements, the world and a third term, which may be persons (what I have called 'subjective relativism'), worldviews or historical (historicism) and cultural situations (cultural relativism). He argues:

> When we use an expression of the form 'Ø is true for W', it seems legitimate to ask the question 'What does "true" mean in this expression?' . . . The correct relativist answer to this question is: 'It means that Ø is true-for-W.' The hyphens in this answer are extremely important. For they show that, the relativist is not talking about truth but instead about truth-for-W. Thus, one can no more reasonably ask what 'true' means in the expression 'true-for-W' than one can ask what 'cat' means in the word 'cattle'. 'True-for-W' denotes a special three-term relation, which does not include the two-term relation of absolute truth as a distinct part.
>
> (Meiland 1977: 574)

According to Meiland, then, relative truth, a three-term relation, is both distinct from the absolutist, two-term relation notion of truth and is philosophically viable. The relativist can even make use of a schema similar to the one used by the correspondence theorists of truth and argue that 'P is true relative to W' means something like 'P corresponds to the facts from the point of view of W'. The thought is that the correspondence theory of truth, when correctly understood, does have this implicit reference to points of view, and cultural and historical perspectives.

Harvey Siegel has argued that Meiland's analysis is unsuccessful because it reduces truth to a two-term relation. Siegel argues:

> To be a genuine three-term relation, it must be possible to individuate each relatum and to distinguish each from the other two. On a conception of absolute truth, this condition . . . is easily met: the world, however difficult to apprehend directly, is clearly distinguishable from statements about it. What, however, is the status of the world on the three-term

conception? Is it clearly distinguishable from the other two relata? Unfortunately, the answer is no. On the relativist conception, the world is not distinguishable from the third relatum (either persons, world view, or historical and cultural situation,). What are related by the alleged three-term relation are statements and the-world-relative-to-W (where W is a person, a set of leading principles, a world view, or a situation – in short, where W is the third relatum). On the relativist conception, the world cannot be conceived as independent of W; if it is so conceived the relativist conception collapses into an absolutist one, for it is granted that there is a way the world is, independent of statements of W's. This is precisely what the relativist must deny, however.

(Siegel 1987: 12)

Meiland, however, could reply that there still remains a crucial difference between the absolutist and the relativist. The absolutist claims that truth should be explicated in terms of a relationship between sentences and the world, while according to the relativist, truth is a relationship between sentences and the world-for-X. These two conceptions of truth are not equivalent for the latter still involves a three-term relation, even if the relationship is slightly different from the one characterised by Meiland, i.e., truth/the world-for-X as opposed to true-for-X/the world. The relativist and absolutist both accept that there is a world independent of us; however, the relativist argues that we cannot give substance or content to the abstract conception 'the world as it is', or say what the world is like without implicitly or explicitly referring to our conceptual and cultural framework. There remains an important distinction between thinking that truth is correspondence with 'the world as it is *for X*' and thinking that it is correspondence with 'the world *as it is*', and it is this distinction that Meiland's theory of truth highlights.

Meiland's analysis of relative truth as it stands is not convincing for a different reason. Firstly, the analogy between 'true' in 'true-for-W' and 'cat' in 'cattle' is singularly unhelpful. In order for 'true-for-W' to do the relativistic work expected of it, we should also be able to use locutions such as 'not-true-for-W', 'true-for-Y', 'true-for-both W and Y', etc. So Meiland has to grant that 'true-for' has a meaning independent of 'true-for-W' in ways that the concatenation of the letters c, a, t in 'cattle' does not. To see this we should return to Meiland's original sentence (let's call it TFW): 'Thus, one can no more reasonably ask what "true" means in the expression "true-for-W" than one can ask what "cat" means in the word "cattle"' (Meiland 1977: 575). The disanalogy becomes clearer if we attempt to translate TFW into another language. All languages have readily and independently available equivalences both for 'true' and for 'true for'; while only when we have found an equivalent for the word cattle in the language into which we are translating TFW can we find the equivalent for 'c~a~t'.[8] The successful translation of 'c~a~t' into a foreign language wholly depends on the initial translation of 'cattle' into that language. This is not the case with 'true' and 'true-for-W'. The concept of truth not only exists independently of the concept 'true-for-W', and hence can be expressed in any given language, but also it gives meaning to 'true-for-W', while 'c~a~t' is completely dependent on 'cattle', and hence the literal translation of Meiland's example into any other language would make nonsense of his point.

A further weakness in constructing relativism as a three-term relation 'true-*for*-W' is that it can turn relativism into a species of subjectivism. The subjectivist, like the Meilandian alethic relativist, makes use of the locution 'true for', and as we have seen, ultimately loses her grasp on meaning and intelligibility. The relativist may argue that a possibly more useful reconstruction of the concept of truth for their purposes is to make use of one of the key motivations for adopting relativism about truth, namely the claim that the idea of absolute truth is incoherent or unintelligible. The absolutist, at least in her traditional realist guise, argues that truth is correspondence with a mind-independent world. Relativists, however, may argue that the project of describing a mind-independent world is incoherent, for the very idea of a mind-independent world is inevitably mediated through the human mind.[9] Whenever we speak of correspondence between a sentence and the world, we are in effect talking about the relationship between our beliefs, sentences and the world as mediated by human understanding, interpretation or even construction. Thus, 'P is true' is to be understood as 'P is true *according* to W', where W is a world-view, culture, belief-system, framework or what have you.[10] In addition, if it is accepted that there can be irreconcilable differences between varying frameworks, cultures, belief-systems, etc., then it follows that what is true according to W1 may not be true according to W2. In this conception of truth, any truth-claim will have to be indexed to a perspective, belief-system, worldview, etc. To think otherwise is to succumb to the absolutist illusion of thinking that we can step outside all frameworks and talk about the world as it is. There is no location for our assertions about the world outside of our belief-systems, just as there is no location for our body outside of our skin.

True-for gives an agent-relative view of truth, at the level of either individuals or groups, while true-according-to provides for an agent-independent or what may be called a 'context-relative' criterion of truth and falsity. One advantage of formulating the relativist claim in this way is that it enables us to distinguish between 'P being true (according to W)' and 'believing that P is true (according to W)'. The crucial gap between belief and truth is retained; individuals can make mistakes about what is true (according to W). It also allows for the possibility that a proposition may be true according to a system of belief or worldview, without necessarily being believed to be true; thus it does not make truth co-extensive with what is actually believed at any given time. This conception of relative truth also allows for belief-change and discovery; it allows us to distinguish between true and false beliefs, or being right and thinking that one is right, within a worldview. Furthermore, 'true according to' can be given an epistemic interpretation, where we can talk, for instance, about 'true according to the assertability conditions prevalent in a worldview W'. The thought is that truth can be identified with rational acceptability, but what is rationally acceptable according to one tradition of enquiry may not be so in another, hence we get different conceptions of truth relative to the norms of rational enquiry prevalent at a given time or place. We shall return to the idea of different and incompatible norms of rationality in the next two chapters. The question remains whether this reformulation of strong alethic relativism can withstand the weight of anti-relativist arguments.

4.4 THE SELF-REFUTATION ARGUMENT

Historically, the most trenchant as well as the most popular argument against relativism, at least since Plato, has been the accusation that relativism is self-refuting. The charge of inconsistency arises out of puzzlement over the standing of the claim that '(all) truth is relative'. Is this claim – let's call it R – true absolutely or only relatively? If R is true absolutely, then there is at least one claim that is true non-relatively. If, on the other hand, it is true only *according to* the relativist conception of truth or worldview, then R is still false *according to* the absolutist, and the relativist has no way of convincing her opponent of its truth. The dilemma facing the relativist has been aired periodically and in various forms since Plato (see chapter 1). However, relativism seems to have managed to shrug off or circumvent the accusation of incoherence and has become more sophisticated and nuanced in the process.

The self-refutation argument has been formulated in many different ways. In what follows, we will consider some of these formulations and assess the counter-arguments provided by the relativists. Harvey Siegel has devoted an entire book to attacking relativism on the basis of the self-refutation argument, and hence can act as spokesman for the self-refutationists. He offers two arguments for the incoherence of what he calls Protagorean relativism and what I have called 'strong alethic relativism':

> Argument 1 Relativism is incoherent because it holds that all beliefs and opinions are true, yet, given conflicting beliefs, some beliefs must necessarily be false – in which case relativism cannot be true.
>
> (Siegel 1987: 6)

> Argument 2 Relativism is incoherent because, if it is right, the very notion of rightness is undermined, in which case relativism cannot be right.
>
> (Ibid.: 8)

Argument 1 is a version of Plato's refutation of Protagoras. One problem with Siegel's criticism (as well as Putnam's version of the same argument discussed in chapter 1) lies in the failure to distinguish between agent-relativism and context-relativism. A context-relativist, unlike a subjectivist, can distinguish between being right (according to the norms of one's culture) and thinking that one is right (according to the norms of one's culture). Furthermore, she would readily grant that she is not in a position to distinguish between being right according to the (epistemic) norms of one's culture (and in that sense thinking that she is right) and being right, *sans phrases*, because there is no possibility of such distinction to begin with. The very point of context-relativism is to deny that there is such a state as being right outside the constraints, perspectives and norms of any culture, worldview or belief-system. It may be argued that context-relativists make us prisoners of our own culture, language or worldview. For although we may be able to distinguish between being right and thinking we are right according to our own society's norms, we are rendered incapable of stepping outside these norms to make any claims about other cultures. This is the famous problem of incommensurability, which will be discussed in chapters 6 and 8. But without further arguments on the unacceptable consequences of the incommensurability thesis, the relativist's inability to draw a distinction between thinking one is right and being right cross-culturally will be taken by her as a strength, rather than a weakness, of her doctrine.

Argument 2, as formulated above, may be seen as a variant of Argument 1, but Siegel generalises it into a more troublesome problem. He proposes that the very idea of rightness requires a non-relativistic interpretation:

> For the relativist wants to argue that relativism is right (or true, or cognitively superior) and that non-relativism is wrong (or false, or cognitively inferior) . . . To make this claim non-relativistically, however, is to give up relativism; conversely, to make the claim only relatively is not to make it at all.
>
> (Ibid.: 9)

The same type of argument has been given an epistemic twist by Maurice Mandelbaum, who claims that the relativists commit what he calls the 'self-excepting fallacy', i.e., 'the fallacy of stating a generalisation that purports to hold of all persons but which, inconsistently, is not then applied to oneself' (Mandelbaum 1982: 36). A relativist, if rational, would cite some evidence to support his relativism; but this evidence would only be convincing if it were not interpreted relativistically.

The argument is that the relativist should choose between saying that statements of the form 'X is true relative to person P' are true (or false) absolutely and saying that they are true (or false) only relatively. If the former, then they will be accepting an absolutist notion of truth. If the latter, their position becomes unintelligible, or 'starts to wobble'. Putnam also, as we saw (1.3), has argued that relativism involves a vicious regress of this sort. According to him, 'truth is relative' should be read as 'it is true relative to . . . that truth is relative', and the clause 'it is true relative to . . .' can be added *ad infinitum*. A '*total* relativist' of this sort, according to Putnam, would have to say whether or not a proposition P is relative to a context C is itself relative (Putnam 1981: 121). The question is whether the regress engendered by total relativism is vicious or not, for on the face of it there does not seem to be any difficulty in imagining a hierarchy of language levels, where the statements made at each level are only true relative to that language level.

It may not seem immediately obvious why the suggestion that 'all claims to truth, including the claim that relativism is true, are relative to the persons or social groups who make them' should be self-defeating. The relativist's position will become unintelligible only if he tries to convince the non-relativist of the superiority of his relativist scheme; but so long as the relativist is content to say 'in my conceptual scheme, system of belief, etc., truth is relative, while for the members of society X, or conceptual scheme Y, truth might be an absolutist notion, and I am not in a position to say which of us is right', his position will not be so shaky. The point is, we can avoid the charge of self-refutation by embracing higher-order relativism. If a relativist accepts that 'truth is relative' is itself only relatively true, i.e., true only for people who suggest it, his position will amount to a simple acknowledgement that all statements, including second-order statements about these statements, are true relative to their social or cultural context; and this does not, in any damaging sense, involve a regress. At most what it suggests is that we can have n-order languages, statements of which are only true relative to the person(s) using that language level. The acknowledgement of the possibility of an infinity of language levels is not by itself absurd or vicious. Such a stand would, of course, rob the relativist of the right to argue for the superiority of her position, and would also force her to accept that an absolutist has something equally good to say about truth. Nevertheless, if a relativist is prepared to pay such a price then she cannot be accused of holding an unintelligible position. This feature of strong relativism about truth, however, does not leave much room for relativistic philosophers, since they are trying to convince their opponents of the truth or superiority of their position by arguing for it. Hence, although total relativism is not self-defeating, arguing for relativism with non-relativists is. So long as the relativist does not wish to convert the non-relativist, then she is not committing a fallacy. This may leave the relativist philosophers in an unenviable position but does not wholly undermine their stand, for in a Wittgensteinian mood they can always claim that the wisdom of their position cannot be put into words, but makes itself manifest.[11]

There is, however, a different formulation of the self-refutation argument which makes the relativist claim come out false rather than incoherent. The argument goes something like this:[12]

R1 The truth and falsity of all propositions are relative to their cultural or conceptual context.

R2 One and the same propositions may be true in one context and false in another.

R3 Absolutism is the claim that the truth or falsity of propositions is invariant across different cultural or conceptual contexts.

R4 Absolutism denies the truth of relativism.
R5 (R1) is either absolutely or relatively true.

> If R1 is true absolutely then R1 is false.
> If R1 is true relatively, then there are some contexts (call them CA) in which R1 is false.
> Given R4, absolutism is true in CA.
> But if absolutism is true in CA, then by R3, absolutism is true in all cultural and conceptual contexts and hence relativism is false.

Therefore, relativism is false. QED

The problem with this version of the self-refutation argument, as in many other reconstructions, is that it establishes the falsity of relativism by presupposing a non-relativistic criterion of truth. For instance, R5 presupposes the law of excluded middle, to the effect that every proposition is either true or false, and to deny the truth of a proposition is to affirm its falsity. But this assumption is in tension with R2, according to which the truth of a proposition (in one context) does not exclude its falsity (in another context). The relativist may agree that to deny the truth of a proposition is to commit oneself to its 'un-truth' but argue that 'untrue' and false are not necessarily equivalent.

The implicit assumption in the self-refutation argument is that our understanding of the 'truth' predicate is necessarily non-relativistic – that we cannot formulate a theory or a conception of truth that does not involve an absolutist assumption. Relativists have adopted various strategies to overcome this objection.

4.5 THE COUNTER-ARGUMENT

Until quite recently, at least in analytic circles, the incoherence of relativism was almost an article of faith.[13] As Thomas Bennigson argues:

> The most remarkable feature of many anti-relativist arguments is their brevity; they often consist of little more than announcing that to assert global relativism is implicitly to claim absolute truth for one's assertion, resulting in immediate self-contradiction.
>
> (Bennigson 1999a: 215)

In the past decade there has been a marked change in the perception of the problem of relativism and the solutions offered, in part because it was accepted (somewhat unwillingly) that the charge of self-refutation had not managed to deliver the death-blow for which it was devised. Robert Nozick echoes the sentiments of a number of philosophers working in this area when he tells us: 'For some time now, I have felt uncomfortable with this quick refutation of relativism, a favorite of philosophers and one that I had often used in conversation' (Nozick 2001: 15). In this section, I shall examine two recent proposals for overcoming the accusation of self-refutation.

One strategy for bypassing the self-refutation argument is to modify the concept of truth used by relativists in such a way that relativistic claims would not lead to contradiction. For instance, Joseph Margolis has argued that relativism can survive the charges of self-contradiction, conceptual anarchy and nihilism only if it abandons the classical two-value (or 'bipolar') view of truth, at least within some domains of discourse, and allows for weaker, gradated and intermediate values for the truth predicate. The impetus behind relativism, according to Margolis, as first expressed by Protagoras, comes from the insight that good arguments can be found for the opposite sides of a debate. The way to accommodate that insight is to accept that although no statement can be both true and false, there is scope for evaluating seemingly contradictory statements along a weaker and more nuanced continuum of truth-like values such as 'plausibility, reasonableness, aptness', etc. According to Margolis,

> by introducing logically weaker values, we may admit claims or judgements to be evidentially supported or supportable even where, on a bipolar model of truth-values but not now, admissible judgements would yield incompatible or contradictory claims. We may simply abandon excluded middle or *tertium non datur*.
>
> (Margolis 1989: 251)

There are two independent ideas at work in Margolis's suggestion. The first is the substitution of a realist view of truth and falsehood with the epistemic idea of warrant. Realist philosophers argue that the truth or falsity of a proposition is independent of its epistemic merits, for it is always possible to find a true sentence implausible or think that a false sentence is apt. They maintain that we should not confuse the truth and falsity of propositions with our psychological and epistemological attitudes towards them, for we can always ask of any judgement if it is true even when it is judged to be reasonable, apt or plausible. The debate between realists and anti-realists on truth is beyond the scope of this book; however, any attempt to defend relativism by using an epistemic conception of truth will have to overcome a host of objections directed at such conceptions.

Second, and more significantly, Margolis is suggesting a revision in classical logic. He is arguing against the assumption that every proposition has either the value true or the value false, and never both. There are some areas of discourse, he believes, where the principle of bivalence, stating that every proposition or sentence is either true or false, does not apply. A number of philosophers and logicians who, for a variety of reasons, deny the universal applicability of binary classical logic have resorted to formal semantics with a continuum of values. The standard method in this approach is to give the values true or false, or in numerical terms the values 1 and 0, to the two extreme ends of a predicate. The truth-values of intermediate cases, on the other hand, will be real numbers in the interval between 0 and 1. For instance, a proposition such as 'John is tall' will get the value 0 if John's height is less than five feet, and the value 1 if John's height is six feet or above. The intermediate cases will get the values 0.9, 0.8, 0.7, etc., depending on John's height and the criterion we use for deciding what counts as a tall man. As our powers of discrimination are finite, in practice we will need only finitely many values. For instance, if we cannot measure the height of a person more precisely than the nearest tenth of a millimetre, then in the above example 10,000 values will be sufficient to reflect all the differences we can discriminate in the continuum between being tall and not being tall. Yet, the theory, in principle, allows for infinitely many values. The multi-valued system of logic, despite its bizarre talk of infinitely many truth-values, receives support from ordinary language locutions such as 'very true', 'more or less true', 'to some extent true', etc., and these are probably the locutions that Margolis has in mind.[14] The many-valued relativist may then argue that the same propositions may be very true relative to context or culture A, while only partially or slightly true in culture B. Margolis tends to restrict his relativism to aesthetic judgement, and hence his suggested revision has an appropriately limited scope. However, it is interesting to explore this point further.

As we saw, strong alethic relativism is the dual claim:

R1 The truth and falsity of all propositions are relative to their cultural or conceptual context.

R2 One and the same proposition may be true in one context and false in another.

The suggestion now is to modify R2 as the claim:

R2 One and the same proposition may be true (to some degree) in one context and false (to a greater or lesser degree) in another.

It is unclear how this radical modification of logic can help alethic relativism. Relativism about truth is a response to the empirical observation of conflict in belief and knowledge-claims. The proposed revision amounts to a denial that there is an actual conflict between the beliefs or the truth-claims of different cultures or language groups in the first place, so the motivation for relativising truth disappears. This may be exactly what Margolis and other similarly minded philosophers are hoping for, but the dissolution of the underlying problem motivating relativism seems too easy. Furthermore, the anti-relativist will argue that even within this multi-value-system the proposition 'truth is relative' will have a lower degree of truth than the proposition 'truth is not relative'. The conclusion to draw from the proposed radical revision in classical logic, the anti-relativist will claim, is that relativism is untrue to a greater degree than it is true, although its falsehood can be tempered by the use of modifiers such as 'somewhat', 'to some extent', etc. The relativist has not provided opponents of relativism with any reason to change their mind on this particular issue, and the stand-off between the relativist and anti-relativist still remains.

A further suggestion for the modification of classical logic for the purposes of developing a consistent form of relativism about truth has come from Steven D. Hales, who reconstructs the self-refutation argument as:

> Relativism is the thesis that *everything is relative*.
> Absolutism is a denial of this, or *not everything is relative*.
> 'Everything is relative' is the claim that every proposition is true in some perspective and untrue in another.
> Absolutism is the negation of this, i.e., there is at least one proposition which has the same truth-value in all perspectives.
> The thesis of relativism is true either absolutely or relatively. If relativism is true absolutely then it is true in all perspectives. Therefore, there is a proposition that has the same truth-value in all perspectives. From which it follows that absolutism is true and relativism false.
> If, on the other hand, the thesis of relativism is true only relatively, then there is some perspective in which relativism is untrue, where, then, absolutism is true.

If absolutism is true, then there is some proposition which is true in all perspectives, from which it follows that relativism is false. Therefore, relativism is false. QED.

Hales's response to the self-refutation argument depends on the analogy he draws between modal logic and his proposed new 'intensional logic of relativism'.[15] According to him:

> just as 'it cannot be the case that everything is possible because the claim runs afoul of the principle that whatever is possibly necessary is necessary . . ., it cannot be the case that everything is relative either, because the claim runs foul of the intuitive principle that whatever is relatively absolute is absolute. However, just as we can safely assert that whatever is true is possibly true . . . so too the relativist can claim that whatever is true is relatively true . . . There is nothing self-contradictory or paradoxical abut the claim that everything true is relatively true, just as there is no puzzle engendered by the claim that whatever is true is possibly true.
>
> (Hales 1997: 36–7)

Hales argues that the air of paradox would disappear once we realised that we can index truth to perspectives in the same way that propositions can be indexed to possible worlds in modal logic. According to him, relativism should be understood as a modality similar to possibility and necessity. His construction of a consistent form of relativism, as he admits, depends on (a) the admission of perspectives into our ontology and (b) accepting the truth of the derivation that 'if P is true then P is relatively true'. He compares (a) to the introduction of possible worlds and argues that it is no more incoherent to relativise the truth of propositions to perspectives, given a perspectivist semantics, than it is to relativise the truth of propositions to possible worlds, given a possible worlds semantics, or to relativise truth to languages given an array of languages. He argues:

> Just as we are willing to agree that there are possible worlds that are both non-identical with the actual world and yet accessible from the actual world, so too we should admit perspectives commensurable to (yet non-identical with) one's actual perspective.
>
> (Ibid.: 39)

Leaving aside the adequacy of the details of Hales's solution, one difficulty with his overall proposal is that our philosophical commitment to the existence of possible worlds, despite strong objections by Quine, is justified by the role possible worlds semantics plays in helping us to understand and explain a host of ideas in logic, metaphysics and theories of meaning – including ordinary language locutions of 'necessity' and 'possibility'. By contrast, the notions of perspectives, accessibility and in particular commensurability that Hales introduces as posits in his system are at the heart of the debate on relativism; they are part of the problem, so to speak, and cannot simply be used as a solution to it.

Assumption (b) is unconvincing for an independent reason. Hales's claim that for any proposition P, 'If P is true, then P is relatively true', hardly seems a plausible starting point for settling the disagreement with the absolutists. The absolutist, to remind ourselves, denies the truth of relativism. In effect, he claims that 'if P is true then P is true non-relatively'; and thus the conditional proposed by the relativist will be false in all cases where its antecedent is true. Hales's construction allows that a relative truth can be absolute, which should satisfy neither the relativist nor the absolutist. In discussing the self-refutation argument, I suggested that relativism cannot be refuted through the assumption of a non-relativist view of truth. The converse applies in this case. Hales's reconstruction of the relativist's argument begs the question against the absolutists. The relativist needs stronger justifications for his radical modification of logic than the ones provided here by Hales.

Despite heroic efforts, strong alethic relativism remains problematic. In particular, the consistent relativist has to embrace higher-order relativism. If we define relativism as either the claim that *everything is relative* or all true propositions are only relatively true, i.e., true in some perspective, or according to a culture or context and untrue in others, then we should include the truth of the relativist position within the scope of this claim. And if relativism is true only relativistically (i.e., true according to the worldview of its believers only), then it cannot be put forward as a genuine philosophical proposal, or one that has the potential to convince everyone. Strong relativism is at best only convincing to its adherents. Relativism, however, comes in a variety of strengths. In the next section I shall examine a more restricted form of alethic relativism.

4.6 RESTRICTED ALETHIC RELATIVISM

An alternative way of dealing with the problem of self-refutation is to restrict the scope of relativism. The restrictions can be applied in one of two ways. Firstly, it could be argued that even if strong alethic relativism is inconsistent, relativism in a number of specialised domains of discourse – for instance, ethics and aesthetics, etc. – is sustainable. We shall look at one version of this claim in chapter 9. Alternatively, we can argue that alethic relativism is true for most truth-claims, but there are some exceptions. In particular, relativism does not apply to itself. That is, there is one truth that is non-relative, or absolute, Let R′ be the claim that 'truth is relative'. Restricted (or moderate) alethic relativism is the claim that 'All statements other than (R′), and other than deductive consequences of (R′), are relative' (Nozick 2001: 15). In other words relativism is a metatheoretical claim applying only to lower-level statements. With Robert Nozick we can ask, 'Would the absolutist really be happy if there were only one absolute truth (along with its deductive consequences, and (R′) was that one? Is the absolutist satisfied simply if relativism is not *universally* true?' (ibid.).

Nozick captures the sentiments often expressed by many relativistically inclined students who think that the self-refutation argument, even if formally correct, does not touch the heart of what is at stake in relativism; that it focuses on an almost irrelevant technicality rather than on the crucial insight that when it comes to those truth-claims that play an important role in our encounters with each other and with the world, relativism is the only available option. The thought is that

> all (or almost all) of the important statements that we currently formulate and care about are merely relative truths. Perhaps there are some absolute truths that we haven't yet formulated and don't really care about, perhaps these are abstract structural statements about the framework of truths, but almost all the ones we know of, care about, and act upon are relative. Does the relativist need more than this? Would the absolutist be content if there exists at least one absolute truth, something firm that he can hang onto even if not do much with? . . . Won't this make the absolutist's victory hollow? Isn't the more important issue, or an equally important issue, the question of what proportion of the truth we believe, put forth, and act upon are merely relative?
>
> (Ibid.: 15–16)

Nozick expresses eloquently what many relativists believe. After all, when we defend absolutism about truth we are not necessarily claiming that all truths are absolute. The same holds for relativism about truth: we can coherently believe that truth is relative without committing ourselves to the impossible view that 'all truth is relative'.

Nozick's is one of the most interesting defences of alethic relativism available. He proposes a pragmatist approach to truth, where truth is that which 'explains a person's or group's success in action; it is what is serviceable for the person or group' (ibid.: 58). Relativism follows because different people may have very different goals. Furthermore, 'truth might vary with and be relative to the *decision rule* the person uses to choose among actions' (ibid.: 59). However, according to him, there are sufficient commonalities between human beings, their situations and their societies to prevent this abstract possibility of alethic relativism from being realised in our world. Truth, according to Nozick, is not relative to contemporary human cultures or societies, but it 'may be relative between human beings and other existing or possible beings in the universe' (ibid.: 62). But then who would confidently deny or care to deny this type of relativism?

Absolutists and realists would deny the starting point of Nozick's position; they would not accept that truth should be equated with what is serviceable for the person or group. Although in many circumstances truth helps us to achieve our aims and goals, we can easily imagine scenarios where a false belief is more efficacious in helping us with our goals than a true one (widespread belief in God and other supernatural powers may be one such example). For any truth-claim T, it is almost always possible to imagine circumstances where T is true but not serviceable or false and serviceable. There is more to truth than serviceability, anti-relativists would argue (This criticism applies, as we shall see below, to other pragmatist approaches to truth, including the one proposed by Richard Rorty, as well as my pragmatist construction of Protagoras' view of truth in chapter 1.)

Even if we reject Nozick's conception of truth, his original argument against the efficacy of the self-refutation argument still stands. Defenders of alethic relativism can be content with the weaker claim that relativism is an unavoidable constraint on our truth-claims and not a universally applicable definition of truth. To search for a universal criterion of truth and falsity is to fall prey to the very same cognitive temptation that the relativist wishes to avoid. The anti-relativist, the argument goes, attempts to show relativism to be self-refuting by reconstructing it as an overtly or covertly universalist position and that is to beg the question against relativism.

4.7 PROBLEMATISING TRUTH

Richard Rorty is one of the most influential philosophical voices today to reject the absolutist and realist conceptions of truth. Rorty denies that he is a relativist, but by casting doubt on traditional views of the role and import of truth and by problematising the role of truth in philosophy, he comes very close to embracing alethic relativism.

Rorty's position on truth and objectivity is one manifestation of a philosophical revisionism which has become the intellectual flavour of the day. A not-so-united group of English-speaking philosophers, helped by the distant rumblings of their deconstructionist allies, have set out to free us, willing or not, from what they see as unhealthy, even corrupting, influences of traditional philosophical images and pre-occupations. At the heart of this revisionist attack are the scope and proper subject of philosophy itself, and the battle lines are drawn primarily around issues of truth, objectivity and reason. The revisionary aspirations stem primarily from the perceived failure of two main planks of traditional philosophical concerns – metaphysics and epistemology. Rorty is in the vanguard of this movement and, for the past twenty years, has been trying to undermine our attachment to long-prevailing philosophical concerns with those very questions of truth, knowledge, realism, etc.

One of the main aims of philosophical revisionism is to change the traditional conceptions of the relationship between language and the world. Rorty distinguishes between two philosophical accounts of how we make sense of our lives and our place in the world: first, the objectivist account of the relationship between language and the world which is favoured by 'the traditionalist philosophers'. The main features of the objectivist philosophical approach are:

> Objectivity is defined in relation to non-human reality.
> Reality is described without a reference to particular human beings.
> The search for Truth (with a capital T) is valorised over more practical goals. Truth is seen as something to be pursued for its own sake.
> The possibility of universal, trans-cultural, rather than merely local accounts of rationality is defended.
> An unequivocal distinction is made between knowledge and opinion on the one hand and reality and appearance on the other. It defers to the authority of science and accepts its universalist

and culture-transcendent claims to justification and theoretical adequacy (see Rorty 1991a and 1998).

Many philosophers working within this tradition adhere to some version of the correspondence theory of truth and representationalist theories of mind and language, where mental states model or represent states of affairs in the natural world. Realism and varieties of Platonism are the main philosophical schools falling into this tradition, and the early Wittgenstein, the early Putnam, Jerry Fodor and Michael Devitt are among its practitioners. The objectivists are traditionalists in that they do not seek to abandon long-established philosophical preoccupations with epistemological and metaphysical issues.

The sociological or community-oriented account of truth, championed by Rorty, is favoured by philosophical revisionists such as Nietzsche, Dewey, James, Heidegger, the later Wittgenstein, Habermas and Gadamer. The ultimate aim of these 'ironist' philosophers is to bring about a radical change in the subject matter of philosophy. In their more grandiose moments, they set their aims higher and talk about changing the whole discourse of our culture. Those favouring this approach argue that philosophy takes a wrong turn when it strives to ground beliefs in metaphysical or epistemological foundations. The characteristics of the revisionist sociological approach to philosophy, according to Rorty (1991a and 1998), are:

> The achievement of intersubjective agreement (or solidarity), rather than objective Truth, is seen as the goal of enquiry.
> The distinction between knowledge and opinion is denied. 'Knowledge' is an honorific title bestowed upon opinion or belief on topics where agreement is readily available; where agreement is hard to come by we are said to have only beliefs or opinions.
> Truth, rationality, and objectivity are to be defined in terms of the practices of a community.
> External questions about the relationship between the practices of a community, including linguistic communities, and a reality independent of it are not deemed to be intelligible.
> The terms 'knowledge' and 'truth' have a normative role in our language. They are compliments paid to beliefs that we think to be well-justified, for the moment, so that no further justification is needed.

I believe that Rorty's sociological approach to truth, despite his denials, has strong affinities with alethic relativism. Rorty, like Putnam, rejects what Putnam has called 'Metaphysical Realism' – the view that 'there is a fixed set of "language-independent" objects . . . and a fixed "relation" between terms and their extensions' (Putnam 1999: 27)[16] – and, consequently, the correspondence theory of truth, where truth is explicated in terms of language (or mental content) modelling, picturing or mirroring states of affairs in the world. According to Rorty, the correspondence theory of truth needs the notion of one vocabulary fitting the world better than another, and a criterion for adequacy of representation. However, such criteria are not available to us. He does not deny the existence of a mind-independent world, but distinguishes between causal and representational accounts of world-independence. Most things are causally independent of us but they are not representationally independent. 'For X to be representationally independent of us is for X to have an intrinsic feature (a feature which it has under any and every description) such that it is better described by some of our terms rather than others' (Rorty 1998: 86), and this, Rorty maintains, is a philosophical illusion. So we discard the idea that there is such a thing as '"how things are *anyway*", apart from whether or how they are described'. We can say that the sentence 'there are no chairs in this room' is true or false by virtue of the way things are or the nature of reality, but only in the sense of 'in virtue of the way our current descriptions of things are used and the causal interactions we have with those things' (ibid.: 86), rather than in virtue of the way things are, quite apart from how we describe them.

Rorty contends that we are not in a position to draw a line between the object and our picture of the object as a representationalist view of truth would expect us to do, because 'all we can draw a line between is the object and some other objects (the marks, noises, brain-states, or whatever, which are helping us cope with the initial object)'. He, thus, repudiates the view that language can represent the world, and questions standard conceptions of objectivity and substantive accounts of truth (or what he calls Truth). Simultaneously, he wishes to distance himself from the suggestion that any view is as good as the next one and that we are not in a position to justify the superiority of some evaluative and epistemic judgements over others. He thus places himself in a quandary as to how to distinguish between better and worse descriptions. Rorty takes, what he sees as, a pragmatic approach to truth. In *Philosophy and the Mirror of Nature*, he says '"objective truth" is no more and no less than the best idea we currently have about how to explain what is going on' (Rorty 1979: 385).[17] In 'Pragmatism, Relativism and Irrationalism' he cites, approvingly, James's definition, 'true is what is good in the way of belief' (Rorty 1982: 162), and in the Introduction to the *Consequences of Pragmatism* he calls truth 'what you can defend against all comers' and 'what is good to believe' (ibid.: xxxvii), where what is good to believe is decided in terms of how particular beliefs enable us to *cope* with the world and each other.[18] According to him, we tend to prefer the descriptions that enable us to deal in more productive, innovative or efficient ways with the problems the world throws at us, and it is those descriptions that receive the honorific title 'true'. For pragmatists, he argues,

> The desire for objectivity is not the desire to escape the limitations of one's community, but simply the desire for as much intersubjective agreement as possible, the desire to extend the reference of 'us' as far as we can. Insofar as pragmatists make a distinction between knowledge and opinion, it is simply the distinction between topics on which such agreement is relatively easy to get and topics on which agreement is relatively hard to get.
>
> (Rorty 1985: 5)

Rorty is aware that by linking objectivity and truth to communal agreement he is courting the charges of relativism. He claims, rather disingenuously, that '"relativism" is the traditional epithet applied to pragmatism by realists' (ibid.). He goes on to distinguish between three senses of 'relativism'. Relativism$_1$ is the view that 'every belief is as good as every other' (ibid.). Relativism$_2$ is the view that 'true' is an equivocal term, having as many meanings as there are procedures of justification (ibid.: 6). Relativism$_3$ is the view that 'there is nothing to be said about either truth or rationality apart from descriptions of the familiar procedures of justification which a given society – ours – uses in one or another area of enquiry' (ibid.). Rorty rejects the 'self-refuting' relativism$_1$ because he does not sympathise with the relativist's call for complete forbearance of all views, or the abandonment of any substantive notion of correctness or better and worse accounts of how things stand. He insists that his views do not lead to relativism$_1$, because there is a distinction between better and worse beliefs, beliefs that are justified and those that are not. He also does not hold the 'eccentric' relativism$_2$ because he believes that in all languages and cultures 'true' has the same meaning and role; it is a general term of commendation for the belief we consider well justified. He accepts relativism$_3$, the ethnocentric view, but argues that it should not be equated with relativism since it is not a positive theory of truth saying that 'something is relative to something else' (ibid.).

147

Ethnocentrism, is the view that 'we must, in practice, privilege our own group, even though there can be no non-circular justification for doing so' (Rorty 1991a: 29), because we can justify our beliefs only to those whose beliefs somewhat overlap with ours (ibid.: 31 n.).[19] He defends the inevitability of ethnocentrism by arguing that terms such as 'warranted' and 'rationally acceptable' always invite the question 'to whom?'. Just as the terms 'better' and 'worse' invite the question 'by what standard?'. The answer, he claims, is always 'us, at our best', where the relevant group, the us, consists of 'the educated, sophisticated, tolerant, wet liberals, the people who are always willing to engage in debate and keep an open mind' (ibid.: 52). According to him, 'there is *no* truth in relativism, but this much truth in ethnocentrism: we cannot justify our beliefs (in physics, ethics, or any other area) to everybody, but only to those whose beliefs overlap ours to some appropriate extent' (Rorty 1991a: 19 n. 13).

Despite Rorty's claims, I believe, that ethnocentrism is a form of relativism, because of the formative links it creates between objectivity and truth and the cognitive and social practices of a community of enquirers. Once we accept that there are many such communities, and that their practices tend to vary substantially and even be at conflict with each other, then the sociological account of truth ends up giving us diverse and incompatible conceptions of truth, rationality and objectivity. The same can be said of the claim that truth is a matter of intersubjective agreement. Historically, there have been many occasions when different communities of enquirers have agreed on different – and incompatible – beliefs. To explicate truth in terms of intersubjective agreement is to concede to one of the key posits of relativism: that truth is dependent on local and changing norms and conceptions. Rorty also argues that we can make sense of the notion of objectivity only in terms of intersubjective agreement – 'there is nothing to objectivity except intersubjectivity' (Rorty 1999: 72). But to make truth a matter of intersubjective agreement is to deny the distinction between truth and falsity, as it is usually understood. History is replete with examples of false beliefs which were accorded intersubjective agreement – were seen by a community of enquirers as 'true' and 'justified'.

Rorty acknowledges the force of this point by arguing that the only use of the 'true' which could not be eliminated from our linguistic practice with relative ease is the cautionary use. That is the use we make of the word 'true' when we contrast justification and truth, and say that a belief may be justified but not true. According to him, this cautionary use is used to contrast less informed with better informed audiences, past audiences with future audiences (Rorty 2000: 4). It is the use of 'true' in statements such as 'although your statement satisfies all our contemporary norms and standards, and I can think of nothing to say against your claim but still, what you say might not be true'. Rorty thinks that this cautionary use is a gesture toward future generations, or the 'better us' as Rorty calls them (Rorty 1998: 60–1). So even this cautionary use is interpreted in sociological terms and relies on an ethnocentric approach.

Rorty's ethnocentrism is a relativistic doctrine for several reasons, First, all relativists are ultimately condemned to be ethnocentric. The relativist, through her claim that truth and knowledge, standards of justification and criteria of right and wrong are relative to their socio-cultural background, embraces a type of determinism that makes ethnocentrism inevitable. If truth is decided by the local norms of our culture, then we are condemned to believe what our culture tells us to be true. The relativist of course accepts that members of other cultures are similarly entrapped by their own cognitive and ethical norms, but that acknowledgement does not free the relativist from the bind of ethnocentrism.

Second, by tying the idea of truth to that of justification, and by making justification audience- and context-dependent, Rorty embraces a relativistic position. Rorty readily admits, 'justification is relative to an audience' (Rorty 1998: 22) and that he cannot give 'any content to the idea of nonlocal correctness of assertion' (ibid.: 60).

Third, and most importantly, Rorty wishes to distance himself from relativism because he rejects the conclusion that every point of view is as good as every other. But it's not really clear that his ethnocentrism would achieve this goal. Rorty claims that truth is the best idea *we* currently have about how to explain what is going on. The problem is to decide who the relevant and significant 'we' is. Given a conflict between different scientific explanations or ethical viewpoints, how are we going to decide which 'we' has the best idea? Unless we assume either that there is always a consensus on what the best idea is for an explanation at any given time or in any given society, or that there is a method of grading various explanations, we are left with divergent and conflicting community-dependent 'truths' and hence relativism. The point is, how do we arbitrate between various types of explanations or vocabularies? Rorty argues that he is not advocating a preference for subjective criteria for choosing between vocabularies or explanatory systems; rather, that there are no criteria for changing from one language-game or world description to another. However, if we were to accept this, it is hard to know what to make of a phrase such as 'the best idea for explanation' or 'what is good to believe'. Rorty suggests, 'in the process of playing vocabularies and cultures off against each other, we produce new and better ways of talking and acting – not better by reference to a previously known standard, but just better in the sense that they come to *seem* clearly better than their predecessors' (Rorty 1982: xxxvii). I am not sure what to make of this passage. Does he mean, as the passage tends to suggest, that all new ideas seem to be better than old ones? Furthermore, he seems to identify being better with seeming better, which makes it impossible to distinguish between mistaken and correct judgements of evaluation even in our own case, since it turns all our judgements into correct ones. Clearly, Rorty's ethnocentric 'we' are the 'wet liberal intellectuals', like himself, but even this is not a homogeneous grouping. We need only to look at the differences of philosophical and political opinion between Putnam, Rorty, Chomsky, Nozick, Dummett and Quine to see that there could hardly be a 'we' in the sense that would satisfy Rorty's ethnocentrism.

An unacceptable consequence of Rorty's ethnocentrism, a further feature shared with relativism, is that where 'a neofascist tendency wins out, people cope better in the sense that it comes to seem to them that they are coping better by dealing savagely with those terrible Jews, foreigners, and communists, while if the forces of good win out it will also be the case that people cope better in the sense that it comes to seem to them that they are' (Putnam 1990: 23–4). Putnam is right in arguing that the concept of 'coping better' as used by Rorty is not 'the concept of there being better and worse norms and standards at all' (ibid.: 24). The point is, how do we choose between societies that exemplify toleration, free inquiry and the quest for undistorted communication, and societies that do not have these habits? Rorty claims that anyone who has experienced both would prefer the former to the latter. This seems a rather optimistic assessment. Rorty himself asks the same question in a slightly different context, 'what if the "we" is the Orwellian state?' (Rorty 1982: 173). His reply is to use a pragmatist's version of Habermas's concept of 'undistorted conversation', where '"undistorted" means employing our criterion of relevance, where we are the people who have read and pondered Plato, Newton, Kant, Marx, Darwin, Freud, Dewey, etc' (ibid.). However, this is an extremely dangerous reply, since in the Orwellian state it is O'Brien, the high official of the Ministry of Truth, who is well versed in philosophical discourse and not the proles.

Thus, Rorty's view of truth has relativist consequences, which is problematic for him since he wishes to disassociate himself from such a position. By itself, this is not a deep objection. All that has been done is to attribute a philosophical position to Rorty that he is not very happy to accept. However, the real problem surfaces when we realise that Rorty is vacillating between taking a relativistic position towards truth and also simultaneously claiming that we can decide what sort of belief-systems or explanatory schemes are better (non-relativistically). This is where his position seriously 'starts to wobble'.

4.8 CONCLUSION

In this chapter, we examined progressively weaker versions of alethic relativism. Relativism about truth, be it in its most naïve form of subjectivism, or in the more sophisticated guises proposed by Nozick and Rorty, does not work. This is not just because alethic relativism is self-refuting – for at best only the stronger versions of it are – but because there are some essential features of the very concept of truth that relativism fails to capture. First, there are differences between truth and justification, truth and coping, truth and serviceability to the goals of a community, etc., for it is not only conceivable but also probable that a belief may be justified or pragmatically useful but not true (and vice versa). More importantly, as I shall argue throughout this book, many of our beliefs – the most common and basic ones – are world-invoking; they involve a reference to the world. This feature of our beliefs, or at least what Wittgenstein would call our 'bedrock beliefs', mitigates against alethic and other forms of relativism in two ways. First, it places a limit on the extent and scope of diversity in beliefs. If there is only one world, then however diverse our conceptions of that world may be, they are circumscribed by it – the world sets the limits of our beliefs about the world. Second, the world itself provides us with a way of arbitrating between various beliefs, of distinguishing between good and bad, true and false, correct and incorrect conceptions of it. We will examine this idea more closely in later chapters.

5

Relativism and rationality

5.1 INTRODUCTION

Some of the most interesting debates on the viability of cognitive relativism revolve around the issue of rationality. The starting point for relativism about rationality is the claim that there is a plurality of cognitive systems, modes of reasoning and procedures of justification, and that there is no unique, independent method to adjudicate between them. This plurality, it is further claimed, leads to the conclusion that all judgements as to the adequacy or success of a mode of reasoning can be made only contextually and with due regard to the cultural norms and practices surrounding it. On the face of it, then, the position of a relativist about rationality seems simple and straightforward. She argues that various societies or cultures have different standards and views of rationality and that we are not in a position to evaluate or choose between these divergent standards. At best, we can use only contextually or internally given criteria in our assessments of diverse systems of belief – judgements of rationality have only a local authority. Universalists, on the other hand, argue that certain core features of reasoning are common to all systems of belief, and that these may even be logically necessary for the very possibility of intelligent and intelligible thought.

Despite this initial impression of simplicity, it is quite difficult to pin down the exact content of the claim made by the relativists about rationality, for the very concept of rationality is notoriously elastic. As Steven Stich has pointed out, 'in the literature of this area detailed accounts of rationality are conspicuously lacking. What we get instead are assertions that one or another pattern of cognitive processing is clearly rational (or clearly irrational), buttressed by appeals to our intuitions' (Stich 1990: 29).

Although a strict definition is neither possible nor even desirable in discussing such a central and general issue, it is possible to isolate some common features of the 'rational'. We variously use the labels 'rational' and 'irrational' both to describe and evaluate (blame and praise) persons, their choices, their behaviour, patterns of action, beliefs, etc. There are common threads binding the diverse uses of 'rational'. For instance, a rational person would engage in rational behaviour, and rational behaviour presupposes a certain degree of rationality of beliefs and preferences. Very broadly, we can distinguish between rationality of actions and rationality of beliefs. We judge the rationality of an action in the light of an agent's goals or ends, and her choices of actions (which will involve further reasons, beliefs and desires) – i.e., the means adopted – for the attainment of these goals. An agent, under normal circumstances, is considered irrational if she does not choose the course of action that would be conducive to the attainment of her avowed goals. Goals may be deemed irrational if they are clearly unattainable, or if they are incompatible with other goals or life-plans of the agent. Some of the more interesting and central questions of cognitive relativism concern the issue of rationality of beliefs and, at a further remove, the rationality and irrationality of the cognitive norms of particular cultures or belief-systems, where a belief-system is defined as the web of interconnected beliefs held by the members of a cultural group or society. Since rationality in action, or practical rationality, presupposes a degree of rationality in belief, or cognitive rationality, a discussion of the latter will also have implications for the former.

Rational beliefs are backed by good reason; they are appropriately justified. The relativist argues that 'good reason' and 'justification' can only be defined according to the norms internal to a society or culture. She points out that rationality is a normative rather than purely descriptive notion, that 'rational' and 'irrational' are terms of praise and blame, and that cognitive norms, like all other norms, receive their meaning and sanction in the context of the social and cultural institutions that give rise to them. So what counts as a good reason depends on the social and cultural context that gives sense to such an evaluation. We judge the rationality of a belief on the basis of the reasons offered for holding that belief. So questions about cognitive rationality often hinge on the issue of the conditions under which a reason or set of reasons would be deemed adequate for supporting or justifying a belief, or set of beliefs.

In its most general sense a belief (B) is rational if:

(1) B is backed by reason(s) (R), and
(2) R is deemed adequate for justifying, supporting or explaining B.

All sides of the debate on rationality tend to agree that good reason has the following features:

(1a) reason (R) provides evidence for the belief (B);
(1b) (as a correlate of 1a) R is deemed to be true and B is seen to be more likely to be true in the light of R, and
(1c) there is a reliable method for assessing the adequacy of R for holding B. That is, there is a reliable method for evaluating the inferences and general modes of reasoning involved in arriving at B; where a 'reliable method' would not, as a rule, lead the believer from true beliefs to false ones and would facilitate an increase in the stock of true beliefs.

The scope and strength of the relativist's claims vary. We can distinguish between strong and moderate forms of relativism about rationality. Strong relativism about rationality denies that there are universally valid means or standards for distinguishing between better and worse styles of reasoning. It maintains that no universal method of belief-assessment is available to us, and that even truth, logic and validity should be defined locally, for what counts as a reliable evidence or method of assessment is always context-sensitive. Moderate relativism about rationality distinguishes between universal and local criteria of belief-assessment. Steven Lukes, for instance, has introduced a useful distinction between the universal and the context-dependent criteria of rationality (Lukes 1979: 208).[1] According to him, consistency and truth (by which I think he means having truth as the goal of enquiry) are universal criteria of rationality, and the context-sensitive criteria include:

(1) a local criterion of relevance
(2) contextual definitions of justification for holding a belief
(3) a context-sensitive notion of evidence.

The moderate relativists argue that at least some features of what counts as adequacy of reason-giving are context-relative. Our assumptions about what constitutes satisfactory evidence for a belief depend on the scope and extent of information available to us, which is constrained by our cultural and historical locations. Furthermore, we can assess the adequacy of justificatory claims for a belief often only in the light of the alternatives available in any given context of inquiry. These contexts of inquiry, in turn, are shaped by their socio-historical conditions, including the particular historical stage of cultural (including scientific) development within which the inquiry is being conducted. They also add, as Hartry Field does, that to say that a belief is justified is to evaluate it, and values (moral and epistemic), unlike truth, are relative to systems of belief and evidence (Field 1982).

Moderate relativists about rationality distinguish between external and internal criteria of rationality. They maintain that it is possible to make external judgements about the rationality of a set of beliefs based on the universal criteria of rationality, but argue that such judgements do not capture the most significant and interesting features of the debate about rationality. Following Jon Elster (1983) we can distinguish between 'thin' and 'broad' theories of rationality. A thin theory of rationality focuses on the external (formal and logical) requirements of rationality, the requirement of logical consistency being foremost among them. A 'broad' or thick definition of rationality examines the relationship between the content of beliefs and the specific reasons given for justifying and explaining them, and in that sense has to rely on *internal* considerations. We begin with thin descriptions of rationality.

5.2 RELATIVISM ABOUT LOGIC

In Western scientific cultures, the accepted reliable methods of reasoning, for instance, inference to the best explanation, the hypothetico-deductive method, etc., involve the use of inductive and deductive logic. In fact, adherence to a minimal set of laws of classical logic is often seen as a precondition of rationality.[2] Consequently, relativism about logic is one of the strongest forms of relativism about rationality. If it can be shown that the rules of logic have a local rather than universal authority then any absolutist or universalist claim on behalf of rationality will be seriously undermined. In other words, relativism about logic is a sufficient condition for relativising rationality.

Relativistic views about logic have surfaced in the works of social anthropologists, cognitive scientists and philosophers. Reports by anthropologists about the thinking habits of remote peoples have led to the suggestion that rules of logic may have only a local rather than universal authority. Philosophical grounds for arguing for relativism about logic have been detected in the work of the later Wittgenstein. More recently, Barry Barnes and David Bloor, using a sociological perspective, and Steven Stich, influenced by findings in cognitive psychology, have also argued for relativism about logic. Stich, as we shall see below, uses experimental evidence gathered by psychologists to claim that human beings employ a multiplicity of modes of reasoning and argumentation, and that we are not in a position to make non-relativistic assessments as to their merits. Barnes and Bloor (1982) rely on the purported shortcomings of formal logic in order to question the universal authority of logic, and thereby justify relativism.

The relativist about logic denies the universality of the rules of inference and claims that standards of correct argument and criteria of validity, as well as the rules by which 'correct' inferences are made, can only be defined locally or internally within a given society, culture or linguistic community. Hence, different societies or peoples might have different, incompatible but equally correct systems of logic and rules of inference. The key question separating relativism and absolutism about logic, then, concerns the very status of logic. Are laws of logic necessary, a priori and universal? Do different groups of people, communities, language groups employ the same logical rules and criterion of validity in their process of reasoning and in their assessment of these processes? Can there be different, incompatible but correct 'logics' for different linguistic communities and modes of reasoning?

Logic, from the very beginnings of Western philosophy, has been seen as the most fundamental and universal of all areas of knowledge. The laws of logic were regarded as the laws of intelligible discourse, and their authority was deemed absolute. Aristotle was the first of many philosophers to maintain that it is misguided to demand a justification for the rules of logic. No independent demonstration of the laws of logic can be given since all demonstrations and thought presuppose logic. And as we saw in chapter 1, Aristotle's rejection of relativism was bound up with his defence of the principle of non-contradiction.

The absolutist, universalistic conception of logic was expressed even more strongly by Kant, according to whom logic is:

> the science of the necessary laws of thought, without which no employment of the understanding and the reason takes place . . . [Logic] does not concern itself with the common and merely empirical use of the understanding and the reason, but solely with the universal and necessary laws of thought, therefore it rests on *a priori* principles, from which all its rules can be derived and proved, as rules to which all rational knowledge must conform.
>
> (Kant [1885] 1972: 37)

Ironically, the Kantian emphasis on rules of logic as the determinants of the form of thought led to psychologism, which Frege and Husserl (chapter 2) saw as a form of relativism. Nineteenth-century German psychologism turned the rules of logic into the rules of actual human thinking, and hence opened the way for subjectivist and relativist views of logic. B. Erdmann, for instance, argued that 'logical laws only hold within the limits of our thinking, without our being able to guarantee that this thinking might not alter in character' (Erdmann 1907 in Baker and Hacker 1989: 41).

He continues:

> we cannot help admitting that all propositions whose contra-
> dictories we cannot envisage in thought are only necessary if
> we presuppose the character of our thought, as definitely
> given in our experience: they are not absolutely necessary, or
> necessary in all possible conditions. On this view our logical
> principles retain their necessity for our thinking, but this
> *necessity is not seen as absolute, but as hypothetical.*
>
> (Ibid.)

The laws of logic seem universal because certain psycho-physiological features of human thinking are invariant. Beings with different psychological make-up may use different rules of logic.

On the absolutist side, Frege, the founding father of modern logic and analytic philosophy, argued that the laws of logic are the 'bound-ary stones set in an eternal foundation which our thought can overflow but never displace' (Frege [1893] 1964: xvi). For Frege, the rules of logic are prescriptive rather than descriptive of human thought.[3] They are the laws of truth and not the psychological, empir-ical laws of thought. Their authority is universal and absolute and not contingent upon considerations such as the psycho-physiological make-up of the beings who use them. Such a conception of logic obviously leaves no room for relativism about logic. Frege goes so far as to argue that even if we came across beings whose ways of thinking or reasoning contradicted ours, all we should conclude is that the empirical laws of their thought, the laws actually governing their practice of thinking, deviate from the laws that describe our thinking, but this would not show that they have equally correct rules of logic and standards of validity; even if we found creatures using deviant laws of logic we should react by saying 'we have here a hitherto unknown type of madness' (ibid.).

Frege's anti-relativist arguments seem to miss the main thrust of the relativist's position. The relativist argues that there is no independent standard or criterion for adjudicating between competing systems of logic; all so-called 'objective' accounts, be it of logic or truth, presuppose the cognitive norms prevalent within a particular belief-system. For instance, we cannot give any justification for the validity of the deductive method of argumentation without making use of the very same method.[4] Frege fails to give an independent justification for preferring his system of logic to the competing accounts and hence begs the question against the relativist (Baker and Hacker 1989: 44). The relativist agrees with Aristotle that to demand justification for the rules of logic is misguided, that no independent demonstration of the laws of logic can be given since all demonstrations and thought presuppose logic. However, she argues that since rules of logic may vary from language to language or culture to culture, we cannot have a decision procedure for preferring one logical system over all others. Frege's response is that only by assuming the a priori, objective truth of the laws of logic can we understand how science, mathematics and even language are possible. To the relativist, however, Frege's protestations are reminiscent of his infamous rejection of the possibility of 'alternative' non-Euclidean geometry.

Frege's arguments point to an ambiguity between the following two formulations in discussions of relativism about logic:

(1) The members of an 'alternative community' use rules of logic which are valid for them and not valid for us, i.e., the scope of the very concept of validity is local rather than universal.
(2) The members of an 'alternative community' differ from us in what they believe to be correct rules of logic.

It may be argued that, as it stands, only (1) can give us an interesting relativistic view of logic. The position advocated by (2) might seem parallel to pointing out that certain tribes have beliefs about the physical laws which are different from ours. For instance, they believe that the Earth is flat and stationary. The fact that they have this false belief would not show that the physical laws are true for us and false for them; all it would show is that they have made an error in the description of how the world is. The parallels between empirical and logical errors, however, are not exact. Universalists about logic, Frege's point about logical madness notwithstanding, argue that no one can be systematically mistaken about the laws of logic, in the way that one may be on scientific matters. Logic provides the preconditions of intelligible thought, and hence any judgement about the standing of logical laws would itself depend on the correct application of some logical rules as well as on having at least implicitly accurate views of validity, acceptable rules of inference, etc. Logic sets the conditions for the possibility of thought and hence cuts across the distinction between erroneous and true beliefs.

5.3 RATIONALITY, LOGIC AND CULTURAL VARIABILITY

A variety of arguments has been proposed in support of relativism about rationality in general and relativism about logic in particular. In broad outline, we can distinguish between two relativistic views about logic (and hence rationality thinly construed).

(a) The uniqueness view

According to the 'uniqueness view' of logic, rules of logic are specific to the Western scientific culture and hence their authority is purely local. This version of relativism about logic can be traced back to Lucien Levy-Bruhl's notorious characterisation of 'primitive' thought as 'prelogical'. According to him, primitive thought

> is not constrained, above all else, as ours is, to avoid contra-
> dictions. The same logical exigencies are not in its case always
> present. What to our eyes is impossible or absurd, it some-
> times will admit without seeing any difficulty.
>
> (Levy-Bruhl 1975: 43)

He suggests that to 'the primitive mind "objects, beings, phenomena" could be in a manner incomprehensible to us both themselves and something other than themselves' (ibid.: 44). Thus, he is, in effect, claiming that the primitive mind does not obey the logical rule of identity. Similar views have been voiced by postmodernist thinkers who see logic as a manifestations of Western 'logocentric' and 'phallocentric' metaphysics. They contend that the universalist pretensions of Western logic and rationality are merely expressions of the colonial and expansionist political ideology which attempts to impose homogeneity on the conquered.[5]

Some feminist epistemologists also subscribe to the view that formal logic is the province of the dominant white male and that, despite its pretensions of universality, it is an instrument of intellectual domination and exclusion (see, e.g., Nye 1990). The history of logic, according to this perspective, is 'the story of power to legitimize some ways of speaking at the expense of others . . . it embodies a suspect desire for certainty and power at the expense of an understanding of the mere context in which utterances are produced' (Hass 1999: 191). Logic is the most abstract and general of subjects and 'once separated from lived experience, through its emphasis on form over content, [it] acquires a dangerous kind of power in that actual experience . . . becomes understood as a lesser form of knowledge than the abstract reasoning of the logician' (ibid.: 192).[6] Formal logic, it is argued, undermines the value of the experiences of the oppressed and the marginalised. (We shall return to the claims of feminist epistemology and its relativistic implications in 6.7.)

(b) The culture-dependence view

According to this view, even though rules of logic and norms of rationality exist in all communities, their scope and content vary greatly from one community to another, and their authority is simply local. Laws of logic, criteria of validity, rules of inference are culture-dependent and can only be understood or evaluated by the local standards and 'the way of life' of the peoples and language groups concerned. This view receives its impetus from reports by social anthropologists who suggest that various groups of people hold systems of belief which, by our standards, are false, unsupported and even logically inconsistent. The Nuer, for instance, believe that very young children do not have souls, yet they also believe that the souls of all twins go 'above' at death (Evans-Pritchard 1956: 46). It follows from this that some children, i.e., the young twins, both 'do and do not have souls'.

The most celebrated example of this kind is the Azande belief in and practice of witchcraft. The Azande, according to Evans-Pritchard, believe the following:

(1) Illness and misfortune are caused by acts of witchcraft.
(2) It is possible to verify whether a person is a witch or not by examining the contents of his intestine.
(3) Witchcraft is inherited through the male line.
(4) The Azande clan is a group of people related to each other through the male line.

From the conjunction of beliefs (2) to (4) it follows that if a person is shown to be a witch through the examination of the contents of his intestine, then all the members of his clan must also be witches.

Evans-Pritchard tells us:

[The] Azande see the sense of this argument but they do not accept the conclusion . . . [the] Azande do not perceive the contradiction as we perceive it because they have no theoretical interest in the subject, and those situations in which they express their beliefs in them do not force the problem upon them.

(Evans-Pritchard [1937] 1976: 3, 4)

According to Evans-Pritchard, the Azande simply refuse to apply logical rules and standards of rationality when it comes to their very fundamental beliefs about witchcraft. In such cases, Evans-Pritchard claims, the Zande cannot think that his thoughts are wrong. This is because the Azande belief-system is a web where

all their beliefs hang together, and were a Zande to give up faith in witchdoctorhood he would have to surrender equally his belief in witchcraft and oracles . . . In this web of belief every strand depends upon every other strand, and a Zande cannot get out of its meshes because this is the only world he knows. The web is not an external structure in which he is enclosed. It is the texture of his thought and he cannot think that his thought is wrong.

(Ibid.: 194–5)

A number of philosophers have made use of Azande material to argue for a culture-dependent view of logic. Here are some prominent examples. Peter Winch relies on the Azande case to argue that we should employ only contextually and internally given criteria of reasoning in our assessment of the systems of belief of alien cultures, and hence we are not in a position, as mere observers, to impute irrationality or illogicality to the Azande. Basing his work on the later philosophy of Wittgenstein, Winch has suggested that 'Our idea of what belongs to the realm of reality is given to us in the language we use' and that even 'the criteria of logic are not a direct gift of God, but arise out of, and are intelligible in the context of ways of living and modes of social life' (Winch 1970: 35). We are thus not in a position to impose our laws of reasoning or criteria of validity on the Azande, as the Azande beliefs in witchcraft occur in a context where our notion of validity does not play any role. For Winch, it does not make sense to speak of a universal standard of rationality because rationality means conforming to the cognitive norms inherent within the linguistic and social practices of any given society or form of life. He writes:

161

the context from which the suggestion about the contradiction is made, the context of our scientific culture, is not on the same level as the context in which the beliefs about witchcraft operate. Azande notions of witchcraft do not constitute a theoretical system in terms of which the Azande try to gain a quasi-scientific understanding of the world. This in its turn suggests that it is the European, obsessed with pressing Azande thought where it would not actually go – to a contradiction – who is guilty of misunderstanding, not the Azande. The European is in fact committing a category-mistake.

(Ibid.: 35)

Winch, then, is proposing that the application of the laws of logic, including the law of non-contradiction, is context-relative and hence it is illegitimate to accuse the Azande of contravening a law where such a law, according to the internal dynamics of their system of belief, does not apply. Winch believes that the Azande case make us realise that 'we must, if you like, be open to new possibilities of what could be invoked and accepted under the rubric of "rationality"' (ibid.: 100). Culturally different ways of experiencing the world and prioritising our needs and goals bring with them different conceptions and criteria of rationality. Winch is also echoing the criticism levelled by Wittgenstein against Frazer's discussion of magic and ritual in 'primitive' societies in *The Golden Bough.* According to Wittgenstein 'Frazer's account of the magical and religious views of mankind is unsatisfactory: it makes these views look like errors' (Wittgenstein 1993: 119). Both Frazer and Evans-Pritchard are basing their analyses on the assumption that Western science is right and magical views are not. Winch and Wittgenstein, on the other hand, believe that such a judgement has no place in our attempts to understand other cultures.

Paul Feyerabend has adopted a similar approach and has argued for the culture-dependence of validity and logic. In *Against Method* (1975), for instance, he suggests that an anthropologist trying to understand an alien society must compare the native's background to his own. The comparison will determine whether the native's way of thinking can be reproduced in European terms or whether it has a logic of its own, which is not to be found in any Western language. Feyerabend believes that absolutism and universalism in logic are the offshoots of the most conservative type of empiricism.

David Cooper, on the other hand, suggests that we can make sense of the seemingly contradictory magico-religious beliefs of other cultures by realising that: 'primitive magico-religious thought incorporates an alternative logic to our "standard" one within the terms of which the apparent inconsistencies are not inconsistencies at all' (Cooper 1971: 52). The apparent tension in the Azande belief-system would be resolved if the conclusion 'Every biological relative of a witch is a witch' is regarded as untestable and hence indeterminate. Primitive thought when dealing with supernatural beliefs, he argues, incorporates a three-valued logic where sentences get the values true, false and indeterminate. The logic of ritual discourse in primitive societies, he argues, is non-classical or deviant. Cooper's views are of interest because he is one of the few philosophers working in this area willing to propose that members of other societies may use a specific form of (alternative) logic.

Cooper's main claim is that the propositions of magico-religious beliefs are typically untestable (and hence indeterminate). However, as Cooper himself notes, the Azande have empirical methods for establishing whether someone is a witch and whether witchcraft has been performed. They even test the efficacy of the poison they use. According to Evans-Pritchard, 'they sometimes test new poison or old poison which they fear has been corrupted by asking it silly questions' (Evans-Pritchard [1937] 1976: 159). For example, at full moon they administer the poison to a fowl and tell the oracle to kill the fowl if a particular person is going up to the sky to spear the moon. If the oracle kills the fowl, they conclude that the poison is corrupt. Contrary to Cooper's claim, the Azande belief-system, even if it does not meet the rigorous standards of falsification aspired to in science, is not regarded as untestable.

Barry Barnes and David Bloor have also used the Azande material, together with a relativistic interpretation of Wittgenstein, to argue for relativism about logic. According to their 'Strong Programme', knowledge is a socio-cultural phenomenon; it is those beliefs and assumptions upon which a socio-cultural group agrees. The distinction between valid and invalid modes of argument, they maintain, like any other human belief, is based on and relative to the practices prevalent in a given linguistic community or society and cannot in any sense be seen as universal or context-neutral, for different societies may have incompatible, but internally coherent, systems of logic. Bloor argues:

> The Azande have the same psychology as us but radically different institutions. If we relate logic to the psychology of reasoning we shall be inclined to say that they have the same logic; if we relate logic more closely to the institutional

framework of thought then we shall incline to the view that
the two cultures have different logics.

(Bloor 1976: 129–30)

To return to the argument schema 1–4 attributed to the Azande (see
p. 160 above), Bloor argues that if the Azande were using Western
logic they should draw the conclusion, obvious to Evans-Pritchard and
other Western thinkers, that all Azande clans-members are witches.
However, since they do not reach this conclusion, it follows that they
do not have the same rules of logic and therefore 'there must be more
than one logic: an Azande logic and a Western logic' (ibid.: 124).

In addition, Barnes and Bloor rely on the purported shortcomings
of formal logic, as well as on the discrepancies between formal logical
systems and our 'everyday' standards of reasoning, to advocate relativism about logic. They believe that there is at least a primitive,
biologically based, reasoning propensity, which is in some sense universal. Nevertheless, they deny that the systems of logic, as developed
by logicians, are in any sense comparable to this primitive mode of
reasoning. According to them:

> Logic, as it is systematized in textbooks, monographs or
> research papers, is a learned body of scholarly lore, growing
> and varying over time. It is a mass of conventional routines,
> decisions, expedient restrictions, dicta, maxims, and *ad hoc*
> rules. The sheer *lack* of necessity in granting its assumptions
> or adopting its strange and elaborate definitions is the point
> that should strike any candid observer. Why should anyone
> adopt a notion of 'implication' whereby a contradiction
> 'implies' any proposition? What is compelling about systems
> of logic which require massive and systematic deviation from
> our everyday use of crucial words like 'if', 'then', and 'and'? As
> a body of conventions and esoteric traditions the compelling
> character of logic, such as it is, derives from certain narrowly
> defined purposes and from custom and institutionalized usage.
> Its authority is moral and social, and as such it is admirable
> material for sociological investigation and explanation. In
> particular the credibility of logical conventions, just like the
> everyday practices which deviate from them, will be of an
> entirely local character. The utility of granting or modifying a
> definition for the sake of formal symmetry; the expediency of
> ignoring the complexity of everyday discourse and everyday
> standards of reasoning so that a certain abstract generality

can be achieved: these will be the kinds of justification that will be offered and accepted or disputed by specialists in the field.

The point that emerges is that if any informal, intuitive reasoning dispositions are universally compelling, they are *ipso facto* without any reasoned justification. On the other hand, any parts of logic which can be justified will not be universal but purely local in their credibility. The rationalist goal of producing pieces of knowledge that are both universal in their credibility *and* justified in context-independent terms is unattainable.

(Barnes and Bloor 1982: 45)

They give the following reasons for upholding relativism and rejecting classical logic:

(1) There is no necessity to grant the assumptions made in a formal classical system.
(2) The deductive move in classical logic, whereby a contradiction implies any proposition whatsoever, is not acceptable.
(3) Classical logic ignores the complexity of everyday discourse.
(4) Classical logic requires massive and systematic deviation from everyday use of the logical connectives.

These objections are well known and are rehearsed frequently by proponents of alternative logical systems.[7] However, even if we accept their complaints, the requisite relativistic conclusions do not follow.[8] The argument between classical logicians and the proponents of deviant logics is over what counts as a suitable replacement for classical logic. Some logicians also advocate pluralism about logic, or the view that there is more than one workable formal system of logic. The aim is to expand the horizons of formal logic, not to make it relative or culture-dependent. Furthermore, Barnes and Bloor fail to tell us what the 'Azande logic' is. The fact, if it is a fact, that the Azande ignore the inconsistencies of their belief-system is not enough to show that they have a different logic or that logic is culture-dependent.

5.4 LOGIC AND INTELLIGIBILITY

The 'uniqueness' and 'culture-dependence' views of logic and (and hence thin rationality) coincide in that they both reject the universality of the rules of logic and norms of rationality. The former points to the likelihood of the presence of language groups or communities which do not employ any laws of logic or norms of rationality. The latter suggests the possibility of linguistic communities or societies which use rules of logic and norms of rationality different from the ones used in the West. Both these positions emphasise the local, rather than the universal, character of our processes of reasoning and inference. The arguments for the local authority of logic are unconvincing because of the fundamental role that at least some logical inferences play in human language and thought. In particular, all intelligible thought presupposes:

(1) adherence to the law of non-contradiction – the acceptance that a proposition cannot be both true and not true – in other words $-(P \& -P)$
(2) distinguishing between truth and falsity in such a way that the truth of a proposition would exclude its falsity and vice versa
(3) defining logical constants in such a way that $(P \& Q)$ is true if (and only if) P is true and Q is true and not both $P \& -P$ can simultaneously be true
(4) the use of conditionals and inferences from $P \rightarrow Q$ and P to Q.

Principles 1–4 are preconditions of intelligibility of thought; they are minimum requirements for any coherent language-use. For a belief to have content it has to exclude at least some possibilities; my specific belief about cows cannot at the same time be a belief about everything else in the universe. If it were, then it would not express anything. Contradictory statements do not have an informative content, for they do not exclude anything. If I assert, in all sincerity, that 'all cows are herbivores' and that 'no cow is a herbivore', what belief have I expressed? I have not said anything intelligible, and the unintelligibility cuts across different languages and different cultures.

Once we grant principle 1, then principles 2 and 3 follow immediately, for without them the principle of non-contradiction cannot be stated or understood. If we assume that the connective 'and' is used in a language, then it can also be shown that the derivation rules '& Introduction' and '& Elimination' would operate in that language (principle 3). The rule that a sentence and its negation cannot both be true at the same time, in part, defines the meaning of 'not'. The use of the conditional (principle 4) is essential for forming beliefs (if the birds have returned then warm weather is coming); for using our imagination (if I climbed that tree I could get some fruit); for formulating our goals and plans ('if I run very fast I might be able to attract the attention of that gorgeous person sitting near the brook') – all cognitive

166

activities without which we would no longer be human. The suggestion that some core logical principles and rules of rationality are
universal, however, does not rule out pluralism about logic or the view
that there could be more than one correct system of logic operating
within the above parameters. Furthermore, the above does not
commit us to the unreasonable view that rules of logic, including the
principle of non-contradiction, cannot be violated.

The law of non-contradiction as a precondition of intelligibility
has come under attack in recent decades. Paraconsistent logicians
have objected that there is no reason to suppose that for a sentence to
have determinate and non-trivial content it must exclude anything.
Let us take the two sentences '2 + 2 = 4' and 'Perth is in Australia'; if
paraconsistency is right, neither of these assertions *logically* excludes
its negation, or anything else. Yet each has a different determinate but
non-trivial content. This is so because each carries information that
the other does not include (Priest *et al.* 1986: 513). Graham Priest and
Richard Routley, for instance, have argued that the content of a given
sentence is determined by the set of further sentences that it implies,
rather than by what it excludes. They agree that in any classical system,
the truth of a sentence would exclude its falsity, but this implication is
not acceptable to the paraconsistent logicians, and to insist that it
should be begs the question on behalf of classical logic. So, a relativist
may be able to deny the law of non-contradiction and still make
content-full assertions.

It would be useful to dispel the illusion that this most radical departure in logic can somehow rescue relativism from its traditional
critiques. There are several problems with the strategy of assigning
content to sentences on the basis of what they imply rather than what
they exclude. For one thing, any sentence has potentially infinitely
many implications. Which of these implications are the relevant ones
for determining its content? How are we going to delineate the class of
implications which represents or reflects the determinate content of a
particular sentence? Consider the three sentences:

(a) 'Perth is a city in Australia.'
(b) 'Sydney is a city in Australia.'
(c) 'Paris is a city in Australia.'

How are we to distinguish between the informative content of (a), (b),
(c)? For (a) to have a definite and different informative content from
(b) it must uniquely imply a set of sentences which (b) does not. The
suggestions that Routley and Priest passingly make, that (a) implies

such things as 'there is at least one city in Australia', 'Perth is a city', etc., are not sufficient since (b) implies that 'there is at least one city in Australia' and 'Sydney is a city', and these implications seem hardly sufficient for differentiating between the informative content of (a) and (b). What distinguishes (a) from (b) is the knowledge that 'Perth' designates a certain city in Australia and 'Sydney' designates a different city in Australia, i.e., a city that *is not* Perth, or Melbourne, or any other *non-Perth*. But to say that a certain object C is designated by a name or description N is to say that C has been set apart from anything else which is not designated by N. Hence, whether we wish it or not, we seem to be smuggling in the idea that the sentence 'Perth is in Australia' excludes the sentence 'Perth is not in Australia', and thus we are still adhering to the law of non-contradiction.

The same point can be approached from a slightly different angle if we compare (a) with (c). What is the informative content of 'Paris is a city in Australia'? The answer is 'nil' because (c) gives false information. However, this is not clear from the Routley–Priest suggestion, for even false sentences can have true implications, e.g., 'Paris is a city'. But how would the adherents to paraconsistency express the falsity of (c)? (c) is false because 'Paris is not a city in Australia' is true. This mode of reasoning, however, is not available to Routley and Priest because from their point of view 'Paris is a city in Australia' does not exclude 'Paris is not a city in Australia'. Priest and Routley's paraconsistent view of what gives sentences content, or makes them informative, does not seem to be supportable. However, even if we accepted their theory, their argument would not make explicit contradictions informative, for what are the implications of a sentence such as 'Perth is in Australia and Perth is not in Australia'? Certainly not that 'there is at least one city in Australia', as they had suggested for the original sentence (c), because given the conjunct 'Perth is not in Australia' then we have no grounds for deducing any conclusions about any possible cities in Australia. For any true sentence P, proposed as the logical consequence of a contradiction, its contradictory, –P, could also be proposed and hence no definite content could be given to a contradiction. Priest and Routley have not succeeded in showing that contradictions can have informative content, and Aristotle's rejection of the law of non-contradiction (see chapter 1) stands the test of time.

5.5 RATIONALITY AND JUSTIFICATION

Logic deals with the form rather than the content of rationality. It places formal constraints on the boundaries of intelligibility. The content of what counts as a rational belief (or belief-system) is given to us through the justificatory schemes we use to back our beliefs. Such justificatory schemes, in addition to making use of inferences, include other beliefs that are used as evidence to back our claims. The relativist argues that what counts as a good reason varies with and depends on the cultural and cognitive norms of different cultures. We cannot step out of these local norms to find a metajustification for them. The question then is whether, apart from a skeletal logical framework, there are any universally applicable and acceptable norms of justification and reason.

We justify beliefs either by appealing to the authority of others – their testimony – or by citing as evidence what is available to our senses, the evidence of the world so to speak. Reliance on testimony would not eliminate the possibility of relativism, for what counts as authoritative testimony may vary with cultures and historical epochs. There are complications attached to relying on the reports of our senses, scepticism about our sense-perception being one, but the problem of scepticism, as we have seen, is independent of the problem of relativism. It is the world, I contend, which ultimately furnishes us with the justification for our most basic beliefs. Our most mundane, basic or 'bedrock' beliefs are justified because they are true, because they are in contact with the way things are in the world. They are answerable to the world (see McDowell 1994). My and your beliefs that snow is cold, rain is wet, when hungry we like to eat, etc., receive their justification not from any culture-specific norm or precept but directly from a world we share. Of course, increasingly complex levels of interpretation are imposed on these basic beliefs in various cultures. The prohibition in some Islamic societies against non-Muslims coming out during rain because of the pollution they will cause is a culture-specific belief receiving its justification from rules on how to avoid contamination and pollution, but its starting point is the belief that rain makes things wet, and that belief is vindicated by our common experiences of the world. The same applies to dietary restrictions (kosher vs. non-kosher for instance); such restrictions are obviously cultural constructs and their justification may vary greatly depending on cultural traditions and religious beliefs. However, their starting point – that we want food when hungry – is a shared bedrock belief needing no justification other than this is how things stand with us. The more heavily a belief is coloured by cultural constructions, the stronger the claims of relativism become. One difficult question to address then is whether we can distinguish between bedrock and culturally constructed beliefs; given that all our beliefs are expressed through a conceptual apparatus that is linguistically mediated, and given that language, arguably, is a cultural construct, could we draw any clear boundaries between our basic, or elemental, beliefs and the rest?

Although we may not be able to give a rigorous definition of what counts as a bedrock or basic belief, we can more or less easily make such distinctions on a case-by-case basis. We do know the difference between believing that 'water quenches thirst' and 'water purges our sins', even if we cannot exactly articulate the difference. One way of distinguishing between them is to say that the first belief is held to be true in all cultures while the second is thought of as true only in some. But this formulation is not adequate; there is always the possibility that a false belief may be held true by all, but it would still not be justified by how things are in the world, since only true beliefs are so justified. An alternative way of formulating the difference is to say that basic beliefs are the ones that put us directly in touch with the commonly shared world. This formulation, although true, is ultimately unsatisfactory as well, because it does not amount to much more than restating the original claim. A further difficulty, the relativist would object, is that the idea of having access to the way things are or to the world (as it is) seems unintelligible. I shall argue later that we can agree with the conceptual relativists that it is impossible to have access to the world unmediated by our concepts. However, this concession does not undermine the minimal claim that there is a core of true beliefs common to all human cultures and belief-systems and that these beliefs are true because of our shared world and shared humanity. Furthermore, we form these beliefs and reason from them by using rules of logic some components of which are also universal.

What of the variability of justificatory procedures and beliefs, the starting points of cognitive relativism? To be sure, different cultures and peoples do hold very different views on all kinds of subjects, but this diversity belies a uniformity at the level of the mundane, the day-to-day. In chapter 3 we saw instances of such uniformity and noted its scope. That fire can heat things, that water can wash dirt, that infants cannot feed themselves are beliefs common to all cultures. Differences arise only at a higher lever, where such beliefs are explained and elaborated upon. Relativistic worries arise when we have a clash between beliefs on how a baby should be fed and not whether it should be fed if it is to survive. Having said this, the possibility of moderate relativism about rationality still remains, as we shall see in 5.8 and 6.5,

5.6 RATIONALITY AND EVOLUTION

A strong attack against the relativisation of rationality has been put forward by philosophers and evolutionary biologists who argue that available evidence from the evolutionary history of the human species refutes relativism about rationality. Daniel Dennett, for instance, following Quine, argues that relativism is refuted by empirical evidence, for natural selection guarantees that organisms would be rational or become extinct. According to him, 'natural selection guarantees that most of an organism's beliefs will be true, most of its strategies rational'(Dennett 1987: 96).[9] Any intentional system, he maintains, would reject contradictions and would believe all the logical consequences of its beliefs. It would not avow beliefs that are strongly disconfirmed by the available empirical evidence or that are self-contradictory or contradict other avowals made (Dennett 1978: 6.22). Similarly, Jerry Fodor has argued that 'Darwinian selection guarantees that organisms either know the elements of logic or become posthumous' (Fodor 1981: 21). The evolutionary argument for rationality proceeds in two stages. First, it is argued that natural selection would favour organisms with mechanisms that privilege the acquisition of true beliefs over false ones. Second, it is assumed that rationality is such a mechanism. Therefore, natural selection would favour rational organisms over irrational or even non-rational ones. Since all human beings are products of natural selection, they would possess the evolutionarily advantageous faculty of rationality, irrespective of their social and cultural backgrounds, and relativism about rationality is ruled out. The crucial assumption is that survival necessitates having true beliefs, for true beliefs are more adaptive than false ones. Since rational belief-systems produce more true beliefs, they are more adaptive than irrational ones. As Dennett puts it, 'the capacity to believe would have no survival value unless it were a capacity to believe truths' (Dennett 1978: 17). The argument has come under attack from various quarters. Stephen Jay Gould and Richard Lewontin, for instance, have characterised the attempts to use natural selection as an explanation for every human trait as 'Panglossian' for they resemble Dr Pangloss's argument, in Voltaire's *Candide*, that humans have noses so that their glasses can be kept in place.[10] What is more, it could equally be argued that in many instances a false or unjustified belief is more adaptive than a true one. For instance, religious beliefs and beliefs about life after death have had an adaptive function in all human societies, hence their preponderance. A more damaging criticism of the evolutionary argument comes from the prevalence of irrationality in human reasoning.

5.7 IRRATIONALITY AND COGNITIVE PLURALISM

Psychologists and cognitive scientists, in recent years, have argued that it is not only the members of exotic cultures who flaunt the rules of logic. The members of Western societies are also quite poor at drawing logically valid inferences from available information. Numerous studies by cognitive psychologists point to the prevalence of what might be called 'illogical' thinking among experimental subjects. Here is just one much discussed puzzle:

> Linda studied sociology and cultural studies at the New School. She is single and attends the meetings of Amnesty International regularly and takes part in political rallies. Which of the following statements have greater likelihood?
> (1) Linda is a bank teller.
> (2) Linda is a bank teller and is active in the feminist movement.

Most experimental subjects have ranked (2) as more probable than (1). But this is incorrect, because (2) is true whenever (1) is.[11]

A number of other well-known studies of human reasoning in experimental conditions have been used to highlight the preponderance of irrational thought. For instance, Amos Tversky and Daniel Kahneman, starting from the early 1970s, reported that 'under quite ordinary circumstances, people reason and make decisions in ways that systematically violate familiar canons of rationality on a broad array of problems' (Tversky and Kahneman 1986: 251). The best-known examples of failure to apply appropriate deductive rules of inference in making choices between available alternatives can be found in Peter Wason's studies (beginning in 1966) known as 'the selection task'.[12] Rather than repeat these rather well-documented results, in what follows I will outline the details of two other experiments that cast doubt on the ability of the majority of experimental subjects, members of Western technologically advanced societies, to reason according to what are supposed to be invariant norms of rationality.

Several studies have shown the inability of experimental subjects to make correct probabilistic judgements in their reasoning. According to Bayesian probability theory, the probability of any hypothesis depends, among other things, on the prior probability of the hypothesis. However, experiments conducted by Kahneman and Tversky (1982) have shown that subjects often seriously undervalue the importance of prior probabilities. Casscells *et al.* (1978) presented the following problem to a group of faculty, staff and fourth-year students at Harvard Medical School.

> If a test to detect a disease whose prevalence is 1/1000 has a false positive rate of 5 per cent, what is the chance that a person found to have a positive result actually has the disease, assuming that you know nothing about the person's symptoms or signs?
>
> <div align="right">(Cascells <i>et al.</i> 1978: 999)</div>

The correct Bayesian answer is 2 per cent. But only 18 per cent of the Harvard audience gave an answer close to 2 per cent. Forty-five per cent of this highly educated experimental group completely ignored the base-rate information and said that the answer was 95 per cent.

Another example of failure of norms of rationality is the degree of unwarranted overconfidence that experimental subjects demonstrate in expressing their views. In experiments using relatively hard questions it is typical to find that for cases where subjects say they are 100 per cent confident, only about 80 per cent of their answers are correct; for cases in which they say that they are 90 per cent confident, only about 70 per cent of their answers are correct; and for cases in which they say that they are 80 per cent confident, only about 60 per cent of their answers are correct. Warning the subjects that people are often overconfident has no significant effect, nor does offering them money (or bottles of French champagne) as a reward for accuracy. Moreover, the phenomenon has been demonstrated in a wide variety of subjects including undergraduates, graduate students, physicians and even CIA analysts.[13]

According to the so-called *standard picture* of rationality, rational thought involves the use of appropriate norms of reasoning derived from inductive and deductive logic, probability theory and decision theory (Stein 1996: 4). These experimental results have been seen as signs of failure of the standard picture.[14] The results, taken at face value, undermine the evolutionary arguments for rationality for they cast doubt on the claim that rationality is a common feature of human reasoning. If rationality is to be constructed according to the standard picture, then its canons are frequently violated, even by the most educated and aware of subjects.

Steven Stich has argued that on many sorts of problems experimental subjects tend to reason very badly, in more or less predictable ways (Stich 1990: 4) which shows that human beings do not reason according to a single standard norm of reason or rationality. He advocates what he calls 'cognitive pluralism', a form of cognitive relativism which includes relativism about logic and rationality. He distinguishes between 'descriptive cognitive pluralism' and 'normative cognitive pluralism'. According to descriptive cognitive pluralism, different individuals or groups of people have different ways of thinking and reasoning; they 'go about the business of cognition – the forming and revising of beliefs – in significantly different ways' (ibid.: 13). More generally, 'different people or different cultures use radically different "psychologics" or . . . the revising and updating of their cognitive states is governed by substantially different principles' (ibid.). Descriptive cognitive pluralism is an empirical argument and, as it stands, does not lead to relativism about logic or rationality. Normative cognitive pluralism is a claim about the cognitive processes that people ought to use. It is a claim about what counts as a good cognitive process. 'What is asserted is that there is no unique system of cognitive processes that people should use, because various systems of cognitive processes that are very different from each other may all be equally good' (ibid.). Normative cognitive pluralism then is a consequence of descriptive cognitive pluralism. Given the truth of descriptive cognitive pluralism, the only method available to us for evaluating varying cognitive processes is to use our personal or local standards and ideas of cognitive evaluation which, in the case of most Western thinkers, consist of appeals to the standard picture of rationality – justificatory systems, rules of logic and valid argumentation, etc. However, we should not forget that these are the products of our culture and do not have any intrinsic, universal or ultimate values and should not be considered as a final court of appeal.

According to Stich, many cognitive divergences are likely to be traceable to cultural differences but genetic and individual psychological differences also play a role. 'In attempting to evaluate these divergent strategies and in deciding which of them we ought ourselves to use, we are trying to decide among a variety of cultural products.' In doing so we cannot use our intuitions as a criterion because these intuitions 'themselves are local cultural products' and hence there will be a plurality of such criteria (ibid.: 20).

For Stich, then, there is no single cognitive process or method of reasoning – including rules of logic – that people should use, since various incompatible cognitive processes may all be equally good. This view is relativistic because it entails that different systems of reasoning may be normatively appropriate for different people or cultures. Cognitive relativism, as construed by Stich, is a 'species of normative cognitive pluralism. An account of cognitive virtue – of what makes a system of reasoning a *good* one – is *relativistic* if it entails that different systems are good for different people (or different groups of people)' (ibid.: 160 n. 23).

Stich advocates a pragmatist approach to the evaluation of standards and methods of reasoning. Our cognitive processes, he maintains, can only be evaluated instrumentally by judging how well they perform in bringing about states of affairs that people typically value – states of affairs such as being able to predict or control nature, or contributing to an interesting and fulfilling life. Since such values may vary from person to person and from culture to culture, there would be no question of using a single universal criterion for assessing different methods of reasoning. Stich's pragmatic account is relativistic because

> the pragmatic assessment of a cognitive system will be sensitive to both the values and the circumstances of the people using it. Thus, it may well turn out that one cognitive system is pragmatically better than a second *for me* while the second is pragmatically better than the first *for someone else*.
>
> (Ibid.: 25)

In rejecting the appeals to our ordinary notions of epistemic evaluation – appeals to rationality, justification and the rest, as final arbiters in our efforts to choose among competing strategies of inquiry – Stich is also denying that rationality or justification has any intrinsic or ultimate value. In the process, he also rejects the suggestion that truth is an intrinsically valuable feature of cognitive activities.

One standard criticism of relativism is that it leads to nihilism, that it abandons any serious attempt to separate good cognitive strategies from bad ones, and hence 'anything goes'. Once we agree that there can be no external criterion for adjudicating between incompatible modes of reasoning, then epistemic anarchy would loom large and we might as well give up on any pretensions to having norms of reasoning. But according to Stich, his approach, although relativistic, is not nihilistic for it does allow for criteria of evaluation of reasoning. But such criteria are situational and are applied using pragmatic considerations such as usefulness, efficacy, etc.

A second criticism of relativism is that it leads to scepticism because it drives a wedge between good reasoning and truth. Stich argues:

[One] complaint against relativism is that it threatens the connection between cognitive inquiry and truth. For if the . . . relativist is right, then there may be a pair of people whose systems of reasoning are very different from one another, though each system is optimal for the person using it. We can expect that on being exposed to essentially the same data these people will sometimes end up with very different sets of beliefs. When this happens it is unlikely to be the case that both sets are true; at least one set of beliefs will be substantially mistaken. Since at least one person will end up with false beliefs, and since *ex hypothesi* they are both using optimally good cognitive systems, it cannot be the case that good cognition always leads to true beliefs.

(Stich 1998: 361)

The break between good or valuable cognitive practices and truth is not fatal, Stich goes on to argue. For even if good reasoning does not guarantee truth we can adopt a reliabilist account of cognitive evaluation according to which people who reason well will do the best job possible at producing truths and avoiding falsehoods. 'To expect more than this seems unreasonable' (ibid.).

There is much that is of interest in Stich's approach. However, even if we accept the general outlines of Stich's argument for cognitive relativism, we are still left with the question of the status of the pragmatist approach to the evaluation of standards of reasoning. Is the pragmatist or instrumentalist approach Stich advocates universally applicable? If so, then there is a universal criterion for evaluating differing cognitive strategies, so Stich's approach turns out to rely on some universal criteria for cognitive evaluation and hence is not completely relativistic. If the pragmatist approach itself is context-sensitive, then we are bereft of any means of evaluating standards of reasoning and the danger of cognitive nihilism is not averted. Furthermore, and maybe even more damagingly, Stich needs to address the question of what the criteria are for adjudicating between the right and wrong applications of the pragmatic criterion. Does Stich allow any evaluative questions about the states of affairs and activities that people typically value? How do we assess the value of being able to predict or control nature or contributing to an interesting and fulfilling life? He argues that such values may vary across individuals and cultures, but would he allow that some individuals or even societies may be mistaken in their perception and characterisation of what counts as an interesting or fulfilling life? If yes, then we will be relying on something more than the situationally and contextually given criterion of evaluation. If, on the other hand, the argument is that such values are to be treated as primitives and not amenable to external scrutiny, then we are deprived of the means of evaluating different approaches to cognition – and the cognitive nihilism that Stich was trying to avoid would loom large. Stich could argue that his pluralism is not nihilistic since it rules out the unproductive forms of reasoning or those forms that fail to produce the desired ends, but this would not solve the problem of finding a way of evaluating or ranking the different ends. In other words, we are still unable to distinguish between productive and unproductive forms of reasoning outside of their specific cultural contexts.

Stich seems to think that there are such things as typically valuable states of affairs, predicting and controlling nature for instance. But given the disagreement between radical or 'deep' ecologists and their opponents on the value, scope and extent of human control over nature, it seems that consensus even on this issue would be difficult to come by. The point is that there may be deep disagreements between different ultimate values and rationalities which may not be amenable to the pragmatic approach in the form that Stich advocates. Pluralism can avoid nihilism only if it operates under some constraints. I shall return to this point in chapters 9 and 10.

5.8 MODERATE RELATIVISM AND CONTEXT-DEPENDENCE

The most compelling arguments on behalf of relativism about rationality avoid strong relativism and confine themselves to the more modest proposal that some features of the 'rational' are context-dependent. The context-sensitive features of rationality may include criteria of what is relevant reason, apt argument, convincing evidence, or appropriate justification for a given belief – all those features that give us a broad or thick internal description of rationality. A classic example of relativism of 'thick' rationality is Hugh Trevor-Roper's discussion of the seventeenth-century witchcraze in Europe. Trevor-Roper argues that the seventeenth-century belief in witches should not be detached from its context which included the cosmology, social attitudes and 'mentality' of the time. According to him, 'We recognize that even rationalism is relative; that it operates within a general philosophic context, and that it cannot properly be detached from this context' (Trevor-Roper 1969: 105). A question arising from this moderate form of relativism, as with all other relativistic claims, is how we are going to evaluate (in a non-question-begging way) different belief-systems. Could we ever say that belief in science is cognitively more valuable than belief in witches?

One of the more interesting and subtle discussions of the context-sensitivity of various conceptions of rationality has been put forward by Alasdair MacIntyre. According to MacIntyre, conceptions of rationality are closely related to an overall view of human life and its place in nature. Therefore, each conception of rationality has to be understood in terms of its historical context because it is embodied and embedded in particular types of social relationships. An inquiry into the nature of rationality, as well as other normative concepts such as justice, would not be intelligible without an understanding of the particular history of the forms of social and practical life of which they are a part. Such an understanding is possible only from within. In other words, only thick descriptions of rationality give us a genuine understanding of what a rational belief is.

According to MacIntyre, in order to be able to engage in evaluating practices of other traditions of rationality, the prospective evaluator has to first identify with a tradition, at least to some degree, before she can enter into an argumentative dialogue with it (MacIntyre 1988: 394). According to him, tradition-transcendent, universal standards and criteria do not exist. Anyone engaging in cross-cultural evaluations has to acquire the language-in-use of the rival tradition and, by an act of imagination, place herself within that tradition so that she is able to conceive and perceive the natural and social world the way members of the alternative tradition do. Finally, she has to test dialectically the theses proposed by each competing tradition in order to test the incoherencies, as well as the advantages, of each tradition. The practical upshot is that we can start asking questions about rationality and justice by debating with people from different traditions, but only after we have learned their language as a second first language.

MacIntyre's account of rationality is context-sensitive but far from being straightforwardly relativistic. MacIntyre seems to assume the value and applicability of dialectical reasoning, test of coherence, dialogue, debate and method of argumentation, and advocates their use in all contexts of inquiry (ibid.: 398). One question arising from this assumption is whether these values are universal or peculiar to MacIntyre's own tradition. If they are universal, then MacIntyre is contradicting himself when he rejects the fiction of universal non-tradition-based values. Alternatively, if they are local, then they would not be of any use in confrontations with traditions that reject them. Furthermore, MacIntyre is not in a position to claim that these are tradition-based values shared by all traditions, precisely because there is ample empirical evidence for the existence of traditions which do not share these values. In fact, valorising dialogue, debate and the method of argumentation is a feature of the Western intellectual tradition which had been particularly emphasised by the Enlightenment, the very tradition that MacIntyre, ironically, is at pains to reject.

MacIntyre might argue that he has an independent reason for rejecting the precepts of the Enlightenment traditions – that he has arrived at this conclusion by looking at the failings of the Enlightenment from inside, as well as outside. The internal failures of the Enlightenment, coupled with his tradition-bound view, warrant the emphatic and the externalist-sounding claims he makes. But the anti-Enlightenment camp seems to underestimate the successes of the universalising tendencies of the Enlightenment and the way these successes can be used to undermine rival claims of justice. To take a few examples, the universalising claims about human nature have made slavery morally unacceptable; they made possible universal suffrage and the women's liberation movement; they have given voice to children, the handicapped, gays and other marginalised groups, by emphasising that all human beings have certain basic rights; they have, gradually, rendered the idea of territorial conquest problematic; they have made possible the ideals of equality and non-exploitation.[15] Despite these criticisms, MacIntyre's context-dependent view of rationality manages to address some of the worries that motivate relativism about rationality and is a welcome addition to the polarised debates in this area.

5.9 CONCLUSION

One problem with most discussions of rationality is that rationality has been taken as an all-or-nothing affair. Furthermore, relativism and universalism have been seen as exhaustive and inclusive categories. The distinction between strong and moderate forms of relativism about rationality, at least to some extent, obviates this problem. Strong relativism about rationality proves to be untenable. Moderate relativism about rationality, on the other hand, is a more complex and nuanced position and cannot be dismissed so readily. An analysis of the concept of rationality and the conditions under which we attribute rationality in thought and action to others shows that the boundaries between the rational and the irrational depend, at least to some extent, on historical and social conditions. I shall return to this topic in chapter 6 where moderate relativism about rationality will be discussed in connection with recent developments in philosophy of science.

6

Epistemic relativism

6.1 INTRODUCTION

Epistemic relativism claims that what we know, or claim to know, is always bound up with particular historical, cultural and even individual perspectives and conditions and hence cannot be universal or non-contextual. Epistemology is the area of philosophy dealing with questions concerning the nature and the justification of knowledge. It examines issues such as belief, truth, objectivity, evidence, justification, the requirements for the establishment of epistemic agency, and the challenge of scepticism. One of its main aims has been to produce a theory of knowledge and to answer questions about the conditions under which knowledge-claims can be made. Epistemology, since Plato, has been at the centre of much of philosophy, and in modern philosophy, particularly over the last one hundred years, it has become intertwined with philosophy of science, and questions about the nature and scope of scientific explanations, the status of scientific laws, the appropriate methods for scientific investigation, etc.

The standard analysis of knowledge in philosophical literature takes the following form:

> Subject S knows P (where P stands for a proposition or statement)
> if and only if
> S believes that P
> S is justified in believing that P
> and P is true.

In other words, knowledge is justified true belief. Epistemic relativists claim that this abstract, non-contextual analysis of knowledge is deeply flawed. In particular, they maintain that not only what counts as a true or false belief may be relative, but more significantly, what counts as acceptable justification can and does vary from culture to culture and there is no neutral method or criterion for adjudicating between different justificatory schemes. Thus, relativism about both truth and rationality could be seen as variants of epistemic relativism. For if the truth of what is 'known' is relative to different contexts and cultures, then knowledge-claims cannot be universal or absolute. Similarly, if standards of rationality were culture-dependent, then justificatory procedures involved in establishing claims to knowledge would also be relative. The scope of epistemic relativism, however, extends beyond that of relativism about truth and rationality. In the writings of Thomas Kuhn, for instance, epistemic relativism has more in common with conceptual relativism (see chapter 7).

As well as examinations of the object of knowledge, or what is known and how it is known, epistemic relativism receives its impetus from considerations of the status of the knower, the subject of knowledge-claims. The universality of claims of knowledge has been challenged strongly by focusing on the social, political and psychological conditions of the knowing subject. The epistemic subject – the knower – in traditional definitions of knowledge is generic and abstract; it is not embodied and has no gender, history, race, class, cultural background or sexual identity. The claim is that one knower is as good as another – epistemic subjects (S in the above definition) are interchangeable. This particular view has come under attack from feminist and postmodernist philosophers (see, for instance, Code 1993).

Knowledge-claims in general, and scientific knowledge in particular, are assumed to be universally true, objective and value-neutral. Galileo (1953) for instance, had proclaimed that the conclusions of natural science are true and necessary, and the judgement of man has nothing to do with them. His is a view that has echoed in the works of both practising scientists and commentators on science, certainly until the end of the nineteenth century, and has become an integral part of what is known as 'the scientific method'. The discoveries achieved by scientists, and the explanations provided by them, if true, are applicable to all times and places and hence they are universal. The Nobel laureate Sheldon Glashow proclaims:

> We [scientists] believe that the world is knowable, that there are simple rules governing the behaviour of matter and the evolution of the universe. We affirm that there are eternal, objective, extra-historical, socially neutral, external and universal truths, and that the assemblage of these truths is what

we call physical science. Natural laws can be discovered that are universal, invariable, inviolable, genderless and verifiable.

They may be found by men or by women or by mixed collaborations of any obscene proportions. Any intelligent alien anywhere would have come upon the same logical system as we have to explain the structure of protons and the nature of supernovae.

He finishes by saying: 'This statement I cannot prove. This statement I cannot justify. This is my faith' (Glashow 1989, quoted in Hankinson Nelson 1993: 130).

Glashow's views represent the objectivist, universalist standpoint *par excellence*. Objectivity thus construed is extended beyond the human ken. Knowledge mirrors an independently existing world, the world of mind-independent facts. Scientific discoveries are achieved by using universally valid methods and principles, which can be applied by anyone, anywhere, and their application under similar conditions would always lead to uniform results. Feminist epistemologists complain that according to this approach, 'genuine knowledge does not reflect the subject who produced it' or the context and conditions out of which knowledge arises (Lennon and Whitford 1994: 2).

The epistemic relativist's challenge is directed against such objectivist and universalist conceptions of knowledge, particularly as it pertains to the natural sciences. In this chapter, I shall examine a number of such attacks.

6.2 RELATIVISM ABOUT SCIENCE

Relativism about science arises, in part, out of the rejection of particular conceptions of the status of scientific theories and practice of science. The main features of the traditional 'image of science' are:[1]

(1) Scientific realism. The view that scientific theories are attempts to describe the one real world and that there is a single correct description of any given aspect of that world.
(2) The unity of science. There is one (correct) science, which applies to the one real world.
(3) The universality of science. Scientific laws apply to all times and places and are invariant (3 may be seen as a consequence of 2).
(4) Scientific knowledge is cumulative. There is a steady growth in the range and depth of our knowledge in any given area of science.
(5) Theory–observation distinction. There is a clear and important

distinction between empirical observations and the scientific theories that make use of the data of observation and explain them.

(6) Foundationalism. Observations and experiments are the foundations and justifications of scientific theories.

(7) Scientific method. There is such a thing as a unique and correct scientific method. Induction, and deduction, and the use of experiments are important features of this method.

(8) Meaning invariance. Scientific concepts and theoretical terms have stable and fixed meanings. They retain their meaning across theory changes.

(9) Fact/value and objective/subjective distinction. The domain of values (ethical, aesthetic, etc.) should be sharply distinguished from the natural world. Science deals with the natural world and is both value-free and objective; value judgements, on the other hand, are subjective, or at best intersubjectively agreed conventions.

(10) Context-independence. There is a sharp distinction between the context of justification of a scientific theory and the context of discovery. The social, economic and psychological circumstances that give rise to a scientific theory should not be confused with the methodological procedures used for justifying the theory.

Philosophers of differing persuasions, and not just those associated with relativistic views, have rejected one or more of 1–10. Anti-realists, e.g., instrumentalist philosophers of science, reject 1, while 5 and 6 have been questioned by many contemporary philosophers, including Karl Popper. Epistemic relativists of various hues, however, deny the truth of all the above features of the traditional 'image of science'; in particular they emphasise the failures of 2, 3, 7, 8 and 10 and so

(I) deny the possibility of ahistorical or non-perspectival knowledge;[2]

(II) emphasise the diversity of scientific theories and reject the possibility of convergence among them;

(III) claim that scientific theories expressed through divergent methods and modes of reasoning are incommensurable;

(IV) argue that different historical epochs and cultures produce different standards and paradigms of rationality and 'correct' reasoning, and that no ahistorical criterion of adjudication is available to us;

(V) deny that there is cumulative progress in science.

The most influential arguments for positions I–V are to be found in the writings of Thomas Kuhn and Paul Feyerabend.

6.3 PARADIGMS AND REVOLUTIONS

The central idea in Kuhn's conception of the history of science is that during what he has called a 'period of normal science', theorising, research, and discovery take place within specific research paradigms.[3] Paradigms are the core cluster of concepts associated with a recognised scientific achievement and shape the approach of the scientists to their subject (Kuhn [1962] 1970). They are 'universally recognized scientific achievements that for a time provide model problems and solutions to a community of practitioners' (ibid.: viii). They supply scientists with 'accepted examples of actual scientific practice – examples which include law, theory, application, and instrumentation . . . [they] provide models from which spring particular coherent traditions of scientific research' (ibid.: 10). Scientists whose research is based on a shared paradigm are committed to the same rules and standards for scientific practice. A paradigm provides the scientist with a stable set of theoretical assumptions, which also encompasses standard ways of applying these assumptions to different experimental situations and observational data.[4] Other essential components of a paradigm are: standard procedures for experimentation and accepted ways of interpreting their results; the use of common instruments and techniques for conducting these experiments; and a number of metaphysical and methodological background assumptions and prescriptions:

> In learning a paradigm the scientists acquire theory, methods, and standards together, usually in an inextricable mixture. Therefore, when paradigms change, there are usually significant shifts in the criteria determining the legitimacy both of problems and of proposed solutions.
>
> (Ibid.: 109)

Kuhn distinguishes between two key senses of 'paradigm'. First, paradigms are the accepted ways of conducting research and solving scientific problems. In this sense, paradigms are achievements that then become a model for future scientists. Second, paradigms are the set of shared methods, standards and values of the scientific community at any given time and within particular fields (Kuhn 1970 and 1977). The latter notion of paradigm emphasises the consensual

character of scientific research, that what counts as scientific knowledge is established through agreements within research communities.

From a traditional inductivist perspective, progress in science
occurs through the accumulation of data, the gathering of facts, and
a process of theory-building, by way of induction from available
data. Karl Popper changed the order of things and argued that
progress is achieved by coming up with bold speculations or hypotheses that can explain larger numbers of observations and survive the
tests that have falsified earlier theories. Kuhn, on the other hand,
finds the very idea of linear progress in science problematic. Consensus among scientists and hence the idea of progress, he argues, are
limited only to what he calls 'periods of normal science'. The history
of science consists of a series of radical shifts and fundamental
changes in scientific worldviews or what he calls 'scientific revolutions'. During a scientific revolution the entire theoretical structure
and the methodological and metaphysical framework of a given area
of research – the prevailing paradigm – is replaced with new and radically different ones that are incompatible on many points with their
predecessors. In this sense, paradigm shifts are discontinuous and scientific knowledge is non-cumulative, largely because questions posed
in older paradigms and the answers provided for them may become
irrelevant in a new paradigm.

According to Kuhn, the history of science consists of several iden-
tifiable stages: In the pre-scientific stage, many different theories
compete in their attempt to explain the same phenomenon. Charac-
teristically, at this stage a wide spectrum of observations and data,
related to the phenomenon under investigation in a rather undifferentiated way, is deemed relevant to the investigation. This proliferation
of theories, Kuhn argues, is in line with the thesis of underdetermination of theory by data, since:

> Philosophers of science have repeatedly demonstrated
> that more than one theoretical construction can always be
> placed upon a given collection of data. History of science
> indicates that, particularly in the early developmental stages
> of a new paradigm, it is not even very difficult to invent such
> alternates.
>
> (Kuhn [1962] 1970: 76)

The main activity occurring at this stage is one of random collection
and accumulation of 'facts'. Researchers working in the pre-scientific
stage do not possess commonly agreed theories, procedures for

conducting experiments or standards of practice. The pre-Newtonian study of light, where light was variously described as corpuscles, emanations from the eye, or a modification of the medium between an object and an observer, is an instance of the proliferation of diverse theories in the pre-scientific stage.

As one of the many competing theories gains ascendancy, a period of 'normal science' gradually emerges. Scientists working within this period conduct their research in accordance with the norms established by the prevailing paradigm. They simply assume the validity of the single, dominant theoretical and methodological framework and conduct their research within its parameters. Their activities are directed towards what Kuhn calls 'puzzle-solving'; they concentrate on working out in detail those problems that are deemed both significant and apt to be resolved by the dominant paradigm. As we saw, according to Kuhn, the idea of scientific progress can be understood only in the context of the practices of normal science.

Even in periods of normal science, scientists encounter experimental anomalies and puzzles that resist solution, but normal science tends to suppress such anomalies by either ignoring them or adjusting the existing paradigm to accommodate them. Once the critical mass of such anomalies makes the attempt at readjustment impossible, or when the anomalies seem to threaten the core theses of a paradigm, a period of crisis begins. This is marked by 'pronounced professional uncertainty' leading to the emergence of what Kuhn calls 'extraordinary science', which resembles the pre-scientific stage in that once again there are many competing theories jockeying for supremacy and there is no consensus on what is an acceptable overall research project or avenue of investigation. Scientific revolutions follow such periods of crisis.

A scientific revolution takes place, according to Kuhn, when there is a shift of professional commitment from one paradigm to another. The scientific developments associated with Copernicus and Einstein are examples of such revolutions. In a revolution, scientists reject one respected and well-established paradigm in favour of another; and with this comes a shift of perspective in the choice of problems to be studied. That is, what counts as a legitimate scientific problem or puzzle and what would constitute a solution to it change to such an extent that, Kuhn suggests, different paradigms bring about different and incommensurable ways of looking at and seeing the world and of practising science in it. 'Though the world does not change with a change of paradigm, the scientists after [a scientific revolution] work in a different world' (Kuhn [1962] 1970: 150). The proponents of different, competing paradigms practise their trades in different worlds, Kuhn claims. 'Practicing in different worlds, the two groups of scientists see different things when they look from the same point at the same direction, for instance one sees chemical solutions as compounds and the other sees it as a mixture' (ibid.). A scientific revolution, then, is not simply a change in the theoretical orientation of a scientific community but more like a 'gestalt switch', that occurs all at once or not at all.

Successive paradigms, according to Kuhn, give us different and sometimes conflicting accounts of the world, its constituents and its composition. The research methodology, the theoretical language and the overall worldviews governing different paradigms are irreconcilable and hence incommensurable with one another. This is in part, he argues, because there is 'no theory-independent way to reconstruct phrases like "really there"; the notion of a match between the ontology of a theory and its 'real' counterpart in nature now seems to me illusive in principle' (ibid.: 206). More generally, observation language, Kuhn argues, presupposes a paradigm and a theory, and hence a change in paradigm brings about a change of observation language: after a scientific revolution the data themselves change (ibid.: 135). New paradigms do inherit and incorporate elements from the theoretical vocabulary and apparatus of the older paradigm, Kuhn admits, but these inherited elements are used in new ways. For instance, the concept of space in Newtonian theory was seen as necessarily flat and homogeneous, while 'space' in Einsteinian theory involves the more complex concept of space/time. Consequently, scientists debating the merits of their respective paradigms often are slightly at cross-purposes. Comparisons of paradigms and debates about paradigm choice can be made only from within a paradigm; there is no neutral ground available for surveying the merits of rival paradigms, since they will have conflicting criteria of evaluation built into them.

The relativistic implications of Kuhn's view seem evident. All assessments of the success, and even truth, of a particular scientific theory can be made only within and relative to a given paradigm – there is no room for extra-paradigmatic, non-relative evaluations in Kuhn's view of science. Furthermore, Kuhn maintains that agreement between scientists is the ultimate authority for theory choice, that 'in paradigm choice – there is no standard higher than the assent of the relevant community' (ibid.: 94). According to him,

> the choice between competing . . . paradigms proves to be a choice between incompatible modes of community life . . .

> When paradigms enter, as they must, into a debate about
> paradigm choice, their role is necessarily circular. Each group
> uses its own paradigm to argue in that paradigm's defense.
>
> (Ibid.)

Since different communities practise their trades within the confines
of different paradigms, we are left with a view of science analogous to
cultural relativism.

Kuhn has been widely accused of undermining the very basis for
rational theory choice. Imre Lakatos, for instance, claimed that for
Kuhn theory choice is a matter of 'mob psychology' and Dudley
Sphere argues that, for Kuhn, paradigm choice cannot be based on
good reasons or rational grounds (Earman, 1993: 10). On the other
hand, commentators outside the narrow circle of analytic philosophy
of science – postmodernists, feminist epistemologists, sociologists,
etc. – have embraced Kuhn's views as a harbinger of our liberation
from the universalist authoritarian claims of the natural sciences.
Kuhn himself was shocked by the irrationalist readings of his book,
and in later publications expended much effort to distance himself
from the relativistic implications of the original edition of *The Structure of Scientific Revolutions*. For instance, he argued that accuracy,
simplicity, fruitfulness, consistency and scope provide us with objective and universal criteria for theory choice.[5] Despite Kuhn's
protestations and attempts to dispel what he saw as deep misunderstandings of his views, his work has remained a dominant influence
on epistemic relativism.

6.4 SCIENCE AS ANARCHY

While Kuhn distanced himself from the relativist implications of his
original position, Paul Feyerabend's views on the role and place of
methodology in science became increasingly hospitable to some versions of relativism.[6] Feyerabend advocates an 'irrationalist' view of
science and denies that there is, or ought to be, an objective scientific
method. Progress in science occurs when scientists break the rules of
the accepted methodology of their time. A detailed look at the
history of science, he claims, shows that: 'proliferation of theories
is beneficial to science, while uniformity impairs its critical power'
(Feyerabend 1975: 11). Philosophy of science in the twentieth century, particularly in the hands of the logical positivists, had been
marked by debates on the constituents and the conditions of application of the so-called 'scientific method'. According to Feyerabend:

> None of the methods which Carnap, Hempel, Nagel, Popper or even Lakatos want to use for rationalising scientific changes can be applied ... What remains are aesthetic judgments, judgments of taste, metaphysical prejudices, religious desires, in short, what remains are our subjective wishes: science at its most advanced and general returns to the individual a freedom he seems to lose in its more pedestrian parts.
>
> (Ibid.: 284–5)

The claim that there is cumulative progress in science, based on the applications of 'the scientific method', assumes the 'meaning invariance' of both theoretical and observational terms used in science. It assumes that there is continuity in the use, interpretation and definition of theoretical terms in successive theories within a scientific domain. However, the claims for meaning invariance are not supported by the history of science, for the meaning of scientific terms changes with each scientific revolution. For instance, the term 'mass', as used in Newtonian mechanics, denotes a property, while in relativity theory it means a relation and hence it would be a mistake to assume that 'mass' has an invariant meaning across theories. This is because scientific revolutions bring about a change in the most fundamental assumptions and principles in the theory and practice of science and

> a change of universal principles brings about a change of the entire world. Speaking in this manner we no longer assume an objective world that remains unaffected by our epistemic activities, except when moving within the confines of a particular point of view.
>
> (Ibid.: 19)

Facts and theories are too intimately connected for us to be able to separate them. 'Not only is the description of every single fact dependent on some theory . . . There exist also facts which cannot be unearthed except with the help of alternatives to the theory to be tested, and which become unavailable as soon as such alternatives are excluded' (Feyerabend 1965: 174–5, quoted in Preston 1997: 126). Furthermore, to insist on the desirability of meaning-invariance would impede progress in science. It would place artificial restrictions on theory construction and stifle creativity.

Feyerabend's views on incommensurability and the extent of the theory dependence of facts are influenced by Benjamin Lee Whorf's principle of linguistic relativity (see chapter 3). Feyerabend claims that his view that observers will '*posit different* facts under the same physical circumstances in the same physical world' (Feyerabend 1975: 286), based on their background theoretical framework, is an extension of Whorf's thesis. He also makes use of Whorf's notion of covert linguistic classifications. These classifications, such as the English gender as opposed to gender in Latin, which is overt, operate through 'an invisible "central exchange" of linkage bonds in such a way as to determine certain other words which mark the class' (Whorf 1956: 69). Covert linguistic classifications underpin the cosmology or 'the comprehensive world view of the world, of society, of the situation of man which influences thought, behaviour, perception' (Feyerabend 1975: 223) contained in the grammar of any language. They also give rise to 'patterned resistance' against alternative worldviews (ibid.: 224),[7] thus leading to incommensurability between worldviews. Feyerabend makes use of examples drawn from the work of social anthropologists to illustrate this point. For instance, he argues:

> Space, time, reality change when we move from one language to another. According to the Nuer, time does not limit human action, it is part of it and follows its rhythm . . . For the Hopi a distinct event is real only when it is past, for a Western businessman it occurs in the presence of events he is participating in. The worlds in which cultures unfold not only contain different events, they also contain them in different ways.
>
> (Feyerabend 1987: 105)

Feyerabend's views on the connection between language and ontology has much in common with conceptual relativism (see chapter 7); his maxim 'anything goes', however, has been used by both the conceptual relativists and the anti-relativists of all hues as a catch-word for the most extreme forms of relativism. The extremist interpretations of his slogan, however, do not reflect his position on relativism; rather, the maxim should be understood in the context of debates on scientific methodology. According to Feyerabend, 'The only principle that does not inhibit progress in science is the propagation of theories, and in that sense the only maxim governing science is, or ought to be, "anything goes"'. For him, this is the only methodological 'principle that can be defended under all stages of human development' (Feyerabend 1975: 27), but it does not mean that every statement or theory is as good as any other, or that there is no difference between truth and falsity.

Feyerabend does defend a version of relativism which, he tells us, is 'not about concepts . . . but about human relations'. He calls his position 'democratic relativism' or the view that different societies may look at the world in different ways and regard different things as acceptable (Feyerabend 1987: 59). Democratic relativism is backed by a modified version of epistemic relativism, or the view that 'For every statement, theory, point of view believed (to be true) with good reason there exist arguments showing a conflicting alternative to be at least as good, or even better' (ibid.: 76). This position, as Feyerabend claims, is far removed from the usual relativist claim that truth (knowledge, reality, etc.) is relative to cultural norms or historical contexts. Rather, he argues that a relativist 'who deserves his name will . . . have to refrain from making assertions about the nature of reality, truth and knowledge'(Feyerabend 1987: 78). Relativism, then, in Feyerabend's hands, is not so much a philosophical doctrine to be judged as true or false, but a method for dealing with cultural and individual differences. It is a plea for intellectual and political tolerance and a denunciation of dogmatism. 'It says that what is right for one culture need not be right for another' (ibid.: 85). People have the right to live and believe as they see fit. To privilege one conception of truth, rationality or knowledge in the name of scientific objectivity runs the risk of imposing a repressive worldview on members of other cultural groupings who do not share our assumptions and intellectual framework.

Kuhn and Feyerabend's views on the incommensurability of paradigms and worldviews have become one of the main bulwarks of contemporary epistemic relativism.

6.5 RELATIVISM AND INCOMMENSURABILITY

Since the publication of *The Structure of Scientific Revolutions*, discussions of incommensurability are intimately linked with those of relativism. The usual line of argument is that incommensurability engenders relativism and since relativism is an incoherent position then incommensurability is also incoherent. Or conversely, it is argued that since the thesis of incommensurability is unintelligible then so is relativism. The connection between incommensurability and relativism, at this stage, is usually simply assumed rather than argued for. In this section, I will examine some of these assumptions and the arguments on the perceived connections between the two.

The term 'incommensurability' – meaning the impossibility of comparison by a common measure – has its origins in mathematics and geometry, but its current philosophical usage dates back to Kuhn ([1962] 1970) and Feyerabend (1962).[8] The thesis was apparently developed in conversations between Feyerabend and Kuhn in the early 1960s, but Feyerabend dates back his version to the early 1950s and credits Elizabeth Anscombe as the original source (Preston 1997: 102–3). The incommensurability thesis has been one of the main sources of relativistic interpretations of Kuhn.[9] Kuhn's relativism, it is argued, rests on his assumption that scientific theories cannot be compared or assessed independently of the paradigms in which they are embedded, and each paradigm acts as a unique and untranslatable language. 'Because rival paradigms lack any access to a common [criterion for adjudication or] language, they cannot be meaningfully compared' (Doppelt 1982: 116); they remain self-contained and beyond the critical reach of other paradigms.

Feyerabend insists that, despite a common perception to the contrary, his version of the incommensurability thesis is substantially different from Kuhn's. He says:

> [Kuhn] observed that different paradigms (A) use concepts that cannot be brought into the usual logical relations of inclusion, exclusion, overlap; and (B) make us see things differently (research workers in different paradigms have not only different concepts, but also different perceptions); and (C) contain different methods for setting up research and evaluating its results. According to Kuhn, it is the collaboration of all these elements that makes a paradigm immune to difficulties and incomparable with other paradigms. Incommensurability in the sense of Kuhn . . . is the incomparability of paradigms that results from the collaboration of (A), (B) and (C).
> (Feyerabend 1978: 66–7 in Preston 1997: 103)

Feyerabend's version of the thesis, according to him, emphasises (A) only. By 'incommensurability', he says, he always had meant 'deductive disjointedness, *and nothing else*' (Feyerabend 1978: 68 in Preston 1997: 103).

Kuhn gives a somewhat different account of the genesis and scope of the term. In 1982 he wrote:

> Twenty years have passed since Paul Feyerabend and I first used in print a term we had borrowed from mathematics to

describe the relationship between successive scientific theories. 'Incommensurability' was the term; each of us was led to
it by problems we had encountered in interpreting scientific
texts. My use of the term was broader than his; his claims for
the phenomenon were more sweeping than mine; but our
overlap at that time was substantial. Each of us was centrally
concerned to show that the meanings of scientific terms and
concepts – 'force', 'mass', for example, or 'element' and 'compound' – often changed with the theory in which they were
deployed. And each of us claimed that when such changes
occurred, it was impossible to define all the terms of one
theory in the vocabulary of the other.

(Kuhn 2000: 34)

Leaving aside the exegetical disputes, we can in general distinguish
between the semantic and the epistemic forms of incommensurability in discussions of the topic in philosophy of science. A third form
of incommensurability, the view that ethical claims may be incommensurable, is central to discussion of moral relativism and value
pluralism and will be examined in chapter 9.

Semantic incommensurability is the claim that two conceptual
systems or theories are incommensurable if they are not inter-
translatable, i.e., if the meaning and the reference of terms used in one
theory cannot be equated with or mapped into the terms used in
another. In his late summation of his views. Kuhn says:

Both Feyerabend and I wrote of the impossibility of defining
the terms of one theory on the basis of the terms of the other.
But he restricted incommensurability to language, I spoke
also of differences in 'methods, problem-field, and standards
of solution' (*Structure*, 2nd ed., p. 103).

(Ibid.: 34 n. 2)

Although Kuhn's definition of 'incommensurability' is quite wide,[10]
there is little evidence that he had a *specifically* semantic interpretation in mind. In his earlier writings he had argued that theories
from different paradigms are incommensurable because there is no
neutral 'observation language' into which both can be fully translated
(Kuhn 1970: 126–7). According to him, successive theories are incommensurable in the sense that there is no language into which both
theories can be translated without residue or loss, but this is not the
same as claiming that they are incomparable (Kuhn 2000: 36). He also

maintains that 'communication across the revolutionary divide is inevitably partial' (Kuhn [1962] 1970: 149). But as some of the historical examples he uses in the *Structure* show, he does not believe that incommensurability entails a radical semantic divide between competing theories, where no translation or interpretation would be possible. Feyerabend does link the incommensurability of scientific theories with questions of meaning and translation. For instance he says:

> [Incommensurability] occurs when the conditions of meaningfulness for the descriptive terms of one language (theory, point of view) do not permit the use of descriptive terms of another language (theory, point of view).
>
> (Feyerabend 1987: 272)

But, as with Kuhn, he does not equate incommensurability with a total breakdown of translation. For he says: 'Incommensurable languages (theories, points of view) are not completely disconnected – there exists a subtle and interesting relation between their conditions of meaningfulness' (ibid.).

The semantic interpretation of incommensurability has been the main target of Donald Davidson's arguments against relativism. Davidson maintains that 'Incommensurable is, of course, Kuhn and Feyerabend's word for not intertranslatable' (Davidson 1984: 190) and goes on to argue that this type of incommensurability is not a genuine possibility. We shall take a detailed look at Davidson's arguments in chapter 8; at this point suffice it to say that Davidson's view of language leaves no room for semantic incommensurability and hence for relativism. For, as we have seen, relativism presupposes the possibility that there could be communities or practitioners of paradigms who are radically different from us in the ways they think about the world. However, Davidson argues that we could never be in a position to judge that others have or use concepts that are radically different from ours. He, thus, makes it a priori impossible for there to be significant differences and incommensurability between languages. The idea of a language forever beyond our grasp is incoherent in virtue of what we mean by a system of concepts, so a worldview governed by a paradigm different from ours will, ultimately, turn out to be very much like our own (Davidson 1984).

Putnam also defines incommensurability as the doctrine that 'there . . . are discourses that represent concepts and contents that we, imprisoned as we are in our discourse, in our conceptual frame, can never fully understand' (Putnam 1981: 122).[11] According to Putnam, the incommensurability thesis is self-refuting because 'if this thesis were really true then we could not translate other languages – or even past stages of our own language – at all. And if we cannot interpret organisms' noises at all, then we have no grounds for regarding them as *thinkers*, *speakers*, or even *persons*' (ibid.: 114). Following David-son, Putnam argues that a consistent relativist 'should not treat others as speakers (or thinkers) at all (if their "noises" are *that* "incommen-surable", then they are *just* noises)' (ibid.). Putnam also echoes Davidson, as well as Vico, when he argues that interpretative practice requires us 'to interpret one another's beliefs, desires, and utterances so that it all makes some kind of *sense*' (ibid.: 117). To call something 'a discourse' or 'a system of concepts' we need to assume that we can interpret it and this, in turn, would hinge on the assumption of there being a large number of shared beliefs between the conceptual systems. The type of relativism that entails incommensurability or the possibility of mutual unintelligibility is itself unintelligible. If this interpretation of Kuhn's argument and the thesis of incommensura-bility were correct, then Kuhn may be susceptible to the Davidsonian type of refutation. How can we even begin to speak about rival alter-native theories if the practitioners of any given paradigm are so completely imprisoned within their own languages?

I shall argue that Putnam's and Davidson's arguments against semantic incommensurability fail to diminish the appeal of relativism or undermine any but the most radical versions of it (see below and chapter 8). But, even if we were to take their arguments at face value, it is not clear if they can be applied to Kuhn who in no place has equated incommensurability with *complete* failure of translation. When Kuhn mentions semantic incommensurability it is only to talk about partial failures of translation; for instance, he claims, that pro-ponents of competing paradigms 'are bound *partly* to talk through each other' (Kuhn [1962] 1970: 148; emphasis added) and that com-munication across paradigms or revolutionary divides 'is inevitably partial' (ibid.: 149).[12]

Let us now consider the epistemic interpretations of incommensu-rability. Epistemic incommensurability emphasises the divergence between different styles of reasoning and methods of justification. Different paradigms, societies or cultures, it is argued, have different modes of reasoning, standards and criteria of rationality, and we are not in a position to evaluate or choose between them. Epistemic incommensurability is closely allied with moderate relativism about rationality (discussed in chapter 5), and Kuhn's own account of incommensurability favours this interpretation. According to him, 'the proponents of competing paradigms . . . fail to make complete contact with each other's viewpoints'(ibid.: 148), because:

(1) The proponents of competing paradigms will often disagree about the list of problems they are to solve. Their definitions and standard of science are not the same (ibid.: 148).

(2) The scientific vocabulary, concepts and terms borrowed from older paradigms are employed in new ways. 'Within the new paradigm, old terms, concepts, and experiments fall into new relationships one with the other' (ibid.: 149).

(3) The most fundamental and at the same time the most obscure aspect of the incommensurability of competing paradigms, according to Kuhn, is that 'the proponents of competing paradigms practise their trades in different worlds' (ibid.: 150). It is not a failure of translation that creates incommensurability, but a disjointedness or lack of congruity between the epistemic apparatus – beliefs, concepts, etc., – that different paradigms rely on for their respective interpretations of the world. It may be thought that the suggestion that old terms are used in new ways, or are placed in different networks of concepts in new paradigms, indicates semantic incommensurability and failure of translation between paradigms. But this is not a correct interpretation of Kuhn's view. In fact, the assumption, on Kuhn's part, is that we are able to recognise that the same theoretical term is being located within different networks of concepts in different paradigms.

Epistemic incommensurability leads to relativism in so far as it precludes the possibility of having a cross-paradigmatic method or criterion for adjudicating between different styles of reasoning. We shall examine one instance of epistemic relativism based on the premise of epistemic incommensurability in 6.6. For the moment, I will focus on the connections between relativism and incommensurability.

It is sometimes assumed that incommensurability (semantic or epistemic) is a sufficient condition for relativism, for if theories, worldviews and languages are not inter-translatable or otherwise comparable, then we cannot adjudicate between their possibly conflicting truth-claims, hence relativism ensues. But this argument cannot be right. The conclusion to be drawn from the observation that we cannot adjudicate between two or more rival theories or worldviews, or that we find them mutually untranslatable, is at most a negative claim about the very possibility of knowledge rather than a positive claim that there are many rival true theories.

The point can be made slightly differently. The sceptic argues:

(a)
T is claimed to be true in the context of paradigm P1, and –T is claimed to be true in the context of paradigm P2.
T and –T contradict each other (or at least are mutually exclusive)
We have no criterion to decide between T and –T.
Therefore, we have to suspend judgement on their truth.

The relativist argues:

(b)
T is claimed to be true in the context of paradigm P1, and –T is claimed to be true in the context of paradigm P2.
T and –T contradict each other (or at least are mutually exclusive).
We have no criterion to decide between T and –T.
Therefore, T is true for P1, and –T is true for P2, and there is no more to be said on this subject.

To arrive at relativism from the assumption of incommensurability we need additional arguments, which the incommensurability thesis by itself cannot provide. The unstated argument used to connect incommensurability to relativism is that scientific theories and their underlying paradigms are necessarily attempts to make true or truth-like claims, and hence the sceptical suspension of commitment to the possibility of knowledge is inapplicable in this context. The incommensurability thesis, on its own, is not sufficient for relativism.

In may be suggested that incommensurability is at least a necessary condition for relativism. The argument is that the relativity of the truth of rival theories or worldviews implies that they cannot be compared or ranked in terms of their truth or falsity, hence the incommensurability between worldviews is a logical consequence of the doctrine of relativism. The connection between incommensurability and relativism in this construction, while real enough, becomes rather trivial and uninteresting. If the truth of a theory, as the relativist claims, is a function of certain features that are unique to that theory, e.g., the paradigm, culture or worldview within which it is embedded, then, given the further assumption that there are rival paradigms, worldviews or cultures, it trivially follows that such theories are in some respect incommensurable, for if they were not then the differing paradigms could be compared and ranked.

The important question to ask, then, is: what type of incommensurability is required in order to establish the very possibility of relativism? That is, what are the scope and the nature of the incommensurability involved in establishing a reasonable case for relativism?

Semantic incommensurability, I believe, is neither sufficient nor necessary for relativism. It is not sufficient because from the premise that languages L1 and L2 are not inter-translatable we cannot conclude that the truth of the sentences of L1 is relative to L1 only. Untranslatability, as Noam Chomsky has pointed out, may have more to do with the biological endowments of different language-using species than with questions of truth ascription.

The question of whether semantic incommensurability is necessary for relativism is more complicated. Arguments for relativism begin with empirical observations of diversity of belief-systems, worldviews and practices. The assumption of such diversity is the cornerstone, the essential presupposition, of relativism. Observations of differences are based on the assumption that the utterances and the behaviour of alien communities are not semantically closed to us. The Davidson/Putnam identification of relativism with semantic incommensurability flies in the face of the commonly accepted starting point for relativism: that different cultures and communities think and act in ways substantially different from those familiar to us. As we saw, Putnam and Davidson argue that a consistent relativist cannot treat others as speakers or thinkers. But *modus tollens* here will work just as well as *modus ponens*. The beliefs and practices of inhabitants of diverse traditions are not just noises, for if they were they would not be candidates for belief and practice, hence they cannot be semantically incommensurable. It may be replied that what Davidson and Putnam have shown is that relativism requires the assumption of incommensurable diversity, and this is an incoherent assumption; the alien beliefs and practices that are cited to prove the case for relativism cannot be different to such an extent as to warrant the inference of relativism. The issue at stake is: what measure of diversity is required in order to get the arguments for relativism going – and the answer surely is not untranslatability. Although relativism relies on the assumption of there being a substantial measure of divergence between different cultures, worldviews, frameworks, etc., such diversity does not presuppose semantic incommensurability or untranslatability.

Epistemic incommensurability, on the other hand, can lead to relativism. The epistemic relativist claims that different paradigms and styles of reasoning lead to different, sometimes incompatible, claims about the world. These claims receive their justification from within the paradigm in which they are embedded. There are no extra-paradigmatic means for adjudicating between different epistemic virtues or value claims. Hence, epistemic incommensurability fulfils the necessary conditions for the establishment both of relativism about rationality and of epistemic relativism. In the next section, we shall examine arguments in favour of one version of epistemic relativism.

6.6 MUTED EPISTEMIC RELATIVISM

Ian Hacking has proposed a form of epistemic relativism that presupposes epistemic rather than semantic incommensurability. Hacking argues that the truth and falsity of some assertions are inseparable from the modes of reasoning or ways of thinking – or what he calls 'styles of reasoning' – underlying them. William Newton-Smith has called Hacking's view 'muted relativism' for Hacking is not arguing, as alethic relativists do, that the truth of a proposition varies from culture to culture. Rather, he is saying that 'what can vary from age to age or from social group to social group is the availability of propositions' (Newton-Smith 1982: 121), which in turn is dependent on the ways of reasoning available to a culture or in a particular historic epoch. Styles of reasoning give sense to non-observational propositions, and hence are responsible for making these propositions available to us. Since they can vary greatly from one culture or epoch to another, at least when we go beyond basic observational statements, and in particular when it comes to theoretical claims, there is no possibility of having an atemporal and universal criterion for adjudicating between rival claims. The suggestion is that, for at least certain type of sentences, questions of truth and falsity can only be settled within the framework of reasoning and thought to which that particular sentence belongs, a claim that has much in common with Kuhn's approach to the history of science.

Hacking borrows the term 'style of reasoning' from A. C. Crombie, and by it he means modes of reasoning which have 'beginnings and trajectories of development' (Hacking 1982: 51). These include the use of specific scientific methods, such as experimentation, techniques of observation and recording of data, specific uses of analogies and comparisons, etc. With a new style of reasoning we discover new types of objects, evidence, sentences or new ways of being candidates for truth and falsehood, laws or modalities and possibilities (Hacking 2002: 189).

Hacking argues:

(1) It is a given style of reasoning that determines the truth-or-falsity of propositions that necessarily require reasoning.
(2) There exist many styles of reasoning.
(3) We cannot reason as to whether alternative systems of reasoning are better or worse than ours, because the propositions to which we reason get their sense only from the method of reasoning employed. The propositions have no existence independent of the ways of reasoning towards them.

(Hacking 1982: 64–5)

Accordingly, 'there are neither sentences that are candidates for truth, nor independently identified objects to be correct about, prior to the development of a style of reasoning' (Hacking 2002: 188–9). The result is that a given proposition may be true in one linguistic framework, but not true in others, because that proposition is not available to the participants in that framework.

At first glance, it may seem that there is a fundamental difference between relativism and the suggestion that some propositions are not available to all languages. However, we should remember that relativism is often contrasted with universalism, the view that the truth or falsehood of a proposition is invariant across all languages. Hacking's muted relativism denies this universalist assumption, but differs from stronger relativistic views in the scope of his claim. Some statements may be made in any language, e.g., 'my skin is warm', but there are others whose sense depends on being located within a particular style of reasoning, e.g., 'the heat which has the refrangibility of the red rays is occasioned by the light of those rays'. The latter sentence cannot be considered true or false outside the explanatory framework and style of reasoning in physics introduced by William Herschel. We are condemned to relativism about styles of reasoning, Hacking argues, for we cannot step outside our own mode of reasoning, or occupy a vantage point to compare and rank different styles of reasoning; the spectre of epistemic incommensurability haunts all styles of reasoning. 'There is a real phenomenon of disparate ways of thinking', Hacking maintains. The Renaissance medical, alchemical and astrological doctrines of resemblance and similitude are one such example.

The reasoning to the effect that mercury salve might be good for syphilis because mercury is signed by the planet Mercury, which is the astrological sign of the marketplace where syphilis is contracted, is totally alien to our way of reasoning. The propositions used in alchemy are put forward and defended in a way that makes no sense outside that particular way of reasoning (Hacking 1982: 60). We can translate the writings of the alchemists, often word for word, but in a deeper sense their thinking remains closed to us.

There are a few worries facing Hacking's muted relativism. For one thing, Hacking seems to be assuming a sharp distinction between theoretical and observational statements, an assumption that has been widely questioned. Another concerns the relationship between the propositions towards which we are going to reason and the method of reasoning that embed them. How do these propositions make themselves available to us? Is it that we change our methods of reasoning and subsequently the new propositions make themselves available to us? Or is it that new discoveries change our view of the world and affect our method of reasoning? If the latter, then it is the world and not simply a style of reasoning that makes propositions available to us. Finally, what is the status of a style of reasoning? Does it incorporate a set of propositions? If so, and if the truth and falsity of propositions not universally available are determined by styles of reasoning, then we are left with the question of what the determinants of the truth and falsity of the propositions that go into the making of a style of reasoning are. If the answer is: they receive their truth and falsity from other, more fundamental ways of reasoning, then there is an infinite regress. If, on the other hand, we think that such propositions carry their truth-values on their sleeves, so to speak, or are in some sense true a priori, or are postulates, then there are at least some non-observational propositions whose truth and falsity are not embedded in anything else. Hacking has argued that styles of reasoning are in 'a certain sense "self-authenticating"'. He admits that there is an 'unsettling feeling of circularity' in this claim, but argues that such apparent circularity is to be welcomed because it 'helps to explain why, although styles may evolve or be abandoned, they are curiously immune to anything akin to refutation' (Hacking 2002: 191, 192). Styles of reasoning, then, are not so much a set of propositions with a truth-value, but a set of practices that become obsolete, and thus the threatened regress does not get started. It is, however, difficult to accept the suggestion that in any given domain there could be practices and skills, together with guidelines for their correct implementation, that do not involve claims to truth or falsehood or propositions. After all, knowing how always involves a good deal of knowing that.

Despite these worries, Hacking's approach gives us an interesting instance of moderate relativism about rationality (see chapter 5). A style of reasoning would incorporate broad or thick (internalised) accounts of rationality; for instance the very idea of what counts as evidence, according to Hacking, is internal to a given style of reasoning. To return to Hacking's example drawn from alchemy, within our style of reasoning it is difficult to understand how anyone can reason from mercury salve to a cure for syphilis, as the alchemist did. We are facing epistemic incommensurability in our encounter with their mode of reasoning and its context-dependent (internal) notion of justification and evidence. The possibility of epistemic incommensurability and the attendant relativism does not necessarily leave us entrapped within our own worldview. Hacking floats the idea that we can adjudicate between different styles of reasoning on the basis of pragmatic criteria such as success, but the suggestion, as it stands, is not very helpful, for what counts as success would itself depend on and vary with different styles of reasoning.

A more fruitful approach is to compare the merits of different styles of reasoning in terms of criteria internal to them. In spite of what relativists often state or imply, it is possible, within certain limits, to judge other styles of reasoning, systems of beliefs, etc., according to the norms internal to one's own belief-system, and to find the alternative to be better, more satisfactory, etc., according to one's own standards. The process of comparison can indeed lead to adjustments and changes in the style of reasoning we were employing in the first place. Styles of reasoning, like cultures, need not be self-enclosed, homogeneous or unchanging. They can be porous, malleable and open-ended, often in unpredictable ways. We can discover that some questions posed within our framework are better addressed by the methods of an alternative style of reasoning, worldview or paradigm. Changes, even drastic ones, can be initiated from within the previously held system of belief or paradigms and need not depend on the assumption of an Archimedean vantage point for comparison. It might be objected that this undermines the very assumption of incommensurability, by making other styles of reasoning and paradigms too familiar and accessible. But this objection loses its plausibility once we realise that paradigms, worldviews and styles of reasoning are not purely abstract entities totally detached from our lived experiences of the world. They are, on the contrary, the means of making sense of experiences and coping with the world. The questions they ask, the issues they concern, their very formulations are in response to the challenges that a shared world poses for us. The success or failure of worldviews, paradigms, or styles of reasoning, both in their own terms, and in comparison with others, is to a large degree determined by how well they serve the purposes for which they have been developed and the specific problems they are trying to deal with.

If we accept that a shared world and biological endowment can pose similar problems for the members of different cultures or practitioners of different paradigms, then some, albeit weak, basis of comparison between different styles of reasoning and cultural frameworks becomes available. To return to Hacking's example from alchemy, the hermetic theory that mercury salve might be good for syphilis was motivated, at least in part, by an interest in having a cure or relief for syphilis, a motivation shared by contemporary medical approaches to the illness. When more successful ways of dealing with the illness became available, the discovery of penicillin most recently for instance, the chances of anything resembling the hermetic theory remaining a serious contender for explaining and curing syphilis diminished rapidly. Hacking's point that it is difficult for us to understand how anyone can reason from mercury salve to a cure for syphilis, as the alchemist did, still stands and a degree of epistemic incommensurability remains. But once the starting point of the alchemists' style of reasoning, the assumption of links between astrological signs and various activities, is recognised, then the steps involved in their reasoning become intelligible, if not acceptable.

The point, however, is that even the most radical of relativists, and Hacking is not one of them, should be reluctant to deny our common humanity. Despite our many cultural, historical and conceptual differences, we, as a species, are all united by birth, pain and death, if nothing else. We are embodied creatures, constrained and formed by our physicality and by the common world we inhabit. As a consequence, there are commonalities in human thought, belief-systems and experiences. Conceptual change can happen in one of three ways: the interests that motivate the establishment of a paradigm or style of reasoning may change in such a way as to make an existing paradigm obsolete; alternatively, the interests may remain constant while new avenues are explored, because an existing paradigm or worldview no longer serves its original purpose effectively or at all; or simply because human beings are curious and innovative creatures and in their more or less spontaneous explorations of their environment or their idle musing they hit upon more satisfactory solutions to their ongoing concerns. Throughout all the changes, some elements, those that concern our animality for instance, will remain (fairly) constant.

Human interests are varied and numerous. They are, of course, informed and influenced by historical and cultural conditions, but the role of our common biological make-up and the shared world we inhabit in shaping these interests should not be underestimated. Both universal and local elements go into the making of the complex web of needs, desires and expectations which underpin every paradigm, every worldview and cultural framework. There are a great many variations in the way people engage in and with the world, hence the appeal of relativism and the possibility of incommensurability. Different modes of engagement with the world have consequences for the ways in which people act and conduct their lives, so worldviews may be evaluated by looking at their consequences in the light of the interests and projects that motivated these engagements in the first place. All comparisons take place within a paradigm, worldview or culture, so the problem of finding an Archimedean neutral point or a view from nowhere does not arise. Rather, what is common to all paradigms, the brute existence of the physical and biological world, however varied and diverse its interpretations may be, becomes the link between what may otherwise seem to be closed and incommensurable worldviews (styles of reasoning, etc.). This approach to the problem of incommensurability, and relativism, does not rely on theoretical considerations, such as universal criteria of rationality or principles of justification; rather, the emphasis is on context-bound assessments of how well various theories or worldviews meet their own objectives and serve the interests for the sake of which they have been developed. The point is that while allowing for the context-dependence of all assessments, we should not lose sight of both the commonalities in our interests and, more importantly, the one constant element in meeting these interests – the natural world which of course includes us. One problem with this suggestion, the relativist will point out, is that the natural world is not available to us in a direct or unmediated form; rather, it presents itself to us through our concepts or conceptual frameworks. This is a serious objection and I shall return to it in chapters 7 and 8. But in our zeal to accommodate the conceptual we must not lose sight of the natural.

In the last section of this chapter, however, I would like to examine a view sympathetic to epistemic relativism which is motivated primarily by social and political concerns.

6.7 FEMINIST EPISTEMOLOGY AND RELATIVISM

In traditional approaches to epistemology, knowledge-claims are construed as universal, objective and subject-neutral. Feminist epistemology arises out of scepticism about the possibility and value of any account of knowledge that does not take into account the social and personal conditions of its production.[13] The feminist rationale for advocating an alternative view to the dominant approach to epistemology is primarily political; nonetheless it has far-reaching consequences for our conception of knowledge in general and science in particular. The connections between knowledge and the power structures of a society are varied and complex. However, as a rule, access to and possession of knowledge leads to empowerment – hence Francis Bacon's adage, 'knowledge is power'. Consequently, the routes for access to knowledge have traditionally been controlled and manipulated by those in positions of domination through exclusionary practices. In addition, at least some feminist epistemologists make the stronger claim that 'the legitimation of knowledge-claims is intimately tied to networks of domination and exclusion' (Lennon and Whitford 1994: 1). They contend that even the briefest glance at the history of philosophy and science shows that the supposedly generic, universal epistemic subject is, in fact, the white affluent male.

The earliest works on feminist epistemology emphasised that what passes in general for knowledge, and in particular what passes as scientific knowledge, was inherently 'masculine' and 'androcentric'. This claim took several forms:

> [T]he problems to be investigated /discussed reflected only male experience of the world; that the theoretical frameworks adopted reflected the structure of masculine gender-identity in contemporary culture; that the narratives constructed served the interests of men as a group, promoting their position and legitimating the subordination of women; the whole symbolic order by means of which knowledge claims were articulated privileged the male and conceptualised the female only as that which lacked masculinity.
>
> (Ibid.: 2)

Feminist epistemology was thus developed as a corrective measure to the purportedly androcentric and ethnocentric approaches to knowledge. Traditional epistemologists of course could acknowledge the legitimacy of such criticisms but respond that these are issues concerning the specific circumstances surrounding the context of discovery, production and use of knowledge, circumstances which can be changed through reforms in scientific practice and in the existing social and political structures.

Later, more radical, feminist epistemologists have directed their criticism at the very presuppositions governing science. A major problem with traditional epistemology and the so-called 'scientific method' and its practice is that it does not take the views and the experiences of women seriously, often dismissing them in such terms as 'subjective', 'intuitive', 'irrational', 'illogical', 'emotional', etc. As we saw (6.2), the traditional image of science is committed to a sharp distinction between fact and value, observation and theory, context of discovery and context of justification; it aspires to the ideal of objectivity and denies the role of personal goals, moral values, hunches and intuitions. Feminist epistemologists deny the legitimacy of these commitments (Anthony 1993: 206). Knowledge, they claim, is accorded the epistemic virtues of objectivity, rationality, etc., in part because the end results of 'objective' enquiries have been used to further patriarchal interests at the expense of women and other disadvantaged groups. Traditional epistemology hides its bias under the cloak of impartiality and objectivity and is not prepared even to acknowledge its existence, hence the need for establishing this new discipline whose task is both to expose this deceit and to give a richer and more nuanced account of knowledge.

What gives feminist epistemology its focal point, and its theoretical as well as socio-political strength, is the claim that standard epistemological views and practices, contrary to their theoretical commitment to impartiality, are in fact biased, prejudiced or partial. How the idea of bias is understood and questions surrounding its scope and characteristics are crucial, both at a theoretical and practical level, to debates in feminism in general and feminist epistemology in particular. Of the various characterisations of the question of bias, two opposing positions have gained prominence. One strand of feminist epistemology acknowledges the presence of bias in the practice of science but does not see it as an unavoidable feature or an inevitable consequence of the traditional image of science. Rather, it judges the presence of bias to be the result of failure in the proper application of the rules of the scientific method. For instance, Jane Roland Martin points out:

> Time after time key questions that should have been asked and key experiments that should have been performed are

not . . . Furthermore, data are used selectively and over-
generalizations are frequently drawn from available data . . .
[O]vergeneralizing from the data, selective use of data, failure
to ask key questions; these are mistakes in scientific procedure and method that beginning science students are taught
to avoid.

(Martin 1989: 8–9)

But such instances of bias and sexism can be eliminated by the rigorous and careful application of existing scientific procedures, argue
moderate feminist epistemologists – feminist empiricists, for instance.
They maintain that the many instances of male bias (and racism) in
science constitute examples of a failure to apply the impartial rules
of the scientific method. Partiality or bias can impinge on the proper
and rigorous application of the scientific method, but awareness of its
likelihood, together with due care and good faith, will enable us to
overcome it.

The strength of this conservative approach is that it respects and
accommodates the prevailing standards of scientific enquiry, standards which not only have led to a vast increase in our understanding
of the natural world, but also, in their application to the social realm,
have facilitated the development of critical thinking and the liberation
from oppressive power structures such as the Church. The danger
with its adoption is that we have no guarantee that even the greatest
vigilance in the application of the rules of the scientific method would
eliminate bias. Many instances of androcentric, sexist scientific
research and practice, brought to light by feminist historians of science, were conducted in good faith and with due attention to the
application of the objective, value-free rules of the scientific method.

This approach does not dispel the deep mistrust of the theoretical
structures and the metaphysics of science prevalent in radical feminist circles. Radical feminist epistemologists place the traditional
image of science (6.2) and its epistemic and metaphysical presuppositions at the root of bias against marginal groups; they are not accidental features of science that can be eliminated through care and
vigilance. Scientists neglect to question the interests and values that
shape their practices, because their methodology presents itself as
value-free, context-independent and subject-neutral. However, far
from being subject-neutral, science has a very dominant subject,
which in our community is a group of males with a specific set of
values and interests that informs their assumptions and aims (Harding 1993). The prevailing image of science leaves no room for the

examination of these contextual determinants of the application of the scientific method, and hence manages to present its own specific values and interests as universal and neutral. Bias and partiality are embedded within the very framework of traditional epistemology and are an ineliminable component of scientific methodology. Modern science, according to this view, is irredeemably an instrument of oppression because it rests on presuppositions which serve the needs and interests of the patriarchy. The close study of the practices of science, in fact, shows that under the guise of objectivity, a predominantly male perspective on the world was privileged and ideals of masculinity have shaped the conceptions of rationality and of the scientific method. Scientific theories and explanations are gender-laden and favour an androcentric vision of the world.

The radical wing of feminist epistemology rejects the ideal of objectivity altogether, characterising it variously as incoherent, unapproachable or undesirable. They argue that male bias is not simply a question of intellectual error or bad faith. No human judgement can ever be totally disinterested, emotion-free or non-perspectival. Furthermore, all knowledge, including scientific knowledge, is a social product and bears the imprint of its producers. Objectivity is a masculine invention and hence it would bear the imprint of *its* inventors. They go even further and argue that there are fundamental differences between the male and female cognitive, emotional and social experiences of the world, and hence the ideal of a universal and neutral conception of rationality is simply a chimera. What we need instead, they argue, are gender-specific conceptions of logic, rationality and reason. Thus, in doing science or constructing a theory of knowledge we should take into account the individual, social and historical particularities of the subjects of knowledge in their diverse forms and accord subjectivity the respect it deserves. They exhort epistemologists to ask questions such as 'Who is the subject of knowledge? How does the social position of the subject affect the production of knowledge? What is the impact upon knowledge and reason of the subject's sexed body?' (Alcoff and Potter 1993: 13).

It is at this point that relativism makes an entry. Lorraine Code argues that if we accept the suggestion 'that knowledge is a *construct* produced by cognitive agents within social practices and acknowledges the variability of agents and practices across social groups' we will begin to realise the limitations of monist and universalist conceptions of justification (Code 1993: 15). If all knowledge-claims are inevitably perspectival and are informed by the specific context within which they are made, then their evaluation would also be contextual. Reason, logic, rationality and even truth are gender-relative. Feminine and feminist knowledge have their own justificatory apparatus, and masculine forms of knowledge could be justified within their own cognitive sphere.

Lorraine Code advocates a mitigated epistemological relativism conjoined with a 'healthy scepticism' (Code 1993: 41). She argues that the 'absolutism/relativism dichotomy needs to be displaced because it does not, as a true dichotomy must, use up all of the alternatives' (Code 2000: 40). Knowledge, according to this view, is relative to specifiable circumstances but these circumstances can be known and assessed. There is no univocal, universal and culture-free sense of knowledge. Of course, the circumstances, the context, surrounding any claim to knowledge can be specified only relative to other circumstances, prejudices and theories, but this circularity is not vicious because it is in practice possible to decide which actions and conclusions are reasonable or workable. Code draws parallels between her brand of relativism and Pyrrhonian scepticism (see 1.5), where, faced with uncertainty, we do not succumb to nihilistic despair but acknowledge the need to avoid dogmatism, suspending judgement where no definitive knowledge or conviction is possible. More specifically, Code exhorts us to take into account the claims of divergent, incompatible perspectives and simultaneously attempt to hold on to some notion of objectivity. She believes that we can achieve this goal by abandoning the current paradigm of empirical knowledge, 'perception at a distance', by replacing it with the model of knowing other human beings, which involves interaction with the object of knowledge (Code 1993). The starting point of this critical approach is the detailed study of 'sensitively gathered' evidence from the 'mundane' sources of the daily lives and knowledge sources and claims of various groups of people, but of women in particular.

Code's main inspiration and intellectual ally in advocating this brand of relativism is Paul Feyerabend (see 6.4) who provides her with the necessary intellectual armoury to fight against intellectual tyranny (Code 2000: 69). Relativism is the most effective method against the imposition of universal sameness and the claim by the privileged that they and only they have access to the 'one true story'. Code admits that relativism, at least cultural relativism, may have no basis for condemning even the most oppressive of social systems, but argues that 'even if relativism . . . comes up against its own limits in such circumstances, it is demonstrably preferable to the imperialist alternative that recognizes no limit' (ibid.: 70).

The rejection of objectivity in favour of subjective considerations has unacceptable theoretical and practical consequences. Once the very idea of objectivity is abandoned, it is no longer clear what basis the feminists could have for criticising the dominant (male) perspectives and power structures. If all viewpoints are unavoidably contaminated by the contexts that give rise to them, if they are all biased and partial, then feminist epistemology is as contaminated as the male objectivist views and we are left with no firm grounds for criticising male perspectives. If some sort of bias is built into the very fabric of all knowledge-claims, then the feminist charge of bias against mainstream epistemology itself is a biased and partial view. The point is that, if all claims are the products of their social and political contexts and indelibly bear their marks, then so do the feminist claims and hence there is no reason for the 'masculine subject' to take the feminist criticism seriously, and the attack on mainstream epistemology loses its strength.[14] At a practical level, to embrace the possibility of relativism runs the risk of exiling feminist epistemology into an isolationist ghetto. Feminist epistemology was developed through attempts to criticise dominant modes of thinking. Relativism makes feminist epistemology critically impotent and marginalises women even further, for relativism is rightly equated with quietism. Relativism, at best, leads to a doctrine of 'separate but equal', but in practice it perpetuates current hierarchies of domination and subjugation.[15]

Since the Cartesian and Scientific Revolutions, epistemology has been dominated by a distinction between the subjective and the objective. The scientific realm is securely placed within the realm of the objective, while values, tastes, emotions, personal histories are relegated to the less favoured term of contrast, 'the subjective'. We, in the twenty-first century, are still held by this traditional image of science and a world picture which divides everything into the domains of the objective, i.e., how the world is anyway, and the domain of the subjective, i.e., how the world seems to us. According to this image

> The subjective . . . was not just unscientific but beyond the scope of reason, and perhaps positively irrational. Science presided over the public arena where truth could be rationally established, if not by general agreement, at least by experts who were generally accepted as such . . . Individual judgements and preferences which varied between people were, at a theoretical level, excluded from its concern.
>
> (Trigg 1993: 3)

This approach has had far-reaching consequences, not just for our conceptions of science, but also for ethics (see chapter 9 for a discussion of this point). Since feminist epistemology has arisen out of opposition to the dominant view of knowledge, many theorists in this field have tended to react by valorising the less privileged axis of the objective/subjective pairing. Such a position, though, leaves the feminists in a vulnerable position where, at best, their views are seen as one voice among many and not a direct challenge to traditional epistemological views. The rejection of objectivity in favour of a subject-oriented account of knowledge confines the feminists to the very parameters set by traditional Cartesian epistemology. It also runs the risk of isolating the feminist discourse and makes it susceptible to the type of criticism levelled against subjective relativism. The way forward, as Davidson, McDowell and others have proposed, is to free ourselves from the Cartesian view of the world altogether rather than define our stand in terms dictated by that very same worldview. I shall return to this topic in chapter 10.

6.8 CONCLUSION

In this chapter we have examined some of the ways in which knowledge-claims are seen to be dependent on and relative to their conditions of production. These conditions are construed in various ways by different philosophers. Kuhn's notion of paradigms, Feyerabend's comprehensive worldviews and Hacking's 'styles of reasoning' emphasise the formative role of the epistemic frameworks within which scientific knowledge is produced. Feminist epistemologists, on the other hand, call attention to the determining role of political and economic or gender-related conditions of production of knowledge. What these positions have in common is rejection of the image of scientific knowledge as ahistorical, objective, neutral or value-free. Most forms of epistemic relativism may be characterised as a sub-category of moderate relativism about rationality for there are ineluctable connections between knowledge-claims and recognised norms of rationality. Epistemic relativism, as discussed here, arises out of specific concerns with the implicit and explicit presuppositions of scientific enquiry, while relativism about rationality has a broader scope. However, both the broadly defined moderate relativism about rationality and the narrowly delineated moderate epistemic relativism present some of the more convincing faces of cognitive relativism.

7

Conceptual relativism

7.1 INTRODUCTION

Conceptual relativism, unlike cultural relativism, is primarily motivated by philosophical considerations about the relationship between
the mind, language and the world, rather than empirical observations
of diversity and difference. The starting point of conceptual relativism
is the philosophical position that the world does not come ready-made
or ready-carved; rather, we divide it into various categories and kinds
by applying a conceptual scheme or categorical framework. The
point, as Jaakko Hintikka expresses it, is:

> Whatever we say of the world is permeated throughout with
> concepts of our own making. Even such *prima facie* trans-
> parently simple notions as that of an individual turn out to
> depend on conceptual assumptions dealing with different
> possible states of affairs. As far as our thinking is concerned,
> reality cannot be in principle wholly disentangled from our
> concepts. A *Ding an sich*, which could be described or even as
> much as individuated without relying on some particular
> conceptual framework, is bound to remain an illusion.
>
> (Hintikka 1972: 457)

In addition, it is argued that there are different ways of categorising
and conceptualising the world and that there is no sense in attempting
to decide which of these different conceptual perspectives is better or
superior, for such a judgement would presuppose something outside
our conceptual schemes to which they could be compared, or by the
standards of which they could be judged. However, since, per hypothesis, all thinking and judging are conducted within a conceptual
scheme, this requirement can never be fulfilled. There is no neutral

vantage point available for surveying and comparing various conceptual schemes.

Conceptual relativism has often been seen as a cornerstone of the most important and interesting arguments on behalf of relativism. For instance, Meiland and Krausz, while introducing the problem of relativism, claim:

> In one of its most common forms cognitive relativism holds that truth and knowledge are relative, not to individual persons or even whole societies, but instead to factors variously called conceptual schemes, conceptual frameworks, linguistic frameworks, forms of life, modes of discourse, systems of thought, *Weltanschauungen*, disciplinary matrices, paradigms, constellations of absolute presuppositions, points of view, perspectives, or worlds. What counts as truth and knowledge is thought to depend on which conceptual scheme or point of view is being employed rather than being determinable in a way which transcends all schemes or points of view.
>
> (Krausz and Meiland 1982: 8)

As the above passage shows, the label 'conceptual relativism' is used to cover a wide range of claims and consequently it is quite easy to conflate them. Conceptual relativism would be co-extensive with cultural relativism if it were assumed that conceptual frameworks are products of specific cultures, as for example in the arguments used by Benjamin Whorf concerning the Hopi language and their distinct ways of conceptualising space and time (see chapter 3). Furthermore, conceptual relativism, once appropriately constructed, can lead to epistemic relativism, or the view that there are no non-perspectival and context-independent claims to knowledge. For if all our encounters with the world are mediated through a conceptual framework, so are our beliefs and knowledge-claims; and if we acknowledge that there could be a multiplicity of non-compatible conceptual frameworks, then each knowledge-claim can be seen as dependent on and relative to its own particular framework. Hence philosophers such as Kuhn, Feyerabend and Hacking may be characterised as conceptual, as well as epistemic relativists (see chapter 6). However, it is vital to bear in mind that some of the main proponents of conceptual relativism, as we shall see, strongly reject various versions of cultural and cognitive relativism, in particular relativism about truth, and have argued against it at length.

I shall return to the differences between conceptual and cultural relativism at the end of this chapter. First, I would like to examine some of the different ways in which conceptual relativism has been defined and defended. In particular, I shall concentrate on the work of some key philosophers working within a tradition I call Harvard relativism and look at the implications of their views for more general issues surrounding the problem of relativism.

7.2 SCHEME–CONTENT DUALISM

Conceptual relativism, also known as 'semantic relativism', 'linguistic relativism', 'ontological relativism' and even 'cognitive relativism', has been characterised, by friend and foe, in many different ways. In all its variants, a distinction is drawn between schemes of conceptualisation and organisation and that which is conceptualised, organised or categorised. On the scheme side of the divide, we find the following formulations, which define conceptual scheme(s) as:

S1 the means by which we put constraints on empirical data (Quine)

S2 the rules or the principles that enable us to construct objects from ontologically more basic units (Kraut 1986: 399)

S3 the categories we use for identifying and classifying the content of our experiences, or the principles of classification which we use to group things together based on some criterion or another

S4 means of making sense of experience/the world by conceptualising it in different ways

S5 means of carving up nature or the world (e.g., Quine)

S6 providing us with criteria for individuation

S7 frameworks or a set of basic assumptions or fundamental principles (Popper 1994: 33, 34)

S8 'a form, construction, or interpretation, which represents the activity of thought' (Lewis 1929: 38)

S9 the set of central beliefs that people hold at different stages of history (Rorty 1979: 272)

S10 a set of concepts we use to describe reality

S11 boundaries we draw, the versions of the world we have or the world we make (Goodman 1978)

S12 the alternative ways of describing reality. Different schemes give us different ontologies or alternative ways of describing what there is (Searle 1995: 160)

S13 one of the many possible systems of representation (ibid.: 151)

S14 languages or ideologies (Quine 1960; Davidson [1974] 1984)

S15 the totality of the web of knowledge or beliefs (Quine).[1]

Despite some clear connections and overlaps, these formulations are not equivalent. We can broadly distinguish between

(a) conceptual schemes as the principles for combining or otherwise organising the elements of our experience in different ways (S1–S7), and
(b) conceptual schemes as sets of basic or fundamental beliefs we have about the world. They are ways of describing the world (S7–S15).[2]

One important difference is that (a) may operate at a pre-linguistic level, while (b), depending on what position we take on belief-possession, presupposes at least a proto-linguistic semantic cognitive apparatus.

The content side of the distinction also has been characterised in different ways:

C1 The content of a conceptual scheme may be something neutral, common, but unnameable which lies outside all schemes: the Kantian 'thing in itself', which according to James

> is absolutely dumb and evanescent, the merely ideal limit of our minds. We may glimpse it, but never grasp it; what we grasp is always some substitute for it which previous human thinking has peptonized and cooked for our consumption.
>
> (James 1975: 250)

C2 The content is the world (Davidson [1974] 1984: 192), reality, nature or the universe, which is either unorganised (C2a) or open to reorganisation (C2b). The world is found and not made, but it is in Schiller's words 'plastic', that is it has a certain degree of malleability.

C3 The content may be sense data, surface irritations, sensory promptings, the 'sensuous': what in seventeenth- and eighteenth-century vocabulary was known as 'ideas' or 'impressions' (Kantian 'intuitions') and is known by today's philosophers as 'bits of experiential intake' (McDowell 1994: 27). It is 'the unsullied stream of experience being variously reworked by various minds or culture' (Davidson 1989: 161); in other words, the stuff that falls under the by-now pejorative term 'the sensuously given' (Lewis 1929: 37).

C4 The content is our experience in all its rich variety: what C. I. Lewis has called the 'thick experience of every-day life' rather than the 'thin experience of immediate sensations' (ibid.: 30).

These formulations of 'content' are not equivalent. It is tempting to identify C1 with either C2 or C3. William Child (1994), for instance, thinks that the neutral content could be seen as the uninterpreted, theory-neutral reality or alternatively as the uncategorised contents of experience. But this is clearly wrong. The world is not the unnameable, and neither are our sense data. As Rorty has argued

> The notion of 'the world' as used in a phrase like 'different conceptual schemes carve up the world differently' must be the notion of something *completely* unspecified and unspecifiable – the thing in itself, in fact. As soon as we start thinking of 'the world' as atoms and the void, or sense data and awareness of them, or 'stimuli' of a certain sort brought to bear upon organs of a certain sort, we have changed the name of the game. For we are now well within some particular theory about how the world is.
>
> (Rorty 1982: 14)

Any conception of reality or experience is by definition mediated by a set of concepts, so C1 should be seen as an independent account of content and probably an incoherent notion.

C3 and C4 are not equivalent either. C4 is a far more inclusive category than C3. It includes the 'thick experience of the world of things' (Lewis 1929: 54); it is the world of trees and houses, the experience of love, hate and disappointments. C3 is the 'thin given of immediacy'; it is the glimpsed, but not yet identified, patch of colour, the indescribable sound, the fleeting sensation that cannot quite be articulated. C4, unlike C3, then, does not involve the philosophically questionable suggestion that there are such things as pure qualia or sense data. Rather, the thought is that conceptual schemes organise our already conceptualised experiences of the world. Despite these differences, we can distinguish between two broad characterisations of content. C1 and C2 suggest that the world (preconceptualised and as yet undifferentiated) is the content of conceptual schemes, while according to C3 and C4 the content consists of a stream of experiences.

Various metaphors have been used to characterise the relationship between a conceptual scheme and its content:

M1 The closet metaphor: conceptual schemes are like the principles we might use in order to organise a closet (Davidson 1974: 192).

M2 Conceptual schemes are nets that catch pertinent elements from the sweep of experiences (Lewis 1929).

M3 The cookie-cutter metaphor. Conceptual schemes slice the dough of reality or of what there is (Putnam 1987: 19).

M4 Conceptual schemes cut the pie of reality (Putnam 1987).

M5 Conceptual schemes 'carve up nature at its joints'. The carving may be done with 'a rapier' or a 'blunt instrument' (Quine 1960; Whorf 1956).

M6 The artistic metaphor of carving a world for ourselves out of pre-given material. William James, for instance, suggests that 'We receive in short the block of marble, but we carve the statue ourselves' (James 1983: 277).

These metaphors also give different pictures of what the scheme–content distinction is. M1 and M2 are appropriate for the model of the distinction where the multifariousness of the content of experience is emphasised (C3 and C4). The closet metaphor is useful for the version of the distinction where the schemes are principles of organisation and the content something in need of organisation. The assumption is that the world presents itself to us in an unorganised or disorganised state. A closet, after all, is in need of organisation if it is untidy or too crowded or if things are thrown in it in a haphazard fashion. The net metaphor implies that we need to be selective, at a preconscious level, in our processes of interpretation. M3, M4 and M5 apply to instances where the undifferentiated world is seen as the content of a conceptual scheme. They differ, however, in the degree of malleability they are prepared to ascribe to the world. The cookie-cutter metaphor applies more readily to the undistinguished stuff, be it a stream of experience or an undifferentiated world that can be sliced into a variety of shapes; it also implies that there is a single world, analogous to the piece of dough, which we can slice into pieces in different ways.[3] The pie metaphor, on the other hand, presents a picture of a ready-made world that can be sliced up according to our purposes and interests; after all, a pie is less malleable than the unbaked cookie dough. M5 is probably the most restrictive metaphor, for it suggests that the content of our experience, largely, is pre-organised. Although, like M3 and M4, it uses the metaphor of cutting and slicing, here we seem to have fewer choices and less freedom for it implies that nature's joints are already predetermined. M6 is still different from the previous metaphors, in so far as it implies that we can chip away at the given and discard what is not wanted. It gives a more empowering and creative role to our conceptual apparatus.

As we shall see, the different formulations of conceptual relativism make use of these differing characterisations of the scheme–content distinction (see 8.5 and 10.3.3 in particular).

7.3 HISTORICAL BACKGROUND

The idea of conceptual schemes originated in Kant's distinctions between sensibility and understanding, on the one hand, and necessary and contingent truth, on the other (see chapter 2). According to Kant, all knowledge begins with experience but does not arise solely out of experience, for 'our empirical knowledge is a compound of that which we receive through impressions, and that which the faculty of cognition supplies from itself' (Kant 1929: A 21/B 327). The faculty of cognition supplies 'the forms of intuition' and the 'categories' which enable us to structure and conceptualise our experiences in an orderly and intelligible way. As Rorty points out, 'since Kant, we find it almost impossible not to think of the mind as divided into active and passive faculties, the former using concepts to "interpret" what "the world" imposes on the latter' (Rorty 1982: 3). For Kant, the categories were the universal, necessary conditions of thought and knowledge. His goal was to provide a metaphysical foundation for Newtonian science. The a priori categories of substance, causality and community were to ground the Newtonian concepts of mass, force and interaction within a single unchanging epistemological framework.[4] The Kantian theory has undergone much change in the hands of a succession of philosophers. The contemporary defenders of scheme–content dualism depart from Kant in giving, variously, a linguistic, empirical (psychological) or conventionalist (cultural) turn to the idea of conceptual schemes; furthermore, they do not insist on there being a unique and immutable scheme.

American pragmatist philosophers are responsible for some of the most interesting and systematic discussions of scheme–content dualism and conceptual relativism in the twentieth century. Foremost among them are William James and C. I. Lewis. James argued that our representations of reality are always informed by our interests, perspectives and limitations. We cannot make sense of the idea that reality is ready-made or is presented to us already formed. Rather, human beings contribute to the process of constructing reality in the very act of conceptualising it. 'What we say about reality thus depends on the perspective into which we throw it. The *that* of it is its own; but the *what* depends on the *which*; and the which depends on *us'* (James 1975: 118). Admittedly 'the stubborn fact remains that there *is* a sensible flux, however, what is *true of it* seems from first to last to be largely a matter of our own creation' (ibid.: 122). In passages that foreshadow Quine, James argues that:

> There is nothing improbable in the supposition that analysis of the world may yield a number of formulae, all consistent with the facts. In physical science different formulae may explain the phenomena equally well – the one-fluid and the two-fluid theories of electricity, for example. Why may it not be so with the world? Why may there not be different points of view for surveying it, within each of which all data harmonize, and which the observer may therefore either choose between, or simply cumulate one upon another?
>
> (James 1979: 66)

Furthermore, we cannot single out one conceptual scheme or belief-system as superior. Each belief-system should be assessed according to its own ends.[5] This, for James, leads to a plurality of belief-systems, each appropriate to its own domain and hence in that sense true. At times James seems to be going further and alluding to relativism about truth. For instance, in discussing the pragmatist's conception of truth he argues:

> Platonic astronomy, Euclidean space, Aristotelian logic, scholastic metaphysics were expedient for centuries, but human experience has boiled over those limits, and we now call these things only relatively true, or true within those borders of experience.
>
> (James 1975: 107)

He avoids outright relativism by recourse to a pragmatist conception of truth, where he famously argues: '"The true" is only the expedient in the way of our thinking, just as "the right" is only the expedient in the way of our behaving' (ibid.: 96). What is expedient is conceived extremely broadly and in the long term, but James allows for the possibility of ultimate convergence of different accounts into an 'absolute truth'.[6] However, as Rorty points out (see chapter 4), the pragmatist account of truth is frequently interpreted in a relativistic spirit.

Lewis's scheme–content dualism, on the other hand, is expressed in a Kantian spirit. According to him:

> There are, in our cognitive experience, two elements: the immediate data, such as those of sense, which are presented or given to the mind, and a form, construction, or interpretation, which represents the activity of thought. Recognition of this fact is one of the oldest and most universal of philosophic insights.
>
> (Lewis 1929: 38)

Lewis's principal thesis is that human knowledge consists of two elements: (a) the concept, which is the production of the activity of thought, and (b) the data of our senses, or the 'sensuously given', which is independent of the mind. The conceptual side of the divide gives rise to the a priori truths which are definitive and explicative of concepts. The content of the given, on the other hand, is independent of the pure concept, and 'neither limits the other' (ibid: 37). Conceptual schemes, then, are the concepts, categories and principles which the mind uses as mechanisms or instruments for interpreting what is given to it. Objects do not classify themselves; they do not present themselves to our experiences with an identification tag on them. The mind imposes on our stream of experience its own interpretations, including those of the real, the right, the beautiful and the valid (Lewis 1929: 27). The reality which everyone knows reflects the structure of human intelligence as much as it does the nature of the independently given sensory content (ibid.: 29–30).

The scheme–content distinction is essential to our understanding of human thought because:

> If there be no datum given to the mind, then knowledge must be contentless and arbitrary; there would be nothing which it must be true to. And if there be no interpretation or construction which the mind itself imposed, then thought is rendered superfluous, the possibility of error becomes inexplicable, and the distinction of true and false is in danger of becoming meaningless. If the significance of knowledge should lie in the data of sense also, without interpretation, then this significance would be assured by the mere presence of such data to the mind, and every cognitive experience must be veracious.
>
> (Ibid.: 39)

Lewis tells us that the given is unalterable; it has a sensuous feel or quality which is not a creation of our mind (ibid.: 52). However, it is also ineffable for 'we do not see patches of colour, but trees and houses; we hear, not indescribable sound, but voices and violins' (ibid.: 54). The given is an abstraction and should not be seen as synonymous with 'data of sense'. Rather, 'experience, when it comes, contains within it just those disjunctions which when made explicit by attention mark the boundary of event, "experiences" and things' (Lewis 1929: 59). This is a particular feature of the human mind, setting us apart from other sentient creatures. He argues:

> The buzzing, blooming confusion could not become reality for an oyster. A purely passive consciousness could find no use for the concept of reality, because it would find none for the idea of the unreal. It could take no attitude and so it would not be baulked and make no interpretations which might be conceivably mistaken.
>
> (Ibid.: 30)

The categories of our thought are indeed changeable and malleable; nevertheless, they are answerable to the world in a consistent and uniform manner. In this sense, then, Lewis is not a relativist. The modes of interpreting and classifying our experiences undergo change, but categories such as 'thing and property, cause and effect, mind and body, and the relations of valid inference' have had their counterparts throughout the long existence of the human mind (ibid.: 234). And although even these categories are not immune from revision, they point towards the unifying features of human experience, they are not necessary in the Kantian sense. There is a fundamental likeness in our modes of thought, Lewis believes. This commonality rules out the incommensurable divergences that are presupposed by the total relativist; however, it does not impose a tight grid on our conceptual schemes either. In a philosophical spirit anticipating Kuhn's, Lewis writes:

> Concepts and principles of interpretation are subject to historical alteration and in terms of them there may be 'new truth' . . . New ranges of experience such as those due to the invention of the telescope and microscope have actually led to alternation of our categories in historic time . . . What was previously regarded as real – e.g., disease entities – may come to be looked upon as unreal and what was previously taken

to be unreal – e.g., curved space – may be admitted to reality. But when this happens *the truth remains unaltered and new truth and old truth do not contradict*. Categories and concepts do not literally change; they are simply given up and replaced by new ones.

(Ibid.: 268)

New conceptual frameworks give us new 'truth' and new 'reality', and in that sense our ontologies are relative to our categories.

7.4 QUINE'S ONTOLOGICAL RELATIVITY

Among more recent philosophers, Quine has been the most influential proponent of scheme-content dualism and what he calls 'ontological relativity'.[7] The thesis of ontological relativity is the upshot of Quine's notorious doctrine of the indeterminacy of translation – the claim that numerous incompatible but equally adequate translation manuals can be constructed for any given language, each delivering a different ontological commitment, for there are no facts of the matter, independently of manuals of translation, to determine our or anyone else's ontological commitments. A conceptual scheme, according to Quine, 'is a fabric of sentences accepted in science as true, however provisionally' (Quine 1981a: 40), and he tells us that where he speaks of a conceptual scheme he 'could have spoken of a language' (ibid.: 41). Translation, or the correlation of the sentences of one language or conceptual scheme with those of another, is the criterion for establishing sameness of conceptual schemes (Quine 1969: 5). However, given that there is an unavoidable indeterminacy in all translations, the possibility of unremitting diversity in ontological commitment looms large. In one of its earliest formulations, and expressed in terms of what Quine calls 'intuitive semantics', the thesis of indeterminacy states:

> Two men could be just alike in all their dispositions to verbal behavior under all possible sensory stimulations, and yet the meanings or ideas expressed in their identically triggered and identically sounded utterances could diverge radically, for the two men, in a wide range of cases.
>
> (Quine 1960: 26)

The thesis of indeterminacy of translation, and the resulting relativisation of ontology, are direct consequences of (a) Quine's rejection of the distinction between analytic and synthetic sentences, (b) his behaviouristic view of language (BL) and (c) the thesis of under-determination of theory by experience (UT). Quine famously rejected the traditional notion of analyticity, characterising it as a dogma of empiricism. This sets his scheme–content dualism apart from that of his predecessors, such as Lewis, whose dualism rested on the dualism of a priori and a posteriori, and in that sense the analytic–synthetic distinction. In line with his overall project of naturalised epistemology, Quine sees language as 'the complex of present dispositions to verbal behavior' (ibid.: 27). and argues that 'there is nothing in linguistic meaning beyond what is to be gleaned from overt behaviour in observable circumstances' (Quine 1992: 38).

He uses the method of radical translation, the thought experiment of translating a completely unknown language, in order to see 'how much of language can be made sense of in terms of its stimulus condition' (Quine 1960: 27). According to his behaviouristic view (BL), language is learned through a continuous process of stimulation of nerve endings by environmental stimuli and behavioural responses. Observation sentences are the entry point for learning a language.

> [The field linguist] tries to match observation sentences of the jungle language with observation sentences of his own that have the same stimulus meaning. That is to say, assent to the two sentences should be prompted by the same stimulation; likewise dissent.
>
> (Quine 1993: 2)

According to Quine, part of the process of understanding a term consists in our ability to use that word properly in different contexts, and part of it in reacting to the use of the words by others in an appropriate manner (Quine 1960). Given this, the radical translator has to start his task by finding out the conditions under which the speakers of the unknown language use a given term. The actual process of translation, using the Quinean approach, begins by the linguist first noting the native speakers' utterances and the circumstances under which they are made. He then correlates these utterances with environmental stimuli and the speaker's behaviour and forms a tentative hypothesis. The subsequent task is to test this hypothesis, which he does by questioning the speakers under different conditions (in both the presence and the absence of the stimuli he has correlated with a term) to elicit assent or dissent and hence to verify or falsify his translation. The meaning of a sentence in a language, in so far as one can speak of meanings, is what it shares with its translations in another language (ibid.: 28–32).[8]

The thesis of underdetermination (UT) states that any one set of empirical data can support more than one theory, in that rival hypotheses may be equally justified by the same observations. The underdetermination of a scientific theory is based on the underdetermination of theory by experience, which according to Quine has strong parallels with the indeterminacy of translation. In both cases, the evidence available is not adequate for deciding in favour of a unique system. 'In the underdetermination case, we have two incompatible but empirically equivalent systems of the world' (Quine 1992: 101); while in the case of indeterminacy we have two incompatible manuals of translation, both equally compatible with the totality of the speech dispositions or behaviour of the speakers.

The conjunction of BL and UT gives us the thesis of indeterminacy of translation.

> [T]he thesis of indeterminacy of translation is that these claims on the part of two manuals might both be true and yet the two translation relations might not be usable in alternation; put in another way, the English sentences prescribed as translations of a given Jungle sentence by two rival manuals might not be interchangeable in English context.
>
> (Quine 1993: 5)

The nub of the indeterminacy thesis is that there *are no facts of matter* which could determine the accuracy or inaccuracy of some particular translation scheme. The utterance of 'gavagai' in Jungle English in the presence of a rabbit can be equally translated as 'undetached rabbit parts', 'an instance of rabbithood', 'a slice of rabbitness in space and time', etc., depending on the conceptual scheme we use. Thus any ontology, or theory of what there is, is relative to the language or conceptual scheme. Quine in his more recent work distinguishes between three interconnected types of indeterminacy:

(1) Indeterminacy at the level of sentences. This is the original indeterminacy-of-translation thesis which in *Word and Object* Quine defines as follows:

> Manuals for translating one language into another can be set up in divergent ways, all compatible with the totality of speech dispositions, yet incompatible with one another. In

countless places, they will diverge in giving, as their respective translations of a sentence of the one language, sentences of the other language which stand to each other in no plausible sort of equivalence however loose.

(Quine 1960: 27)

He goes on to say:

There can be no doubt that rival systems of analytical hypotheses can fit the totality of the speech behavior to perfection, and can fit the totality of dispositions to speech behavior as well, and still specify mutually incompatible translations of countless sentences insusceptible of independent control.

(Ibid.: 72)

(2) Indeterminacy at the level of terms, or the thesis of the inscrutability of reference. The claim here is that in constructing a manual of translation there are always alternative ways of fixing or assigning reference. This level of indeterminacy leads to ontological relativity, i.e., the view that reference can be fixed only within the background of some specific manual of translation or theory.

(3) The underdetermination of scientific theory. Here the indeterminacy occurs at the level of scientific theories. 'Different theories of the world can be empirically equivalent' (Quine 1993: 8). That is, they can have the same empirical content and imply all the same possible data while remaining non-reducible.

The central thesis of indeterminacy of translation, according to Quine's most recent view, is the holophrastic thesis (1), which states that divergences in translation can remain unreconciled even at the level of the whole sentence, 'and are compensated for only by divergences in the translations of other whole sentences' (ibid.: 9). Indeterminacy of translation, however, does not obtrude in practice because the field linguist inevitably assumes that the native's attitudes and way of thinking are like his own and hence he imposes his own ontology and linguistic patterns on the native (Quine 1960).[9]

In what sense, if any, should Quine be seen as a relativist? What are the connections between ontological relativity and other types of relativism discussed in this book? Quine's belief that there can be a variety of incompatible conceptual schemes or languages and that to be able to 'talk about the world we must impose upon the world some conceptual scheme peculiar to our own special language' (Quine 1953: 78) opens the way for relativistic interpretations. Quine argues:

> The totality of our so-called knowledge or belief, from the most casual matters of geography and history to the profoundest laws of atomic physics or even mathematics and logic, is a man-made fabric which impinges on experience at the edges.
>
> (Ibid.: 42)

We can have different conceptual frameworks for coping with our experiences. Ontologies, our conceptions of what exists, are based on particular conceptual schemes by which we interpret experiences (ibid.: 10). One important question facing Quine is whether we have the means to choose between these varied frameworks. Quine's reply is in line with his pragmatism. Conceptual schemes are tools we use to cope with our experiences of the world, to make sense of them and to make predictions with them. He argues:

> I continue to think of the conceptual scheme of science as a tool, ultimately, for predicting future experience in the light of past and present experience. Physical objects are conceptually imported into the situation as convenient intermediaries – not by definition in terms of experience, but simply as irreducible posits comparable, epistemologically, to the gods of Homer. For my part I do, qua lay physicist, believe in physical objects and not in Homer's gods; and I consider it a scientific error to believe otherwise. But in point of epistemological footing the physical objects and the gods differ only in degree and not in kind. Both sorts of entities enter our conceptions only as cultural posits. The myth of physical objects is epistemologically superior to most in that it has proved more efficacious than other myths as a device for working a manageable structure into the flux of experience.
>
> (Ibid.: 44)

Radically different scientific theories, with incompatible ontological commitments, could be equally supported by the evidence available and we have the choice to switch from one theory to another according to pragmatic considerations. The phenomenalistic scheme, which accounts for the world in terms of our sense experiences, and the physicalist scheme, which accounts for the world in terms of folk physics postulating medium-sized objects, are cases in point. Each of these schemes has its own advantages: 'each has its special simplicity in its own way. Each, I suggest, deserves to be developed. Each may be said, indeed, to be more fundamental, though in different senses: the one is epistemologically, the other physically, fundamental' (ibid.: 17).

Remarks such as the above have led a number of commentators to emphasise the relativistic implications of Quine's positions.[10] Quine, however, strongly rejects cultural relativism and argues against relativism about logic, truth and rationality. Cultural relativism, he maintains, is incoherent, because someone 'cannot proclaim cultural relativism without rising above it, and he cannot rise above it without giving it up' (Quine 1975: 328). Furthermore, attributions of bizarre and illogical beliefs to alien cultures are in all likelihood the outcome of bad translations (see chapter 8). In our encounters with more exotic cultures and languages we acknowledge the possibility of indeterminacy of translation and ontological relativity because 'any one intercultural correlation of worlds and phrases and hence of theories, will be just one among various empirically admissible correlations . . . there is nothing for such a correlation to be uniquely right or wrong about' (Quine 1969: 25); ultimately, however, we always choose our own existing conceptual scheme. We always 'philosophise from the vantage point only of our own provincial conceptual scheme and scientific epoch, true; but I know not better' (ibid.: 25). Is Quine's position tantamount to relativism about truth and cultural relativism? Quine does not think so. He says:

> Have we now so far lowered our sights as to settle for a relativistic doctrine of truth – rating the statements of each theory as true for that theory, and brooking no higher criticism? Not so. The saving consideration is that we continue to take seriously our own particular aggregate science, our own particular world-theory . . . Within our own total evolving doctrine, we can judge truth as earnestly and absolutely as can be; subject to correction, but that goes without saying.
>
> (Quine 1960: 24–5)

This certainly is nothing like cultural relativism, but Quine's position is uncomfortably reminiscent of Rorty's ethnocentrism (see chapter 4). Alethic relativism is ruled out; but the possibility of other types of relativism still remains. In 'Relativism and Absolutism' Quine (1984) attempts to clarify the extent and nature of his commitment to relativism. He distinguishes between various types of relativisms that, given his framework, may obtrude:

(1) Relativity of observations to background assumptions. Sentences, such as 'it's raining' and 'that's a dog' count as observational sentences for all normal observers. A sentence such as 'that's an X-ray machine' qualifies as an observational sentence only for an expert or initiate, so in that sense what counts as an observation sentence is relative to the background assumptions, knowledge and theoretical framework of the observer. However, this type of relativism can be overcome because the 'empirical evidence for a theory is reducible ultimately to what can be conveyed in observation sentences at the novice's level' (Quine 1984: 293).

(2) Relativism to one's language. 'The sentences, observational and otherwise, of one language are the gibberish of another' (ibid.). This relativism, Quine argues, can be transcended because the act of observation is independent of language, even though observational terms and sentences are not.

(3) Quine allows for one type of relativism: relativity to standards of similarity shared by mankind. As we saw, Quine remains constant in insisting that divergences in translation can remain unreconciled at the level of whole sentences, but believes that the indeterminacy is a problem only at a theoretical level and that, in practice, all human languages are translatable. The radical interpreter, according to Quine, can overcome the indeterminacy of language ascription and choose between indefinitely many languages because of a biologically endowed sense of similarity that is fundamental to our thought and language. Without a sense of similarity, he argues, learning in general and language learning in particular would not be possible, and neither would induction and prediction. The existence of this innate trait is explained in terms of the evolutionary advantages it has accrued for our species. According to him

> A sense of comparative similarity [. . .] is one of man's animal endowments. Insofar as it fits in with regularities of nature, so as to afford us reasonable success in our primitive inductions and expectations, it is presumably an evolutionary product of natural selection.
>
> (Ibid.: 123)

He maintains that subjects radically different from each other in their biology could never learn observation sentences or anything else from one another. Our training of children – and even of animals such as dogs and seals – depends on having shared, inarticulate standards of similarity. But standards of similarity can undergo a great deal of change over the history of a species. Furthermore, as scientific theories progress and become more sophisticated, our views on what counts as similar may also become more developed. This is the residual relativism of empirical evidence, Quine maintains (ibid.). We are left with this 'irreducible kernel of relativism', but it has little in common with the various types of cognitive relativism discussed in chapters 5 and 6. Quine's work, nevertheless, has had a marked impact on the development of relativistic views in the twentieth century. Kuhn and Feyerabend's brands of epistemic relativism, for instance, rely on the idea of underdetermination (see chapter 6). Quine's influence is also evident in the work of his colleagues in Harvard, Nelson Goodman and Hilary Putnam.

7.5 GOODMAN'S MANY WORLDS

Nelson Goodman's brand of conceptual relativism is influenced by both James and Quine, but takes an original turn in an important respect. According to Goodman, conceptual relativists are wrong to speak of different 'world pictures', as James had done, or alternative descriptions of the world or of our experiences. Rather, even though it may sound highly paradoxical, a conceptual relativist must accept that there are many worlds, all of which are of our own making. Goodman's position stems from the long-standing dispute between realist and anti-realist philosophers. Realist philosophers traditionally have argued that our beliefs and statements are true or false depending on whether they represent or are adequate to the world or a reality independent of human language and thought. Anti-realist philosophers, on the other hand, argue that the talk of a reality that is completely independent of our judgements is incoherent. The realist distinction between the world and the representations or descriptions of that world does not make any sense to the anti-realist; we cannot even begin to formulate the realist position in a coherent manner, for the only way we can begin to express any views about the mind-independent world is through our representations.

The anti-realist, however, faces a different problem – that of specifying what various perspectives are perspectives of. David Papineau, a staunch realist, puts the issue at stake between the realists and anti-realists as follows:

> Realists . . . think of 'reality' as something which exists independently of human judgement, to which judgement is striving more or less successfully to conform. And because of this, when realists are faced with different communities with conflicting beliefs, they can happily say that all but at most one have things wrong, all but at most one have beliefs that do not correspond to reality. Anti-realists, on the other hand, suggest that at some point 'reality' simply is the picture presented by human judgement, not some unreachable abstraction we are perpetually striving to grasp. But then anti-realists cannot allow that at that point different humans can have different views. For to do so would commit them to the apparently absurd conclusion that different humans live in different realities.
>
> (Papineau 1987: 10)

The point is that if we take the metaphor of the social or conceptual construction of reality literally, then we have to conclude that different groups of people using different conceptual schemes live in different worlds with different realities. This 'apparently absurd conclusion' is exactly the position that Goodman embraces. According to him, there are many right versions of the world, some of which may be incompatible, and none occupies a privileged position. Furthermore, these incompatible versions refer to different worlds, for there is no sense in asking about what the world is like, or what its true ontology is, independently of various systems of descriptions. Goodman calls his position 'a radical relativism', where even truth is relativised to different worlds or versions, but distinguishes it from the unrestrained relativism advocated by cultural relativists – where 'anything goes' and where there is no criterion for adjudicating between right and wrong versions.

Goodman is unwilling to accept the relativistic scenario whereby two incompatible descriptions are true of one and the same world, for such a view would entail the denial of the law of non-contradiction. Using examples that support Quine's underdetermination and indeterminacy theses, he maintains, for instance, that it cannot be true of one and the same world that the space–time points are both abstractions and individual things. Contrary, contradictory and incompatible sentences cannot be simultaneously true of the same world. The equal rightness of incompatible descriptions or versions, therefore, shows that they must be true of different worlds. He argues:

> I maintain that many world versions – some conflicting with each other, some so disparate that conflict or compatibility among them is indeterminable – are equally right. Nevertheless, right versions are different from wrong versions: relativism is restrained by considerations of rightness. Rightness, however, is neither constituted nor tested by correspondence with a world independent of all versions.
>
> (Goodman 1996: 144)

A central notion in Goodman's relativism is the idea of worldmaking. There is a sense in which we are engaged in the act of worldmaking, he claims:

> Now we thus make constellations by picking out and putting together certain stars rather than others, so we make stars by drawing certain boundaries rather than others. Nothing dictates whether the sky shall be marked off into constellations or other objects, we have to make what we find, be it the Great Dipper, Sirius, food, fuel, or a stereo system.[11]
>
> (Ibid.: 145)

We make or construct worlds, or world versions, for specific purposes, but the 'Willingness to accept countless alternative true or right world versions does not mean that everything goes, that tall stories are as good as short ones, that truths are no longer distinguished from falsehoods' (Goodman 1978: 94). Not all systems of worldmaking are equally good. There are many right versions, but there are also many wrong versions of the world, and we can discriminate between them by examining the effectiveness of each version in light of the purposes for which they have been constructed. There are various right versions, and each right version would not be equally good for every purpose, but that does not obliterate the distinction between right and wrong versions.

Goodman's views can be characterised as pluralistic rather than relativist. The pluralist, like the relativist, accepts that there can be more than one true or correct account of how things stand in any domain, but rejects the relativist's conclusion that truth or correctness is relative to the norms of each domain. A pluralist argues that we are still in a position to distinguish between right and wrong versions across worldviews. As he puts it, 'A true version is true in some worlds, a false version in none' (Goodman 1984: 31); hence Goodman's pluralism respects the distinction between truth and falsehood in its traditional sense, or at least aims to do so, and cannot be equated with alethic relativism. One problem facing Goodman, as for all those who espouse pluralism but do not wish to embrace relativism, is how to distinguish between right and wrong versions – how to maintain consistently that there are many non-compatible or alternative right versions, and yet rule out some other versions as wrong. As we saw, Goodman argues that a description or representation is right, and in that sense true, if it fits with the prac-tice for which the version has been constructed. For instance, the truth or rightness of a scientific theory is a matter of how it fits with the scientific practices of explaining and predicting events in the natural world. The rightness of deductive or inductive inferences is decided by how they fit with the practices of drawing inferences, constructing arguments, etc. Metajudgements about fitness of pur-pose, on the other hand, can be made only relative to the system that the design serves. Thus, he tells us:

> rightness of design and truth of statements are alike relative to a system: a design that is wrong in Raphael's world may be right in Seurat's, much as a description of the stewardess's motion that is wrong from the control tower may be right from the passenger's seat.
>
> (Goodman 1978: 139)

But what is the status of these various, at times incompatible, systems? Could we rank them in any way, and if so, then by what criterion? and if not, would we not end up with the unrestrained relativism that Goodman wishes to reject? The dilemma is that, on the one hand, Goodman insists that there can be genuinely incompatible right versions or worlds, and on the other, that there can be standards of rightness and not everything goes. There are criteria of rightness or 'fit', but they are based on the specific purposes that a version serves. This allows us to assess judgements within a given system or version, but we are left with no metacriteria to adjudicate between all those versions that are internally coherent or workable. It will not do to argue that the different versions or worlds are not incompatible, for to do so would undercut the pluralism that was Goodman's starting point. But if we accept that there could be a plurality of incompati-ble versions or worlds, then the problem that Goodman was trying to avoid at the level of different interpretations of the same world re-appears at the metalevel of different versions or worlds.

Harvey Siegel has argued that Goodman's relativism, like all other relativistic claims, is self-refuting because Goodman believes his 'restraints on radical relativism, his criteria of rightness to be version-neutral, and to pick out his version as right. But, by his own scheme, those restraints, those criteria cannot be seen as version-neutral, but rather must be seen as part of his meta-version – and so cannot non-question-beggingly pick out his version as right' (Siegel 1987: 155–6). Goodman wishes to reject the type of relativism that obliterates the distinction between right and wrong versions. But he faces the very difficulty he wishes to avoid at higher or metalevel. How is he going to deal with the relativist who argues that there is no version-neutral distinction between right and wrong versions? Goodman's response seemingly is that the distinction between workable (and in that sense right) and unworkable (wrong) versions holds across all versions, even though, in each individual case, the criterion for what counts as a workable version is internal to the version, and depends on what it aims to achieve. With this response, however, he seems to be offering a version of the world which would (or should) be accepted by anyone. But given his earlier arguments what, at most, he can say is that his metaversion would be accepted only by those who share his particular interests, and this qualification reopens the spectre of unrestrained relativism.

Goodman at times resorts to the rhetoric favoured by the pragmatists, as well as neo-pragmatists such as Rorty, and contends that we try to sell the world that seems right to us. He also argues that whatever world version we take to be right depends on our varied purposes and habits. But in what way is this preferable to the cultural relativism which he wishes to reject? Why is the argument that what is right is relative to our purposes and habits preferable to the argument that what is right is relative to our culture and customs? After all, our purposes are also part of the fabric of the culture to which we belong, and our habits are largely shaped by our customs.

A further difficulty with Goodman's argument concerns the notion of worldmaking. The idea of worldmaking is both ambiguous and misleading, for Goodman seems to imply that we make stars and constellations, in the same way that we make food and radios, and consequently denies the distinction between natural kinds and artefacts.[12] Radios are paradigm instances of artefacts. They are objects literally constructed based on specific man-made designs in order to perform a specific function. Food shares some, but not all, the features of constructed artefacts. Some edible items are found in nature 'ready-made', so to speak, while others require more direct human intervention. However, what counts as food, largely, is determined by the role pre-existing natural ingredients play in the context of both our shared biology and local cultures. We can also make some sort of sense of the idea that constellations are man-made. To call a group of stars a constellation, the Orion for instance, depends on specific cultural and linguistic conventions. The question whether the Big Dipper exists or not does not make sense independently of very specific human ways of observing the sky and the stars. Not only is the concept *the Big Dipper* conventional, in the sense that all of language is conventional, but also the question of what group of stars the concept should be applied to is based on cultural conventions and practices. But what about stars? Could the same argument not be applied to stars? The answer, despite some caveats to be discussed below, is no, because although the concept *star* is man-made what it applies to is not. Putnam expresses the position in the following terms:

> we didn't make Sirius a star. Not only didn't we make Sirius a star in the sense in which a carpenter makes a table, *we didn't make it a star*. Our ancestors and our contemporaries (including astrophysicists), in shaping and creating our language, created the concept *star*, with its partly conventional boundaries, with its partly indeterminate boundaries, and so on. And that concept *applies* to Sirius. The fact that the concept *star* has conventional elements doesn't mean that we make it the case that that concept applies to any particular thing, in the way in which we make it the case the concept 'Big Dipper' applies to a particular group of stars.
>
> (Putnam 1992a: 114)

What complicates the picture is the admission that the application of any concept inevitably depends on man-made conventions. The concept *star*, like all other concepts, has vague boundaries. There are, of course, instances where we cannot be certain of its applicability or appropriateness. For instance, are loosely bound masses of gas stars? Are only glowing masses of gas to count as stars? etc. Such cases will often have to be decided by fiat. However, the admission that there is an element of convention in all applications of concepts does not support Goodman's view that we make stars in the same way that we make radios. Goodman's position is based on a conflation of the sense in which we engage in constructing semantic representations of objects with constructing the objects themselves. To put the point graphically, if rather crudely, you can burn your fingers making fire, but not while creating the concept of fire.[13] Goodman seems to concede this point when he argues that 'we do not make stars as we make bricks; not all making is a matter of molding mud. The worldmaking mainly in question here is making not with hands but with minds, or rather with languages or other symbol systems' (Goodman 1996: 145). But he then adds: 'Yet when I say that worlds are made, I mean it literally . . .' (ibid.). Yet the literal meaning of 'making a world' has exactly the connotations that 'brickmaking' does. If God made the world in six days, *literally*, he did not make it in Goodman's ways.

7.6 PUTNAM'S CONCEPTUAL RELATIVITY

Starting in the late 1970s Hilary Putnam, originally a staunch defender of realism, entered a new phase of philosophical thinking characterised by the rejection of his earlier work, in particular what he has called 'Metaphysical Realism' or the 'Realism (with a capital R) of the philosophers'. In his new philosophical incarnation Putnam questions what he sees as 'the traditional assumptions' of realism, including:

(a) The world consists of a fixed totality of all objects, a view defended by, among others, Wittgenstein in the *Tractatus*.
(b) The world has a fixed totality of properties.
(c) There is a sharp distinction between properties we 'discover', i.e., the world, and the properties we 'project' onto the world.
(d) There is such a thing as a fixed relation of 'correspondence' in terms of which truth is supposed to be defined.
(e) The empirical sciences describe a concept-independent and non-perspectival reality.
(f) The quest for achieving a 'God's-eye view' or the epistemic ideal of achieving a view from an 'Archimedean point' is coherent (Putnam 1981: 49 and 1990).

Putnam finds these assumptions not false but unintelligible, because they rely on an untenable separation between the mind and the world (Putnam 2000: 181). In this new departure, he is greatly influenced by the views of Goodman and has echoed many of Goodman's sentiments on the multiplicity of versions, without accepting the more radical conclusion that there are many incompatible worlds.

His new position, which for a period he called 'internal realism', is defined by the following key beliefs.[14]

(I)   Both (cultural) relativism and realism are impossible attempts to view the world from nowhere.

(II) All our views of the world reflect our interests and values but we are also committed to regarding some views of the world as better than others.

(III) We can both retain the notion of objectivity and jettison absoluteness, by realising that an interpretation of the world or an explanation is correct given the interests relevant to the context of the interpretation.

(IV) There is no genuine or philosophically worthwhile distinction between an agent's point of view, or the view from within a conceptual system, and the way things really are in themselves.

(V)   Realist philosophers (e.g., Bernard Williams) are wrong to think that the very concept of knowledge requires convergence to a big picture. The requirement of absoluteness within any epistemic domain, and not only in the domain of ethics, is incoherent (Putnam 1987, 1990; Rorty 1998: 43–4).

The above beliefs are motivated by the general philosophical doctrine that 'elements of what we call "language" or "mind" penetrate so deeply into what we call "reality" *that the very project of representing ourselves as being "mappers" of something "language independent" is fatally compromised from the very start*' (Putnam 1990: 28).

Conceptual relativity is an important feature of 'internal realism' – internal because according to Putnam the ontological question of what the furniture of the world is, or what the world consists of, can be made sense of, and hence answered, only within a theory, description or conceptual scheme (see, e.g., Putnam 1981: 49). The key point of Putnam's conceptual relativity is the conviction that we cannot step outside our language, our mind-set, or perspective and compare our beliefs about the world to the world as it is in itself. The very *idea* of an unconceptualised world is incoherent. To give any substance to such a view we need to postulate a God's-eye view of reality, but even if such a view exists, it certainly is not available to us mere humans. He argues, 'There is no God's Eye point of view that we can know or usefully imagine; there are only the various points of view of actual persons reflecting various interests and purposes that their descriptions and theories subserve' (ibid.: 50). Conceptual relativity, Putnam warns us, should not be confused with cultural relativism. Cultural relativism amounts to the claim that 'there is no truth to be found . . . "true" is just a name for what a bunch of people can agree on' (Putnam 1987: 17–18), that truth is only a matter of convention, while according to his conceptual relativity, although concepts may be culturally relative, 'it does not follow that the truth or falsity of everything we say using those concepts is simply "decided" by the culture' (ibid.: 20).

> The doctrine of conceptual relativity, in brief, is that while there is an aspect of conventionality and an aspect of fact in everything we say that is true, we fall into hopeless philosophical error if we commit a 'fallacy of division' and conclude that there must be a part of the truth that is the 'conventional part' and a part that is the 'factual part'. A corollary of my conceptual relativity – and a controversial one – is the doctrine that two statements which are incompatible at face value can sometimes both be true (and the incompatibility cannot be explained away by saying that the statements have 'different meaning' in the schemes to which they respectively belong).
>
> (Putnam 1990: x)

According to Putnam's internal realism, objects do not exist independently of conceptual schemes. 'We cut up the world into objects when we introduce one or another scheme of description' (Putnam 1981: 52). For instance, the 'same' world may be described as consisting of chairs and tables or consisting of space–time regions, or particles and fields. These descriptions need not, and may not, be reducible to a single version of the world (Putnam 1990: 20). To show the force of the argument he proposes a scenario where one and the same situation can be described as involving very different numbers and kinds of objects (Putnam 1987, 1989, 1990). Let us take a world or domain containing objects a, b, c. It seems perfectly natural or commonsensical to say that there are three objects in that world. However, according to the basic assumption of 'mereology', a type of logic invented by Polish logicians in the 1940s, for every two particulars there is an object that is their sum. Given this basic mereological starting point, our world will contain not three but seven objects. Putnam calls the first (three-object) view an 'atomist conceptual scheme' and the second (seven-object) view a 'mereological conceptual scheme' and argues that the atomist and the mereologist would have substantial disagreements on how many objects exist in a particular space. He asks: faced with a world with three individuals, does the question how many objects are there in this world have a determinate reply? The answer is no, because any reply would depend on how we interpret the word 'object'. From an atomist perspective, the perspective most of us use and take for granted, there would be three independent, unrelated objects a, b, c in this world; while, according to the mereological conceptual scheme the world we were describing will consist of seven objects, a, b, c, a + b, a + c, b + c, a + b + c. Putnam goes on to argue:

> Internal realism denies that there is a fact of the matter as to which of the conceptual schemes that serve us so well – the conceptual scheme of commonsense objects, with their vague identity conditions and their dispositional and counterfactual properties, or the scientific-philosophical scheme of fundamental practices and their 'aggregations' . . . is 'really true'. Each of these schemes contains, in its present form, bits that are 'true' (or 'right') and bits that will turn out to be 'wrong' in one way or another – bits that are right and wrong *by the standards appropriate to the scheme itself* – but the question 'which kind of "true" is really Truth' is one that internal realism rejects.
>
> (Putnam 1990: 96)

The problem confronting Putnam's position is similar to the one facing Goodman. If all our views reflect our interests and values, then how could we adjudicate between differing worldviews? In what sense can we ever claim that another worldview is better than ours? As we saw, Putnam argues, on the one hand, that we can retain the notion of objectivity and argue for the superiority of some worldviews over others, and on the other hand, that our views of the world reflect our interests and values (II and III above). He tries to overcome the air of paradox surrounding these statements by recourse to an objectivist notion of warrant (short for the Deweyan technical notion of 'warranted assertibility'). The following five principles define the notion of warrant for Putnam:

(1) In ordinary circumstances, there is usually a fact of the matter as to whether the statements people make are warranted or not.

(2) Whether a statement is warranted or not is independent of whether the majority of one's cultural peers would *say* it is warranted or unwarranted.

(3) Our norms and standards of warranted assertibility are historical products; they evolve in time.

(4) Our norms and standards always reflect our interests and values. Our picture of intellectual flourishing is part of, and only makes sense as part of, our picture of human flourishing in general.

(5) Our norms and standards of anything – including warranted assertibility – are capable of reform. There are better and worse norms and standards.

(Putnam 1990: 21)

There is something unsettling in Putnam's use of the term 'facts of the matter'. Traditionally, what counts as 'a fact of the matter' is supposed to be interest-free, non-perspectival and objective. Facts are mind-independent, hence the contrast between facts of the matter and mere beliefs and opinions. Facts are what propositions, in correspondence theory of truth, supposedly correspond to. Putnam, as we have seen, denies the possibility of there being such mind-independent entities. However, if we take seriously his pleas for objectivity as well as his insistence, in (1), on there being 'facts of the matter', then we have to accept that he is becoming enmeshed in the very picture of the relationship of language and the world that he wished to reject. If, on the other hand, we accept that all interpretations are interest-relative then it is difficult to understand what he means by 'objectivity'. Objectivity is usually identified with impartiality and neutrality, while normally we are partial towards what is of interest to us.

1 and 2, according to Putnam, are conceptually interconnected – the existence of such a thing as warrant, Putnam argues, and its independence from majority opinion are conceptually interdependent. That is, 'it is central to our conception or picture of warrant that whether or not a judgement is warranted in a given problematical situation is independent of whether a majority of one's peers would *agree* that it is warranted in that situation (ibid.: 22). To say that warrant and truth are simply expressions of 'communal agreements' is a misdescription of the notions we already have.

Putnam's point holds for our notion of truth. When the alethic relativist suggests that truth is a matter of cultural convention, then she is misdescribing the concept of truth and the role it has in our cognitive economy. Alternatively, she is suggesting a radical revision of an existing concept. This is not true of the concept of warrant. As Rorty has argued, 'the term "warranted" always invites the question "to whom?" just as the terms "better" and "worse" invite the question "by what standard"'? (Rorty 1998: 52). But as soon as we start using the term 'warranted (to us)' the spectre of relativism makes an un-welcome return. What decides whether a statement is warranted depends on local knowledge, historic and cultural conditions and the presuppositions that inform the epistemic judgements of a group of thinkers. For that reason a judgement may be warranted at a given time but not true, or true and unwarranted.

It may be argued that the rupture between truth and warrant comes about only in cases where we mistakenly had assumed that we had a warrant for a belief, and not in all instances where we actually have genuine warrant. To distinguish between thinking that one is warranted and actually being warranted *is* the distinction between truth and falsity and it is no longer clear what role the internalist, interest-relative notion of warrant plays.

Putnam also argues (3 and 4) that although our norms and stan-dards are 'historical objects' (Putnam 1990: 25), they can change for the better and be seen as having changed for the better. The only way in which we can judge whether there has been an improvement is from within our picture of the world, but, from within that picture itself, better is not the same as '*we* think that it's better' (ibid.: 26). The diffi-culty with Putnam's claims arises in cases where the perceived improvement is considered a clear case of disimprovement by those who subscribe to a different picture or worldview (the clash between liberal and fundamentalist, or modernist and traditionalist, points of view comes to mind). In what sense and from whose perspective could Putnam still speak of one's norms changing for the better?

The difficulty Putnam faces is that, on the one hand, he denies that anything could have intrinsic, non-description-relative, and in that sense objective, features, and yet, on the other hand, he tries to retain a hold on more traditional notions of objectivity, trans-cultural stan-dards, etc. Thus, as he admits (ibid.: 21), there seems to be a tension between Putnam's rejection of what he sees as the presuppositions of metaphysical realism and his desire to retain a substantial notion of 'correctness'. Despite these criticisms, I believe Putnam's conceptual relativity, or conceptual pluralism as he now prefers to call it, is a fruitful approach to discussion of conceptual diversity and relativism. I shall argue in chapter 10 that the objectivity Putnam seeks can be achieved only if we accept that ultimately all our conceptions of the world are answerable to the same world.

7.7 RELATIVISM: CONCEPTUAL AND CULTURAL

Despite the criticism levelled against particular versions of the Harvard relativists, discussed in this chapter, their philosophical outlook reflects a deep and genuine concern that motivates not only anti-realism but also many versions of relativism. Although we can agree that there is a world that's 'already there' prior to and independent of our experiences, conceptions and beliefs, we are not in a position to talk about the world that exists independently of our experiences and conceptions. In chapter 6, I argued that we can largely overcome epistemic incommensurability by admitting that we live and believe in the same world and that behind all the many differences there is the unifying core of a common world and common biology. However, as the arguments of this chapter have indicated, this common world, even if acknowledged, may be beyond the reach of our descriptions. Bernard Williams expresses the dilemma facing us thus:

> On the one hand, the 'world' may be characterised in terms of our current beliefs about what it contains; it is a world of stars, people, grass, or tables. When 'the world' is taken in this way, we can of course say that our beliefs about the world are affected by the world, in the sense that for instance our beliefs about grass are affected by grass, but there is nothing illuminating or substantive in this – our conception of the world as the object of our belief can do no better than repeat the beliefs we take to represent it. If, on the other hand, we try to form some idea of a world that is prior to any description of it, the world that all systems of belief and representation are trying to represent, then we have an empty notion of something completely unspecified and unspecifiable. So either way we fail to have a notion of 'the world' that will do what is required of it.
>
> (Williams 1985: 138)

Williams believes that it is possible to provide what he calls 'an absolute conception of the world'. This is a 'conception of the world that might be arrived at by any investigators, even if they were very different from us' (ibid.: 139). It is a conception 'consisting of non-perspectival materials available to any adequate investigator, of whatever constitution' (ibid.: 140). But the problem that Williams, as well as any other realist, faces is that it is logically impossible to give an instance of what the world is like without smuggling in a point of view or perspective. Thomas Nagel has argued that it is possible to have a bare idea or conception of the world as it is, even if we cannot give substance to this conception (Nagel 1986: 5). Bill Child, with some reservations, has echoed the same point and argues that even if we are unable to 'form a detailed conception of the world without using our concepts . . . it does not follow from this that we cannot form the bare idea of the world as it is in itself without reading a structure into it, we just do understand the idea of the world as it is in itself' (Child 1994: 57). It is unclear what 'the bare idea of the world' as used here is. I have a bare idea of chemistry in so far as I know what the subject matter of chemistry is, and also have a vague notion of what sorts of experiments and formulas are used in that field, and a minimum amount of knowledge of the entities involved in these experiments and formulas. But what does it mean to say that I have a bare idea of the world? If the world is the totality of what there is, then a bare idea of the world would be a bare idea of the totality of what there is and not of something else. How could we ever possess a bare idea of the totality of what there is beyond simply repeating tautologically that 'the world is the totality of what there is'? We might be able to make sense of the suggestion that we can possess the bare idea of a world if we think that the world possesses certain basic inherent and hence invariable features. But such an argument would not satisfy the disquiet felt by anti-realists for when all is said and done, we are still left with the human conceptions of what there is.

Conceptual relativists also argue that there is a plurality of incompatible conceptions. The world as conceived by us is not one but many, and how each of these worlds is depends on the conceptual apparatus that we bring into play. Our world is never the world, or if it is, then it is the world for us. Cultural relativists share this philosophical intuition but emphasise the historical, social, and cultural conditions that go into the construction of worldviews. They also deny the possibility of access to any culture-transcendent criterion for adjudicating between different worldviews. The danger is that conceptual relativism can easily slide into the type of relativism where any view, so long as it is sincerely held by a group of people, would be as good as any other – a scenario unequivocally rejected by all the conceptual relativists discussed in this chapter. Regrettably, the solutions to this dilemma offered by Goodman and Putnam do not quite work. We are then left with two options: we might be inclined to abandon conceptual relativism by accepting the criticisms levelled against it, or we might begin, heroically, to look for an alternative which would accommodate the pluralist and objectivist intuitions shared by Goodman and Putnam. Exploring this possibility is the task of the last chapter.

7.8 CONCLUSION

This chapter has focused on the work of a number of twentieth-century philosophers who have proposed views that come under the general rubric of conceptual relativism. There are interesting similarities and differences between the positions of the Harvard relativists – so called because of their affiliation with Harvard University.[15] What unites the Harvard relativists – from James to Putnam – is their questioning of the coherence of the realist claim that there can be a view from nowhere, that it makes sense to talk about an uninterpreted reality. This philosophical intuition or temperament is one of the strongest motivations for all varieties of relativism. What all these philosophers have in common is their insistence that there are no facts of the matter independent of the scheme in which the 'facts' are represented. 'What there is' becomes our world by the interpretive acts of the human mind, through the application of conceptual schemes, belief networks, worldviews, etc. The world does not come to us ready-made, even though 'what there is' may be, and probably is, there independently of our worldmaking.

What is common to them all is the rejection of realism on the one hand and cultural – or 'anything goes' – versions of relativism, on the other. Their anti-realism is accompanied with the acceptance of some version of scheme–content dualism, although each construes the dualism in his own particular way. Furthermore, there are parallels in their conviction that there is a plurality of interpretations (Quine), conceptions (Putnam), versions (Goodman) and world-pictures (James) and also in their attempts to find a way of adjudicating between diverging worldviews, etc., by applying pragmatic criteria. These similarities, however, should not blind us to fundamental differences in their philosophical orientation. Quine for instance is a thoroughgoing naturalist, while in rejecting metaphysical realism Putnam has come to repudiate naturalism as well. Both Quine and Putnam reject Nelson Goodman's insistence that we literally make worlds, even though Putnam acknowledges the strong influence Goodman has had in the development of his position on conceptual relativity (Putnam 1992a).

Despite these differences, the Harvard relativists offer a not-so-unified front against realism in their rejection of the possibility of a vantage point, outside of all conceptual schemes, for surveying how things stand, and denial of the prospect of a 'cosmic exile' (Quine 1960: 275). A second unifying feature is their opposition to cultural relativism – strong alethic relativism in particular. Quine and Putnam, for instance, have claimed that cultural relativism is self-refuting and ultimately incoherent. Goodman, as we saw, wishes to disassociate himself from 'anything goes' relativism and insists that it is possible to distinguish between right and wrong (true and false) versions of the world. However, the distinction between cultural and conceptual relativism is not always very easy to draw. The issue is not one of simple terminological confusion, or sloppy taxonomy. Rather, there is a plethora of issues common to relativisms of different hues that makes the task of classification quite difficult. Quine, as we saw, relativises ontologies to conceptual schemes or languages, Goodman advocates the plurality of world versions or the relativity of existence to conceptual systems (Harré and Krausz 1996: 24). Putnam thinks that our descriptions and categorisations of the world always take place within conceptual schemes and that it is possible to have more than one correct system of categorisation. James occupies a position that is equidistant between Goodman's worldmaking and Putnam's worldthinking. But as both Putnam and Quine admit, different conceptual schemes could be co-extensive with the languages and belief-systems of different cultures. Once we accept that different cultural groups may be the users and bearers of different conceptual schemes, then the distinction between cultural and conceptual relativism starts to disappear. The Harvard relativists, however, wish to distance themselves from one particular implication of cultural relativism, namely that all criteria of truth and falsehood are culturally determined. Putnam and Goodman do so by embracing pluralism but rejecting 'anything-goes relativism'. Quine relies on arguments arising out of translations between different languages or conceptual schemes to argue against relativism about logic (and, by extension, rationality and truth). I turn to this type of refutation of relativism in chapter 8.

8

Relativism, interpretation and charity

8.1 INTRODUCTION

In chapter 4 we examined what, since Plato, has been considered the most decisive argument against relativism – that is, self-refuting – and looked at some of the reasons for its failure to convince the relativistically inclined. In recent years, a new type of criticism has been proposed which aims to show that cognitive relativism is incoherent because it relies on an untenable premise of diversity of conceptual schemes, languages or cultures. Davidson, Putnam, Quine, Martin Hollis and David Papineau, to name just a few, have argued that to grasp linguistic meaning through interpretation presupposes extensive agreement on what is true and reasonable – a presupposition that undermines the arguments for diversity, the very starting point of relativism. This criticism relies on the requirements for translating a hitherto unknown language into a home language, in other words, the thought experiment of 'radical translation'. In this chapter, I shall discuss the ways in which various presuppositions involved in radical translation have been used to undermine relativism about logic, truth and rationality.

As discussed in chapter 7, Quine coined the term 'radical translation' to refer to hypothetical situations of translating a hitherto completely unknown language into our home language. Examining the conditions for radical translation allows us to spell out the requirements and the preconditions for learning and translating a language. The argument arising from radical translation runs as follow.

All languages have a syntax and semantics. Regularities in the use of various speech patterns help an interpreter to decipher the syntactical properties of a language, while working out the way various units of the language relate to the world, and the goings-on in the speaker's environment would point a translator towards the semantics of the language. We would not impute the possession of a common language to a group of people, or other living beings, unless we had some behavioural evidence indicating they understood each other's verbal behaviour. Part of this evidence will be based on what we judge to be a fairly regular pattern of reactions to the vocal sounds they emit and hear. The first requirement for calling certain noises a speech-act is the discernment of a pattern of relationships connecting these sounds to the behaviour of their originators, to the goings-on in their immediate environment and to the behaviour of those in their proximity (whom we take to be their audience). Undoubtedly, the triangular relationship between the speaker, the hearer and the environment will be complex and not fully specifiable. Yet, at least in principle, it should be expressible in terms of a number of generalisations and informed guesses which will be the starting point of constructing a manual of translation; for, otherwise, we would have no grounds for thinking that the creatures were engaged in communication rather than merely making pointless, random noises or gestures.

The attribution of meaningful patterns of behaviour to a group of people and the interpretation of their speech-acts in turn involve a great deal of interpretation of their non-linguistic behaviour. It would be very difficult (impossible, according to Davidson) to impute a language to a group of people without also imputing beliefs, desires and intentions to them; consequently a radical translator will have to assume a great deal about the speakers' beliefs, intentions and desires. Such assumptions, in effect, amount to ascribing propositional attitudes to other speakers broadly similar to ours, because our understanding of what beliefs and desires are is bound up with our experiences of them. Furthermore, the understanding of a language depends on sharing, or learning to share, at least the outlines of a system of interrelated beliefs that the speakers of that language hold. Of course, this does not mean that interpretation and translation of a language depend on total agreement on every belief or utterance; there can be huge differences in what is believed to be true, real, reasonable or desirable, but these differences can be identified only when we assume a great deal of agreement on background shared beliefs.

8.2 LOGIC IN TRANSLATION

Quine is the originator of the argument arising from radical translation against cognitive relativism. He employs the behaviourist approach to translation and meaning, outlined in chapter 7, as the entry point for interpreting a native's utterances. The data to be considered are 'the forces that [the translator] sees impinging on the native's surfaces and observable behaviour, vocal and otherwise, of the native' (Quine, 1960: 28). As we saw in chapter 7, Quine uses the thought experiment of a radical interpreter to make the case for his thesis of indeterminacy of translation. In the process, however, he also argues that it is a presupposition of translation that agreement between the native and the translator should be maximised. He argues: 'It behoves us in construing a strange language, to make the obvious sentences go over into English sentences which are true and, preferably, also obvious . . . For translation theory, banal messages are the breath of life' (ibid.: 69). This is Quine's version of the principle of charity. The principle as originally formulated by Wilson states that 'we select as designatum that individual which makes the largest possible number of statements true' (Wilson 1959 in Quine 1960: 59). Quine maintains: 'assertions, startlingly false on the face of them, are likely to turn on hidden differences in language' (Quine, 1960: 59). 'The common sense behind the maxim is that one's interlocutor's silliness, beyond a certain point, is less likely than a bad translation – or, in the domestic case, linguistic divergence' (ibid.).[1] The principle is needed because without the assumption of a great deal of agreement, the task of the radical translator would not even get off the ground.

According to Quine, the two main types of sentences whose truth should be carried over from the native's language to the translator's are occasion sentences – that is, simple singular observation sentences – and compound sentences constructed through the use of logical connectives such as 'and', 'or', 'not', 'if . . . then'. The radical translator observes the behaviour of the natives and by eliciting assent and dissent from them she can wholly specify the semantic criteria both for occasion and compound sentences. He argues:

> Take . . . the case of trying to construe some unknown language on the strength of observable behaviour. If a native is prepared to assent to some compound sentence but not to a constituent, this is a reason not to construe the construction as conjunction. If a native is prepared to assent to a constituent but not to the compound, this is a reason not to construe the construction as alternation. We impute our orthodox logic to him, or impose it on him, by translating his language to suit. We build the logic into our manual of translation. Nor is there cause here for apology. We have to base translation on some kind of evidence, and what better?[2]
>
> (Quine 1970: 86)

247

This method of radical translation, together with the principle of charity, blocks the relativist's claim that logic is culture-dependent (see 5.2). Quine's manual of translation would impute to the native a logic identical to ours; the unargued assumption is that the translator (in this instance an English speaker) is using a classical truth-functional logic, and therefore so do the natives.[3]

Quine's approach also rules out the 'uniqueness-view' of logic (see 5.3a), or the view that logic is a peculiarly Western phenomenon and that there could be societies or languages which do not use any rules of logic. He tells us:

> This approach ill accords with a doctrine of 'prelogical mentality'. To take the extreme case, let us suppose that certain natives are said to accept as true certain sentences translatable in the form 'p and not p'. Now this claim is absurd under our semantic criteria. And, not to be dogmatic about them, what criteria might one prefer? Wanton translation can make natives sound as queer as one pleases. Better translation imposes our logic upon them, and would beg the question of prelogicality if there were a question to beg.
>
> (Quine 1960: 58)

David Papineau has used Quine's approach to argue that if we are going to translate certain alien terms as equivalents to our 'not, 'and', 'all', 'or', etc., then we must conclude that these people will be making the same logical inferences as we do, because the meaning of logical particles is given by the rules of inference that involve their use. He also rejects the possibility of an alien culture having a logic which simply fails to translate into ours. According to him:

> If a people can be said to have beliefs at all, it must be that they distinguish between things actually being as a belief represents them and things not being so. And as such they cannot but have the notion of negation, of things not being as a given belief represents them.
>
> (Papineau 1978: 150)

Papineau's argument neglects the possibilities offered by alternative logics. In classical logic, every proposition receives the value either true or false, and this is the assumption underlining Papineau's, as well as Quine's, method of translation. Many of the postulates of classical logic, however, have been under attack in the past sixty years or so by developments in deviant logics.[4] For instance, it is not clear why propositions should not be assigned one of the three values true, false and indeterminate.[5] Why could there not be alien belief-systems where the natives distinguish between (1) things actually being as their beliefs represent them, (2) things not being as their beliefs represent them, and (3) things being indeterminate *vis-à-vis* how their beliefs represent them? According to this scenario, sentences expressing the native's beliefs would be interpreted along the lines suggested by a three-valued semantics, and the appropriate form of non-classical logic incorporated into the radical translator's manual. Alternatively, why could there not be language-users who define negation in accordance with the rules of intuitionistic logic, rather than classical logic, and reject the classical rule of double negation?

Similarly, should we assume that necessarily all languages respect the rule of bivalence – the view that for every proposition, either it or its negation must be true? Admittedly, we will have difficulty translating a speaker who does not respect the law of non-contradiction, who makes no distinction between truth and falsity at all, but it is not obvious that languages which rely on deviant logical systems will also be untranslatable.

Papineau, as a devout realist, assumes that classical logic has universal and unequivocal validity and absolute authority, and hence begs the question against relativism about logic. Quine, on the other hand, is more circumspect and is even willing to concede that there may be scope for translating the linguistic behaviour of the natives along the lines suggested by intuitionistic logic. In his later writings, he distinguishes between truth-function and 'something more primitive', which he calls 'verdict function'. A 'verdict logic' assigns to sentences one of the three values of assent, dissent and abstention. According to Quine, 'Two-valued logic is a theoretical development that is learned, like other theory, in indirect ways upon which we can only speculate. Some theorists, notably the intuitionists, favour another logic, and there is nothing in the observable circumstances of our utterances that need persuade them to assign meaning to our two-valued scheme' (Quine 1974: 77).

However, even if we accept that some logical connectives, e.g., 'or' and 'not', may be translated non-classically, this concession does not prove the case for relativism about logic – at most what it shows is that there may be a plurality of workable logical systems. To remind ourselves: relativism about logic is the claim that what counts as a correct formal rule of deduction may vary from culture to culture and that there is no universal criterion for adjudicating between alternative logical systems. What the above arguments show, and what Quine seems to allow, is that there could be a plurality of logics – but not that what counts as correct logic is context- or culture-dependent. I argued in chapter 5 that adherence to the law of non-contradiction is a requirement of intelligibility. If that is correct, then pluralism about logic, unlike relativism, excludes certain types of logic (paraconsistent logic, for instance) and hence blocks the relativist's more radical claim that what counts as logic depends on what a cultural grouping believes it to be.

8.3 TRUTH, MEANING AND CHARITY

Alethic relativism requires that a sentence or statement would be true in one framework or culture, and false in another; and many philosophers find this position unintelligible.[6] The question is whether we can identify and compare the sentences of two languages whose users have radically different views of what is true and what is false. Donald Davidson, in a series of articles, has launched an original and influential attack on relativism about truth and conceptual relativism, the main thrust of which is the denial of such identification. According to him:

> The dominant metaphor of conceptual relativism, that of differing points of view, seems to betray an underlying paradox. Different points of view make sense, but only if there is a common co-ordinate system on which to plot them; yet the existence of a common system belies the claim of dramatic incomparability.
>
> (Davidson [1974] 1984: 184)

Language, for Davidson, is the common co-ordinate system. Conceptual schemes are languages, for without a language we will not be able even to formulate the network of concepts that would make up a conceptual scheme. Davidson's theory of meaning applies the apparatus of a Tarski-style theory of truth to natural languages.[7] According to Alfred Tarski's (1902–80) influential semantic theory of truth, any satisfactory theory of truth should meet the conditions of being (a) materially adequate and (b) formally correct. The conditions of 'material adequacy' state (1) that truth is predicated of sentences of a particular language (let's call it L) and (2) that 'for a definition of truth in the meta-language of a language L to be adequate it must have for its consequences all sentences of L which are obtained from the expression "x is true if and only if p" by substituting for "x" a name or structural description of any sentence of L and for "p" the expression which is the translation of that sentence into the meta-language' (Tarski 1983). This is the so-called convention T, the main component of Tarski's semantic theory of truth. The convention T provides the truth conditions of sentences of any language in the following way:

> 'It is snowing' is true iff (if and only if) it is snowing.
> 'Grass is green' is true iff grass is green.
> Etc.

On the left-hand side of the biconditional (iff), in quotation marks, we place the name of the sentence, and on the right-hand side the trans-lation or the expression of that sentence in the metalanguage; such equivalences are called T-sentences and can be schematised as: X is true iff p (where X is the name of a sentence and p stands for the translation of that sentence into the metalanguage). The schema can generate a T-sentence for every indicative sentence of any given language, and this ensures the material adequacy of Tarski's definition of truth.

Davidson's theory of meaning is constructed on the basis of Tarski's theory of truth which Davidson then applies to individual speakers of particular languages. According to his approach, in constructing an adequate theory of meaning every sentence of an object language L should be matched with a corresponding sentence in the metalanguage that has exactly the same truth conditions. A complete theory of mean-ing for a language, then, will provide T-sentences of the form '"La neige est blanche" is true in French if and only if snow is white', for all the sentences of the object language and thus will specify the meaning of each sentence of that language. Thus, when applied to particular languages, Davidson's theory acts as an empirical theory of meaning and hence its results should be empirically testable. For instance, the test should ensure that we do not end up with T-sentences such as '"La neige est blanche" is true in French if and only if grass is green'.

Davidson's holistic view of language, the view that the meaning of a sentence depends on the meaning of other sentences in the lan-guage, is an essential component of his theory of meaning (and a main rationale for the adoption of the principle of charity, see 8.4). The reason why we must assume that most beliefs are correct is that a belief is identified by its location in a pattern of beliefs and it is this pattern which determines the subject matter of the belief. Davidson's holism, together with the rules regarding the compositionality of language, also ensure that T-sentences such as '"La neige est blanche" is true in French if and only if snow is green' will not be accepted into our final manual of translation or theory of meaning. To take the simplest example, it is difficult to see how one can assign the value true to 'snow is green' in an object language, and the value false to 'the rabbit is green', and retain the conventional meaning of 'rabbit', 'grass', 'white', etc.

Thus, according to Davidson, any language, including ours, incorporates and depends upon a largely correct, shared view of how things are. Communication, or interpretation, across various languages proves the existence of a shared and largely true view of the world. In the absence of successful communication, or interpretation, however, we shall not have any criterion for ascribing beliefs to a biological entity. Hence, we can either communicate and translate and thus share a view of the world or fail to communicate and hence fail to identify a linguistic community which is radically different from us. The failure, Davidson claims, shows that in fact there cannot be such a linguistic community.

There is a close logical connection between the meaning of assertoric sentences, their translation conditions and their truth conditions, Davidson argues. The truth of an utterance depends on just two things: (1) what the words, as spoken, mean and (2) how the world is arranged. Once meaning and truth are tied so closely, then it becomes impossible to conceive of situations where two sentences could have the same meaning and different truth conditions. 'Two interpreters, as unlike in culture, language and point of view as you please, can disagree over whether an utterance is true, but only if they differ on how things are in the world they share, or what the utterance means' (Davidson 1986: 309). Alethic relativism, he argues, entails that one and the same sentence is true in one conceptual scheme, framework (and hence language) and false in another. Davidson believes this suggestion to be hopelessly incoherent. He formulates his argument against relativism, both conceptual and cognitive, as follows:

Pr.1: Conceptual schemes are languages.

Pr.2: For anything to count, and be identified, as a language it must be translatable.

C1: Conclusion: In order to be able to identify a conceptual scheme/language we must be able to translate it.

Pr.3: Translation, at least in its initial stages, requires the application of the principle of charity, or the assumption of substantial agreement on a large number of beliefs/truths.

Pr.4: A conceptual scheme (language) is either wholly translatable into ours or it is not. No partial translation is possible.

C2: If a conceptual scheme is translatable then it cannot be very different from ours. If it is not translatable, then, given C1, we have no justification for claiming that there is such a scheme.

Supplementary argument 1: If we cannot show that there are different conceptual schemes we also cannot show that there are identical conceptual schemes.

C3: Therefore, there can be no such things as conceptual schemes.

Supplementary argument 2: Relativism about truth is the claim that one and the same sentence can be true in one language and false in another.

C4: If we cannot translate without assuming agreement on truth, then we cannot be relativists about truth.

C5: Therefore, we cannot be relativists about truth.

The conclusion reached is that if translation succeeds, we have shown there is no need to speak of two conceptual schemes, and if it fails, there is no intelligible ground for speaking as if there is one. 'For if we cannot intelligibly say that schemes are different, neither can we say that they are one' (Davidson [1974] 1984: 198).

8.4 THE LIMITS OF CHARITY

The success of Davidson's argument depends on several fundamental assumptions. We will begin with Pr.3 and the principle of charity. Davidson's version of the principle states:

> If all we know is what sentences a speaker holds true, and we cannot assume that his language is our own, then we cannot take even a first step towards interpretation without knowing or assuming a great deal about the speaker's beliefs. Since knowledge of beliefs comes only with the ability to interpret words, the only possibility at the start is to assume general agreement.
>
> (Ibid.: 196)

Charity is a precondition of translation and not an empirical constraint or heuristic device. Davidson argues:

> Charity is not an option, but a condition of having a workable theory. [. . .] Until we have successfully established a systematic correlation of sentences held true with sentences held true there are no mistakes to make. Charity is forced on

us; whether we like it or not, if we want to understand others, we must count them right in most matters.

(Ibid.: 197)

The main role of the principle of charity is to render the speaker intelligible, so we can make maximum sense of the words and thoughts of others when we interpret them. In order to be able to identify something as a belief, Davidson argues, we must be able to interpret it, and in order to be able to interpret it or to assign meaning to it, we will have to regard the beliefs on the whole as true or in agreement with us.[8] The principle, in fact, is a prerequisite for establishing that a person has any beliefs, for a correct understanding of the beliefs and other propositional attitudes of a person leads to the conclusion that most of his beliefs must be true. It also has the consequence of making it impossible to hold that anyone could be totally wrong about how things are, so it can be used as an argument against scepticism, Furthermore, the principle shows that truth is objective and independent of human thought and language. In 'Empirical Content' Davidson summarises the purpose of the method of radical interpretation and the principle of charity:

> My main point is that our basic methodology for interpreting the words of others necessarily makes it the case that most of the time the simplest sentences which speakers hold true *are* true. It is not the *speaker* who must perform the impossible feat of comparing his belief with reality; it is the *interpreter* who must take into account the causal interaction between world and speaker in order to find out what the speaker means, and hence what that speaker believes. Each speaker can do no better than make his system of beliefs coherent, adjusting the system as rationally as he can as new beliefs are thrust on him. But there is no need to fear that these beliefs might be just a fairy tale. For the sentences that express the beliefs, and the beliefs themselves, are correctly understood to be about the public things and events that cause them, and so must be mainly veridical. Each individual knows this, since he knows the nature of speech and belief. This does not, of course, tell him *which* of his beliefs and sentences are true, but it does assure him that his overall picture of the world around him is like the picture other people have, and is in its large features correct.

(Davidson 2001: 174)

Davidson does allow for divergence between belief-systems, but claims 'we can make sense of differences all right, but only against a background of shared belief: We can quarrel with different world views but ... without a vast common ground, there is no place for the disputants to have their quarrels' (Davidson 1984: 200).

A requirement of cognitive relativism in general, and alethic relativism in particular, is the acceptance that there could be communities which are radically different from us in the ways they think about the world. Davidson's conception of the relationship between truth and meaning and his methodology of translation makes it impossible to accept that there can be concepts and beliefs radically different from ours. Hence cognitive relativism becomes impossible. Relativism about truth, he argues, if it is to be more than the reiteration of the obvious point that people have different beliefs, would be tantamount to denying the existence of a common ground. But without a common ground we cannot make any inroads into any alien culture and hence have no way of determining whether they do have views on truth and falsity, or a criterion of truth, different from ours.[9]

Davidson uses his argument to rule out, in an undifferentiated manner, a whole host of relativistic views, including the scheme–content dualisms of both Lewis and Quine, the conceptual relativism of Feyerabend and Wolf, the incommensurability theses of Kuhn and Goodman, as well as cultural relativism.

In its original formulation, the principle of charity emphasised consistency and agreement on truth. Davidson had argued that 'To the extent that we fail to discover a coherent and plausible pattern in the attitudes and actions of others we simply forgo the chance of treating them as persons' (Davidson 1980: 222) and in our need to make sense of other speakers 'we will try for a theory that finds him consistent, a believer of truth, and a lover of the good (all by our own lights, it goes without saying)' (ibid.). In his later work, however, he has argued that in attributing beliefs and hence meaning to users of language, at least in some basic cases, the object of a belief should be identified with the cause of that belief.[10] He now distinguishes between two elements in the principle of charity: the 'principle of coherence' and the 'principle of correspondence'.

The Principle of Coherence prompts the interpreter to discover a degree of logical consistency in the thought of the speaker; the Principle of Correspondence prompts the interpreter to take the speaker to be responding to the same feature of the world that he (the interpreter) would be responding to under similar circumstances.

(Davidson 1991: 158)

The principle of coherence endows the speaker with a modicum of logical truth; the principle of correspondence endows him with a degree of true belief about the world. The latter thus ensures that there is a 'fact of the matter' common to different but empirically equivalent languages. In other words, Davidson thinks that we are able to interpret a speaker and hence assign a specific language to her, because we share a world with her. The principle of coherence provides us with a means of correlating the two languages.

A causal view of the relationship between the world and our more basic beliefs does not allow for massive divergence or error. If my belief that it is raining is caused by the fact that it is raining then there is no room for error because the cause of my belief has determined the object of my belief. If my belief were different, then *ipso facto* it would have had a different cause, and vice versa. A false belief that 'it is raining', on the other hand, would not be caused by the fact that it is raining. Of course, not all beliefs are causally determined in this straightforward manner, e.g., the higher-order theoretical, ethical or aesthetic beliefs; but the beliefs that have the most direct and immediate connection with the world are. The more theoretical beliefs, on the other hand, are often extrapolations or abstractions from the basic beliefs. Once we agree that all belief-systems, conceptual schemes or languages share a large number of basic beliefs, then relativism is ruled out. A causal view of the origins of beliefs is also tantamount to the denial of relativism about truth, for according to the relativist, true beliefs are products of diverse cultures or conceptual frameworks, while according to the causal view, the unique world is the determining factor in the productions of our most basic beliefs.

One difficulty with this approach lies with Davidson's use of the notion of causality. The concept of causality, as Quine and Putnam have pointed out, is applied to the world according to and in the light of human interests. Davidson agrees that specific causal relations are often singled out of a multitude based on the interests of the speakers involved. Consequently, there can always be many potential 'common causes of any utterance' – for example, any large slice of the history of the universe up to a time before the speaker or speakers were born. That particular slice may be a common cause of two speakers being disposed to assent to the claim 'that's red' but it would also be a cause of all other dispositions of both speakers. The converse is also true.

That is, one and the same slice of the world, or event, may be the cause of very different utterances (Davidson 1990a: 77). Thus, everything can be the cause – and hence the content – of a given belief, and so the project of interpretation and belief-ascription will not get off the ground.

Davidson argues that it is possible to narrow down the choice of the relevant cause by taking into account what is salient both for the speakers and for their interpreters, where 'salience' is defined in terms of similarity of responses. Communication is made possible, he argues, through the sharing of acquired and inherited similarity responses. A speaker and her interpreter cannot communicate unless they class together or identify the same objects and events (ibid.: 78). Similarly in learning a new language

> the innate similarity responses of child and teacher – what they naturally group together – must be much alike; other-wise the child will respond to what the teacher takes to be similar stimuli in ways the teacher does not find similar. A condition for being a speaker is that there must be others enough like oneself.
>
> (Davidson [1992] 2001: 120)

But he maintains that there is no need to be 'worried by the dependence of the concept of cause on our interest; it is our shared interests, our shared similarity responses, which decide what counts as a relevant cause' (Davidson 1990a: 78).

The Davidsonian framework gives ample reason for worry. A new element has been added to the principle of charity which makes quite strong empirical demands on the a priori conditions of translation. A radical interpreter should not only assume the fundamental reasonableness and truthfulness of all speakers, but also that in their interaction with their environment and the verbal categories used for this interaction, the speaker and the interpreter share fundamentally the same interests. Does the Davidsonian approach entitle us to make such an assumption? Quine and Putnam, in very different ways, have argued for the thesis of the interest-dependence of ascriptions of causal relations. As we saw in chapter 7, Quine has argued that our sense of similarity is fundamental to our thought and language. Without it, learning in general and language-learning in particular would be impossible and so would induction and prediction.

The assumption that human beings share an innate similarity-standard is in line with Quine's project of naturalised epistemology, since for him the boundaries between philosophy and science are artificial and unnecessary. Davidson's arguments, however, have always had a transcendental rather than a naturalistic flavour (see for instance his argument on the role of charity in interpretation, quoted above). He compromises this dimension of his work once he allows biological assumptions to become a part of the principle of charity.

Putnam has also argued that the ascription of a causal nexus is interest-relative, in that whether we say that A *caused* B or not depends on what we take to be the relevant alternative. According to Putnam, 'The truth of a judgement of the form A caused B depends upon the context and the interests of the people making the judgement (for example what the speakers want to know in a particular context)' (Putnam 1992a: 64). He goes on to argue that causal statements can be considered true or false

> Only when a certain framework of pre-understandings is in place, including which conditions should be considered 'background conditions' and which conditions should be considered 'bringers-about' of effects . . . [But] there isn't a distinction in the physical facts themselves between background conditions and bringers-about of effects independent of the existence of human beings with human interests and human capacities.
>
> (Ibid.: 209 n. 5)

Putnam embraces these conclusions since he believes that conceptual relativity is an unavoidable but non-threatening consequence of our correct understanding of the relationship between mind, language and the world. Given Davidson's dismissal of the scheme–content division, the conclusions should be unwelcome to him.

The addition of the idea of the uniformity of similarity responses, the principle of charity has some further unwelcome consequences for the Davidsonian project. Davidson has argued that inter-translatability is the necessary condition for the existence of a language. Without being able to translate we cannot attribute beliefs, desires and intentions to a creature. Hence, we cannot make sense of the idea that there can be beings with propositional attitudes, i.e., thinking beings, whose language is not translatable into ours. In addition, Davidson tells us that interaction among similar creatures is a necessary condition for speaking a language and that communication is possible between these similar creatures in so far as they share a common stock of similarity responses. Putting these theses together, we have the rather surprising conclusion that all language users in the universe must be largely alike in their similarity responses. We have arrived at an interesting empirical result by engaging in a priori philosophy of language! The assumption that all human and non-human speakers, despite their differing evolutionary histories and biological make-up, must share roughly uniform interests and similarity responses may help to undermine the threat of relativism, but it does so at the cost of imposing a highly implausible quasi-empirical assumption on language possession. Yet, this seems to be a consequence of Davidson's views of language and understanding. By accepting that shared trans-socio-historical interests and cross-species similarity responses are the preconditions of language possession, we impose a questionable degree of homogeneity on the speakers of all languages – homogeneity that does not stop at the level of ascription of beliefs, desires and truth but also intrudes into the biological substratum. It may be objected that Davidson's arguments are meant to apply to human languages only, and hence counter-arguments, using hypothetical speakers from other species, do not meet their target. This could be a good response were it not for Davidson's categorical statement that for something to be a language – and not just a human language – it must be translatable into ours (Pr.2).

8.5 CONCEPTUAL SCHEMES AND LANGUAGES

Even if we put aside the above objections to Davidson's extended principle of charity, we still can detect several questionable assumptions in the schematised version of his argument against relativism (pp. 252–3). I shall examine two:

Pr.1: Conceptual schemes are languages.
Pr.2: For anything to count as a language it must be translatable into our language.

The discussion will also touch upon a third questionable premise:

Pr.4: A language is either translatable into ours or it is not.[11]

The straightforward identification of conceptual schemes with languages is too facile. Conceptual schemes can be seen as means of organising, categorising and systematising our experiences and languages as the means for giving expression to these categories. At first glance, this objection may seem trivial, as Davidson could reply that a language is the only means of individuating a conceptual scheme and hence the distinction between a language and a conceptual scheme is spurious. His reply is anthropocentric, as it excludes the possibility that animals may possess cognitive schemes. It is plausible to assume that animals, particularly higher mammals, organise, categorise and systematise their experiences. If this is right then it is unreasonable to claim that simply because these are non-linguistic creatures they cannot possess conceptual schemes. Davidson objects to the claim that conceptual schemes are the means, not necessarily linguistic, of organising and categorising a stream of experience. He argues that whereas it makes sense to say that one can organise a group of things, it does not make sense to say that one is organising a single thing such as experience. This reply seems to beg the question about the nature of unorganised experience. It is sufficient for our claim to accept that either (1) data, sensory input, information, etc., reach the senses in a jumbled fashion and a cognitive scheme is the means by which they are packaged and made sense of, or (2) there is a continuum of sense experiences, information input, etc., which is then divided up and categorised. Davidson may object that the above account does not provide us with a criterion for identifying and individuating a conceptual scheme. We may be able, at least in principle, to individuate conceptual schemes that are expressed in a linguistic form, but the claim that conceptual schemes are non- or pre-linguistic leaves us with no criterion for their identification or individuation. This may well be true – we may never be able to find out what type of a conceptual scheme bats have – and this may be part of the reason why we can never know what it is like to be a bat.[12] However, the fact that we cannot conceive what the conceptual schemes of other species of animals may be does not undermine the plausibility of the claim that there could be such schemes, as the evidence for the existence of such schemes can come indirectly from observations of their behaviour.

Davidson has an even stronger objection to the suggestion that conceptual schemes are non- or pre-linguistic. In attributing a conceptual scheme to a living organism we are implying that the organism is capable of having some (maybe very primitive) concepts and hence a modicum of thought or mindedness. Davidson, however, maintains that 'only creatures with a language can think' (Davidson 2001: 96), so language possession becomes a necessary condition for possessing a conceptual scheme. This anthropocentric claim is unnecessarily and unreasonably strong. Observations of the behaviour of some primates give us ample evidence for attributing goals and plans to them, (e.g., when they improvise tools to secure a piece of food), which in turn shows that they are capable of thought, be it at a very rudimentary level. Thus, Davidson has failed to establish convincingly the first premise (Pr.1) of his argument against the very idea of a conceptual scheme.

The second premise (Pr.2) states that translatability into our language is a condition for language, i.e., if we cannot interpret and translate the verbal and non-verbal behaviour of certain creatures then we would have no basis for attributing a language to them. The premise can be given a strong and weak interpretation. Taken at face value, Davidson seems to be making an a priori claim about all languages (i.e., for *anything* to count as a language it must be translatable into our language). The weak interpretation restricts the scope of his claim to human languages only. The stronger claim is untenable. Imagine the following scenario:

A spaceship lands in Times Square, several bizarre-looking creatures descend from it and engage in very complicated behaviour involving the manipulation of what look like hand-held instruments and the utterance of certain complex and, to human ears, strange sounds. Other spaceships arrive and more of these creatures congregate in New York carrying out amazing feats, such as affecting the biosphere in the immediate vicinity of the landing area. The combined forces of the greatest philosophers, linguists, and psychologists in New York do their utmost to translate and interpret the alien vocalisations, with no success; this despite having ample opportunity to observe and record the alien behaviour.

Given the intelligibility of the above scenario, do we have a basis for claiming that the aliens do not have a language? I think not. The aliens' advanced technology, which is an indication of a highly developed intelligence and consciousness, and their general demeanour give us a strong ground for attributing the possession of a language to them. Translatability into our language is not the sole criterion of language. Furthermore, Davidson does not distinguish between the learnability and the translatability of languages – there could be languages whose sentences do not map in any simple way into English, French, Russian, etc., and yet remain learnable. The requirements for acquiring a second language are not the same as the requirements for translating that language; learning a language through translation is a very different experience from learning it as a first language. To accept that a language may be untranslatable is not equivalent to the claim that it is unlearnable. Furthermore, it is not at all obvious that in learning a language from scratch we need to apply the principle of charity to the extent that Davidson recommends. To make translation into our language a criterion of languagehood, or conformity to our patterns of behaviour a precondition of interpretive success, is to impose artificial limits on our conceptual and behavioural possibilities.

Some of Davidson's arguments on the conditions of translation will be tenable if Pr.2 is given a weak interpretation – if its scope is restricted to human languages only. For instance, in discussing the way radical translation can get off the ground, he argues that we have to assume that the subjects of our translation share our basic, core, beliefs, i.e., those beliefs that we most stubbornly hold and which are central to our whole worldview. Core beliefs are the simple beliefs that are caused by the goings-on in the world. They are the non-explicit assumptions that inform all our judgements. The stronger interpretation of Pr.2 implies that such beliefs are shared by all language users. It is implausible to assume that creatures biologically distinct from us, inhabiting environments substantially different from ours, will have the same core beliefs as humans do. Davidson's arguments, then, despite appearances to the contrary, should be interpreted as applying to human languages only. The weaker interpretation of Pr.2 does have some plausibility. As has been argued in previous chapters, underlying the many differences, beyond all diversity, we are all of one world – this world – and share the same biological make-up. It is a reasonable assumption that there would be a stock of shared beliefs among the speakers of different languages. However, Davidson seems to assume that the core beliefs of all speakers will completely overlap. This, together with Davidson's holistic view of language, gives us Pr.4, or the argument against the possibility of partial failure of translation. But even in considering the more restricted class of human languages, is it plausible to assume that all languages share the same core beliefs? We live in a world of great ecological and environmental diversity. Human societies, at least up to quite recently, exploited their environments in hugely diverse manners, from hunter–gathering societies, to farming communities, to industrialised societies. What is most salient to the inhabitant of the Amazon jungle may not be always salient to the inhabitants of Northern Europe and vice versa. If the core or basic beliefs are caused by how things are in the world, then radically different environments (e.g., the monsoon countries of the Indian sub-continent compared to the sub-Saharan desert) will give rise to *some* differences in the stock of core beliefs, which in turn can lead to partial failures of translation.

If the above arguments are correct, then Davidson has failed to show that the idea of a conceptual scheme is incoherent. Nor has he proven the unintelligibility of relativism about truth. As we saw, by applying the principle of charity the radical translator ensures that speakers of other languages agree with her on the truth and falsity of their most basic beliefs. She thus ensures that there is a substantial degree of agreement across different belief-systems or languages. The assumption of such wide-ranging agreement is neither warranted nor desirable. There are many instances where we can make better sense of a person's utterances by attributing false beliefs to them. This is the criticism levelled at Davidson by Richard Grandy in his development of his alternative 'principle of humanity'.

8.6 RATIONALITY AND HUMANITY

The principle of humanity, originally formulated by Richard Grandy, has been proposed as an alternative to the principle of charity. Grandy suggests that, at least in some situations of radical translation, considerations of rationality advise us to ascribe false beliefs to our subjects of interpretations. Take the following scenario:

> Suppose Paul has just arrived at a party and asserts: 'The man with a martini is a philosopher'. And suppose that the facts are that there is a man [let's call him Biff] in plain view who is drinking water from a martini glass and that he is not a philosopher. Suppose also that in fact there is only one man at the party drinking martini, that he is a philosopher, and that he is out of sight [let's call him Ludwig].
>
> (Grandy 1973: 445)

Using the principle of charity as our guideline, we have to conclude that Ludwig is a philosopher since this will make Paul's statements true. However, what Paul was asserting was the false statement that Biff, or the man drinking water from a Martini glass, is a philosopher. So the application of the principle of charity prevents us from interpreting Paul's statement correctly. What we need to do, in this and many other instances, according to Grandy, is to place ourselves in Paul's shoes and try to imagine what we would be saying or thinking in similar circumstances. The conclusion Grandy draws is that we interpret other people's utterances in such a way that they make sense to us, even if this means attributing false beliefs to them. This is the principle of humanity according to which:

> If a translation tells us that the other person's beliefs and
> desires are connected in a way that is too bizarre for us
> to make sense of, then the translation is useless for our pur-
> poses. So we have, as a pragmatic constraint on translation,
> the condition that the imparted pattern of relation among
> beliefs, desires and the world be as similar to our own as
> possible.
>
> (Ibid.: 443)

The principle of humanity enjoins us to interpret the utterances and
behaviour of others in such a way as to make the connections between their speech, beliefs and desires rational by our standards. The
underlying assumption is that we can make sense of other people's
patterns of beliefs, desires and actions only if we assume them to be
similar to ours. Furthermore, in so far as it is presumed that, by and
large, 'we' are rational it follows that others also must, by and large,
be rational.

The principle of humanity requires us to ascribe both behavioural
and cognitive rationality – that is rationality both in action and
thought – to those whose language and behaviour we are interpreting.
In attributing behavioural rationality, we are assuming that the subjects of our interpretations have desires, plans and goals which they
aim to achieve by appropriate and relevant behaviour. By attributing
cognitive rationality we are assuming that they engage in reasoning
using the inductive and deductive method, that they aim to be consistent and largely are, and that they make use of justificatory principles
and procedures (similar to ours) in establishing their beliefs.

The principle of humanity can be given a weak (minimal) and a
strong (maximal) interpretation. In its strong sense, the wholesale
application of the principle would turn the members of other cultures
into dull replicas of idealised models of the Western rational man. In
Western societies actions are often seen as rational, or optimising
rationality, if they involve the choice of the best means for a particular end. However, judgements of what constitutes the best means to a
given end are dictated by the circumstances of a highly technological
urban lifestyle, where there is a sharp distinction between the sacred
and the profane, work and play, the public and the private and where
great emphasis is placed on material success. This ideal of behavioural
rationality was developed within the context of Western industrialised
societies, which are distinguished from many others by their advanced
scientific and technological knowledge and by their free-market econ-
omies, where efficiency, punctuality, productivity and competitiveness

are all seen as highly laudable virtues. Such ideals cannot easily be projected onto non-industrialised societies the members of which often tend to have very different priorities and goals. Furthermore, as we saw in chapter 5, even in Western societies, the idealised models of rationality bear little resemblance to how human beings actually behave or think. Thus the principle of humanity interpreted in the strong sense places unwarranted restrictions on our understanding and interpretation of human behaviour.

The weaker interpretation of the principle of humanity, on the other hand, allows for substantial dissimilarities between cultures and societies, and is consequently inadequate for ruling out relativism about rationality. In this weaker version, the principle simply enjoins us not to ascribe disagreement where we cannot explain how such a disagreement or error could have come about. Thus, if we were able to give an account of the alien patterns of reasoning or action, however incompatible with ours they may be, we would be satisfying the requirement of this weaker version of the principle. By doing so, however, we would rule out the possibility of irrationality. Grandy argues that 'the purpose of translation is to enable the translator to make the best possible predictions and to offer the best possible explanation of the behaviour of the translatee' (ibid.: 447). However, this does not require us to attribute to other people our standards of rationality, or even a pattern of beliefs and desires very similar to our own. The point is illustrated when we look at the work of psychiatrists who not only interpret the behaviour and utterances of their severely psychotic patients but also succeed in making correct predictions about their behaviour. The overall pattern of the patients' beliefs and desires frequently would not resemble ours very closely, otherwise they would not be considered abnormal. Furthermore, no assumptions about the patient's rationality can be made; if anything, a psychotic patient is often seen as a paradigm case of irrationality. The following extract taken from a session between a patient suffering from schizophrenia and his doctor demonstrates the point:

Dr: How are you at the moment?
P: I felt very afraid to come here, this morning
Dr: Oh why?
P: Well because I think everyone hates me
Dr: yeah
P: An doesn't like me because I'm <u>God right</u> they (want) they are (.) against me I can't give them what they want . . .

P: and people you know sometimes they walk past me and they look at me and they spit on the floor to insult me . . . an when they walk past me I notice that as well when(ever) I'm walking on the street I feel uncomfortable and unsafe . . . so I try to stay indoors most of the time

Somewhat later . . .

P: Why don't people believe me doctor when I say I'm God . . . so do you believe what I'm telling you. Even when I was working in . . . I asked my supervisor because she was dealing with the psychiatry people an do do they exist that there are people that are causing this eh sickness.

(McCabe *et al.* 2003)

We, like the doctor, have little difficulty in interpreting and understanding what the patient is saying. Of course, we implicitly assume some basic similarities between the patient and ourselves, at least in so far as we are attributing beliefs and desires and other intentional states to her, but these similarities exist in virtue of our common humanity and not because of a common rationality. We also have an understanding of the patient's psychological states such as feeling insulted and feeling ill. Our interpretation is also based on our beliefs about mental illness. The successful interpretation of the patient's behaviour, however, does not presuppose her rationality or any *close* resemblance between the patient's and the interpreter's patterns of beliefs and desires. Thus the link between rationality and successful interpretation breaks down. It may be objected that the above is not a situation of radical translation, that the psychiatrist, the patient and we already share a home language. But Grandy's principle of humanity, and Davidson's principle of charity, are not simply devices for translating unknown languages – they are proposed as necessary tools for interpreting and understanding *all* speech behaviours.[13]

Grandy's principle of humanity, when interpreted in the strong sense, rules out relativism about rationality but at the price of postulating implausible uniformity between cultures and people. In its weaker version, it fails to allow for irrationality. Furthermore, Grandy fails to explain how it is that we can identify certain types of behaviour as irrational. To be able to distinguish between rational and irrational behaviour we need to interpret them both. Ascriptions of irrationality are just as much the outcome of a long chain of interpretation of the verbal and non-verbal behaviour of the subject as are ascriptions of rationality.

8.7 CONCLUSION

In this chapter we have examined some influential contemporary arguments, using the thought experiment of radical translation, against a variety of relativistic positions and found them to be unconvincing. What should be conceded, however, is that when translating or learning a completely alien language, or when attempting to interpret the most bizarre and seemingly irrational behaviour, we are still obliged to make *some* (maybe provisional) assumptions about the subjects of our interpretation. Without a very loose interpretative framework it is difficult to know how we can start the task of translation, and inevitably the elements of the framework will rely on our parochial cognitive apparatus and cultural assumptions. We will have to assume that the behaviour under consideration (verbal or otherwise) *is intelligible* in the broadest possible sense, which of course means intelligible from our point of view and by our own lights. An alien pattern of behaviour or language can become intelligible to us only when we find an entry point into their system of thought or action. But such entry points may be numerous and varied. I have argued (see 5.4) that we must assume that, by and large, our subjects of interpretation will avoid contradictions (but of course, as we know there are many exceptions to this rule). In interpreting the behaviour of living beings we will also make some assumptions about their physical needs and wants – often based on our own experiences. In addition, we shall assume that we inhabit the same physical world and are reacting to the 'same' physical events and goings-on, however variously they may be interpreted.

These provisional assumptions will provide us with entry points to other points of view, languages and conceptual schemes. When attempting to interpret other human beings, our common animality – our genetic, biological and psychological make-up – provides us with a variety of points of contact. In chapter 3, we looked at some anthropological data on common features across cultures. The commonality required for making other human beings intelligible by our standards need not be as extensive as that listed in 3.3. A small number of basic assumptions will suffice. Facts of physical birth, death, hunger and thirst, sleep and wakefulness, love and desire, happiness and grief, pain and pleasure give us enough points of contact to make at least some of our behaviour mutually intelligible and hence provide us with entry points for interpretation. The relativist will have to agree that the assumption of a significant degree of overlap between our differing belief-systems is necessary for mutual understanding. To return to the example of the Azande belief in witchcraft (discussed in 5.3b), in interpreting the Azande we accept that we and the Azande have roughly similar beliefs as to what counts as an illness and misfortune, and a (broadly similar) conception of causality. The overlap between the Azande and Western beliefs and conceptions does not need to be complete; indeed there may be, and probably are, substantial differences, including differences in the core or basic beliefs. In particular, each belief-system may have a different explanation and hence conception of what they judge to be the same physical event (e.g., a tree falling on a hut and killing its inhabitants). The Western outlook, influenced by science, would explain the event as an unfortunate accident caused by the physical laws governing trees, as well as everything else in nature. The Azande, on the other hand, would in part accept this explanation, but add that further forces were at work, e.g., that the ill will of the witches in the neighbourhood was responsible for causing the exact conditions that led to the death of these particular persons. For instance, they would question why all the inhabitants of the hut should have moved uncharacteristically into one particular corner at that particular moment. Furthermore, the role that the common beliefs and the concepts play within their respective framework can also be quite different. For instance, the concepts of *witchcraft* and *magic* play an explanatory role in the Azande accounts of the natural world, which is absent from the Western accounts. Thus conceptual overlap does not preclude deep diversity.

We do not, however, require either a stable a priori bridgehead or blanket charity in order to understand each other. Our humanity is not a principle, it simply is. All we need is the assumption of some overlap and family resemblance. As Ernest Gellner has pointed out:

> It is an interesting fact about the world we actually live in that no anthropologist, to my knowledge, has come back from a field trip with the following report: *their* concepts are *so* alien that it is impossible to describe their land tenure, their kinship system, their ritual . . . As far as I know, there is no record of such a total admission of failure.
>
> (Gellner 1982: 185)

There are cases of partial incomprehension, for instance when the West Africans talk about washing their souls, or when an Ethiopian old man asks Dan Sperber to hunt for the dragon with the golden heart (Sperber 1982: 149). But such partial failures of intelligibility simply highlight the extent of agreement and understanding.

Once we start to traverse the vast distances of the Universe, in our thought experiments if not in fact, we begin to lose hold of these common points. It is intellectual hubris worthy only of the greats in philosophy to assume that all thinking beings will necessarily be language users and hence transparent to us. All human languages are inter-translatable but not because of any a priori constraints on what counts as a language; they are translatable because they are *human* languages. But we also should not forget that perfect translation is never possible. Some important shades of meaning, colour and nuance are lost in most translations. With patience and empathy we can understand the behaviour of others, including those distant from us by cultural norms, historical conditions or psychological make-up. We can even interpret and ultimately come to understand those who have become distanced from the routine and ordinary. If relativism requires untranslatability in language and incoherence in behaviour, then the physical facts of our existence refute relativism. What remains is the possibility of vast differences, untranslatability, incommensurability and unintelligibility across much larger chasms than those separating human cultures and histories. The common contact points between different languages, cultures, etc., do not rule out the possibility of conceptual diversity and plurality. The difficulty is to find a way to allow for substantial diversity while avoiding the type of relativism that makes all criteria of truth and falsehood, right and wrong simply a matter of local cultural norms. In chapter 10 I shall outline the beginnings of a solution. Before that we should examine the crucial issue of ethical relativism.

9

Moral relativism

9.1 INTRODUCTION

Relativism about moral standards (moral or ethical relativism) is probably the most popular of all relativisms. In its broadest terms, the ethical relativist claims that moral judgements, adjudications of right and wrong, good and bad, just and unjust, etc., are embedded in specific cultural, historical or conceptual backgrounds, and that their authority is restricted and relative to their context. In other words, the moral relativist denies that there is a single true morality. Moral relativism relies on several interconnected evidentiary sources and assumptions:

(1) Empirical evidence tends to make us aware of the extent of diversity of ethical viewpoints. Members of different cultures and societies conduct their lives according to moral precepts that not only vary greatly from one another, but also may conflict with each other.
(2) Moral beliefs and judgements are determined by their social, cultural or psychological settings.
(3) There are no objective, universal criteria for adjudicating between conflicting ethical worldviews. All attempts to establish such a standard, be it in terms of religious or philosophical doctrines, have failed. Moreover, this failure is not due to our epistemological shortcomings; rather it is proof that ethical judgements are different from empirical judgements. Moral diversity would not entail relativism if there were a dependable path towards the discovery of ethical truths or the establishment of a universal framework for arbitrating between incompatible moral claims. Ethical relativists also claim that any rational decision procedure will inevitably have deeply seated normative, historical and cultural presuppositions embedded in it. Reason and rationality

are themselves evaluative concepts, constrained in turn by cultural and historical influences, and hence are incapable of leading to a set of neutral and universally applicable standards of evaluation.

(4) Ethical relativism also, implicitly or explicitly, assumes that diverse moral judgements are incommensurable. Incommensurability in the domain of ethics is cashed out in terms of the absence of a unique procedure or criterion for adjudicating between different moral claims or the impossibility of comparing or ranking such claims.

We can, accordingly, distinguish between three varieties of claims on behalf of moral relativism.

(a) Descriptive moral relativism, or the empirical claim that as a matter of fact different individuals, societies or historical groupings adhere to different ethical norms and act according to diverse and often mutually incompatible moral standards and beliefs. Descriptive moral relativism relies on (1) as its source and justification.

(b) Normative moral relativism, or the view that what is morally right or wrong can and should be decided only in the context of and relative to the social and ethical norms of different societies, and since both social contexts and ethical norms tend to vary greatly, relativism ensues. Normative moral relativism relies on (1) and (2) in support of its position and often assumes (4).

(c) Metaethical relativism, or the view that the moral domain is such that objective, absolute or universal judgements within it are impossible. Metaethical relativism is frequently contrasted with ethical realism, or the view that there can be objectively true or false moral judgements, as well as with moral cognitivism, the view that there are procedures to ascertain objectively what constitutes a good or right act. Although metaethical relativism relies on (3) above, its claims go beyond that of denying the truth of cognitivist and objectivist views of ethics. It also relies on evidence drawn from descriptive relativism and the assumptions of normative relativism to claim that nothing can be said about morality outside the local claims of what constitutes right and wrong, good and bad. John W. Cook, for instance, characterises metaethical relativism in the following terms:

> Because no action can rightly be thought of as (or said to be) wrong in and of itself, that is, absolutely wrong, a

> moral principle cannot be properly formulated in an entirely general way . . . rather, a moral principle is properly formulated only when a 'relativizing clause' is attached to it, so that you would have something like '*For Americans* headhunting is wrong' or '*Americans* are morally obligated to do such and such'.[1]
>
> (Cook 1999: 14)

He goes on to argue that this definition is not descriptive of the concept of morality as it occurs in various cultures or language groups; rather, it is a metaethical statement about how morality should (correctly) be viewed.

Discussions of moral relativism often focus on normative moral relativism, and the truth of metaethical relativism is implicitly assumed. The argument usually starts from the premise that moral values are grounded on societal conventions, historical conditions, metaphysical beliefs, etc., which vary from one society or social grouping to another; that questions of right and wrong, good and bad, etc., are inexorably bound with specific societal or cultural conventions. Furthermore, it is argued that there are no neutral standards available to us for adjudicating between such competing claims. The idea is that the truth or falsity, the appropriateness or inappropriateness, of an ethical position is internal to its socio-historical framework and cannot be judged independently of it. The argument relies on the denial of ethical objectivism, absolutism and universalism, and assumes the truth of metaethical relativism. Objectivists in ethics maintain that moral judgements have truth-values, i.e., they are either true or false and it is not our beliefs or practices of forming moral judgements that make them so; furthermore, they maintain that it is possible to discover, at least in some instances, whether they are true or false. Objectivism in ethics, then, amounts to the claim that there is one ultimate, true or correct morality and that when two moral viewpoints seem to conflict then at least one of them must be false, and if not, then these seemingly incompatible moral precepts could converge into one true morality. Moral absolutism is the belief that some moral principles have unconditional authority. They are binding on all moral agents – they apply to everyone and everywhere. There are of course variations in local practice, but such variations are ultimately explainable in terms of general and universal moral principles. Absolutists also admit that in most cases we have not yet established with any certainty what is ethically true, but hold that such epistemic failure is due to the complexity of the issues and to failings in human nature rather than being any indication that moral truths are anything but absolute. Gilbert Harman defines the respective positions of the absolutist and the relativist as follows:

> According to moral absolutism . . ., there is a single moral law that applies to everyone, in other words, there are moral demands that everyone has sufficient reasons to follow, and these demands are the source of all moral reasons. Moral relativism denies that there are universal moral demands, and says different peoples are subject to different basic moral demands depending on the social customs, practices, conventions values, and principles that they accept.
>
> (Harman 2000: 105)

Absolutism also entails the universal validity of moral principles. Universalism is the claim that the scope of at least some moral claims or principles goes beyond the beliefs and practices of particular cultures or historical epochs. Universalism is often contrasted with moral particularism, or the view that ethical judgements are applicable to particular cases and situations only. Relativism, however, should be distinguished from moral particularism in that particularists, unlike the relativists, maintain that a given moral judgement can be objectively true or right for a particular occasion. Absolutism and universalism in ethics imply monism, or the view that on every ethical question there is no more than one correct answer. The relativists, on the other hand, are pluralists. They believe that for any moral question there could be more than one correct answer. And above all, they object to the absolutist contention that it is possible to pass judgement on the ethical worth of the practices of other cultures and societies. As Cook has aptly pointed out, 'It is the absolutist's confidence in this matter that distresses the relativist, for the relativist insists that it is a mistake for anyone to think that he knows what is right and wrong for everyone and everywhere, including the people of cultures very different from his own' (Cook 1999: 8). This absolutist position, known as ethnocentrism, is often seen as crass and unreflective and a hallmark of the bigots who, despite an awareness of differences in ethical thinking and practices across cultures, still insist on the correctness of their parochial values and reject all else. Relativism, on the other hand, it is argued, counteracts ethnocentrism and parochialism and leads to tolerance and open-mindedness, even if the price is the tolerance of the intolerant. In this chapter, I shall examine some key arguments in favour of various versions of ethical relativism.

9.2 NAÏVE MORAL RELATIVISM

Some versions of ethical relativism, despite their popularity, are quite easy to dismiss. One instance, dubbed 'vulgar relativism' by Bernard Williams, argues that 'right' means, and can be understood only as, 'right for a given society'. And therefore it is 'wrong for people in one society to condemn, interfere with, etc., the values of another society' (Williams 1972: 22). The position, as Williams points out, is clearly inconsistent since the conclusion makes use of a non-relativist understanding of 'wrong'.

One version of what may be called 'naïve moral relativism' relies on ethical justifications for its case. The outline of this type of argument is already present in the vulgar relativism dismissed by Williams. This defence of ethical relativism emphasises the inherent dangers of ethical absolutism in judging the actions, character and ways of life of others. In its original form, the argument relied on the virtue of tolerance and extolled relativism for instilling such a moral outlook. The anthropologist Melville Herskovits, for instance, has argued that relativism is a philosophy of tolerance and thus it helps to bring about greater understanding and forbearance in a conflict-ridden world (Herskovits 1972: 31). Feyerabend's defence of democratic relativism is another case in point (6.4). The ethical justification of moral relativism, stated in this way, is vulnerable to the charge of inconsistency as outlined by Williams. Its defenders, however, see the attack as a failure to distinguish between an ethical precept about what is the best way to live and abstract formal arguments about the structure of moral reasoning. The point of relativism, they argue, is that it prevents us from imposing our viewpoints on others; it stops us from interfering in the affairs of other cultures and their ways of life, which, as history has shown, can have disastrous consequences. Relativism turns us into more open-minded and self-critical human beings. Admittedly, to extol the virtues of relativism in this way is to make non-relativistic judgements about the value of tolerance, non-interference and open-mindedness, but such a position would seem contradictory only if we thought of relativism either as descriptive of all moral judgements or as a metaethical statement concerning the status of all moral judgements. Relativism, it is argued, is the best weapon we have against the temptations of moral arrogance and cultural imperialism; to forget the role of moral relativism as a guideline for leading better lives is to miss its main point.

A more recent version of the same type of argument has appeared in the work of postmodernist cultural theorists, including feminist thinkers, who explicitly or implicitly embrace relativism by rejecting all objectivist and universalist approaches to ethics. They argue that absolutist theories of ethics sacrifice the importance of individual and cultural differences at the altar of the 'universal good'. The result, they say, is a denial of the scope and importance of difference, which typically disenfranchises the weak and the voiceless in society, women, children, minorities and the poor. The so-called 'universal' human rights and the slogans of equality and liberty are Western products with illegitimate pretensions of culture-transcendence.

Leaving aside the logical defects of this type of argument, at an empirical level, the normative defence of relativism remains unconvincing. It is far from obvious that the adoption of ethical relativism will have the laudatory consequences attributed to it. Ethical relativism can lead to moral paralysis that could damage the cause of the disenfranchised groups that the theory champions. Furthermore, it is not clear if relativism leads to tolerance. The sociologist Orlando Patterson argues:

> True enough, [relativism] is often associated with a liberal and tolerant attitude. But it is doubtful whether the association is in any way causal . . . Relativism, in fact, can be associated just as easily with a reactionary view of the world, and can easily be used to rationalize inaction, complacency, and even the wildest forms of oppression. It is all too easy for the reactionary white South African, or American, to say of the reservation Bantus or Indians, that it is wrong to interfere with their way of life since what might appear to be squalor and backwardness to us, may be matters of great virtue to them.
> (Patterson 1973–4: 126 in Krausz and Meiland 1982: 227)

Most damningly, as Uma Narayan has pointed out, the claims by feminists and other champions of the cause of the oppressed that ideas of equality, human rights, liberty, etc., are simply local 'Western' values, ironically, risk echoing the illiberal rhetoric of some of their main targets, i.e., 'Western cultural supremacists', such as Bloom (1987), and 'Third World fundamentalists', such as Ayatollah Khomeini (1902–89).[2] Naïve moral relativism can give succour to the most illiberal ethical and political positions, and can also lead to political inaction. If naïve ethical relativism is true, then even tolerance and non-interference could not be seen as universal values and could not be recommended to those cultures that do not already subscribe to them. The moral relativist faces the ethical problem that complete moral tolerance can lead to moral indifference and even nihilism or the denial of all moral values. A relativist will have neither the intellectual tools nor the moral certitude to condemn unconditionally even the most reprehensible acts – genocide, torture, child-abuse, slavery, to take just a few examples – so long as such actions are seen as part of the fabric of the social and cultural life of the people who commit them.

Ethical relativism is treated as a normative doctrine in so far as it prohibits interference with the ways of life and the moral practices of other cultures. But, as we have seen, there is an obvious inconsistency in advocating relativism as a universally applicable ethical doctrine. Alternatively, the position is sometimes construed as an attempt to bring about a sea change in our current views of morality, but this too is paradoxical. The relativist argues that judgements of right and wrong are relative to their social and cultural context, from which it follows that we have to believe that *our* societal rules are the correct ones. The dominant moral framework that the relativist wishes to debunk is, per hypothesis, non-relativistic – it holds that at least some actions are right for everyone. Therefore, prevailing social norms also refute naïve moral relativism.

What at times gives credibility to naïve moral realism is the tone used by the reactionary political and social institutions in their unanimous condemnation of it. The Catholic Church, religious fundamentalists in America and elsewhere, right-wing ideologues are all united in their fear and loathing of relativism, which they demonise as the source of many of the ills of the Western world. James Q. Wilson, for instance, has argued that if relativism is accepted then at least some people will feel 'that they are free to do whatever they can get away with'. Consequently

> the moral relativism of the modern age has probably contributed to the increase in crime rate . . . by supplying a justification for doing what they might have done anyway. If you are tempted to take the criminal route to the easy life, you may go further along that route if everywhere you turn you hear educated people saying – indeed, 'proving' – that . . . moral standards [are] arbitrary.
>
> (Wilson 1993: 8–10 in Cook 1999: 41)

Wilson's argument is an extreme example from among a host of alarmist stories about the consequences of accepting relativism. The 'fear of relativism', as Scanlon has called it (Scanlon [1976] 2001), is in part a reaction to a Nietzchean tendency on the part of some relativists to debunk morality – to show it to be merely an expression of power relations and authoritarian societal conventions. If we accept, with the relativist, that morality ultimately is nothing but a matter of social convention, then the authority of all moral precepts is compromised. The worry is that by denying the absolute authority of ethical principles, relativism opens up the way for the erosion of all moral authority, including that prevailing within the relativist's moral system. The relativists, on the other hand, would argue that this is a complete misunderstanding of their position. As Scanlon has argued, most relativists are defending a 'benign' form of the doctrine, 'according to which the requirements of morality vary but are not for that reason to be taken less seriously' (ibid.: 145). Social anthropologists, for instance, frequently argue that the moralities of other cultures are 'just as good as ours' and should be respected as much as ours (ibid.: 146) and that such a view should not be equated with a call to relinquish our desire and obligation to be moral. Frequently, the most vociferous anti-relativists prove to be the most unconvincing. But the fear remains that by opposing moral relativism we are forging an unintended and unwelcome moral alliance with groups whose views we otherwise condemn. What we need to bear in mind, however, is that relativism and reactionary absolutism are not the only ethical options available to us. I shall outline an alternative approach at the end of this chapter.

The extreme reaction to relativism at times stems from a confusion between relativism and crude versions of subjectivism – the view that what is morally right or wrong is relative to the beliefs, emotions, likes and dislikes of individuals.[3] According to this brand of subjectivism, moral decisions are nothing more than the expressions of the egotistical and even non-rational preferences of individuals; a moral statement such as 'torture is wrong' is equivalent to 'torture is wrong for the individual x'. Were this view of morality to be accepted then moral judgements, such as 'individual human rights are more important than a country's national security', would be on a par with expressions of personal preferences, such as 'vanilla ice-cream is nice but chocolate doesn't do anything for me'. Subjective judgements, statements of personal preferences, likes and dislikes, etc., are seldom amenable to rational procedures of criticism, argumentation and justification. In discussions of personal taste and preferences, the statement 'I just like it' often ends the debate; this is not true of moral debates. The subjectivist, also, is in danger of underestimating the social dimension of ethics. Moral rules help us to regulate both our public and private lives and place constraints on our interactions with others and with our environment. Moral principles we adopt and choices we make are subject to criticism and debate by others in ways that subjective judgements often are not. To equate moral relativism with crude subjectivism would deprive it of this essential feature of moral reasoning. The unreflective form of moral subjectivism amounts to the denial of the very possibility of ethics and if it is co-extensive with moral relativism, then critics such as Wilson are vindicated. Moral relativism, however, can be seen as an attempt to confine the authority and scope of ethical judgements to the parameters of their social or historical background. The question is whether there can be a sustainable version of this attempt. Varieties of more or less sophisticated versions of ethical relativism have been proposed. In what follows, I shall examine some of them.

9.3 NORMATIVE ETHICAL RELATIVISM

Normative ethical relativism is the claim that the moral obligations of any individual are determined by the ethical rules prevalent in her society and, more generally, that ethical judgements derive their authority from the norms or moral codes of that society. The thought is that the norms of a social or cultural group are the only appropriate or valid basis for moral appraisal.[4] To take an example from contemporary anthropological literature, Richard Shweder writes:

> On September 4, 1987, Roop Kanwar, a beautiful eighteen-year-old, college-educated Rajput woman, received national press coverage in India when she immolated herself in front of a large supportive crowd, with her dead husband resting on her lap. Immediately the scene of the event became a popular pilgrimage site. The cremation ground was enshrined a romantic memorial to an extraordinary act of devotion and as a place in a sacred geography, that could be pointed to as tangible evidence of the reality of the divine and the descent of the gods.
>
> (Shweder 1991: 16)

According to Shweder, suttee is a manifestation of some of the deepest properties of Hinduism's 'moral world'. In Hindu moral thinking, husbands and wives live in the world as gods and goddesses, and the death of the husband has a metaphysical meaning that cannot be captured by Western views of the relationship between spouses. Consequently, the practice of suttee cannot be judged based on the presuppositions of Western moral thinking. Similar sentiments had been expressed much earlier by W. G. Sumner who had argued that all moral judgements are relative to the customs or 'folkways' that give rise to them, and 'everything in the mores of a time and place must be regarded as justified with regard to that time and place' (Sumner 1906: 11).

This brand of normative moral relativism, although not overtly self-refuting, is nonetheless untenable, for it relies on a crude and simplistic view of the relationship between individual moral agents and their social or cultural backgrounds. First, individuals typically belong to more than one social and cultural group. Even in societies with less complex social structures than modern Western countries, we do not find the homogeneity that this view implies, and, even if we allow for the existence of a dominant cultural or ethical outlook within a given society, in all societies there are sub-cultures, or currents which frequently subvert the dominant view. Women, their lives, their relationships with their children, and their modes of interaction are notable examples of such sub-cultures. Furthermore, as argued in chapter 3, societies and socio-cultural units are not tightly defined closed systems – their boundaries are loose and porous. Hence, the identification of a self-enclosed social or cultural grouping of people with a shared moral code that is exclusive and internal to its members is empirically much more difficult than this type of argument for relativism leads us to expect. Furthermore, the relationship between a moral agent's ethical viewpoints and the societal norms is more complex than the relativist's deterministic picture of moral enculturation implies. For one thing, ethical relativism makes it difficult for us to understand the phenomenon of individual dissent that can become a catalyst for moral change in society. Not all Hindu women are willing participants in suttee. The history of human cultures is replete with the drama of dissent by individuals and groups against prevailing moral and cultural norms – a litany of attempts to reshape dominant moral outlooks and effect fundamental change. The determinism informing moral relativism does not allow for moral rebellion and attempts at moral change.

Even if we accept the case for determinism, the interpretation of the ethnographic evidence used to establish the case for normative relativism is often quite flawed. In many instances, once we take the social and cultural background of seemingly strange ethical beliefs into account, as the relativist exhorts us to do, the 'alien' practices become familiar and intelligible. To look at one example, Edward Westermarck's discussion of the Eskimo custom of leaving their old people to freeze to death has often been seen as a prime instance of a non-ethnocentric approach to ethics. According to Westermarck, the custom of killing or abandoning parents worn out with age or disease shows how moral evaluations across cultures can vary. The Eskimo practice seems atrocious to Western eyes, but to the Eskimo it seems an act of kindness and is 'commonly approved of, or even insisted upon, by the old people themselves' (Westermarck 1932: 184). According to Westermarck, cultural differences bring about irresolvable moral differences, such that no general agreement can be reached. He says:

> We find . . . among many people the custom of killing or abandoning parents worn out with age or disease . . . This custom is particularly common among nomadic hunting tribes, owing to the hardships of life and the inability of decrepit persons to keep up in the march. In times when the food-supply is insufficient to support all members of a community it also seems more reasonable that the old and useless should have to perish than the young and vigorous.
>
> (Ibid.)

Contrary to Westermarck's claim, once the motivations behind the Eskimo's seemingly cruel acts are explained, then their behaviour becomes morally intelligible by standards prevalent in Western societies. Once we accept that they were acting for the greater good of their group, we realise that they were behaving according to a moral principle which, although open to debate, has parallels with those also espoused in Westermarck's own society. The Eskimos are prioritising the well-being of their community over that of its individual members. The issue at stake between 'them' and 'us' is a clash of two fundamental values or moral principles (let's call them 'collectivist' and 'individualist' principles). We can see the point of both these principles, why each may be prioritised and how they can come into conflict not only in cross-cultural comparisons, but also within our own society or personal experiences. The Eskimo case throws into relief the plurality of moral norms and values and not their relativity. (I shall return to moral pluralism below.)

A similar point has been made by David Wong, according to whom 'a recognition of moral relativity is the best explanation of moral experience' (Wong 1984: 7). Basing his arguments, in part, on comparisons between moralities of Eastern and Western cultures and between rights-centred and virtue-centred moralities, he maintains that the truth of moral judgements is always relative to some adequate moral system. Wong defines the adequacy of a moral system primarily in terms of its ability to resolve and regulate social and personal conflicts. According to him, morality arises out of a set of rules that a given society uses in order to resolve interpersonal conflicts of interests (ibid.: 38). Different societies have developed different systems of rules and 'there are many possible systems of rules that would fit the description of a moral system' (ibid.: 39). We distinguish between adequate and inadequate moral systems based on their success in meeting the objective of conflict resolution. At the same time, we accept that there are many different moral systems that can perform this task equally well. Wong's position is closer to the pluralism advocated in this book than to the normative relativism discussed in this section. Where I disagree with Wong is on the limited scope he assigns to ethical systems. Conflict resolution is only one of the many roles that ethical rules play in our lives. The scope of morality is wider than the one Wong ascribes to it.

Normative moral relativism proves unconvincing on many fronts. Other, more sophisticated versions of moral relativism, as we shall see, also make use of the descriptive premise of moral diversity but supplement it with additional philosophical considerations.

9.4 METAETHICAL RELATIVISM AND NATURALISM

The naturalistic or scientific conception of the world has provided for a philosophical environment conducive to ethical relativism. Before the Scientific Revolution of the sixteenth and seventeenth centuries the Christian Church in Europe was seen as the guardian of truth and the ultimate arbiter on matters moral and scientific. The Reformation and the inception of modern science and philosophy undermined the Church's authority. Where, before the Enlightenment, God's revelations were the ultimate source of truth, by the seventeenth and eighteenth centuries human reason in general, and the scientific approach in particular, had become the main instruments for gaining knowledge of the world (see 2.3). The reliable method of establishing truths was regarded as a preserve of science, in part because science is supposed to be dealing with facts which are public, mind-independent and in principle open to general agreement (see 6.1). Reason and the scientific method came to be seen as co-extensive, while that which was not identified as scientific or associated with the rule of reason was categorised as subjective and irrational (or at least non-rational). This scientific worldview rendered the idea of value judgements particularly problematic, as values are notoriously hard to agree upon and do not seem to fit the category of the 'publicly observable'. Hence the distinction between facts and values was introduced. David Hume (see also 2.4), in a seminal passage in the *Treatise*, argued:

> In every system of morality, which I have hitherto met with, I have always remark'd, that the author proceeds for some time in the ordinary way of reasoning, and establishes the being of a God, or makes observations concerning human affairs; when of a sudden I am surpriz'd to find, that instead of the usual copulations of propositions, *is*, and *is not*, I meet with no proposition that is not connected with an *ought*, or an *ought not*. This change is imperceptible; but is, however, of the last consequence. For as this *ought*, or *ought not*, expresses some new relation or affirmation, 'tis necessary that it shou'd be observ'd and explain'd; and at the same time that a reason should be given, for what seems altogether inconceivable, how this new relation can be a deduction from others, which are entirely different from it.
>
> (Hume [1739] 1978: 469)

The perceived chasm between 'is' and 'ought', or fact and value, the absence of entailment relationships between descriptive statements and value judgements, has come to dominate much of moral philosophy since Hume. The scientific is thus characterised as not only objective but also value-free, while the personal and the subjective are deemed to be value-laden. The scientific conception of the universe motivates us into thinking that if ethical knowledge were possible, then such knowledge would be on a par with scientific knowledge as to its sources and methods of discovery. Since there are no observable or independently discoverable mind-independent entities called 'ethical facts', then the claims of morality are relegated to the area of the emotive, the prescriptive and the conventional (*pace* the logical positivists). For those who believe that there is no room for ethics in the scientific conception of the world, both ethical subjectivism and relativism become a metaethical, if not an action-guiding, option. In this section, I shall discuss two accounts of ethical norms which rely on a strong distinction between the natural and evaluative domains.

John Mackie (1917–81), who has been credited with the popularity of ethical subjectivism and relativism in recent times, exemplifies this approach to ethics. According to Mackie, the very idea of ethics presupposes the existence of objective values; values, however, are not objective – they are not part of the fabric of the world. Therefore, there can be no ethical knowledge. Rightness and wrongness, duty and obligation, as well as aesthetic values such as beauty and artistic merits, are not part of 'what there is', Mackie argues. To say that 'there are no objective values is to say that value statements cannot be either true or false' (Mackie 1977: 25). Of course, it is possible to talk about the truth or falsity of a moral judgement in the context of pre-existing standards or value-systems. For instance, we can ask questions about just actions or judgements in the context of standards of justice prevalent in a society at a given time; but questions about the objective standing of these standards do not make sense, for all moral standards are subjective. Mackie puts forward the thesis of 'moral scepticism' or alternatively 'subjectivism' – a second-order, or metaethical, thesis about the status of moral judgements, rather than a first-order thesis about how one should behave. Crude moral subjectivism, discussed in 9.2, is usually understood as the doctrine that moral judgements are equivalent to reports of a speaker's feelings, preferences and other psychological attitudes. Mackie's version differs from this view in that he offers subjectivism as a negative doctrine, a denial of the objectivity of moral values.

Mackie, in a manner reminiscent of Pyrrhonian sceptics, argues that the empirical fact of moral diversity across cultures and historical epochs – what he calls the 'argument from relativity' – gives indirect support to moral scepticism and subjectivism, because 'radical differences between first-order moral judgements make it difficult to treat those judgements as apprehensions of objective truths' (ibid.: 36). This is because 'the actual variations in the moral codes are more readily explained by the hypothesis that they reflect ways of life than by the hypothesis that they express perceptions, most of them seriously inadequate and badly distorted, of objective values' (ibid.: 37). The empirical fact of diversity in the goals that people pursue and find satisfying also 'makes it implausible to construe such pursuits as resulting from an imperfect grasp of a unitary true good' (ibid.: 48). He is in effect employing the empirical assumption of moral relativism (9.1) to support a thoroughgoing moral scepticism. Interestingly, Mackie's moral scepticism, the denial of objective moral values, is presented as a corrective measure to a 'common cognitive mistake'; he accepts that a belief in objective values is built into ordinary moral thought and language, but holds that this ingrained belief is false (ibid.: 49). Moral scepticism, he claims, needs to be defended from the 'common-sense' view that ethics deals with an objective realm. Although most people in making moral judgements believe and implicitly claim that they are invoking objective values, their beliefs are wrong.[5] This is Mackie's 'error theory' of morality, or the view that all moral judgements claiming to be objectively true are mistakes or errors (ibid.).

Mackie considers a general objection to the argument from relativity, namely that 'the items for which objective validity is in the first place to be claimed are not specific moral rules or codes, but very general basic principles which are recognised at least implicitly to some extent in all societies' (ibid.: 37). The principle of universalisability or some utilitarian principle to promote general happiness are instances of such general basic principles. He acknowledges the force of this argument in countering, at least partly, the argument from relativity of moral norms and practices but maintains that such principles are 'far from constituting the whole of what is actually affirmed as basic in ordinary moral thought' (ibid.). There is much more to our ethical life than what such principles can deliver. Our varied moral reactions in diverse situations are not based on reasoning but on something closer to a 'moral sense' or 'intuition' and such intuitions are culture-specific.

Mackie calls his argument against objectivist views of ethics 'the argument from queerness' and assigns to it both a metaphysical and an epistemological component. The metaphysical component is the claim that 'if there were objective values, then they would be entities or qualities or relations of a very strange sort, utterly different from anything else in the universe' (ibid.: 38). The epistemological counterpart of the argument is that knowledge of objective moral values would require us to have some special faculty of moral perception or intuitions, utterly different from our ordinary ways of knowing everything else. Another way of bringing out this 'queerness', Mackie argues, is by showing that so-called 'objective' moral qualities cannot be seen to have causal or logical connections with the natural features of an action or the world, and therefore we are unable to explain how they can be part of the natural world. To establish that values can have causal connections with actions would involve postulating some queer entities, i.e., assuming that there exist 'value-entities or value-features of quite a different order from anything else with which we are acquainted, and of a corresponding faculty with which to detect them' (ibid.: 40).

For centuries, human beings have believed moral values to be objective because of the role they play in establishing and regulating socially necessary patterns of behaviour. According to Mackie:

> We need morality to regulate interpersonal relations, to control some of the ways in which people behave towards one

another, often in opposition to contrary inclinations. We therefore want our moral judgements to be authoritative for other agents as well as for ourselves: objective validity would give them the authority required.

(Ibid.: 43)

Objectivity in ethics, then, is a deeply rooted pretence, necessary for giving weight to our moral precepts. However, an informed analysis of the place of ethics in the order of things shows that subjectivism, moral scepticism and moral relativity are the correct approaches to take.

Before evaluating this position, I would like to turn to the work of Gilbert Harman who is one of the most influential contemporary voices supporting moral relativism. Harman argues that ethical relativism is the logical consequence of the naturalist attitude towards the world. Like Mackie, Harman believes that in the scientific picture of the world there is no room for such non-natural entities as values. Given the truth of the scientific conception of the world, ethics, in so far as it strives to be objective, universal and absolutist, rests on false presuppositions. A variety of non-cognitivist theories, such as emotivism and prescriptivism, as well as Mackie's version of moral scepticism and subjectivism, are motivated by naturalism. Harman, however, believes that 'the most plausible versions of naturalism involve a moral relativism that says different agents are subject to different basic moral requirements depending on the moral conventions in which they participate' (Harman 2000: 100). His view, like Mackie's, may be seen as a metaethical position as he theorises about the standing of ethics. The general outline of Harman's argument is:

(1) Morality arises from established conventions, agreements or understanding among various groups of people about their relation with one another (Harman 2000).

(2) Different groups of people use different conventions and have different understandings of ethical requirements.

(3) Therefore there is no single moral demand that applies to all human beings (ibid.: 77). Rather, moral right or wrong, judgements about the moral worth of an action or an agent are relative to a choice of moral framework. 'What is morally right in relation to one moral framework can be morally wrong in relation to a different moral framework. And no moral framework is objectively privileged as the one true morality' (Harman 1996: 4). There is no single true morality.

Harman bases his argument for moral relativism on the logical properties of what he calls 'inner judgements', or judgements to the effect
that someone ought or ought not to have acted in a certain way. Inner
judgements have the feature that where the agent has reasons to do
something, she endorses these reasons. For it would be quite odd,
Harman claims, to say that an agent ought to do something when she
has no reason for doing it. Inner judgements are intelligible only in
the context of moral agreement. Moral agreements, which provide the
agent's motivating attitude, come about when a number of people
subscribe to a set of principles. Only a person who participates in
such an agreement will have the appropriate motivational attitude to
behave as specified by that agreement. The hypothesis that morality is
based on agreement among people of varying power and resources
also provides a plausible explanation, for instance, as to why our society should give priority to the moral precept of not harming one
another rather than the injunction to distribute wealth equally.
Harman claims that:

> The rich, the poor, the strong, and the weak would all benefit
> if all were to avoid harming one another. So everyone could
> agree to that arrangement. But the rich and the strong would
> not benefit from an arrangement whereby everyone would try
> to do as much as possible to help those in need. The poor and
> weak would get all of the benefit of this latter arrangement.
> (Harman [1985] 2000: 11)

However, even the most seemingly obvious moral precepts, e.g., not
harming the innocent, could have only a local rather than universal
and absolute scope, as the following argument (ibid.: 86–7) shows:

Pr.1 If a person does not intend to do something, and this is not
   because of failure in his reasoning, then that person does not
   have a sufficient reason to do that thing.
Pr.2 There are many instances when people in different societies or
   social groupings, e.g., cannibals, the Nazis or the society of professional criminals incorporated, fail to act according to the
   moral norm in question, and this is not due to any failure in their
   powers of reasoning.
Conclusion There are people or groups of people who do not have
   sufficient reason not to harm others. Such people cannot be condemned for not doing what they have no reason to do. There
   is no failure on their parts, as individuals, in living their lives

according to the agreements prevalent in their society or the moral group to which they belong.

There are many problems with Harman's argument. First, the idea that morality is based on agreement is hugely under-described. How are such agreements achieved? Why should there be agreement on one set of moral principles rather than another? Why is it that different societies may come to different sets of agreements? How do we understand and evaluate the actions of those who rebel against the moral norms of their society, in other words, break the agreement, and, as a consequence, bring about moral change? If morality is based on a society-wide agreement, how can we account for internal criticisms of the moral norms of a society or a social group? Second, are we simply to assume, in a manner reminiscent of Mackie's error theory, that in all the instances where human beings have been willing to pass judgement on the moral norms of other societies, based on their own moral norms, in all the instances where it has been assumed that moral injunctions go beyond merely parochial outlooks, they have been in the throes of an error in reasoning and judgement?

Harman offers relativism as the best available explanation for moral diversity. He believes that 'Moral relativism is a plausible inference from the most plausible account of existing moral diversity' (Harman 1996: 63). So his argument is based on inference to the best explanation. In any instance of such inferences, a counter-strategy is to show that there is an explanation equally or more plausible for the available data. Judith Jarvis Thomson, for instance, has argued that there is a variety of explanations for the existence of intractable moral diversity. According to her:

> In some cases, the source of the apparent intractability is the fact that the issues in dispute are just plain hard, hard in that deciding what to think about them has implications for a wide variety of kinds of action. Abortion, euthanasia: coming to a view about them has a bearing on what we should think about taking life and allowing death quite generally, about the limits to freedom, about the duties we do or do not have to others, and so on.
>
> (Jarvis Thomson 1996: 205)

A further, maybe less significant but nonetheless plausible explanation for the persistence of moral disagreement is what Jarvis Thomson calls 'walling off', or to use the Sartrean, more elegant explanation, the phenomenon of 'bad faith': people protecting their cherished worldviews, ignoring evidence that does not support the beliefs, moral or otherwise, in which they have an investment. Finally, intractable moral disagreements may also be the result of moral indeterminacy – there just being no answer to the question of which action is right or preferable in particular circumstances.[6]

Alternatively, it may be argued that perceived moral differences are not as deep or irreconcilable as all that, that in spite of many cultural variations, there are some core ethical values that underpin all moral systems. A number of philosophers have argued that there are some universal features of our common humanity which, although interpreted differently in different contexts and cultures, give us the beginnings of the denial of the relativist assumption of irreconcilable cultural diversity. Our mortality, embodiedness, experience of pleasure and pain, our cognitive capabilities, our ability to love and hate and to engage in social rituals having to do with these feelings, point to the bedrock of all moral thought: our common humanity. Martha Nussbaum, for instance, has argued that certain key human capabilities are central to any account of not only what it is to be human but also what the minimum requirements are for human flourishing. To take a few examples, 'being able to live to the end of human life of normal length', 'being able to have good health', 'being able to move freely from place to place', 'being able to use the senses, to imagine, to think, and reason', 'being able to have [emotional] attachments', are some of the capabilities that any moral and political system should respect and endeavour to provide (Nussbaum 2000: 210–11).[7]

My main worry, however, is with the very starting point of both Mackie's and Harman's metaethical positions. As we have seen, the naturalist view of the world, presupposed by these authors, posits a sharp division between facts and values; a dichotomy that, following Hilary Putnam, we can call into question. The point is that, on the factual side, the empirical hypotheses that are supposed to describe the world of natural facts bear the mark of epistemic values such as rationality, simplicity, truthfulness, etc., and in that sense are value-laden. On the evaluative side, on the other hand, many of our thick ethical concepts have an inescapable factual or descriptive component. To call someone 'truthful', 'resilient', 'forthright', 'duplicitous', etc., is both to describe and evaluate her. The idea that the world presents itself to us as neatly packaged facts, and that values are subsequently imposed on them by our psychological states or societal conventions, is untenable. The 'mind-independent' world is invariably mediated through – and hence contaminated by – our conceptual contributions. Our conceptions of the world have descriptive and normative elements, but the dividing lines between them are fuzzy and porous. A statement such as 'making videotapes of child pornography is wrong' is no less true than a statement such as 'the Rocky Mountains were formed when the Pacific Plate collided with the American Plate' (in fact the truth of the former is far more unassailable than that of the latter). Both statements carry the imprint of our concepts and categories, and when all is said and done, their truth is established by the method of 'what is agreeable to reason' (Putnam 2002: 32), a method which in turn is coloured by our encounters with the world. The fact–value dichotomy is one manifestation of the philosophical Manichaeism that has haunted modern philosophy. Moral relativism and subjectivism seem plausible in the face of a sharp division between objective facts and non-objective (subjective) values. Once we deny the legitimacy of the dichotomy, once we accept that 'the natural' and 'the normative' come in an inseparable mix, then Harman's and Mackie's positions lose much of their appeal.

9.5 INCOMMENSURABILITY AND CULTURAL DISTANCE

Even if we accept, with Nussbaum and other universalists, that our common humanity limits the scope of diversity in moral outlooks and hence undermines some stronger versions of moral relativism, there remains enough scope for variety to satisfy the relativistically inclined. As Williams has argued, once we have put aside the cruder versions of relativism, we still face some of the deeper concerns of the relativists – the concern of being able to give an account of differences between moral outlooks. Williams believes that the idea of incommensurability across different scientific paradigms (discussed in chapter 6) is highly implausible but that there is scope for incommensurability in the ethical outlook of societies that are separated by great cultural and historical distances.

The idea of the incommensurability of values is central to moral relativism, yet it is quite difficult to find a unified account of it. In discussions of moral relativism, 'incommensurability' is used for at least three distinct doctrines. First, following Davidson, it has been identified with untranslatability. But to think of ethical incommensurability as tantamount to the absence of a criterion for translation is to rob the topic of ethical differences and disagreements of any significance. Interesting questions about relativism arise only when we are able to understand the moral outlook of an alien culture but are unable to agree with it. Second, incommensurability, true to its origins in Pythagorean geometry, has been equated with the absence of a single scale or unit of measurement in assessments of conflicting values. The idea is that when faced with opposing moral positions, the utilitarian felicific calculus notwithstanding, we are unable to find a universally acceptable or objective method of ranking them or a common denominator for assessing them. Third, incommensurability has been understood as incomparability of a more general sort, where the issue is the absence of a method to compare competing moral claims.[8] Values may be in conflict or incomparable in three different ways:

(a) There may be irresolvable conflicts among ultimate values espoused by a single moral system. These values may exclude each other or be uncombinable, e.g., conflicts between equality and liberty or justice and compassion.

(b) Each ethical value, for instance justice for all, may contain conflicting or incompatible elements.

(c) Different cultures may generate different moralities and values, containing many overlapping features but also specifying different virtues and conceptions of the good (Gray 1995a: 45). Relativism is closely aligned with this variety of incommensurability.

Williams has argued that both universalism and relativism in ethics are attempts to explain away conflict. Relativism does so by indexing judgements to their cultural or historical milieu. Universalism minimises the extent of diversity by claiming that the perceived differences are more apparent than real. However, there are cases where conflict cannot be explained away, when belief-systems prove to be genuinely exclusive. Williams wishes to find a middle path between the extremes of arguing either that all moral outlooks are right for the group that holds such outlooks, or that only one moral outlook is right for everyone. Both the relativists and universalists make the mistake of drawing a single line between 'ourselves' and 'others'. Rather, we 'must not draw a line at all, but recognize that others are at varying distances from us' (Williams 1985: 160). The outlooks of some cultures, for instance a hyper-traditional society, may be incommensurable with that of a modern society. But, for Williams, these conflicts are the limit cases and do not impinge on our moral judgements in the way suggested by relativists. Accordingly, he distinguishes between real and notional confrontations of diverse moral outlooks and ways of life:

A real confrontation between two divergent outlooks occurs at a given time if there is a group for whom each of the outlooks is a real option. A notional confrontation, by contrast, occurs when some people know about two divergent outlooks, but at least one of those outlooks does not present a real option.

(Ibid.)

A moral outlook is a 'real option' if it can be adopted as part of a way of life, if the practitioners 'could live inside it in their actual historical circumstances and retain their hold on reality' (ibid.). Many social or moral outlooks are not real options for us – Williams cites the examples of a Bronze Age chief and a medieval samurai. The historical and cultural distance between our way of life and that of the medieval samurai is so great that our normal terms of appraisal – 'good', 'bad', 'right' or 'wrong' – cannot be applied to their actions and ways of life; their moral outlook is incommensurable with ours. In general, we can intelligibly appraise ways of life which are in real, and not notional, confrontation with ours. The socio-cultural distance that makes the confrontation notional also makes relativism, with its consequent suspension of ethical judgement, possible. This type of relativism, as opposed to vulgar relativism, he says, is coherent because:

(a) It allows that in order for us to be able to think about and assess other societies we must have a form of thought that is not relativised to our existing social norms and standards.
(b) There are societies which do not have strong enough connections with our concerns for our appraisal to have any real substance.

One important question in assessing the force of Williams's argument is how to understand and assess the idea of cultural distance – or how to distinguish between real and notional confrontations. Williams says: 'Sometimes [the distance] is a matter of what is elsewhere, and the relativism is applied to the exotic. It is naturally applied to the more distant past. It can also be applied to the future' (ibid.: 162). He also adds:

Relativism over merely spatial distance is of no interest or application in the modern world. Today all confrontations between cultures must be real confrontations, and the existence of exotic traditional societies presents quite different, and difficult, issues of whether the rest of the world can or should use power to preserve them, like endangered species.

(Ibid.: 163)

Williams, then, believes that relativism of distance is not applicable to our contemporary world. However, he also argues that the life of surviving traditional societies is not a real option for the members of technologically advanced countries. But if the lives of a Bantu tribesman in Africa or a Qashqai nomad in Iran are not real options for us, then why would Williams's version of relativism not be applicable to their cases? What if we looked at the situation from the perspective of the Bantu tribesman surveying the moral outlook of a technologically advanced society – would Williams's relativism of distance not be applicable to the here and now, and hence come much closer to the type of cultural relativism that he wishes to reject?

A second related problem with Williams's account arises when assessing the moral outlooks of societies whose ways of life are not real options for members of Western societies, but are in actual social and political conflict with Western ways and hence, according to the criterion applied by Williams, are legitimate subjects of appraisal and criticism. A currently prominent example is the lifestyle imposed by political systems driven by fundamentalist religions. Could we ever be in a real confrontation, in Williams's sense, with their moral outlook? In what way is it more plausible to think that a convinced atheist and liberal may live the life of a fundamentalist Muslim but not the life of a medieval samurai? (The answer cannot be that we don't know enough about the life of the samurai, for this is a purely empirical problem). Only a complete conversion to the brand of Islamic fundamentalism that the Taliban, for instance, espouse would make their lifestyle a real option for the atheist liberal; and as Williams has argued, non-rational conversion involves extensive paranoia and self-deception. But does this render fundamentalist autocracies beyond the reach of criticism? Are the Western liberals to take a tolerant relativist approach to them? If the Muslim fundamentalist outlook is as far from a Western liberal one as that of the Teutonic Knight or the samurai, as I maintain it to be, why should we believe that we are deprived of the philosophical licence to criticise the samurai and not the fundamentalists such as the Taliban? The relativist, of course, maintains that as onlookers we do not have the licence to criticise either, but this is not the conclusion Williams favours.

Williams might argue that the fundamentalists do not fall within the ambit of his relativism of distance because there are enough connections between the concerns of the society within which they operate and ours. For instance, we can identify with the concerns of women living in such societies and this would give us enough leverage to take a moral stand about the belief-system that leads to their oppression and exclusion. The reply, however, is not completely satisfactory. What is the difference between the women victimised by a Bronze Age Greek chief and those victimised by Shariah courts? The source of our concern for the plight of both sets of victims is our feelings of sympathy for their pain, our identification with their suffering, and the concern applies equally to the victims of Islamic fundamentalism and the Greek warring chiefs. The difference is that we may be able to take some action on behalf of the former only. Williams might reply that the legitimacy of our condemnation of contemporary repressive systems and the possibility of a non-relativistic appraisal of them arise out of a common concern for social justice. Muslim fundamentalists are violating the precepts of justice laid down within their own religious beliefs and hence we do not need to resort to Western liberal values in order to condemn their actions. How we should interpret Islamic precepts on the treatment of women is beyond the scope of this book, but the interpretive stand we take towards the teachings of Islam on such issues is irrelevant here because our condemnation of oppressive religious and political belief-systems is external to the ('true') values that underpin the practices under scrutiny.

I have focused my criticisms on Williams's distinction between real and notional confrontations. Philippa Foot, on the other hand, has criticised Williams for assuming that genuine appraisal is always possible in cases of real confrontation. She thinks that we cannot criticise the moral outlook of societies that are real options for us because terms of appraisal, such as 'true' and 'false', 'get a substantial use where there are objective criteria, or at least methods of some kind for settling disputes' (Foot [1975] 1982: 164). In making this criticism, Foot is drawing our attention to one key motivation behind moral relativism: the absence of objective criteria or a decision procedure for settling moral disputes. We should accept, with Foot and Williams, that there is 'truth in relativism' in so far as it is an attempt to come to terms with the genuinely perplexing phenomenon of moral diversity and the absence of the means to settle some moral disputes. But the correct response is not to embrace either moral absolutism or relativism but to accept that there is a plurality of moral values and that any satisfactory ethical outlook should accommodate this fact. This is the task of the final section of this chapter.

9.6 RELATIVISM AND PLURALISM

Although Williams's relativism of distance ultimately proves unsatis-factory, it points to a difficulty in any attempt to accommodate diver-sity and simultaneously to reject the moral *laissez-faire* that relativism can entail. Could we adopt a moral stand that at once acknowledges the variety of ethical points of view and also allows us to engage critically with those which we find reprehensible? The question has practical as well as theoretical import. Relativism provides no solu-tion to a practical dilemma facing members of multi-cultural modern societies. Western societies are no longer homogeneous groupings. We live in a world that is increasingly pluralistic in its social fabric. In such societies there are inevitable conflicts between varying moral claims. Relativism, with its advocacy of 'to each culture according to their beliefs', does not give us the means for resolving such conflicts.

In this section, I will argue that 'value pluralism' suggests a way to overcome the failed dichotomy between absolutism and relativism. Value pluralism claims that there can be no univocal criterion for adjudicating between all conflicting ethical frameworks. The pluralist perspective warns against the error of supposing that 'all goals, virtues and ideals are compatible and that what is desirable can ultimately be united into a harmonious whole without loss' (Williams in Berlin 1978: xvi). Instead, it recommends tolerance and respect for beliefs that vary from those held by us, while maintaining that not all moral positions are deserving of equal respect. Isaiah Berlin is one of the most original and influential defenders of this approach. According to him, ethical life is characterised by the existence of a plurality of values and worldviews, which are in principle irreducible to a single overarching value. He distinguishes between two major theoretical outlooks which he calls 'Platonic idealism' and 'pluralism'. 'Platonic idealism' is the view that both in the natural sciences and in ethics all genuine questions must have one, and only one, true answer. There must be, and presumably is, a dependable path towards the discovery of these truths, and convergence between the discovered answers – the true answers would not only be compatible with each other but would also form a single whole. Platonic idealism defines the moral outlook of not just Plato, but also the Stoics, the Judaeo-Christian religions, the rationalists and the empiricists. The only significant difference between them is in the methods they recommend for discovering the ultimate, universal moral truths. Revelation, light of reason, and empirical investigation are some of the favoured methods, but the ultimate goal is the One True Answer.

The pluralist moral outlook on the other hand, can be understood in terms of its denial of the tenets of Platonic idealism. It is marked by the recognition that there can be, and are, many incompatible moral systems and moral values, without there being an overarching criterion to decide between them. In addition, pluralism emphasises (as in Vico) that ultimate ends, recognised by different cultures, can fail to converge or to be reconciled with each other. Pluralism, then, according to Berlin, is the view that

> there are many objective ends, ultimate values, some incompatible with others, pursued by different societies at various times, or by different groups in the same society, by entire classes or churches or races, or by particular individuals within them, any one of which may find itself subject to conflicting claims of uncombinable, yet equally ultimate and objective, ends.
>
> (Berlin 1991: 80)

Instances of such incompatible moral ends are: rigorous justice versus mercy and compassion in particular cases; spontaneity and organised planning; loyalty to one's country or fellow human beings versus love and loyalty in the private sphere and concern for immediate relatives.

Values can clash between cultures, groups in the same cultures or even within an individual. The clash does not necessarily entail a contradiction in the sense that some values have to be true and others false. Moral norms are intelligible only in terms of the social historical context out of which they emerge and cannot be correctly understood or interpreted in the absence of this background knowledge and these assumptions. Once these contexts are taken into account, we have a richer array of possible evaluations than offered by the monistic view advocated by the moral absolutist.[9]

Although pluralism has frequently been equated with relativism, Berlin denies that he is a relativist. Pluralism should not be confused with relativism because a pluralistic outlook does not preclude the possibility of

> members of one culture [being able], by the force of imaginative insight, [to] understand the values, the ideals, the forms of life of another culture or society, even those remote in time or space. They may find these values unacceptable, but if they open their minds sufficiently they can grasp how one can be a full human being, with whom one could communicate, and at

the same time live in the light of values widely different from one's own, but which nevertheless . . . can be seen to be values, ends of life, by the realisation of which men could be fulfilled.

(Ibid.: 10)

Relativism for Berlin boils down to something like 'I prefer coffee, you prefer champagne. We have different tastes' (ibid.: 11),[10] a position reminiscent of crude subjectivism discussed above. Gray also echoes Berlin's distinction between relativism and pluralism by arguing that cultural pluralism, or incomparability among values, is easily confused with moral relativism – the view that human values are always internal to particular cultural traditions and cannot be the objects of any sort of rational assessment or criticism. But, for the pluralist, Berlin stresses, 'there is a world of objective values'. These are the ends that 'men pursue for their own sakes, to which other things are means' (ibid.).

There are strong similarities between moral relativism and value pluralism: the starting points for both are the perceived empirical fact of moral diversity and the theoretical assumption that disagreement resulting from such diversity is rationally irresolvable. They are both opposed to monism. They both deny that there could be a unique, overarching criterion for or conception of the good life, a single true system of value or an overriding criterion for adjudicating between incompatible ethical belief-systems. Furthermore, both are frequently seen, by liberal theorists, as offering resistance to ethical and political imperialism.

There are also important differences between pluralism and relativism. Pluralism entails the existence of many 'right' incompatible ways of conducting our lives, but some conducts are unacceptable by any standard. Relativism, on the other hand, makes it impossible to rule out any ethical system so long as that system is deemed acceptable by some moral agent or community. Relativism does not allow us to adjudicate between incompatible ethical claims. On the face of it, this seems to be true of pluralism as well. All value judgements receive their justification from the specific context from which they arise, the relativist argues, and we are not in a position to choose between conflicting moral claims independently of the context to which we belong. This, at least on Berlin's account, seems to be true of pluralism as well. Pluralists, because of their rejection of the very possibility of there being any overriding values, are equally unable to adjudicate between conflicting values. However, Berlin claims that in practice collisions . . . can be softened. Claims can be balanced, compromises can be reached: in concrete situations not every claim is of equal force – so much liberty and so much equality; so much for sharp moral condemnation, and so much for understanding a given human situation; so much for the full force of the law, and so much for the prerogative of mercy; for feeding of the hungry, clothing the naked, healing the sick, sheltering the homeless. Priorities, never final and absolute, must be established.

(Ibid.: 17)

Despite these caveats, Michael Sandel has argued that pluralism 'comes perilously close to foundering on the relativist predicament. If one's convictions are only relatively valid, why stand for them unflinchingly? In a tragically-configured moral universe, such as Berlin assumes, is the ideal of freedom any less subject than competing ideals to the ultimate incommensurability of values?' (Sandel 1984: 8). Could we, then, accommodate value pluralism without becoming a moral relativist?

One way to avoid the extremes of relativism, Berlin argues, is to realise that incompatibility between values should not be over-dramatised as there is much in common between human societies.

I am not blind to what the Greeks valued – their values may not be mine, but I can grasp what it would be like to live by their light, I can admire and respect them, and even imagine myself as pursuing them, although I do not – and do not wish to, and perhaps could not if I wished. Forms of life differ. Ends, moral principles, are many. But not infinitely many: they must be within the human horizon.

(Berlin 1991: 11)

Berlin thus rejects the possibility of complete incommensurability of values. Our common humanity brings about our common morality. There are no universal values, but there is a minimum without which societies cannot survive, for instance avoiding extremes of suffering for people. Furthermore, there are limits to what counts as a human value. Moral values have to fall within 'the limits of the human horizon'. They have to be intelligible by our lights; for instance, the idea that some human beings may worship trees simply because they are made of wood, and for no other reason, does not make sense to us.

In the public realm, the upshot of all this is that there cannot be such a thing as a perfect political state, but we still can find ways of accommodating multi-cultural and pluralistic societies. We can agree that in all societies the first public obligation is to avoid extremes of suffering and also that the most fruitful approach is to engage in trade-offs and negotiations, but at all times we should remember that choices between incompatible values are not a subjective matter. They are guided by the form of life of the society to which one belongs.

Have we managed to show that pluralism does not collapse into relativism? Is there a way of accounting for the plurality of moral values without falling into the moral paralysis that an outright relativistic position threatens? To remind ourselves, relativism implies that any moral point of view, even that of the Nazis, is right for those who accept and practise it and that although we can judge the Nazi ideology and actions to be wrong 'for us', we should accept that the ideology is right for its practitioners. Since value judgements receive their justification from the specific context from which they arise, the relativist argues, we are not in a position to adjudicate between various moral claims. A Berlinian pluralist would accept that any moral judgement concerning someone's actions must be sensitive to norms of the value-system within which that person operates. But the pluralist, unlike the relativist, is willing to say that even with due consideration of the diversity of moral outlooks, there are cases where we are in a position to distinguish between right and wrong actions of people from moral traditions very different from ours. The difficulty is to spell out how such judgements can be made. It may be helpful to look at examples drawn from areas other than ethics, where a plurality of approaches and assessments is accepted and put into practice, to see if we can find a useful model for value pluralism.

The first analogy I would like to draw on is from the area of performing arts – music in particular. There are some interesting parallels between performances in music and their evaluation and ethics. Although we may make use of abstract ethical principles in our moral thinking, ethics ultimately deals with human action and has a strong element of practical knowledge incorporated into it. Michael Luntley, for instance, has advocated a model of moral knowledge as a practical skill – rather than that of cognitive symbol manipulation, analogous to the skills acquired by a performing musician (a jazz soloist for instance) (Luntley 1995). The suggestion is that, just as in music we can have non-subjective judgements of what counts as a displeasing or even incorrect rendering of a piece, in the same way in ethics we can arrive at context-dependent but objective judgements of right and wrong. Of course some degree of familiarity with musical styles, background knowledge of pieces, etc., are necessary for achieving such a non-subjective judgement, but given the presence of this background knowledge, a substantial degree of agreement in matters musical is achievable. The agreement that a particular performance is not aesthetically acceptable, however, does not rule out that there could be many 'right' or 'pleasing' accounts of the same piece. In matters of musical performance, plurality of divergent interpretations is seen as a virtue of the art of music-making, rather than a problem to be overcome. Could the same be said of ethics?

One problem with this analogy, as it stands, is that in music a pre-given set of rules, or at least norms, provide us with a procedure for judging whether a particular note was played correctly or whether a particular interpretation was convincing. The perennial difficulty posed by ethical questions is that, utilitarianism notwithstanding, often there are no pre-given rules for deciding whether a particular ethical judgement is right or wrong. This feature of ethics is of course at the heart of Berlin's pluralism, but it leaves us with the problem of how to avoid relativism and still remain a value pluralist. The answer might lie in how we respond to the foundational question: what counts as a moral system? An ethical outlook outlines what is to be done by way of human conduct so that it would be conducive to a good life. Moral values and injunctions aim to contribute to the achievement of better lives, better societies and better human beings. The difficulty starts with the attempt to specify what counts as a 'good life'. To return to our analogy, something counts as a musical system if it specifies the organisation of sounds and silence, rhythm and pulse, such that the end-result stimulates a range of feelings and excites a variety of emotions. Many different musical systems are considered emotionally rewarding – pleasing, stirring, moving, etc. – but not every sound-pattern is. The judgement as to what counts as an emotionally rewarding sequence of sound and silence is made within the flexible limits of our psychological and physical possibilities – the parameters of artistic appreciation – and is ultimately based on what we find 'good by way of rewarding hearing'. Similarly, what is good by way of the human life is circumscribed by what Berlin calls 'the human horizon', a horizon that is curtailed by our biological and psychological endowments, by the realities of the world, and ultimately by what we as a species find 'good by way of living'.

The analogy between a musical and a moral system can be furthered in two other ways. First, there are many distinct musical traditions (e.g., Indian raga, Japanese gagaku, and Argentine tango) using different sound intervals and rhythmic patterns, all aesthetically rewarding, at least to the trained ear. In the same way, there are different right or good ways of conducting our lives. Second, and even more tellingly, there is often a plurality of interpretations of the same piece of music, which cannot be simultaneously realised and hence, in that sense, are incompatible, and our choice or preference for one over others does not negate the value of those not selected. In the same way, there are many – sometimes incompatible – ways of conducting our lives, of reacting to ethical problems and responding to the moral demands of our fellow human beings. To give preference to one does not negate the value of those not selected.

The second analogy I wish to draw on is from a radically different domain and is somewhat more controversial. It has become commonplace to argue that there can be rival systems of logic. Formal logic gives us guidelines as to how to reason well; it also reflects the modes of human reasoning. In this sense, logic has both an evaluative and descriptive role. Since the early days of modern logic, many different and at times incompatible systems of logic have been proposed and utilised in assessing human reasoning. It has been argued that rules of logic enable us to make valid inferences, but different rules may be best suited to different contexts or subject matters. For instance, Putnam argues that the reasoning in the area of quantum mechanics, i.e., reasoning about the micro-world, may warrant the choice of non-classical quantum logic over classical logic. Fuzzy logic, according to its originator Zadeh (1975), is the logic suited to approximate reasoning, and reasoning with vague predicates. The intuitionists L. E. Brouwer and A. Heyting, based on their views of mathematical proofs, have proposed a modification of classical logic that involves the rejection of the law of excluded middle. Michael Dummett has extended their arguments to non-mathematical reasoning.[11]

Instrumentalists about logic, such as Graham Priest, see logic simply as a tool for drawing inferences. From this perspective, a logical theory is right in so far as it produces the right results, where 'right' is defined in terms of pragmatic criteria such as fruitfulness, adequacy to data, simplicity and ease of use, etc. For a realist the story would be very different. For her, 'correct' logic describes an objective, theory-independent reality. But how do we decide which logic is successful in capturing reality correctly? As Priest has pointed out, the criterion used by the realist would be exactly the same as that used by the instrumentalist: the logic that gives us the right results, the one that enables us to conduct our enquiry more fruitfully, is the logic we should adopt. If it is true that different formal systems fulfil this function more or less successfully in different contexts of enquiry, or that more than one system of logic can be successfully applied to a given domain of enquiry, then we will have pluralist conceptions of 'right' logic. The interesting point about logical pluralism, however, is that although there can be many rival systems of logic, not every symbolic system would be acceptable. Even Priest's controversial paraconsistent logic, which rejects the law of non-contradiction, operates within certain formal constraints. While music provided an analogy with the practical side of moral knowledge, pluralism about logic offers an analogy with the more abstract or cognitive features of moral reasoning. Logic provides us with principles and guidelines for reasoning or thinking well; ethical principles fulfil a similar function in giving us guidelines for living and acting well. Given the rich tapestry of our lives, the complexities of the human mind, and the seeming intractability of the theoretical and practical problems we face, there is often more than one right answer to the question 'how should I live?' as there is more than one right solution to the puzzle 'how should I reason?'. Yet, just as relativism about logic had to be ruled out, so too should ethical relativism. In both logic and ethics, there is a difference between right and wrong which is independent of local norms or conventions. But, for many complex questions, there can be many right answers and many more wrong ones.

Although there are many correct formal logical systems it does not follow that any system will count as correct. Similarly, although there are many aesthetically rewarding ways of performing a given piece of music, some renditions are neither correct nor rewarding. In the same way, there are many good, appropriate, right modes of ethical conduct and moral judgement, some of which are in mutual conflict – e.g., virtue-based ethics versus a right-based ethics – yet not all ethical judgements are equally good, even when they are fully adopted by a society or an individual – the Nazi moral outlook being a case in point. It is important to take the two analogies together since moral knowledge has both practical, skills-oriented and cognitive components. Furthermore, by focusing on the analogy from music alone it might be assumed that ethical judgements, like aesthetic judgements as some people have claimed, are purely subjective and a matter of personal taste. Neither of these analogies reflects the concerns of ethics very exactly, but there are enough parallels to give us the hope that there may be a way to accommodate value pluralism without denying ourselves the authority to dismiss at least some value-systems as untenable or unacceptable. Being conducive to human flourishing is the overall criterion for distinguishing between acceptable and unacceptable values. Human flourishing, unlike pleasure and even happiness, is a rich and complex concept which could never be fully specified.[12] It is, however, easier to see what is not conducive to human flourishing. Murder, torture, physical, material and psychological deprivation, lack of freedom and opportunity to express oneself emotionally, intellectually and artistically (to name just a few examples) will all hinder human flourishing, wherever they take place, and should be condemned. Yet, within these broad universal parameters there is much scope for diversity and conflict of perspectives.

The pluralistic approach does not solve the difficulty of finding out which ethical precepts should be chosen in particular circumstances or which course of action should be preferred, but it does reassure us that, frequently, there is more than one right course of action open to us. It also fulfils the promises of tolerance and open-mindedness that relativists have been heralding, without forcing us into a position where we are unable to condemn even the most heinous of political and social systems. The difficulty, of course, is in distinguishing between acceptable and unacceptable moral values, but the core ideas of human well-being and flourishing are good starting points for any discussion of ethics.

9.7 CONCLUSION

Moral relativism attempts to account for moral diversity and the intractability of moral problems but it runs the risk of moral paralysis in the face of injustice and cruelty. Moral pluralism, I have argued, addresses the concerns of the moral relativist but also affords us an opportunity to evaluate moral judgements irrespective of their social and historical contexts. The difficulty is to specify how such pluralism will resolve the ethical dilemmas we face. The devil, as they say, is in the detail. But to assume that ethical problems are open to easy and quick resolution is to misconstrue the human condition.

10

Conclusion
Relativism, pluralism and diversity

10.1 INTRODUCTION (AND CONCLUSION)

Relativism, for more than two thousand years, has shrugged off numerous attempts to refute it, and continues to tempt and lure. Part of the explanation for its perennial appeal and its periodic prominence lies in the fact that it captures some essential insights, albeit in an exaggerated fashion, about what we know, think and believe. The relativist rightly argues that our dealings with the world, whether through our perceptual experiences, thoughts or feelings, always take place from within a perspective or worldview. They are permeated by our concepts, our interests and our historical conditions. Our encounters with our social and natural environment can be described and to that extent, one might even say, experienced in many different ways. Different modes of conceptualisations have consequences for the ways in which we act or conduct our lives, which show that there is a practical side to conceptual diversity. There are numerous, at times conflicting, ways of conceptualising our lives, our experiences and the world. The conceptual schemes through which we think, judge, interpret and act are diverse and not always fully compatible with each other; we live in a world of pluralities, and do not have access to univocal answers to our diverse problems. Here lies the truth in relativism.

The power of relativism stems from its correct diagnosis of the significance of irreconcilable diversity and contingency; its failing is its response to this. Relativists since Protagoras have been accused of inconsistency and incoherence. More recently this charge, in the hands of Quine and Davidson, has been given a new twist. However, the accusations of incoherence and self-refutation, be they in the form of the traditional self-refutation argument or the new form of the requirements of translation, have not really diminished the popularity of the doctrine. They fail in part because they are seen either as irrelevant to one of the main aims of relativism – the denial of absolutist and monist conceptions of truth, goodness, reason, etc. – or as presupposing the very absolutist and monist viewpoint that the relativist wishes to deny. Still the cost of countering absolutism by relativising truth and goodness is too high. The price is either intellectual and moral paralysis – the inability to compare and evaluate what lies outside our immediate cultural and conceptual surroundings – or the very predicament that the relativist wishes to avoid: parochialism and ethnocentrism. Faced with differing cultural and conceptual perspectives, the relativist can do no more than either retreat from intellectual and social engagement with them – opt for quietism of the most extreme form – or accept that she can only use her purely local standards to judge others, and thus become indistinguishable from the provincial bigot she condemns. Neither option should satisfy her.

There is a way out. Some of the legitimate worries that give rise to relativism can be addressed by espousing a moderate form of pluralism. In chapter 9 I discussed how value pluralism can help us to overcome the unwelcome dichotomy between moral relativism and absolutism. Here, I will give a tentative outline of how we can accommodate conceptual pluralism.

10.2 CONCEPTUAL PLURALISM

Following Huw Price (1992), we can distinguish between vertical and horizontal pluralisms. Vertical pluralism is the claim that questions of truth and falsity in different subjects or domains of discourse, e.g., the ethical, scientific and religious domains, should be treated as distinct and maybe even unique and cannot be reduced to a single overarching idea of truth. Crispin Wright (2001) and Michael Lynch (1998) have offered a defence of this type of pluralism. Horizontal pluralism is the claim that there can be more than one correct account of how things are in any given domain. Horizontal pluralism is opposed to monism. It claims that for many questions in the domains of metaphysics, aesthetics, ethics and even science, there could be more than one appropriate or correct answer. It is this more controversial but nonetheless defensible version of pluralism that can be offered as a substitute for relativism. Pluralism, at least in the moderate form defended in this book, agrees with relativism on the issue of conceptual diversity but parts company from it by insisting that not only are there limits to the scope of such diversity but also that in many instances we can distinguish between better and worse, or more and less fruitful or productive, conceptual systems. The pluralist, unlike the relativist, believes that there are culture-transcendent constraints on what is an acceptable belief- or value-system.

Conceptual schemes are the sets of concepts, categories and beliefs human beings use to make sense of the world and their experiences therein. They are broad frameworks for interpreting and describing the world and our lives in all their variety. They comprise the cognitive apparatus we bring to the world for the purposes of interpreting and understanding it, and include metaphysical tools such as criteria of identity and individuation of the objects of our experiences. These schemes are the cognitive components of the perspective we have on the world, and their content is the world (natural and social) as it impacts on us. Conceptual schemes need not be co-extensive with specific natural languages or historically constituted cultural traditions. As Putnam's example of mereological and common-sense conceptual schemes shows (see chapter 7), incompatible conceptual schemes may make use of the linguistic apparatus of a single natural language (in this case English). Different scientific frameworks or Hacking's modes of reasoning are a further example of conceptual diversity occurring within the broad framework of a single linguistic tradition. That there can be and is a multiplicity of such schemes is a philosophical hypothesis backed by empirical observations of how we engage with the world in our day-to-day lives, as well as on purely abstract grounds. We realise that our life-experiences can be variously described most clearly when we look at how other cultures (both diachronically and synchronically individuated) describe, experience and cope with 'the same world'. Cognitive scientists in recent years have highlighted such differences. To take a few examples:

In Dyirabil, an aboriginal language of Australia, all objects and experiences in the universe are classified into four groups:

(1) *Bayi*: Chiefly classifies human males and animals; but also the moon, storms, rainbows and boomerangs.
(2) *Balan*: Classifies human females; but also water, fire, fighting, most birds, some trees, etc.
(3) *Balam*: Classifies non-flesh food, but also cigarettes.
(4) *Bala*: Everything not in the other categories including noises and language, wind, some spears, etc.[1]

This fourfold classification provides us with a rather striking instance of how familiar experiences such as noises, as well as pre-individuated objects such as food and animals, can be further conceptualised in ways that make them seem strange and unfamiliar to non-Dyirabil thinking. Furthermore, this alternative way of conceptualising and categorising their lived world also has consequences for how Dyirabil-speaking people conduct their lives and react to various events and experiences involving these categories. In this sense, then, alternative conceptual schemes are also alternative ways of life.

Psychological states and experiences such as emotions and feelings are also conceptualised differently in different schemes and languages. The Tahitians, for instance, categorise sadness with sickness, fatigue or the attack of an evil spirit and do not have a separate word or an independent concept for it. The Tahitians, of course, do experience sadness; but they conceptualise their experiences differently from the way Europeans do (Levy 1991).

The above gives us an example of how core human experiences can be further categorised and conceptualised according to differing conceptual schemes. Sadness is one of the basic emotions felt by all normal human beings, and in that sense it is part of our common humanity, yet the way it is further interpreted, categorised and classified can vary substantially depending on the conceptual scheme or framework that a particular culture brings to its understanding.

A further example comes from Richard Nisbett who in a number of publications provides interesting instances of a rather different type of conceptual diversity. He and his colleagues have argued that there are large and systematic differences in the cognitive processes of East Asians and Westerners. These differences range over cognitive processes such as perception, attention and memory, as well as the ways these groups tend to categorise objects, explain and describe events or even react to paradoxes and contradictions. J. Weinberg *et al.* give a useful summary of some of Nisbett's findings.

> According to Nisbett and his colleagues, the differences [between the East Asians and Westerners] 'can be loosely grouped together under the heading of holistic vs. analytic thought.' Holistic thought, which predominates among East Asians, is characterised as 'involving an orientation to the context or field as a whole, including attention to relationships between a focal object and the field, and a preference for explaining and predicting events on the basis of such relationships.' Analytic thought, the prevailing pattern among Westerners, is characterised as 'involving detachment of the object from its context, a tendency to focus on attributes of the object in order to assign it to categories, and a preference

for using rules about the categories to explain and predict the object's behavior.' One concomitant of East Asian holistic thought is the tendency to focus on chronological rather than causal patterns in describing and recalling events. Westerners, by contrast, focus on causal patterns in these tasks. Westerners also have a stronger sense of agency and independence, while East Asians have a much stronger commitment to social harmony. In East Asian society, the individual feels 'very much a part of a large and complex social organism . . . where behavioral prescriptions must be followed and role obligations adhered to scrupulously.'

(Weinberg *et al.* 2001: 430)

The authors use Nisbett's findings to argue that 'there really are people whose reasoning and belief forming strategies are very different from ours. Indeed, there are over a billion of them!' (ibid.: 432). This talk of strategies of belief-forming gives the misleading impression that members of different groups make explicit and transparent choices as to what overall cognitive approaches they should utilise in dealing with the world. I think what Nisbett's studies, as well as the Dyirabil and Tahitian cases, show is that members of different cultural, historical or linguistic traditions bring different conceptual and belief-forming frameworks to their encounters with the world and in that sense they possess different conceptual schemes.

10.3 THREE CRITICISMS

The idea of conceptual relativism has been criticised in several ways. Some of these criticisms will also affect the conceptual pluralism I am defending here. Below, I examine these criticisms under the headings of triviality, confinement and dogmatism, and show in what way pluralism can counter their challenges.

10.3.1 The charge of triviality

It may be argued that we can easily accept the above claims on behalf of scheme–content dualism and attendant conceptual relativism (and pluralism) without accepting that any philosophically substantive or interesting claim has been made on behalf of pluralism. In other words, scheme–content dualism is philosophically trivial. John Searle's views on the topic are a case in point. Searle believes that conceptual schemes are the different vocabularies and sets of concepts used to carve up a language-independent reality, and agrees with the main presuppositions of conceptual relativism in so far as:

> Any system of classification or individuation of objects, any set of categories for describing the world, indeed, any system of representation at all is conventional, and to that extent arbitrary. The world divides up the way we divide it, and if we are ever inclined to think that our present way of dividing it is the right one, or is somehow inevitable, we can always imagine alternative systems of classification.
>
> (Searle 1995: 60)

He goes on to add: 'From the fact that a *description* can only be made relative to a set of linguistic categories, it does not follow that the *facts/objects/states of affairs/etc., described* can only *exist* relative to a set of categories' (ibid.: 66). According to Searle, conceptual relativism is wholly compatible with what he calls 'external realism',[2] the view that the world, or reality, exists independently of our representations of it. 'The fact that alternative conceptual schemes allow for different descriptions of the same reality, and that there are no descriptions of reality outside all conceptual schemes, has no bearing whatever on the truth of realism' (ibid.: 165).

Conceptual pluralism rests on the assumption that there can be, and indeed are, incompatible correct or true descriptions in various domains and that what is true or correct can only be decided within a conceptual scheme, worldview or vocabulary. Searle, on the other hand, believes that any appearance of conflict between the verdicts of different theories or conceptual schemes is trivial and easily settled by attending to the different criteria involved in reaching our verdict on what the facts of the matter are.

A similar line of thought has been pursued by Donald Davidson when arguing against Quine's thesis of indeterminacy of translation and ontological relativity. As we have seen, Quine's thesis of indeterminacy of translation plays a formative role in his arguments for ontological relativity. Davidson, contra Quine, has argued that indeterminacy should not be seen as a threatening phenomenon and, once correctly understood, it will not result in any type of relativism – ontological, conceptual or otherwise. Davidson claims that the thesis of indeterminacy is neither mysterious nor threatening, or at least is 'no more mysterious than the fact that temperature can be measured in Centigrade or Fahrenheit . . . And it is not threatening because the very procedure that demonstrates the degree of indeterminacy at the same time demonstrates that what is determinate is all we need' (Davidson 1986: 313).

Both Searle and Davidson trivialise conceptual pluralism by focusing on cases where there is no real conflict between various ways of describing the world. (Searle, like Davidson, gives the example of metric and imperial measurements (Searle 1995: 165).) However, the phenomenon of conceptual diversity is not confined to trivial instances of differing standards of weight or temperature. The issue at stake is not the surface differences about units of measurement; rather, it concerns fundamental ontological commitments, incompatible methods of classification, cognitive values and priorities.

One way to show that conceptual pluralism is not a trivial thesis is to look at the disanalogies between the localised examples, such as different conventions of measurement, that Davidson and Searle cite, and the examples of diversity in core conceptions of the world that cognitive scientists point out. One important disanalogy, as noted by Davidson himself, is that, in the cases of measurement of temperature or weight, our linguistic interactions with others allow us to agree

> on the properties of the numbers and the sort of structures in nature that allow us to represent those structures in the numbers. We cannot in the same way agree on the structure of sentences or thoughts we use to chart the thoughts and meanings of others, for the attempt to reach such an agreement simply sends us back to the very process of interpretation on which all agreement depends.
>
> (Davidson 1991: 164)

To put it slightly differently, in the case of measurements of temperature, there are certain pre-existing conventions which allow us to correlate the two structures. Such conventions are not present for the totality of a language or conceptual schemes. The issues at stake in debates on conceptual diversity are philosophically deeper than Searle's or Davidson's discussions lead us to believe.

10.3.2 *The charge of confinement*

Karl Popper has argued that incommensurability and diversity of the kind required by the relativist (and by the same token by the pluralist) are a consequence of the pernicious 'myth of frameworks'. The myth construes historical periods, cultural norms, theoretical systems and conceptual or grammatical structures as prisons from which no escape is possible. The clash of cultures makes us aware of the existence of conceptual and cultural frameworks, but to conclude from this awareness that there is no possibility of transcending our particular language or culture is a grave error. The awareness of alternative worldviews, languages and cultural posits 'allows us to break out of the prison. If we try hard enough, we can transcend our prison by studying the new language and by comparing it with our own' (Popper 1994: 52).

The conceptual pluralism I am proposing does not entail the type of imprisonment that Popper rightly criticises. For one thing, pluralism, unlike relativism, does not presuppose a deterministic relationship between social and cultural frameworks and individual beliefs. We can accept the anti-realist intuition that it is not possible to step outside all frameworks, that the view from nowhere does not exist, that each time we transcend a particular prison we enter 'a larger and wider prison' (ibid.: 52). At the same time, we should not be seduced by the relativist illusion that we are barred from occupying different perspectives or frameworks, or that we are unable to make any comparisons between them.

Those sympathetic to relativism would argue that Popper subscribes to another myth, *the myth of the possibility of transcendence* or the assumption that there exist methods of criticism and rational evaluation that are framework-transcendent. Popper does not believe in the force of such a criticism. He argues that we can pursue an aim or a goal, such as the aim of better understanding the universe, which is independent of the theories or frameworks that we construct to try to meet this aim. But of course the very idea of 'understanding the universe better' cannot be understood or evaluated independently of all frameworks. This, however, is not a fatal problem, for the very understanding of what counts as 'understanding something better' itself can undergo a process of critical revision. All our conceptions and evaluations are not only informed by our conceptual frameworks, but are also provisional and fallible. The important point to remember is that we can, and we do, revise our frameworks, but working from inside.

10.3.3 *The charge of dogmatism*

A third criticism of conceptual relativism and pluralism is an attack on the very idea of conceptual schemes. In chapter 8, we examined Davidson's first line of attack against scheme–content dualism and conceptual relativism. Davidson's second line of attack may be called 'the charge of dogmatism'. According to him, the very idea of a conceptual scheme is 'a dogma of empiricism, the third dogma of empiricism. The third, and perhaps the last, for if we give it up it is not clear that there is anything distinctive left to call empiricism' (Davidson [1974] 1984: 189).

At its most basic, empiricism is the claim that knowledge of the world is achieved through our sense experiences. Empiricism as a theory of knowledge and justification was, in part, shaped by its encounter with scepticism. The empiricist reaction to scepticism was to claim that sense data can act as the ultimate evidence for our knowledge of the world, and hence the foundation of empirical knowledge. But in so doing empiricism gave rise to the notorious question of how we can be sure that we can transcend the veil of ideas or senses and gain access to the real world.

The dualism of scheme and content has been seen as a response to the epistemological worries about the relationship between mind and the world. The sceptical challenge intensifies the worries about our ability to retain our hold on the empirical world and underlines the need to have some unassailable source for justifying our claims about the connection between our minds, with their conceptual apparatus, and the external world. This is John McDowell's point when he argues:

> The point of the dualism is that it allows us to acknowledge an external constraint on our freedom to deploy our empirical concepts . . . The putatively reassuring idea is that empirical justifications have an ultimate foundation in impingements on the conceptual realm from outside.
>
> (McDowell 1994: 6)

According to Davidson, 'the idea that there is a basic division between uninterpreted experience and an organizing conceptual scheme is a deep mistake, born of the essentially incoherent picture of the mind as a passive but critical spectator of an inner show' (Davidson 1989: 171). He argues that 'Empiricism is the view that the subjective is the foundation of the objective empirical knowledge', but goes on to suggest that 'empirical knowledge has no epistemological foundation, and needs none' (ibid.). What motivated this type of foundationalism is the thought that it is 'necessary to insulate the ultimate sources of evidence from the outside world in order to guarantee the authority of the evidence for the subject' (ibid.: 162). The difficulty with this approach, as McDowell has pointed out, is that by making sense-impressions the means of our contact with the external world, it turns them into intermediaries between us and the world and hence prevents us from having an unmediated contact with the world.[3] Once we begin characterising the mind/world relationship in terms of a distinction between conceptual schemes and an unsullied stream of experience, or the given, as the content, then the next, almost inevitable step is the claim that all we have access to in our experiences of the world are the immediate contents of our senses, our impressions, or ideas. Instead of finding any justifications for our epistemological claims, we have saddled ourselves with unnecessary philosophical anxieties about our hold on reality.

What Davidson objects to here is the view of conceptual schemes as an intermediary between the human mind and the world. The aim is to find ways in which we can be directly in touch with the world, without needing to have any basic, incorrigible or otherwise privileged or foundational epistemic items at our disposal. A naturalistic account of knowledge, Davidson argues, that makes no appeals to such epistemological intermediaries as sense data, qualia or raw feels will give us that unmediated hold. If, on the other hand, we accept that sensations do not play an epistemological role in determining the content of our beliefs about the world, then we are giving up the third dogma of empiricism.

We can agree with Davidson on the desirability of relinquishing the Cartesian model of the mind/world relationship and still find use for the idea of scheme–content dualism. The scheme–content distinction as outlined in this chapter provides us with a way to explain the prevalence of differing conceptions of the world, including the erroneous ones. The scheme–sense-data distinction, on the other hand, is a response to the worries raised by scepticism. The content of conceptual schemes, as construed here, need not be 'the given' or the flow of sense data, for these are philosophical myths; rather, the content is the world as it directly impinges on us. But the world is us as well, so the opposition between the mind and the world is spurious – it is simply a remnant of the worldview that accorded man a special place in God's scheme of things. The content of conceptual schemes is the world as experienced by us. It is what Lewis calls the thick experiences of our lives (Lewis 1929: 54).[4]

All human experiences already bear the mark of our concepts and categories. The dualism of scheme and content gives us a way of talking about different ways of conceptualising our lived experiences in the world. Conceptual schemes enable us not only to describe and organise our experiences of the world, but also to understand and to cope with these experiences. They are the tools by which we interpret, account for and understand the rich variety of our encounters with the world, with each other and with life. McDowell has argued that 'Conceptual schemes or perspectives need not be one side of the exploded dualism of scheme and world. Thus innocently conceived, schemes or perspectives can be seen as embodied in languages or cultural traditions' (McDowell 1994: 155). This innocent version of conceptual schemes accommodates the philosophical intuition that there are no non-perspectival views of things. To admit the existence of conceptual perspectives does not prevent us from having access to the world. What is being emphasised is that all our life-experiences are from, in McDowell's words, a 'stand-point of engagement' (McDowell 1986: 381). But from such a standpoint 'languages and traditions can figure . . . as constitutive of our unproblematic openness to the world' (McDowell 1994: 155).

We can admit one of the philosophical intuitions informing relativism: that our encounters with the world, our beliefs and judgements are always perspectival. However, we should remind ourselves that we are not trapped within a single perspective. Even a small step to the left or right gives us a new and sometimes completely different perspective on a given landscape. We can always shift between different perspectives, move backward and forward between them, compare and contrast them and choose what we judge to be the best or most convenient or most rewarding for a particular purpose. What is true of visual perspectives also holds for conceptual and cognitive perspectives. We are not prisoners of any one single perspective. Incommensurability of the type that prevents us for ever from gaining entry into different frameworks is yet another philosophical myth.

We can deny, with McDowell, that there can be a purely unconceptualised content to our experience and hence avoid the 'myth of the given', without renouncing either the claim that experience is a rational constraint on thinking, or the claim that our content-full experiences can be made sense of in differing ways. We can reassure Davidson that there is no gap between thought and the world, without making the connection between the mind and the world so robust as to be unable to account for non-trivial diversity.

The crucial point to remember is that by accepting conceptual pluralism we are not surrendering our powers of discrimination between better and worse schemes. Throughout this book I have criticised relativisms of differing kinds for undermining the possibility of distinctions between right and wrong, good and bad, true and false. The question now is: can pluralism avoid this charge?

10.4 SCHEMES, MAPS AND OTHER PLURALITIES

The way forward, I believe, is to supplement pluralism with a minimum-cost representationalist theory of the mind–world relationship. This might be achieved if we embrace some version of a metaphor that has been out of favour with many realist and anti-realist philosophers alike: the metaphor of human beings as mappers, and conceptual schemes as maps or systems and principles of mapping the world. The suggestion is that conceptual schemes provide us with ways of mapping both the natural and the social world. They enable us to find our way in ethical and epistemic terrains, in ways not dissimilar to how physical maps guide us through physical terrains. The metaphor is rejected by Rorty, Putnam and various other anti-realist philosophers, as they interpret it as a variant of the correspondence theory of truth. It is also rejected by realists such as Paul Horwich for very similar reasons. The correspondence theory of truth saddles us with an ontology of facts, and many contemporary realists believe that this is unnecessary metaphysical baggage.

Despite these objections, I believe that the metaphor of mapping can provide us with a way of being conceptual pluralists while avoiding relativism. Let us look at some of the features of map-making and see how far this metaphor can take us.[5]

(1) A map is always a view from somewhere. This is true of our conceptual schemes. Therefore, the anti-realist rejection of the possibility of a God's-eye view stands.

(2) There is no single correct way of constructing or drawing a map. Depending on their function and purpose, different types of maps are constructed using very different approaches and principles. Map-making is pluralistic. The same may be said of conceptual schemes. The conceptual scheme of Dyirabil is one of the many ways in which different language-users can conceptualise the world.

(3) Different types of maps serve different purposes and satisfy different needs. A map of the London Underground will be useless for a tourist wishing to walk from Trafalgar Square to Oxford Street, but does its job very well if the aim is to travel using the tube. The same may be said of conceptual schemes. The conceptual scheme of theoretical physics is unsuitable for dealing with our daily encounters with the world at macro-level. The 'mereological' conceptual scheme proposed by Putnam is not

very helpful for counting the number of students attending a particular course.

(4) There are better and worse, more accurate and less accurate maps. A sixteenth-century map of the world is superior to the ones constructed in the Middle Ages but inferior to later ones in respect of accuracy of representation. However, the older maps can be aesthetically superior to later ones and rich in symbolism through the imagery they use and hence they can provide us with a different set of useful information. In the same way, a belief-system that incorporates the discoveries made by Newtonian physics gives us a better grip on the world than one relying on Ptolemic physics only, but can also carry unwelcome philosophical baggage (e.g., the fact–value dichotomy, materialism, a mechanical view of the world).

(5) Whether a map is good or bad depends, in part, on the purpose for which it has been constructed or is being used. The same is true of belief-systems. Any judgement concerning the efficacy of different belief-systems in dealing with the world will have to be made in the light of the aims it serves. Furthermore, maps can be made sense of in the context of the interests they serve; we can distinguish between better and worse maps but only in the context of our interests and projects.

(6) Although it does not make sense to say that a map is made true by the world, it makes sense to say that a map may or may not be true to what it attempts to depict. Conceptual schemes or frameworks of beliefs are not made true by the world either, but we can ascertain whether they are true to the world. Our beliefs about the world are tested directly and indirectly through our experiences of and encounters with it. True beliefs stand the test of time and place.

(7) Map-making is an evolving art. Standards of map-making are historically conditioned. We cannot even begin to decipher or understand a map unless we have an insight into the presuppositions involved in drawing it, and these presuppositions will vary across time and space. The same is true of conceptual schemes. Our belief-systems undergo change. Our views of the world, the priorities we assign to certain beliefs and ideas, the way we construct the connections between different elements in a belief-system are all subject to change. To understand the belief that mercury can cure syphilis (see chapter 6) we need to gain an understanding of the alchemical belief-system resulting in it. Belief-making is also an evolving art.

(8) There is no such thing as a single absolutely correct map. Within a given domain, a map may be exhaustive. That is, we may come to think that no further information or detail would add to the proper functioning of it, but exhaustiveness should not be confused with absoluteness. This is true of conceptual schemes. No conceptual scheme can give us an absolute conception of the world. Conceptual schemes are always partial – not least because the universe is infinite while human conceptions are inevitably finite.

(9) Since maps are drawn for different, sometimes incompatible, purposes, the notion of global convergence (e.g., a map of all maps) does not make sense.

(10) The metaphor of mapping can be applied to a variety of contexts, including charting the domain specific to human relations. We can readily talk about a map of the human heart or indeed the human mind. Metaphors of the moral, emotional and psychological terrains are all useful ways of thinking about our understanding of the human condition.

(11) Maps aim to represent the features of a given landscape in such a way that there is structural isomorphism between the representation and the represented. This is also true of certain usages of language. In descriptive usages of language, where the primary aim is to give an account of how things stand in the world, we aim to achieve isomorphism between our descriptions and that which we are describing. Structural isomorphism does not rule out pluralism as such. Isomorphism is established from within a conceptual scheme, a belief-system, or a point of view; however, it does anchor maps (and conceptual schemes) to the world or what there is.

The above points (1–9 in particular) have been constructed in such a way as to reflect Putnam's views on conceptual relativity (see chapter 7). Putnam, as we noted, explicitly rejects the metaphor of mapping. He argues that 'elements of what we call "language" or "mind" penetrate so deeply into what we call "reality" *that the very project of representing ourselves as being "mappers" of something "language independent" is fatally compromised from the very start*' (Putnam 1990: 28). However, Putnam's approach, particularly his use of the idea of warrant, does not give us the means for distinguishing between better and worse conceptual schemes. The metaphor of mapping, on the other hand, allows us to see how we can retain a pluralist outlook and yet rely on something outside of our conceptual schemes for comparing and evaluating them.

It has been objected that maps involve pictorial representation which is very different from linguistic representation. Paul Horwich, for instance, has argued that 'the difference between a map . . . and a sentence of a natural language is that the interpretation of maps is more "natural" – or in other words, less "conventional" – than the interpretation of a sentence' (Horwich 1990: 115). According to him, maps are less conventional than language because:

> In the case of certain maps, a representation that consists in some set of objects (symbols) standing in some relation to one another is supposed to be interpreted as saying that the referents of those objects stand in the very same relation. For example:
>
> (a) The fact that *point y* is on a straight line between points x and z expresses
> (b) the fact that the *place represented by y* is on a straight line between the places represented by x and z.
>
> (Ibid.: 116)

What is natural or non-conventional, Horwich claims, is that (a) and (b) share a pictorial form, namely:

> (c) That . . . is on a straight line between . . . and . . .
> That is not shared between a language and what it is mapping because maps share a pictorial form with the world while – the *Tractatus* notwithstanding – languages do not.

It is extremely odd to claim that maps are in any sense natural or non-conventional. Horwich is relying on a narrow definition of what is conventional in making his claim. A 'pictorial form' – what is shared between a map and the mapped – according to him is natural or non-conventional. But this is to completely misunderstand the art of map-making. Maps are unintelligible scribbles for anyone who is not familiar with the conventions for constructing and reading them. However, even if we accept Horwich's point in the case of 'certain maps', the simplest and most rudimentary, his criticism does not apply to the much broader metaphor of mapping as used here.

It may also be objected that the above account of conceptual schemes lands us in the realist camp as it involves the assumption of correspondence between language and the world, the very view that informs the metaphysical realism that philosophers such as Putnam and Rorty have rejected. The suggestion is that the type of representation involved in mapping amounts to a relationship of correspondence or structural resemblance between the map and what is being mapped. But to suggest that our conceptual schemes, among other things, are the means for representing the world we live in does not commit us to the existence of facts or any other spurious ontological entities. Furthermore, different conceptual schemes, even in Putnam's account of them, ultimately deal with the same world. The mereologists and the Carnapians (see 7. 6) inhabit the *same world* and count the contents of that world, even though they come up with very different answers to the question 'How many objects are there in that world?'. We use language to describe our world, our emotions, our lives, etc. These descriptions often are attempts at representing what we believe to be true, real or important. To think that by admitting that there are many instances of such innocent representation we are being trapped in a spurious metaphysical picture is to let our philosophical Puritanism get in the way of commonsense. It may seem that Searle is proven to be correct after all and that the suggested model of conceptual pluralism leads to realism, because it presupposes a language-independent reality that can be carved up or divided in different ways. Searle has claimed: 'unless there is already a territory on which we can draw boundaries, there is no possibility of drawing any boundaries' (Searle 1995: 166). The same may be said of maps.

The problem with most accounts of conceptual relativism is that if the doctrine is true then what counts as a fact, object or a state of affairs can only be individuated by the conceptual tools available within a conceptual scheme. It simply does not make sense to talk about different conceptual schemes representing the same fact or object differently when what counts as the same object or fact cannot be decided prior to and independently of the way in which it is to be defined or individuated by that scheme. To speak of a scheme–world or a scheme–reality distinction is to presuppose that we can understand, and hence individuate, the already existing world or reality and then impose our conceptual schemes on it. If 'the world' is a name for the objects that our worldview or conceptual scheme individuates, then it cannot play the role we wish to assign to it in defence of conceptual pluralism.

This claim is true of some versions of conceptual relativism and pluralism. However, what is being suggested here is that what counts as a territory, as well as how the boundaries of a territory are demarcated, are internal to a conceptual scheme. As Putnam has suggested,

318

our conceptual schemes, languages or mind-sets interpenetrate 'reality' to such an extent that the very idea that we can intelligibly conceive of a pre-schematised territory, world or reality is irrevocably compromised. The point is that although the very idea of the world is already contaminated by our concepts; those concepts in turn are in a non-trivial way informed and constrained by the world. We cannot *talk* about that which our conceptual schemes map outside the parameters set by the maps we currently have at our disposal, but this does not mean that there is nothing outside our maps to speak of. Our schemes and maps bear the ineluctable signs of what they are mapping, but the subject of our maps, that which we are attempting to map, is also contaminated by our conceptual map-making. It may seem deeply paradoxical to claim that conceptual schemes are our different ways of mapping what there is (in the broadest sense of the term), but we are not in a position to say what it is that we are mapping independently of such maps. But the paradox results in what is required of us by our opponents. No one, not even the scientific realist, can step out of his conceptual skin to tell us what the world is like outside of all conceptions. To demand such a division is to fall prey to yet another version of philosophical Manichaeism

The conceptual maps we draw operate under various constraints. Logic in general, and the principle of non-contradiction in particular, is one such general constraint. This does not mean that all conceptions are necessarily internally consistent. There can be hidden contradictions in a belief-system that do not readily manifest themselves (as in the case of the Azande belief in witchcraft). But such inconsistencies, by and large, will remain on the periphery of a conceptual scheme and will not affect the core, everyday, mundane beliefs. Secondly, our conceptual frameworks, or at least the bits of them that specifically deal with the world, are constrained by that world. For if they were not they would not perform the functions they are supposed to serve. Again, we feel the impact of the world most when dealing with the practical and the humdrum. The further we are removed from the commonplace, the more abstract and speculative our conceptions, the less the impact of the natural world. In the furthest reaches of the human imagination, the world, or what there is, stops having any noticeable impact and even logic loses some of its grip. Conceptual schemes provide us with ways of discovering, charting and navigating the natural and cultural world we inhabit. Their comparative merits depend on their usefulness and success – and their success, to a significant degree, is contingent upon the world they are mapping.

Pluralism, conceptual and evaluative, is not at one with relativism. There are many ways of conceptualising and evaluating the world but these ways are not relative to different cultures, historical epochs, etc. Although the diversity of conceptual systems is at its most obvious when we come across different cultures or societies, a variety of incompatible conceptual systems may be operative in the same society or historical period. There may be good historical and sociological explanations for the existence of diverse conceptual systems, but to explain diversity is not to admit to its relativity. Pluralism is not relativism for it allows for comparisons between different conceptual frameworks and perspectives. It also, unlike relativism, acknowledges the possibility of giving preference to one framework over others, without embracing ethnocentrism or parochialism.

Finally, 'is it all relative'?

NO. But some things are and many things are not. And that's the way things map out in the pluralistic universe we inhabit and conceptualise.

Notes

INTRODUCTION

1 See Geertz (1989) for a discussion of anti-anti-relativism.
2 See chapter 4 for a more detailed discussion of these issues.
3 As we shall see in chapters 4 and 7, despite their common rejection of a–d, there are significant differences between Rorty, Putnam and Goodman that militate against the use of the blanket term 'relativism', even in this narrower negative sense, to cover their distinct positions.
4 For a detailed and interesting definition of relativism on the above lines see Nozick (2001: 17–19).
5 I would like to thank Tim Williamson for this point.
6 See also Gilbert Harman's formulation of moral relativism in chapter 9 of this book.
7 I am skirting around a further complication here, namely, that the same predicate as uttered in different contexts can express different properties. Similarly, the same sentence uttered in different circumstances or contexts may express different propositions. I am not going to discuss this form of linguistic contextualism or meaning relativism in this book. Although the topic is of interest, it does not have the same philosophical urgency that other types of relativism discussed here possess.
8 Subjectivism like relativism is a multifaceted doctrine with its own history and trajectory of development. In this book I use the term as a shorthand for all attempts to relativise cognitive, evaluative and even perceptual states to an *individual* (see chapters 1, 4 and 9). More subtle subjectivist positions require a book-length treatment.
9 As pointed out above, we can also distinguish between relativising a value to the social, cultural or historical context of the evaluator and relativising it to the context of the object of evaluation, contexts which may not always coincide.
10 Social scientists often distinguish between worldviews or the cognitive aspects of the beliefs and practices of a culture, and what they call 'ethos', the evaluative aspects of the beliefs and practices of cultures. Clifford Geertz, for instance, claims that 'A people's ethos is the tone, character, and quality of their life, its moral and aesthetic style and mood; it is the underlying attitude toward themselves and their world that life reflects' (Geertz 1973: 126). In many places in this book, in line with my rejection

of the fact–value dichotomy (see chapter 9), unless specifically qualified, I use the term 'worldview' in an inclusive manner covering both cognitive and evaluative aspects of a belief-system.

11 A number of conceptual relativists tend to relativise only specific elements of δ to IV (e.g. ontology); the issue is quite complicated and will be examined in detail in chapter 7.

12 It is useful to compare the above scheme with the one proposed by Harré and Krausz (1996). The authors draw two catalogues of relativism. They first distinguish between different types of relativism by concentrating on its topics and second, as we saw, they look at what relativism denies. The following catalogue is the result of their classificatory scheme by topic (ibid.: 23–4):

(a) semantic relativism or the relativity of meaning to language (e.g., Quine)
(b) ontological relativism or relativity of existence to conceptual systems (e.g., Goodman)
(c) epistemic relativism or the claim that knowledge is relative to persons, standards of evaluations, epistemic framework or conceptual schemes (e.g., Protagoras, Kuhn, MacIntyre)
(d) moral relativism, or the relativity of moral worth to societies and epochs (anthropologists such as Boas and Ruth Benedict)
(e) aesthetic relativism: relativity of aesthetic values to culture and epochs.

From the above list, (a), (b) and some versions of (c) fall under what I have called 'conceptual relativism', while (d), (e) and some versions of (c) can be characterised as variants of cultural relativism. One major difference between the above scheme and the one adopted in this book is that while Harré and Krausz concentrate on what it is that is being relativised, I find it useful also to look at the contexts of relativisation. For instance, languages, conceptual systems and epistemic frameworks, as we shall see in chapter 7, are variants of conceptual schemes and hence we can simplify our classificatory schemes by grouping them together.

1 THE BEGINNINGS: RELATIVISM IN CLASSICAL PHILOSOPHY

1 See Guthrie (1971) among others for a discussion of this point.
2 A number of philosophers with relativistic inclinations fit the profile of insider–outsiders: Jacques Derrida (Jewish–Algerian–French), Ludwig Wittgenstein (Jewish–Austrian–British) (see chapter 3), Isaiah Berlin (Jewish–Russian–British) (chapter 9), Paul Feyerabend (Austrian–American) (chapter 6), etc.
3 It is very likely that this passage is a direct quotation from Protagoras' *Truth*, as the same passage also appears in Plato's *Cratylus* (1997b: 386a).
4 This is the interpretation favoured by Cornford (1935).
5 This passage seems suggestive more of a doctrine of relativity than of relativism. For a discussion of the distinction see 1.5 below.
6 For a more detailed reconstruction of Plato's argument see Burnyeat (1976a) on whose work some of the discussion here is based.

7   See Putnam (1981) and Burnyeat (1976a) for various explanations of this omission.

8   Hilary Putnam interprets Plato as arguing that if every statement X means 'I think that X' then I should (on Protagoras' view) really say (1) I think that I think that X and the process of adding 'I think' can go on indefinitely. 'This Plato took to be a *reductio ad absurdum*. However, Plato's argument is not a good one as it stands. Why should Protagoras not agree that his analysis applies to itself? It doesn't follow that it *must* be self-applied an infinite number of times, but only that it *can* be self-applied an *infinite number of times*' (Putnam 1981: 123). But Putnam believes that there is much to be said on behalf of Plato's argument.

9   Hankinson (1995) distinguishes between restricted and radical relativism. I prefer Putnam's suggested locution of 'total relativism'. But leaving aside terminological differences, the real issue is whether second-order relativism is coherent.

10 There are interesting parallels between contemporary debates on truth between the neo-pragmatists and their realist opponents and the dispute between Plato and Protagoras. See for instance chapter 4 and the discussion of Rorty's position on truth.

11 Putnam bases his argument on Wittgenstein's famous Private Language Argument. See 4.2 for a brief discussion of this argument and 3.4 for a more detailed account of Wittgenstein's views on language.

12 Discussions of the Protagorean doctrine appear in Books Γ and K of Aristotle's *Metaphysics*.

13 Vasilis Politis has also argued that Aristotle was careful to distinguish between relativism and what he calls 'phenomenalism' (or what I have called 'subjectivism'). He cites in particular the passage '[those who think about these things] must take care to assert not that appearance is true [i.e., phenomenalism], but rather that appearance is true to the one to whom it appears, and at the time when it appears, and in the respect in which it appears, and in the way in which it appears [i.e., relativism]' (Politis 2004, forthcoming).

14 To look at a more recent expression of this type of argument, according to Michael Luntley 'It is in the nature of what it is to make an assertion that, in asserting that P, we rule out certain states of affairs as obtaining. In making an assertion we must, at least, confer a sense upon the utterance that divides all the possible experiences in two: those that are excluded by the assertion and those that are not. But in doing so, we ensure that it cannot be the case that neither of these two classes of states of affairs obtains and that both classes cannot obtain simultaneously' (Luntley 1988: 120–1). His argument is for the acceptance of the *tertium non datur* as well as non-contradiction but the weaker claim is sufficient for the present purposes.

15 Despite Aristotle's strong criticism of Protagorean relativism, certain passages in the *Nicomachean Ethics* make it clear that he was not totally unsympathetic towards the claims of societal conventions, and hence relativism and pluralism of sorts, concerning ethical duties. For a discussion of this point see Evans (1996).

16 Also in Hankinson (1995: 138).

17 See Annas and Barnes (1985: 130–45) for these points.

2 RELATIVISM IN MODERN PHILOSOPHY

1 At least there were no public expressions of relativism, for none would have been tolerated. Indeed, heretical movements were often castigated for preaching 'libertine' or 'anything goes' doctrines.

2 Montaigne, however, was not the only philosopher of the period to discuss relativism. For instance, in *Les Dialogues de Guy de Brués, contre les nouveux Academiciens* (1557), de Brués presents the sceptics Baif and Auber adducing arguments in favour of relativism on the basis of the diversity of human opinions, and concludes that ethical and legal views are mere beliefs and hence do not have the absolute or universal authority of genuine knowledge-claims (Popkin 2003: 33).

3 Given the closeness of Montaigne's arguments for relativism and scepticism to modern views we should credit him, as Popkin does, with a greater role in the foundation of modern thought. It must, however, be added that Montaigne, unlike Descartes, never developed a systematic approach to philosophy.

4 It is instructive also to remember that Montaigne was writing in the shadow of the heretic Giordano Bruno who posited the existence of an infinity of worlds and speculated about recurrent incarnations, and was burned at the stake for his views.

5 Descartes believed that reason is the same in all men; any apparent variation is due to the fact that some men use it wisely and others do not.

6 It is also important to note that Descartes' moral maxims are provisional and tolerant, a view that would distance him from universalist and absolutist conceptions of ethics, unless we assume that he believed in the absolute validity of a principle of toleration.

7 Descartes was also aware of the diversity in religious beliefs; for instance, he mentions that the Hurons in Canada believe that God is a tree or a stone. However, he thinks that this shows that all human beings have an innate and universal idea of God.

8 Montesquieu's position arguably is not simply an instance of moral particularism. Moral particularists, in one version of the theory, agree with relativists that there are no universal moral generalisations but argue that individual moral judgements are capable of expressing absolutely true or absolutely false propositions on the occasions where such judgements are applied to specific actions and events. Montesquieu's position is relativistic as he believes that the assessment of the truth and falsity of moral judgements can be made only in the light of, and relative to, further environmental and social considerations.

9 Or at least finite thought, since God's thoughts are not constrained by the categories.

10 There are alternative interpretations of these philosophers' works. J. C. O'Flaherty (in Hamann 1967), for instance, has argued that Hamann is in fact a 'child of the Enlightenment' and a defender of reason properly understood.

11 See chapter 3 for a discussion of the linguistic relativism of Whorf.

12 Wittgenstein, for example, whose views are discussed in chapter 3.

13 But, as we saw, this blanket characterisation of the French Enlightenment is mistaken.

14 The writings of the founders of the Counter-Enlightenment also fore-

shadowed the rejection of values of rationality, reason and objectivity by the nineteenth-century romantics. When Johann Gottlieb Fichte argues that values and principles are not objectively given, either by nature or by God, or William Blake proclaims that 'Reasoning is secret murder' and 'Art is the tree of life. Science is the Tree of Death', or when George Sorel or E. T. A. Hoffmann castigates '*la petite science*' and the common notion of reality reified by science and technology, we also see the first intimations of what has become a renewed revolt against the Enlightenment, truth, rationality and reason by twentieth-century postmodernist philosophers.

15 I am grateful to my colleague Brian O'Connor for pointing this out to me. This chapter was much improved by his helpful comments.

16 Pragmatist interpretations of Nietzsche are emphasised by Danto ([1965] 1980: 75) and Warnock (1978) but are denied by Hales and Welshon (2000: 207 n. 21)

17 There are, I believe, unresolved tensions in Nietzsche's writing on the possibility of comparison between different perspectives and on the question of how there could be multiple perspectives on the same 'thing'. For instance, shortly after telling us that all seeing and all interpretations are perspectival he continues: 'and the more affects we allow to speak about one thing, the more eyes, different eyes, we can use to observe one thing, the more complete will our "concepts" of things, our "objectivity" be' (Nietzsche 1968: §540). The topic, however, is beyond the scope of this book.

18 See Danto ([1965] 1980) for one instance of this type of criticism of Nietzsche. The version of the self-refutation argument I have used here against Nietzsche is based on his work.

3 CONTEMPORARY SOURCES OF RELATIVISM

1 There are also some dissenting voices. Cook (1999), for instance, denies that Boas was a relativist.

2 See chapter 5 for a more detailed discussion of the Azande belief in witchcraft.

3 Haack uses the locution 'shallow and deep relativism' to make similar distinctions and thus adds to the terminological miasma surrounding the topic. Shallow relativism 'corresponds to the more familiar . . . descriptive relativism . . . to the effect that different communities or cultures accept different epistemic, moral or aesthetic values' (Haack 1993: 299). She says that 'deep relativism' parallels what is usually called 'philosophical cultural relativism' and is the claim that 'talk of epistemic, moral or aesthetic value makes sense only relative to some culture or community' (ibid.). The evidence gathered by anthropologists in support of descriptive relativism is used to support philosophical or deep relativism. Haack dismisses the philosophical significance of shallow varieties of relativism which she believes are 'sometimes taken to have more philosophical interest than they deserve because they are confused with, or wrongly taken to imply, the corresponding forms of deep relativism' (ibid.).

4 The problem of incommensurability and its connections with relativism are discussed in chapter 6.

5 This runs contrary to the famous accusation levelled by Donald Davidson

(see chapter 8) that Whorf's conceptual relativism entails incommensurability and untranslatability.

6 The data used by Mead and Evans-Pritchard have also been called into question. For criticisms of Mead's work see Freeman (1983) and Pinker (1994). For an excellent discussion of the Azande material see Moody-Adams (1997).

7 For the full list of these common traits see Brown (1991) and Pinker (1994).

8 For a most illuminating account of the history of social anthropology see Kuper (1999). I have relied heavily on his work in this section, in particular on the connections between social anthropology and postmodernism (ibid.: 206–27)

9 For a discussion of Winch and of Barnes and Bloor see chapter 5. Lyotard's views are discussed in 3.5.

10 For instance, Hanjo Glock (1996) equates Wittgenstein's approach with cultural relativism and Robert Kirk (1999) argues that Wittgenstein's views on language-games lead to relativism.

11 There are also some strong dissenting voices. Hilary Putnam, for instance, has resisted drawing the relativistic conclusions that seem to follow from the above passages. Putnam's discussion of Wittgenstein's alleged relativism and the passages §§608–12 of *On Certainty* are in Putnam (1992a: 168–79).

12 See chapter 6 for a discussion of different types of incommensurability and their connections with relativism.

13 Ernest Gellner has remarked that the confrontation between the postmodernists and their opponents might be seen as a replay of the battle between classicism and romanticism, the former associated with the domination of Europe by a French court and its manners and standards, and the latter with the eventual reaction by other nations, affirming the values of their own folk cultures (Gellner 1992: 26 in Kuper 1999: 220).

14 These passages are discussed by Baldwin (2001). I am grateful to my colleague Tim Mooney for bringing them to my attention and for his generous comments on this section of the book.

15 For a discussion of some of Derrida's qualifications of his more extreme pronouncements see Mooney (1999).

16 See chapter 2 for a discussion of Nietzsche's views.

17 From Mooney (1999: 42).

18 I put the question to Derrida at a round table on ethics and deconstruction held in the Department of Philosophy, University College Dublin, in February 1997.

19 I shall return to this type of argument in chapter 4 where the question of the coherence of relativism is discussed.

4 RELATIVISM ABOUT TRUTH

1 A number of philosophers have argued this point; see Karl Popper (1963) for instance.

2 The assessment of realist theories of truth is beyond the scope of this book. For an accessible account sympathetic to realism see Engel (2002).

3 See for instance the discussion of Ian Hacking's views in chapter 6.

4 For a useful discussion of the point see Swoyer (1982: esp. 94–5).

5 See 1.4 and 5.4 for further discussions of this point.

6 The same type of sentiment has been expressed in Davidson's theory of triangulation. According to this view, for language to be possible one needs to assume a triangular relationship between at least two speakers and a world that is shared by them (Davidson 2001).

7 It is unusual to characterise relativistic truth as a three-term, rather than a two-term relation (see Introduction). Meiland's motivation, as I understand it, is to cash out both absolute and relative truth in terms of correspondence with the world. My arguments against Meiland, however, would still stand even if we defined relative truth as a two-term predicate.

8 For instance, c~a~t would be translated into *b~é~t*, in French, but that's only when we have discovered that 'cattle' should be translated into *bétail*, while we can translate 'true' as '*vrai*', even if we were unaware that 'true-for' would be translated into '*vrai-pour*'.

9 It is not only the relativists who take this position. Anti-realists of various hues, Kantians and neo-Kantians included, argue for the interdependence of mind and reality without necessarily embracing alethic relativism.

10 These ideas will be examined in chapter 7.

11 In his article 'Why Reason Can't Be Naturalised', Putnam spells out his regress argument in greater detail. He maintains that when a relativist says that an utterance P is true by the norms of the culture of A then what he is saying is that according to the norms of the relativist's culture, the utterance P is true by the norms of the culture of A. This would make other cultures, systems of belief, etc. simply logical constructions out of the conceptual schemes, practices and procedures of the relativist's own culture. If the relativist then adds "'the situation is reversed from the view point of the *other* culture", he lands in the predicament that his transcendental claim of a symmetrical situation cannot be understood if the relativist's doctrine is right' (Putnam 1983b: 237–8).

The point is, as Putnam rightly recognises, for the relativist, other cultures, their beliefs, etc. are constructs viewed from the prism of her own culture. Any attempt by the relativist to express the position of other cultures ends up being a restatement of his own cultural viewpoint. This is, I think, yet another version of the incommensurability argument to be discussed in chapter 6.

12 This construction is a compilation of the arguments by Hales (1997) and others.

13 This is true of at least some non-analytic philosophers as well. Some years ago, in a private conversation, Jürgen Habermas expressed great surprise that I was spending time on a book on relativism. His reaction was 'but relativism is self-refuting' QED.

14 A general problem with many-valued logics is that in all instances where a sentence (P) receives the value 0.5 then (P & –P) also receives the value 0.5, and hence contradictions in this system come out as 'half-true' rather than false. Less surprisingly, the principle of excluded middle (P v –P) in this system can be assigned the value 0.5 or 'half true' instead of true, and hence what would be seen as a logical truth in classical logic receives the same truth-value, or is true to the same degree, as a contradiction. Even if we choose to reject the authority of the law of excluded middle we need to explain this anomalous result.

15 Hales provides an elegant formal semantics for language RL where he introduces the perspectival operators ■ and ◊, and the non-empty set P of perspectives and a commensurability relation C on P are added to standard models for predicate modal logic.

16 See 7.6 for a discussion of Putnam's views.

17 Rorty has modified this claim somewhat, but the main thrust of the sociological account of truth has remained constant.

18 Similarities with Nozick's view of truth as 'what is serviceable' are interesting. Both philosophers assign a functional role to the notion of truth, rather than giving it an abstract characterisation. In chapter 1 I argued that this is what Protagoras may have been doing as well.

19 Rorty's use of the term 'ethnocentrism' is heavily ironic (I am sure), for the rejection of a sense of superiority by colonialist societies, or what became known as 'ethnocentrism', was one of the main motivations for cultural relativism as advocated by anthropologists whose liberal sympathies Rorty shares (see chapter 3).

5 RELATIVISM AND RATIONALITY

1 Lukes (1979: 207) defines an irrational belief or set of beliefs as having one or more of the following characteristics:

(1) if they are illogical, i.e., inconsistent or self-contradictory, consisting of or relying on invalid inferences, etc.
(2) if they are partially or wholly false
(3) if they are nonsensical
(4) if they are situationally specific or *ad hoc*, i.e., not universalised because bound to particular occasions.

(Lukes 1979: 207)

In addition, a rational person will seek to have reliable evidence, justification and good reasons for her beliefs or choice of actions. Lukes's conditions 1–4 are, as they stand, too strong for delineating rational from irrational beliefs. Any belief set will almost certainly contain some false beliefs as well as beliefs which are held unreflectively or uncritically.

2 By classical logic I mean the standard Russell–Whitehead *Principia Mathematica* system. Examples of such a system can readily be found in elementary logic books such as *Beginning Logic* by E. J. Lemmon (1965). Two main features of such a system are:

(1) It has a truth-functional, two-valued, semantics. That is, every proposition (sentence or statement) gets either the value 'true' or the value 'false' and there are no truth-value gaps and truth-value gluts.
(2) It has all of the following formulas as part of its theorems or axioms:

$$\text{(i)} \quad -(P \mathbin{\&} -P)$$
$$\text{(ii)} \quad (P \lor -P)$$
$$\text{(iii)} \quad (P \Leftrightarrow P)$$

It also has a number of rules of deduction. Among them are the rules for conditional reasoning which state P → Q, P therefore Q (or *modus ponens*) as well as its converse P → Q, – Q therefore –P (or *modus tollens*); the laws governing the application of conjunction to the effect that if two propositions P and Q are jointly true, then so is P on its own and Q on its own, i.e., P & Q therefore P, and P & Q, therefore Q; and P, Q therefore P & Q. Many of these presuppositions have been questioned by philosophers who for technical or philosophical reasons advocate non-classical logics, e.g., many-valued logic, intuitionistic logic, relevance logic. Deviant (non-classical) logics are formal systems which use the same vocabulary as classical logic does but drop some of its rules and axioms. Deviant logics may also have a non-truth-functional or non-bivalent semantics. Examples of deviant logics are 'intuitionistic logic', 'quantum logics', 'many-valued logics'. Intuitionistic logic, for instance, rejects (P v –P) and (–P → P). The various versions of many-valued logics, as we saw in chapter 4, assign to propositions or sentences values intermediary between truth and falsity.

3 By which of course Frege means the rules of standard classical logic. See note 2.

4 See Lewis Carroll's 'What Achilles Said to the Tortoise' (1895) and the host of debate it has engendered.

5 The arguments for the uniqueness view of logic are notoriously unconvincing. Levy-Bruhl renounced it later in life and the postmodern arguments often show a lack of familiarity with and understanding of the fundamentals of formal logic.

6 Hass makes this point while discussing Andrea Nye's rejection of logic as masculine and androcentric but does not subscribe to her position.

7 2 is denied by paraconsistent and relevant logicians. 3 is the starting point of relevance logic. Classical negation has also been questioned in intuitionistic logic.

8 For instance, relevance logicians attempt to devise a new system of logic that would address the perceived problems of classical systems. They claim that relevance logic, the main point of which is to provide a formal system which allows only those deductions that, in addition to being truth-preserving, ensure the relevance of the premises of the argument to the conclusion, is the 'one true logic' (see Anderson and Belnap 1975; Baghramian 1988–90). Relevance logic, they argue, reflects our ordinary-language arguments and reasoning much more accurately than classical logic. However, they do not argue, as Barnes and Bloor do, that its introduction in any way justifies relativism about logic.

9 Dennett has an even stronger line of argument against relativism about rationality. According to him, attributing rationality is a prerequisite of our ability to ascribe intentionality to other beings. Even creatures from another planet would share with us our beliefs in logical truths. This is because the assumption that something is an intentional system is the assumption that it is rational; that is, one gets nowhere with the assumption that entity x has beliefs p, q, r, . . . unless one also supposes that x believes what follows from p, q, r, . . .; otherwise there is no way of ruling out the prediction that x will, in the face of its beliefs p, q, r, . . . do something utterly stupid, and, if we cannot rule out *that* prediction, we will have acquired no predictive power at all (Dennett 1978: 10–11).

10 For a discussion of this and other criticism of the evolutionary accounts of rationality see Stein (1996).

11 See Stein (1996) and Papineau (2000) for a discussion of this and other similar cases.

12 For detailed surveys of these results see Nisbett and Ross (1980), Kahneman, Slovic and Tversky (1982), Baron (1994), Piatelli-Palmarini (1989), Dawes (1988) and Sutherland (1994).

13 For a survey of the literature see Lichtenstein *et al.* (1982).

14 The material in what follows has been drawn from Samuels *et al.* (1999).

15 MacIntyre also believes that the Enlightenment view turns us into 'rootless cosmopolitans', belonging everywhere and hence nowhere (MacIntyre 1988: 397). On a personal note, as a self-confessed rootless cosmopolitan I tend to resent MacIntyre's conclusion that intellectually or morally I am in a worse position than those who firmly belong to a single moral (religious) tradition. After all, we are bipeds and not trees.

6 EPISTEMIC RELATIVISM

1 The list is based on Hacking (1981: 1–5). However, in several places I have departed from his original nine points.

2 See Siegel (1996 and 2004) for informative discussions of these points.

3 Harré and Krausz (1996) have argued that 'The "thought-styles" and "thought-collectives" of Ludwick Fleck ([1935] 1979) are ancestors in modern times of much of the relativism in the interpretation of natural science, attributed to Kuhn'. Although many of Fleck's ideas anticipate Kuhn's discussion of paradigm change in science, it was only with the publication of Kuhn's work that the issue of relativism in science became a central concern and point of debate. Hence, in terms of intellectual impact, rather than historical precedence, Kuhn's work is of far greater significance.

4 Kuhn's views on paradigms are influenced by the assumption, shared by many other philosophers of science, that all observations are theory-laden. However, he also extends this view to the more radical claim that even truth is theory-dependent.

5 See, for instance, the postscript to Kuhn (1970) and 'Objectivity, Value Judgments, and Theory Choice', in Kuhn (1977), where Kuhn attempts to counter the accusation of relativism and avoid the more radical consequences of the incommensurability thesis.

6 But also see Preston (1997) for arguments against interpreting Feyerabend as a relativist, at least in his earlier writings.

7 See also Preston (1997: 183–5). Preston's book provides a systematic detailed analysis of Feyerabend's work; however, I find myself in disagreement with some of his views on the extent of Feyerabend's commitment to relativism.

8 Kuhn says: 'Remember briefly where the term "incommensurability" came from. The hypotenuse of an isosceles right triangle is incommensurable with its side or the circumference of a circle with its radius in the sense that there is no unit of length contained without residue an integral number of times in each member of the pair' (Kuhn 2000: 35).

9 See for instance Shapere (1966), Sheffler (1967), Davidson (1984) and

Putnam (1981). Davidson's views will be discussed in greater detail in chapter 8.

10 Kuhn has progressively weakened the claims he made in the first edition of *The Structure of Scientific Revolutions* in order to avoid the relativistic implications of his doctrine. See Kitcher (1982) for a discussion of this point.

11 It is interesting that despite disagreements on many points Putnam and Davidson agree on this particular criticism of incommensurability and of relativism.

12 As we shall see in chapter 7, the view that a proposition can be true in one language but not true in another has been found unintelligible by Donald Davidson. Furthermore, Davidson, unlike Kuhn, does not allow for partial translatability.

13 I owe many of the points in this section to discussions with Cynthia McDonald and her unpublished paper on the paradox of bias.

14 Various solutions to this so-called 'paradox of bias' have been proffered. For instance, Louise Anthony (1993) has argued that we should distinguish between 'good and bad bias'. Good bias facilitates the search for truth, while bad bias (as in androcentric bias) leads to bad science because it leaves out the feminist perspective and hence does not provide us with a complete account of knowledge. The problem with this approach is that the mainstream epistemologists can equally claim that feminist epistemology is not able to capture all the knowledge that there is either, and hence mainstream and feminist epistemologies suffer from exactly the same (inescapable) defects. That is, they each give only a partial account of knowledge (I owe this point to Cynthia McDonald).

15 Some feminist epistemologists have tried to overcome such objections by proposing a new outlook on the very definition of knowledge, a view that emphasises the communitarian, holistic and public nature of knowledge rather than the individualistic view taken by mainstream epistemologists. See, e.g., Hankinson Nelson (1993) and Potter (1993).

7 CONCEPTUAL RELATIVISM

1 In listing these various accounts of scheme and content I have not distinguished between the accounts given by those who uphold the distinction between scheme and content (e.g., Quine) and those who reject it (e.g., Davidson). Furthermore, particular accounts of scheme or content have been discussed in order to be rejected by the philosophers cited. For instance, Putnam introduces the cookie-cutter metaphor only to deny its usefulness (Putnam 1987).

2 I believe S7 straddles the two interpretations.

3 See Hilary Putnam for an interesting discussion of this point, in Putnam (1987, 1990).

4 See Friedman (1993: 37–55) for an illuminating discussion of the relationship between the a priori and developments in science.

5 For an excellent discussion of Jamesian pluralism see O' Shea (2000).

6 Richard Rorty has argued that James and Dewey are 'metaphilosophical relativists, in a certain limited sense. Namely: they think there is no way

to choose, and no point in choosing, between incompatible philosophical theories of the typical Platonic or Kantian type. Such theories are
attempts to ground some elements of our practices on something external
to these practices. Pragmatists think that any such philosophical ground-
ing is, apart from the elegance of execution, pretty much as good or as
bad as the practice it purports to ground' (James 1979: 77). Rorty, hence,
gives yet another nuance to the term 'relativism'.

7 Quine's views were influenced by, and were a reaction to, Rudolph
Carnap's. Carnap believed in the plurality of linguistic frameworks, each
embodying logical principles and governed by 'meaning postulates'. Our
choice between various frameworks is governed by conventions which
are, in turn, chosen by pragmatic considerations of usefulness, fruitfulness of research, simplicity, etc. Because according to Carnap, when it
comes to logic: 'everyone is at liberty to build up his own logic, i.e., his
own form of language, as he wishes'. This is Carnap's 'principle of tolerance'. The question of the correct or incorrect application of the rules of
logic can occur only within a linguistic framework – an internal question,
as Carnap calls it – while the external question of the truth or falsity of
these frameworks cannot be made sense of, as there are no transcendental
standards available to us to settle such a question.

8 There are many theoretical and practical problems with this description
of the work of the radical translator. For instance, how does she identify
and translate the natives' signs of assent and dissent? How would she
convey to the natives that she is asking a question? Quine is assuming that
the native would share the linguist's disposition to volunteer certain types
of sentences in the presence of certain types of stimuli and that there is
large communality between the speakers of diverse languages. I shall
return to this last point.

9 Under the influence of his former student, Donald Davidson, Quine
increasingly modified his commitment to the thesis of underdetermination and indeterminacy and came to argue that 'We are thus left only
with empirically equivalent theory formulations that are logically reconcilable. If we subscribe to one of them as true, we can call them all true
and view them as different descriptions of one and the same world. We
are no strangers, after all, to strange languages. If this be relativism make
the most of it' (Quine 1984: 295).

10 See for instance J. F. Harris who argues that 'Willard Van Orman Quine is
certainly one of the most important early figures in the current wave of
relativism' (Harris 1992: 27).

11 The influence of James is striking. He says: 'We carve out groups of stars
in the heavens, and call them constellations, and the stars patiently suffer
us to do so' (James 1975: 121).

12 Goodman is willing to question the distinction between natural kinds and
artefacts as well as the dividing line between the natural and conventional. See Goodman (1989: 80–5). But the questioning of these
distinctions is a consequence of the position he is proposing and cannot
be used as premise of his argument.

13 There is also an important distinction, as Putnam has pointed out,
between the ways in which concepts apply to artefacts as opposed to natural kinds. Natural kind concepts, such as *star*, *tiger*, *gold*, hook up with

the world in ways that concepts applicable to artefacts do not. This topic, however, is beyond the scope of the present book.

14 Putnam's views have undergone further changes in the past few years. For instance, he has moved away from the position he had called 'internal realism' in *Reason, Truth and History* (Putnam 1981) in so far as that doctrine had verificationist assumptions, and this move was in large part motivated by the types of concerns outlined here. However, he continues to reject what he calls 'metaphysical realism'. He now is more willing to talk about 'truth' as opposed to just 'warrant', where truth has a substantive, non-disquotational interpretation but is not defined in terms of traditional correspondence theories. For a detailed discussion of Putnam's work see Baghramian (forthcoming).

15 Robert Nozick, another Harvard philosopher, in his last book (Nozick 2001) defends a very weak version of relativism and hence can be seen as an affiliate member of the Harvard relativists. See chapter 4 for a discussion of Nozick's position.

8 RELATIVISM, INTERPRETATION AND CHARITY

1 Quine's formulation is rather unfortunate. Judgements as to the 'silliness' of any behaviour are invariably culture-dependent. The most solemn and serious ceremonies in one culture may (and often do) seem quite 'silly' to observers from other cultures.

2 According to Quine: 'The semantic criterion of negation is that it turns any short sentence to which one will assent into a sentence from which one will dissent, and vice versa. That of conjunction is that it produces compounds to which (so long as the component sentences are short) one is prepared to assent always and only when one is prepared to assent to each component. That of alternation is similar with assent changed twice to dissent' (Quine 1960: 57–8).

3 In other words, the process of translation then necessitates the ascription of a classical truth-functional logic to the natives and consequently blocks the possibility of their using 'alternative logical' systems.

4 For an outline of the main axioms and rules of derivation of classical logic and the differences with deviant logics see chapter 5, note 2.

5 Even more radically, positions can receive any of infinitely many numerical values falling between 0 and 1, e.g., 0.1, 0.2, 0.3.

6 Among the philosophers who have relied on considerations of translation to argue against cognitive relativism is Martin Hollis who has argued that we need to postulate a 'bridgehead' or assume that natives share our concepts of truth, coherence and rational interdependence of beliefs, and will make similar perceptual judgements in simple situations (Hollis 1970a and b). William Newton-Smith, on the other hand, has argued that 'it is a necessary (but not sufficient) condition of two sentences having the same meaning that they have the same truth conditions' (Newton-Smith 1982: 108). According to him, any two sentences S and S1 cannot have the same meaning but different truth conditions, and hence relativism about truth is unintelligible. Newton-Smith, like many other anti-relativists, seems to be assuming an objectivist theory of truth and meaning, hence begging the question against the relativist.

7 See Baghramian (1998b).

8 Davidson prefers the term 'radical interpretation' to Quine's radical translation as it has a wider application and can be applied to speakers of the same language (Davidson 1984).

9 Davidson's arguments also rule out some versions of relativism about logic; for relativism about logic can be construed as the claim that logical truth is culture-relative and this is what Davidson is denying.

10 It would take us well beyond the scope of this book to try to show why Davidson found this additional element necessary. Briefly put, I think Davidson realised (rightly) that he needed to anchor basic beliefs, as well as the principle of charity, in the real (physical) world.

11 Pr.4, even when taken independently of other premises, does not withstand a close scrutiny. However, a discussion of the problems it faces would take us well beyond the scope of this book.

12 See Nagel (1974).

13 Hence Davidson's dictum that all interpretation is radical interpretation.

9 MORAL RELATIVISM

1 Given the prevalence of 'head-hunting' in American academic circles, Cook's use of this example is somewhat unfortunate; the point of the example, however, stands.

2 Narayan argues:

> Feminist claims that 'equality' and 'rights' are 'Western values' also risk echoing the rhetoric of two groups of people who, despite their other differences, share the characteristic of being no friends of the feminist agenda. The first are what I shall call 'Western cultural supremacists', whose agenda of constructing flattering portraits of 'Western culture' proceeds by claiming ideas of equality, rights, democracy and so on as 'Western ideas' that prove the West's moral and political superiority to all 'Other' cultures (Bloom 1987; Schlesinger 1992). The second are Third World fundamentalists who share the views of Western cultural supremacists that all such notions are 'Western ideas'. Fundamentalists deploy these views to justify the claim that such ideas are 'irrelevant foreign notions' used only by 'Westernized and inauthentic' Third World subjects and to cloak their violations of rights and suppression of democratic processes in the mantle of cultural preservation (Howard 1993; Mayer 1995).
>
> (Narayan 2000: 91–2)

3 Crude subjectivism is to be distinguished from various philosophically sophisticated doctrines such as the 'reasonable subjectivism' of David Wiggins. Wiggins (1991) denies that his views of ethics imply relativism. Crude subjectivism is also distinct from prescriptivism (R. M. Hare) and projectivism (Simon Blackburn) even though these doctrines have also been characterised as 'subjectivist'.

4 David Lyons attributes this type of relativism to the social anthropologists (Lyons 1982).

5 There are some indications that both subjectivism and relativism are becoming a part of the common reaction to ethical issues in the West. Moral scepticism has penetrated the 'common-sense' conception of morality, at least in northern European countries, in ways that were not anticipated by Mackie in the early 1970s.

6 Jarvis Thomson believes that moral concepts operate in a quasi-absolutist fashion, in so far as we use terms of moral appraisal and approbation within the security of our own moral framework (Jarvis Thomson 1996: 206).

7 For a full list of the human capabilities and their requirements see Nussbaum (2000).

8 For a useful discussion of these last two senses of 'incommensurable' see Chang (1997).

9 As we saw in our discussion of moral incommensurability, values may be in conflict in several different ways: (i) There may exist plurality of values which are not compossible or they may be incompatible. (ii) Values may be incommensurable, which strictly means they cannot be compared. (iii) Alternatively, it may be argued that values can be compared but we do not have a single criterion or a decision procedure for choosing or adjudicating between them. (iv) Incommensurability may be defined as untranslatability. Berlin, however, is not explicit as to which of the many options he has in mind.

10 Berlin is not alone in identifying relativism with subjectivism. See also Kekes (1993: 15).

11 See chapters 5 and 8 for discussions of non-classical logics.

12 But see Martha Nussbaum above.

10 CONCLUSION: RELATIVISM, PLURALISM AND DIVERSITY

1 The case study originally analysed by R. M. Dixon can be found in Lakoff (1990: 92). Similar examples are plentiful in anthropological literature and are often employed in discussions of conceptual schemes by psychologists and cognitive scientists.

2 As opposed to Putnam's internal realism (see chapter 7).

3 McDowell puts the point this way: 'even as it tries to make out that sensory impressions are our avenue of access to the empirical world, empiricism conceives impressions in such a way that they could only close us off from the world, disrupting our "unmediated touch" with ordinary objects' (McDowell 1994: 155).

4 Davidson, in his argument against the very idea of a conceptual scheme, also introduces this possibility, only to dismiss it with other varieties of scheme–content dualism. He says: 'The notion of organisation applies only to pluralities. But whatever plurality we take experience to consist in – events like losing a button or stubbing a toe, having a sensation of warmth or hearing an oboe – we will have to individuate according to familiar principles. A language that organizes such entities must be a language very like our own' (Davidson [1974] 1984: 192). Stubbing a toe or hearing an oboe are instances of what Lewis has called thick experiences rather than thin, contentless sensations of pain or sound.

5 James O'Shea has drawn my attention to some of the similarities of my proposal to James's idea of 'conceptual map-making'. A discussion of the similarities and differences between the two views would take me beyond the scope of this book. Briefly put, James's pluralism is a richer and philosophically more ambitious idea than the moderate pluralism supported here. However, much of what I have said in this book is in sympathy with a Jamesian philosophical tone.

Bibliography

Alcoff, L. and Potter, E. (eds) (1993) *Feminist Epistemologies*, London: Routledge.

Alston, W. P. (ed.) (2002) *Realism and Antirealism*, Ithaca, NY: Cornell University Press.

Anderson, A. and Belnap, N. (1975) *Entailment: The Logic of Relevance and Necessity*, vol. 1. Princeton, NJ: Princeton University Press.

Anderson, D. L. (1992) 'What is Realistic about Putnam's Internal Realism?' *Philosophical Topics:* 20(1): 49–83.

Anderson, R. (1958) 'Mathematics and the Language-Game', *Review of Metaphysics*, 11: 254–70.

Annas, J. and Barnes, J. (1985) *The Modes of Skepticism: Ancient Texts and Modern Interpretations*, Cambridge: Cambridge University Press.

Anthony, L. (1993) *A Mind of One's Own: Feminist Essays on Reason and Objectivity*, Boulder, CO: Westview Press.

Appiah, A. (1992) *In My Father's House*, Oxford: Oxford University Press.

Aristotle (1908) *Metaphysics*, in *The Works of Aristotle Translated into English*, vol. 8, ed. W. D. Ross, trans. J. A. Smith and W. D. Ross, Oxford: Clarendon Press.

Aristotle (1924) *Rhetoric*, in *The Works of Aristotle Translated into English*, vol. 11, ed. W. D. Ross, trans. W. Rhys Roberts, Oxford: Clarendon Press.

Arrington, R. L. (1989) *Rationalism, Realism, and Relativism: Perspectives in Contemporary Moral Epistemology*, Ithaca, NY: Cornell University Press.

Ashman, K. M. and Baringer, P. S. (eds) (2001) *After the Science Wars*, London: Routledge.

Aune, B. (1987) 'Conceptual Relativism', in James E. Tomberlin (ed.) *Philosophical Perspectives*, 1, *Metaphysics*, Atascadero, CA: Ridgview: 269–88.

Baghramian, M. (1988–90) 'The Justification for Relevance Logic', *Philosophical Studies*, 32: 32–43.

—— (1990) 'Rorty, Davidson and Truth', *Ratio*, 3(2): 101–16.

—— (1998a) 'Why Conceptual Schemes?', *Proceedings of the Aristotelian Society*, 98(2): 287–306.

—— (1998b) *Modern Philosophy of Language*, London: J. M. Dent and Washington, DC: Counter Point.

—— (2000) 'On the Plurality of Conceptual Schemes', in M. Baghramian and A. Ingram (eds) *Pluralism: The Philosophy and Politics of Diversity*, London: Routledge: 44–59.

—— (forthcoming) *Hilary Putnam: Mind, Language and the World*, Cambridge: Polity Press.

Baghramian, M. and Ingram, A. (eds) (2000) *Pluralism: Essays on the Philosophy and Politics of Diversity*, London: Routledge.

Baker, G. P. and Hacker, P. M. S. (1979) *An Analytical Commentary on Wittgenstein's Philosophical Investigations*, vol. 1, Oxford: Blackwell.

—— (1989) *Frege: Logical Excavations*, Oxford: Oxford University Press.

Baldwin, T. (2001) 'Death and Meaning: Some Questions for Derrida', in S. Glendinning (ed.) *Arguing with Derrida*, Oxford: Blackwell: 89–101.

Baringer, P. S. (2001) 'Introduction: The "Science Wars"', in K. M. Ashman and P. S. Baringer (eds) *After the Science Wars*, London: Routledge: 1–13.

Barkow, J., Cosmides, L. and Tooby, J. (eds) (1992) *The Adapted Mind: Evolutionary Psychology and the Generation of Culture*, Oxford: Oxford University Press.

Barnes, B. (1977) *Interests and the Growth of Knowledge*, London: Routledge.

Barnes, B. and Bloor, D. (1982) 'Relativism, Rationalism and the Sociology of Knowledge', in M. Hollis and S. Lukes (eds) *Rationality and Relativism*, Oxford: Blackwell: 21–47.

Barnes, J. (1988–90) 'Scepticism and Relativity', *Philosophical Studies*, 32: 1–31.

Baron-Cohen, S. (1995) *Mindblindness: An Essay on Autism and Theory of Mind*, Cambridge, MA: MIT Press.

Barrett, R. and Gibson, R. (eds) (1990) *Perspectives on Quine*, Oxford: Blackwell.

Battersby, C. (1978) 'Morality and the Ik', *Philosophy*, 53: 201–14.

Bayle, P. (1992) *De la tolérance. Commentaire philosophique*, ed. J. M. Gros, Coll. Agora–Les classiques, Paris: Presses Pocket.

Bayley, J. E. (ed.) (1992) *Aspects of Relativism: Moral, Cognitive and Literary*, Lanham, MD: University Press of America.

Bearn. G. C. F. (1985) 'Relativism as Reductio', *Mind* (N.S.) 94(375): 389–408.

Beiser, F. C. (1987) *The Fate of Reason: German Philosophy from Kant to Fichte*, Cambridge, MA: Harvard University Press.

Benedict, R. (1934a) 'A Defense of Moral Relativism', *The Journal of General Psychology*, 10: 59–82.

—— (1934b) *Patterns of Culture*, London: Penguin.

Bennett, J. (1989) *Rationality: An Essay towards an Analysis*, London: Routledge and Kegan Paul.

Bennigson, T. (1999a) 'Is Relativism Really Self-Refuting?' *Philosophical Studies*, 94(3): 211–35.

—— (1999b) 'The Truth in Vulgar Relativism', *Philosophical Studies*, 96(3): 296–301.

Berlin, I. (1969) *Four Essays on Liberty*, Oxford: Oxford University Press.

—— (1978) *Concepts and Categories*, introduction by B. Williams, Oxford: Oxford University Press.

—— (1981) 'The Originality of Machiavelli', in Berlin, *Against the Current*, ed. H. Hardy, Oxford: Oxford University Press: 25–79.

—— (1991) *The Crooked Timber of Humanity*, ed. H. Hardy, New York: Knopf.

—— (1999) *The Roots of Romanticism*, ed. H. Hardy, Princeton, NJ: Princeton University Press.

—— (2000) *Three Critics of the Enlightenment: Vico, Hamann, Herder*, ed. H. Hardy, Princeton, NJ, and Oxford: Princeton University Press.

Bernstein, R. J. (1989) *Beyond Objectivism and Relativism: Science, Hermeneutics, and Praxis*, Oxford: Blackwell.

Bianchi, E. (ed.) (1999) *Is Feminist Philosophy Philosophy?* Evanston, IL: Northwestern University Press.

Bird, A. (2000) *Thomas Kuhn*, Princeton, NJ: Princeton University Press.

Bloom, A. (1987) *The Closing of the American Mind*, foreword by S. Bellow, London: Penguin.

Bloor, D. (1976) *Knowledge and Social Imagery*, London: Routledge and Kegan Paul.

Boas, F. (1940) 'The Aims of Ethnology', in Boas, *Race, Language and Culture*, New York: The Free Press: 626–38.

Boghossian, P. (1996) 'What the Sokal Hoax Ought to Teach Us', *Times Literary Supplement, Commentary*, 13 December: 14–15.

Brandom, R. B. (ed.) (2000) *Rorty and his Critics*, Oxford: Blackwell Publishers.

Brown, D. E. (1991) *Human Universals*, New York: McGraw-Hill.

Brown, H. I. (1990) *Rationality*, London: Routledge.

Brown, S. C. (1979) *Philosophical Disputes in the Social Sciences*, Brighton: Harvester Press.

—— (ed.) (1984) *Objectivity and Cultural Divergence*, Cambridge: Cambridge University Press.

Burnyeat, M. F. (1976a) 'Protagoras and Self-refutation in Plato's *Theaetetus*', *The Philosophical Review*, 85(2): 172–95.

—— (1976b) 'Protagoras and Self-refutation in Later Greek Philosophy', *The Philosophical Review*, 85(1): 44–69.

Campbell, R. (1992) *Truth and Historicity*, Oxford: Clarendon Press.

Carnap, R. (1937) *The Logical Syntax of Language*, London: Routledge.

—— (1950) 'Empiricism, Semantics and Ontology', *Revue Internationale de la Philosophie*, 4(11): 20–40.

Carroll, L. (1895) 'What the Tortoise Said to Achilles', *Mind*, 14: 278–80.

Casscells, W., Schoenberger, A. and Grayboys, T. (1978). 'Interpretation by Physicians of Clinical Laboratory Results', *New England Journal of Medicine*, 299: 999–1000.

Chalmers, A. F. (1978) *What Is This Thing Called Science?* 3rd edn, Buckingham: Open University Press.

Chang, R. (ed.) (1997) *Incommensurability, Incomparability, and Practical Reason*, Cambridge, MA: Harvard University Press.

Child, W. (1994) 'On the Dualism of Scheme and Content', *Proceedings of the Aristotelian Society*, 94(1): 53–71.

Chomsky, N. (1992) 'Explaining Language Use', *Philosophical Topics*, 20(1): 205–32.

Cinelli, A. (1993) 'Nietzsche, Relativism and Truth', *Auslegung* 19(1): 35–45.

Clark, M. (1990) *Nietzsche on Truth and Philosophy*, Cambridge: Cambridge University Press.

Clifford, J. and Marcus, G. E. (eds) (1986) *Writing Culture: The Poetics and Politics of Ethnography*, Berkeley: University of California Press.

Coburn, R. (1976) 'Relativism and the Basis of Morality', *The Philosophical Review*, 85(1): 87–93.

Code, L. (1993) 'Taking Subjectivity into Account', in L. Alcoff and E. Potter (eds) *Feminist Epistemologies*, London: Routledge: 15–48.

—— (2000) 'How to Think Globally: Stretching the Limits of Imagination', in U. Narayan and S. Harding (eds) *Decentring the Center: Philosophy for a Multicultural, Postcolonial, and Feminist World*, Bloomington: Indiana University Press: 67–79.

Collin, F. (1997) *Social Reality*, London: Routledge.

Conant, J. (1992) 'The Search for Logically Alien Thought: Descartes, Kant, Frege and the *Tractatus*', *Philosophical Topics*, 20(1): 115–36.

Cook, J. W. (1999) *Morality and Cultural Differences*, Oxford: Oxford University Press.

Cooper, D. E. (1971) 'Alternative Logic in 'Primitive Thought'', *Man* (N.S.), 10: 238–56.

—— (1985) 'Anthropology and Translation', *Proceedings of the Aristotelian Society*, 2: 51–68.

Cornford, F. M. (1935) *Plato's Theory of Knowledge: The 'Theaetetus' and the 'Sophist' of Plato*, New York: Harcourt, Brace and Company.

—— (1952) *Principium Sapientiae*, Cambridge: Cambridge University Press.

Cosmides, L. and Tooby, J. (1992) 'Cognitive Adaptations for Social Exchange', in J. Barkow, L. Cosmides and J. Tooby (eds) *The Adapted Mind: Evolutionary Psychology and the Generation of Culture*, Oxford: Oxford University Press: 163–228.

Cowan, J. L. (1961) 'Wittgenstein's Philosophy of Logic', *The Philosophical Review*, 71: 87–105.

Danto, A. C. ([1965] 1980) *Nietzsche as Philosopher*, 2nd edn, New York: Columbia University Press.

Davidson, D. ([1974] 1984) 'On the Very Idea of a Conceptual Scheme', reprinted in D. Davidson (1984) *Inquiries into Truth and Interpretation*, Oxford: Oxford University Press: 183–98.

—— (1980) *Essays on Actions and Events*, Oxford: Oxford University Press.

—— (1984) *Inquiries into Truth and Interpretation*, Oxford: Oxford University Press.

—— (1986) 'A Coherence Theory of Truth and Knowledge', in E. LePore (ed.) (1986) *Truth and Interpretation*, Oxford: Blackwell: 307–19.

—— (1989) 'The Myth of the Subjective', in M. Krausz (ed.) *Relativism: Interpretation and Confrontation*, Notre Dame, IL: University of Notre Dame Press: 159–72.

—— (1990a) 'Meaning, Truth and Evidence', in R. Barrett and R. Gibson (eds) *Perspectives on Quine*, Oxford: Blackwell: 68–79.

—— (1990b) 'The Structure and Content of Truth', The Dewey Lectures 1989, *Journal of Philosophy*, 87: 279–328.

—— (1991) 'Three Varieties of Knowledge', in A. Phillips Griffiths (ed.) *A. J. Ayer: Memorial Essays*, Royal Institute of Philosophy Supplement, 30, Cambridge: Cambridge University Press: 153–66.

—— ([1992] 2001) 'The Second Person' in D. Davidson, *Subjective, Intersubjective, Objective*, Oxford: Clarendon Press: 107–22.

—— (2001) *Subjective, Intersubjective, Objective*, Oxford: Clarendon Press.

Davidson, D. and Hintikka, J. (eds) (1969) *Words and Objections: Essays on the Work of W. V. Quine*, Dordrecht: Reidel.

Dennett, D. (1978) *Brainstorms*, Montgomery, VT: Bradford Books.

—— (1987) *The Intentional Stance*, Cambridge, MA: MIT Press.

Derrida, J. ([1967] 1997) *Of Grammatology*, trans. G. C. Spivak, Baltimore, MD: The Johns Hopkins University Press.

—— ([1972] 1981) *Positions*, trans. A. Bass, Chicago: Chicago University Press.

—— ([1972] 1982) *Margins of Philosophy*, Chicago: University of Chicago Press.

—— ([1982] 1988) *The Ear of the Other: Otobiography, Transference, Translation: Texts and Discussions with Jacques Derrida*, Lincoln: University of Nebraska Press.

—— (1988) *Limited Inc*, ed. G. Graff, Evanston, IL: Northwestern University Press.

—— (1999) 'Hospitality, Justice and Responsibility', in M. Dooley and R. Kearney (eds) (1999) *Questioning Ethics: Contemporary Debates in Philosophy*, London: Routledge: 65–83.

Descartes, R. (1641) *Meditations Concerning First Philosophy*, in *Philosophical Works* (1955) ed. E. Haldane and G. R. T. Ross, 2 vols. New York: Dover.

Diderot, D. (1956) 'Supplement to Bougainville's "Voyage"', in *Rameau's Nephew and Other Works*, trans. J. Barzum and R. H. Bowen, New York: Doubleday: 183–239.

Dilthey, W. (1961) *Meaning in History*, trans. and ed. H. P. Rickman, London: George Allen and Unwin.

—— (1988) *Introduction to the Human Sciences*, trans. R. J. Betanoz, London: Harvester Press.

Diogenes Laertius (1925) *Lives of Eminent Philosophers*, trans R. D. Hicks, Cambridge, MA: Harvard University Press.

Doppelt, G. (1982) 'Kuhn's Epistemological Relativism: An Interpretation and Defense', in M. Krausz and J. Meiland (eds) *Relativism: Cognitive and Moral*, Notre Dame, IL: University of Notre Dame Press: 113–46.

Dreben, B. (1992) 'Putnam, Quine – and the Facts', *Philosophical Topics*, 20 (1): 293–316.

Dummett, M. (1978) *Truth and Other Enigmas*, London: Duckworth.

Duran, J. (2001) *Worlds of Knowing: Global Feminist Epistemologies*, New York: Routledge.

Earman, J. (1993) 'Carnap, Kuhn, and the Philosophy of Scientific Methodology', in P. Horwich (ed.) *World Changes: Thomas Kuhn and the Nature of Science*, Cambridge, MA: MIT Press: 9–36.

Ebbs, G. (1992) ' Realism and Rational Inquiry', *Philosophical Topics*, 20(1): 1–34.

Ellis, B. (1979) *Rational Belief Systems*, Oxford: Blackwell.

Elster, J. (1978) *Logic and Society: Contradictions and Possible Worlds*, Chichester: John Wiley and Son.

—— (1983) *Sour Grapes: Studies in the Subversion of Rationality*, Cambridge: Cambridge University Press.

Engel, P. (2002) *Truth*, Chesham: Acumen Press.

Engels, F. ([1886] 1985) *Anti-Dühring* in John Ladd (ed.) *Ethical Relativism*, Lanham, MD: University Press of America: 16–28.

Envine, S. (1991) *Davidson*, Cambridge: Polity Press.

Erdmann, B. (1907) *Logische Elementarlehre*, 2nd revised edn, Halle: Niemeyer.

Evans, J. D. G. (1996) 'Cultural Realism: The Ancient Philosophical Background', in *Philosophy and Pluralism*, Royal Institute of Philosophy Supplement 40, ed. David Archard: 57–8.

Evans-Pritchard, E. E. ([1937] 1976) *Witchcraft, Oracles, and Magic among the Azande*, abridged and with an introduction by E. Gillies, Oxford: Clarendon Press.

—— (1956) *Nuer Religion*, Oxford: Oxford University Press.

Feyerabend, P. (1962) 'Explanation, Reduction and Empiricism', in H. Feigl and G. Maxwell (eds) *Scientific Explanation: Space and Time*, Minneapolis: University of Minnesota Press: 28–97.

—— (1965) 'Problems of Empiricism', in R. G. Colodny (ed.) *Beyond the Edge of Certainty*, University of Pittsburgh Studies in the Philosophy of Science, Englewood Cliffs, NJ: Prentice-Hall.

—— (1975) *Against Method*, London: New Left Books.

—— (1978) *Science in a Free Society*, London: Verso.

—— (1987) *Farewell to Reason*, London: Verso.

—— (1991) *Three Dialogues on Knowledge*, Oxford: Blackwell.

Field, H. (1982) 'Realism and Relativism', *Journal of Philosophy*, 79: 553–67.

Fish, S. (2002) 'Don't Blame Relativism': 27–31, www.communitarian network.org.

Fleck L. ([1935] 1979) *Genesis and Development of a Scientific Fact*, ed. T. J. Trenn and R. K. Merton, Chicago: University of Chicago Press.

Fodor, J. A. (1981) *Representations: Philosophical Essays on the Foundations of Cognitive Science*, Cambridge, MA: MIT Press.

—— (1983). *The Modularity of Mind*. Cambridge, MA: MIT Press.

—— (1990) *A Theory of Content and Other Essays*, Cambridge, MA: MIT Press.

Fodor, J. and LePore, E. (1992) *Holism: A Shopper's Guide*, Oxford: Blackwell.

Foot, P. ([1975] 1982) 'Moral Relativism', in M. Krausz and J. Meiland (eds) *Relativism: Cognitive and Moral*, Notre Dame, IL: University of Notre Dame Press: 152–66.

Foster, L. (1988) 'Strong Relativism Revisited', *Philosophy and Phenomenological Research*, 49(1): 145–50.

Foucault, M. (1970) *The Order of Things*, trans. A. Sheridan, London: Tavistock.

—— (1977) 'Nietzsche, Genealogy, History', trans. D. Bouchard and S. Sherry, in D. Bouchard (ed.) *Language, Counter-Memory, Practise*, Ithaca, NY: Cornell University Press.

—— ([1977] 1992) 'Prison Talk', trans. C. Gordon, in C. Gordon (ed.) *Power/Knowledge: Selected Interviews and Other Writings, 1972–1977*, New York: Pantheon. Also published in *Radical Philosophy*, 16: 10–15.

—— (2001) 'Truth and Power', in M. P. Lynch (ed.) *The Nature of Truth*, Cambridge, MA: MIT Press.

Freeman, D. (1983) *Margaret Mead and Samoa: The Making and Unmaking of an Anthropological Myth*. Cambridge, MA: Harvard University Press.

Frege, G. (1960) *Translations from the Philosophical Writings of Gottlob Frege*, ed. P. Geach and M. Black, Oxford: Blackwell.

—— ([1883] 1964) *The Basic Laws of Arithmetic: Exposition of the System*, trans. and ed. M. Furth, Berkeley: University of California Press.

—— (1973) *Posthumous Writings*, trans. P. Long and R. White, Oxford: Blackwell.

Friedman, M. (1993) 'Remarks on the History of Science and the History of Philosophy', in P. Horwich (ed.) *World Changes: Thomas Kuhn and the Nature of Science*, Cambridge, MA: MIT Press: 37–55.

Fuller, S. (2000) 'The Reenchantment of Science: A Fit End to the Science Wars', in K. M. Ashman, and P. S. Baringer (eds) *After the Science Wars*, London: Routledge: 183–208.

Gadamer, H. G. (1975) *Truth and Method*, London: Methuen.

Galileo. (1953) *Dialogue on the Great World Systems*, ed. Giorgio de Santillana, Chicago: University of Chicago Press.

Geertz, C. (1973) *The Interpretation of Cultures*, New York: Basic Books.

—— (1989) 'Anti-anti-relativism', in M. Krausz (ed.) *Relativism: Interpretation and Confrontation*, Notre Dame, IL: University of Notre Dame Press: 12–34.

Gellner, E. (1982) 'Relativism and Universals', in M. Hollis and S. Lukes (eds) *Rationality and Relativism*, Oxford: Blackwell: 181–200.

—— (1992) *Postmodernism, Reason and Religion*, London: Routledge.

Glendinning, S. (ed.) (2001) *Arguing with Derrida*, Oxford: Blackwell.

Glock H. J. (1996) *Wittgenstein Dictionary*, Oxford: Blackwell.

Goodman, N. (1978) *Ways of Worldmaking*, Indianapolis: Hackett Publishing Company.

—— (1984) *Of Minds and Other Matters*, Cambridge, MA: Harvard University Press.

—— (1989) 'Just the Facts, Ma'am!', in M. Krausz (ed.) *Relativism: Interpretation and Confrontation*, Notre Dame, IL: University of Notre Dame Press: 80–5.

—— (1996) 'On Starmaking', in P. J. McCormick (ed.) *Starmaking: Realism, Anti-Realism, and Irrealism*, Cambridge, MA: MIT Press: 143–50.

Grandy, R. E. (1973) 'Reference, Meaning and Belief', *The Journal of Philosophy*, 70: 439–52.

Gray, J. (1995a) *Berlin*, London: Fontana Press.

—— (1995b) *Enlightenment's Wake*, London: Routledge.

Grote, J. (1865) *Exploratio Philosophica: Rough Notes on Modern Intellectual Science*, Cambridge: Deighton, Bell and Co.

Guthrie, W. K. C. (1971) *The Sophists*, Cambridge: Cambridge University Press.

Haack, S. ([1974] 1996) *Deviant Logic: Some Philosophical Issues*, Cambridge: Cambridge University Press.

—— (1993) *Evidence and Inquiry*, Oxford: Blackwell.

—— (1996) 'Reflections on Relativism: from Momentous Tautology to Seductive Contradiction', in James E. Tomberlin (ed.) *Philosophical Perspectives, 10, Metaphysics*, Oxford: Blackwell: 297–315.

Hacking, I. (1975) *Why Does Language Matter to Philosophy?* Cambridge: Cambridge University Press.

—— (1982) 'Language, Truth and Reason', in M. Hollis and S. Lukes (eds) *Rationality and Relativism*, Oxford: Blackwell: 48–66.

—— (1983) *Representing and Intervening*, Cambridge: Cambridge University Press.

—— (2002) *Historical Ontology*, Cambridge, MA: Harvard University Press.

—— (ed.) (1981) *Scientific Revolutions*, Oxford: Oxford University Press.

Hales, S. D. (1997) 'A Consistent Relativism', *Mind* (N.S.), 106: 33–52.

Hales, S. D. and Welshon, R. (2000) *Nietzsche's Perspectivism*, Champaign: University of Illinois Press.

Hamann, J. G. *(1967)*, *Hamann's Socratic Memorabilia. A Translation and Commentary*, trans. and ed. James C. O'Flaherty, Baltimore, MD: The Johns Hopkins University Press.

Hankinson, R. J. (1995) *The Sceptics*, London: Routledge.

Hankinson Nelson, L. (1993) 'Epistemological Communities', in L. Alcoff and E. Potter (eds) *Feminist Epistemologies*, London: Routledge: 121–60.

Harding, S. (1986) *The Science Question in Feminism*, New York: Cornell University Press.

—— (1993) 'Rethinking Standpoint Epistemology: "What is Strong Objectivity"' in L. Alcoff and E. Potter (eds) *Feminist Epistemologies*, London: Routledge: 49–82.

Harman, G. ([1975] 2000) 'Moral Relativism Defended', in G. Harman (2000)

Explaining Value and Other Essays in Moral Philosophy, Oxford: Oxford University Press: 3–19.

—— ([1985] 2000) 'Is There a Single True Morality', in G. Harman (2000) *Explaining Value and Other Essays in Moral Philosophy*, Oxford: Oxford University Press: 77–99.

—— (1996) 'Moral Relativism' in G. Harman and J. Jarvis Thomson (eds) *Moral Relativism and Moral Objectivity*, Oxford: Blackwell: 1–64.

—— (2000) *Explaining Value and Other Essays in Moral Philosophy*, Oxford: Oxford University Press.

Harman, G. and Jarvis Thomson, J. (1996) *Moral Relativism and Moral Objectivity*, Oxford: Blackwell.

Harré, R. and Krausz, M. (1996) *Varieties of Relativism*, Blackwell: Oxford.

Harris, J. F. (1992) *Against Relativism: A Philosophical Defense of Method*, La Salle, IL: Open Court.

Hass, M. (1999) 'Can there be a Feminist Logic?' in E. Bianchi (ed.) *Is Feminist Philosophy Philosophy?* Evanston, IL: Northwestern University Press: 190–201.

Hegel, G. W. F. (1929) *Science of Logic*, trans. H. Johnston and L. G. Struthers, London: Allen and Unwin.

—— (1975) *Lectures on the Philosophy of World History. Introduction: Reason in History*, trans. H. B. Nisbet, Cambridge: Cambridge University Press.

Heisenberg, W. ([1958] 1959) *Physics and Philosophy. The Revolution in Modern Science*, London: George Allen and Unwin.

Hekman, S. J. (1986) *Hermeneutics and the Sociology of Knowledge*, Oxford: Polity Press.

Helvétius, C. A. (1758) *De l'esprit, or, Essays on the Mind and its Several Faculties*, London: Dodsley.

Herder, J. G. (2002) *Philosophical Writings*, trans. and ed. M. N. Forster, Cambridge: Cambridge University Press.

Herodotus (1988) *The History*, trans. D. Grene, Chicago: University of Chicago Press.

Herskovits, M. J. (1960) *Man and His Works*, New York: Knopf.

—— (1972) *Cultural Relativism: Perspectives in Cultural Pluralism*, ed. F. Herskovits, New York: Random House.

Hintikka, H. (1972) 'Semantics for Propositional Attitudes', in A. Marras (ed.) *Intentionality, Mind and Language*, Chicago: University of Illinois Press: 457–72.

Hobhouse, L. T. (1951) *Morals in Evolution: A Study in Comparative Ethics*, London: Chapman and Hall.

Hollis, M. (1970a) 'The Limits of Irrationality', in B. R. Wilson (ed.) *Rationality*, Oxford: Blackwell, 214–20.

—— (1970b) 'Reason and Ritual', in B. R. Wilson (ed.) *Rationality*, Oxford: Blackwell, 221–39.

—— (1995a) 'A Prayer for Understanding', in C. M. Lewis (ed.) *Relativism and Religion*, London: Macmillan: 16–34.

—— (1995b) 'Perspectives', in C. M. Lewis (ed.) *Relativism and Religion*, London: Macmillan: 129–34.

Hollis, M. and Lukes, S. (eds) (1982) *Rationality and Relativism*, Oxford: Blackwell.

Hookway, C. (1992) *Scepticism*, London: Routledge.

Horwich, P. (1990) *Truth*, Oxford: Blackwell.

—— (ed.) (1993) *World Changes: Thomas Kuhn and the Nature of Science*, Cambridge, MA: MIT Press.

Humboldt, W. von ([1836] 1999) *On Language*, trans P. Heath, ed. M. Losonsky, Cambridge: Cambridge University Press.

Hume, D. ([1739] 1978) *A Treatise of Human Nature*, Oxford: Clarendon Press.

—— (1972) *Essays and Treatises on Several Subjects*, London: T. Cadell.

Husserl, E.([1900] 1970) *Prolegomena to the Logical Investigations*, London: Routledge.

Israel, J. I. (2001) *Radical Enlightenment: Philosophy and the Making of Modernity 1650–1750*, Oxford: Oxford University Press.

James, W. (1975) *Pragmatism: A New Name for Some Old Ways of Thinking*, Cambridge, MA: Harvard University Press.

—— (1979) *The Will to Believe*, Cambridge, MA: Harvard University Press.

—— (1983) *The Principles of Psychology*, Cambridge, MA: Harvard University Press.

—— (1997) *A Pluralistic Universe*, Lincoln: University of Nebraska Press.

Jarvie, I. C. (1984) *Rationality and Relativism: In Search of a Philosophy and History of Anthropology*, London: Routledge.

—— (1995a) 'The Justificationist Roots of Relativism', in C. M. Lewis (ed.) *Relativism and Religion*, London: Macmillan: 52–70.

—— (1995b) 'Responses', in C. M. Lewis (ed.) *Relativism and Religion*, London: Macmillan: 125–8.

Jarvis Thomson, J. (1996) 'Moral Objectivity', in Gilbert Harman and J. Jarvis Thomson (eds) (1996) *Moral Relativism and Moral Objectivity*, Oxford: Blackwell: 67–153.

Jencks, C. (1986) *What is Post-Modernism?* London: Academy Editions.

Jenkins, K. (ed.) (1997) *The Postmodern History Reader*, London: Routledge.

Johansen, K. F. ([1991] 1998) *A History of Ancient Philosophy*, trans. Henrik Rosenmeier, London: Routledge.

Johnson-Laird, P. N. and Wason, P. C. (1970) 'Insight into a Logical Relation', *Quarterly Journal of Experimental Pyschology*, 22: 49–61.

Kahneman, D. and Tversky, A. (1973) 'On the Psychology of Prediction', *Psychological Review*, 80: 237–51. Reprinted in Kahneman *et al.* (1982).

—— (1982) 'Subjective Probability: A Judgement of Representativeness', *Cognitive Psychology*, 3: 430–54.

Kahneman, D., Slovic, P. and Tversky, A. (eds) (1982) *Judgment under Uncertainty: Heuristics and Biases*, Cambridge: Cambridge University Press.

Kant, I. ([1885] 1972) *Introduction to Logic*, trans. T. K. Abbott, in I. M. Copi and J. A. Gould (eds) *Readings in Logic*, New York: Macmillan: 35–9.

—— (1929) *Critique of Pure Reason*, trans. N. Kemp Smith, London: Macmillan.

Kearney, R. (1991) *Poetics of Imagining from Husserl to Lyotard*, London: Routledge.

Kekes, J. (1993) *The Morality of Pluralism*, Princeton, NJ: Princeton University Press.

Kirk, R. (1999), *Relativism and Reality*, London: Routledge.

Kitcher, P. (1982) 'Implications of Incommensurability', *PSA* 1982: 589–603.

Knight, K. (ed.) (1998) *The MacIntyre Reader*, Cambridge: Polity Press.

Krausz, M. (ed.) (1989) *Relativism: Interpretation and Confrontation*, Notre Dame, IL: University of Notre Dame Press.

Krausz, M. and Meiland, J. W. (eds) (1982) *Relativism: Cognitive and Moral*, Notre Dame, IL: University of Notre Dame Press.

Kraut, R. (1986) 'The Third Dogma', in E. LePore (ed.) *Truth and Interpretation*, Oxford: Blackwell: 398–416.

Kroeber, A. (1948) *Anthropology*, New York: Harcourt Brace.

Kroeber, A. and Kluckhohn, C. (1952) 'Culture: A Critical Review of Concepts and Definition', *Papers of the Peabody Museum of American Archaeology and Ethnology*, 47(1): 181.

Kuhn T. S. ([1962] 1970) *The Structure of Scientific Revolutions*, Chicago: University of Chicago Press.

—— (1977) *The Essential Tension*, Chicago: University of Chicago Press.

—— (1981) 'A Function for Thought Experiments', in I. Hacking (ed.) *Scientific Revolutions*, Oxford: Oxford University Press: 6–27.

—— (2000) *The Road since Structure: Philosophical Essays, 1970–1993, with an Autobiographical Interview*, ed. J. Conant and J. Haugeland, Chicago: University of Chicago Press.

Kuper, A. (1999) *Culture: The Anthropologists' Account*, Cambridge, MA: Harvard University Press.

Kusch, M. (1995) *Psychologism*, London: Routledge.

Ladd, J. (ed.) (1985) *Ethical Relativism*, New York: University Press of America.

Lakoff, G. (1990) *Women, Fire, and Dangerous Things: What Categories Reveal about the Mind*, Chicago: University of Chicago Press.

Larmour, C. (1996) *The Morals of Modernity*, Cambridge: Cambridge University Press.

Latour, B. (1993) *We Have Never Been Modern*, trans. C. Porter, Cambridge, MA: Harvard University Press.

Laudan, L. (1990) *Science and Relativism: Some Key Controversies in the Philosophy of Science*, Chicago: University of Chicago Press.

Leibniz, G. W. (1966) *New Essays: Concerning Human Understanding*, trans. A. Langley, Oxford: Clarendon Press.

Lemmon, E. J. (1965) *Beginning Logic*, London: Nelson.

Lennon, K. and Whitford, M. (1994) *Knowing the Difference: Feminist Perspectives in Epistemology*, London: Routledge.

LePore, E. (ed.) (1986) *Truth and Interpretation*, Oxford: Blackwell.

LePore, E. and McLaughlin, B. (1985) *Actions and Events*, Oxford: Blackwell.

Levine, J. (1993) 'Putnam, Davidson and the Seventeenth-Century Picture of Mind and World', *International Journal of Philosophical Studies*, 1(2): 193–230.

Levison, A. B. (1984) 'Wittgenstein and Logical Laws', *Philosophical Quarterly*, 4: 57–68.

Levy, R. I. (1991) *Tahitians, Mind and Experience in the Society Islands*, Chicago: University of Chicago Press.

Levy-Bruhl, L. (1966) *How Natives Think*, trans. L. Clare, Oxford: Clarendon Press.

—— (1975) *The Notebooks of Lucien Levy-Bruhl*, trans. P. Rivière, Oxford: Blackwell.

Lewis, C. I. (1929) *Mind and the World Order*, New York: Dover Publications.

—— (1983) *Collected Papers*, vol. 1, Oxford: Oxford University Press.

Lewis, C. M. (ed.) (1995) *Relativism and Religion*, London: Macmillan Press.

Lichtenstein, S., Fischoff, B. and Phillips, L. (1982) 'Calibration of Probabilities: The State of the Art to 1980' in D. Kahneman, P. Slovic and A. Tversky (eds) *Judgement under Uncertainty: Heuristics and Biases*, Cambridge: Cambridge University Press: 306–34.

Locke, J. (1959) *An Essay Concerning Human Understanding*, Oxford: Oxford University Press.

Long, A. A. (1974) *Hellenistic Philosophy*, London: Duckworth.

—— (ed.) (1999) *The Cambridge Companion to Early Greek Philosophy*, Cambridge: Cambridge University Press.

Łukasiewicz, J. (1966) *Elements of Mathematical Logic*, Oxford: Pergamon Press.

—— (1971) 'The Law of Non-contradiction in Aristotle', *The Review of Metaphysics*, 24: 485–509.

Lukes, S. (1979) 'Some Problems about Rationality', in B. R. Wilson (ed.) *Rationality*, Oxford: Blackwell: 194–213.

Luntley, M. (1988) *Language, Logic and Experience*, London: Duckworth.

—— (1995) *Reason, Truth and Self: The Postmodern Reconditioned*, London: Routledge.

Lynch, M. P. (1998) *Truth in Context: An Essay on Pluralism and Objectivity*, Cambridge, MA: MIT Press.

—— (2001) *The Nature of Truth*, Cambridge, MA: MIT Press.

Lyons, D. (1982) 'Ethical Relativism and the Problem of Incoherence', in M. Krausz and J. W. Meiland (eds) *Relativism: Cognitive and Moral*, Notre Dame, IL: University of Notre Dame Press: 210–11.

Lyotard, J.-F. (1984) *The Postmodern Condition: A Report on Knowlege*, trans. G. Bennington and B. Massumi, Manchester: Manchester University Press.

McCabe, R., Burns, T. and Priebe, S. (2003) 'Engagement of Patients with Psychosis in the Consultation: Conversation Analytic Study', *British Medical Journal* – bmj_com McCabe et al_ 325 (7373) 1148 Data Supplement – Transcripts and their conventions.htm, 2003.

McCormick, P. J. (ed.) (1996) *Starmaking: Realism, Anti-Realism, and Irrealism*, Cambridge, MA: MIT Press.

MacDonald, G. and Pettit, P. (1981) *Semantics and Social Science*, London: Routledge and Kegan Paul.

McDowell, J. (1986) 'Critical Notice: *Ethics and the Limits of Philosophy* by Bernard Williams', *Mind*, 95: 377–86.

—— (1992) 'Putnam on Mind and Meaning', *Philosophical Topics*, 20(1): 35–48.

—— (1994) *Mind and World*, Cambridge, MA: Harvard University Press.

McGinn, C. (1977) 'Charity, Interpretation, and Belief', *The Journal of Philosophy*, 28: 521–35.

MacIntyre, A. (1984) *After Virtue*, Notre Dame, IL: University of Notre Dame Press.

—— (1985) 'Relativism, Power and Philosophy', *Proceedings and Addresses of the American Philosophical Association*, 59: 5–22.

—— (1988) *Whose Justice? Which Rationality?* London: Duckworth.

—— (1990) *Three Rival Versions of Moral Inquiry*, Notre Dame, IL: University of Notre Dame Press.

Mackie, J. L. (1977) *Ethics: Inventing Right and Wrong*, Harmondsworth: Penguin.

Macklin, R. (1999) *Against Relativism*, Oxford: Oxford University Press.

Madison, G. B. (1991) 'Philosophy without Foundations', *Reason Papers*, 16: 15–44.

Malotki, E. (1983) *Hopi Time: A Linguistic Analysis of the Temporal Categories in the Hopi Language*, Berlin: Mouton.

Malpas, J. (1992) *Donald Davidson and the Mirror of Meaning*, Cambridge: Cambridge University Press.

Mandelbaum, M. (1982) 'Subjective, Objective, and Conceptual Relativism', in M. Krausz and J. Meiland (eds) *Relativism: Cognitive and Moral*, Notre Dame, IL: University of Notre Dame Press: 34–61.

Margolis, J. (1983) 'The Nature and Strategies of Relativism', *Mind* (N.S.), 92(368): 548–67.

—— (1984) *Science without Unity*, Oxford: Blackwell.

—— (1986) *Pragmatism without Foundations: Reconciling Realism and Relativism*, Oxford: Blackwell.

—— (1989) 'The Truth about Relativism', in M. Krausz (ed.) *Relativism: Interpretation and Confrontation*, Notre Dame, IL: University of Notre Dame Press: 232–55.

—— (1991) *The Truth about Relativism*, Oxford: Blackwell.

Martin, J. R. (1989) 'Ideological Critiques and the Philosophy of Science', *Philosophy of Science*, 56: 1–22.

Marx, K. and Engels, F. (1963) *The German Ideology*, New York: International Publishers.

May, S. ([1999] 2002) *Nietzsche's Ethics and his War on 'Morality'*, Oxford: Oxford University Press.

Mead, M. ([1920] 1963) *Growing up in New Guinea*, London: Penguin.

—— ([1928] 1978) *Coming of Age in Samoa*, London: Penguin.

Mead, M. and Metreaux, R. (eds) (1953) *The Study of Culture at a Distance*, Chicago: University of Chicago Press.

Meiland, J. W. (1977) 'The Concept of Relative Truth', *Monist*, 60: 568–82.

—— (1979) 'Bernard Williams' Relativism', *Mind* (N.S.), 88(350): 258–62.

Merquior, J. G. (1985) *Foucault*, London: Fontana Press/Collins.

Miller, C. (2002) 'Realism, Antirealism and Commonsense', in W. P. Alston (ed.) *Realism and Antirealism*, Ithaca, NY: Cornell University Press: 13–25.

Miller, R. W. (1992) 'Realism without Positivism', *Philosophical Topics*, 20(1): 85–114.

Montaigne, M. (1987) *An Apology for Raymond Sebond*, trans. M. A. Screech, London: Penguin.

—— (1991a) 'On Coaches', in M. Montaigne, *Essays:* 330–50.

—— (1991b) 'On the Resemblance of Children to Fathers', in M. Montaigne, *Essays*: 202–31.

—— (1991c) ' On the Cannibals', in M. Montaigne, *Essays*: 79–92.

—— (1991d) *Essays*, trans. M. A. Screech, London: Penguin.

Montesquieu, C. de Secondat ([1748] 1989) *The Spirit of the Laws*, trans. A. M. Cohler, C. M. Basia and H. S. Stone, Cambridge: Cambridge University Press.

—— ([1821] 1964) *The Persian Letters*, trans. G. R. Healy, Indianapolis, IN: Hackett Publishing Company.

Moody-Adams, M. (1997) *Fieldwork in Familiar Places*, Cambridge, MA: Harvard University Press.

Mooney, T. (1999) 'Derrida's Empirical Realism', *Philosophy and Social Criticism*, 25(5): 33–56.

Moore, A. W. (1997) *Points of View*, Oxford: Clarendon Press.

Nagel, T. (1974) 'What is it Like to Be a Bat?', *Philosophical Review*, 83: 435–50.

—— (1986) *The View from Nowhere*, Oxford: Oxford University Press.

Narayan, U. (2000) 'Essence of Culture and a Sense of History: A Feminist Critique of Cultural Essentialism', in U. Narayan and S. Harding (eds) *Decentering the Center: Philosophy for a Multicultural, Postcolonial, and Feminist World*, Bloomington: Indiana University Press: 80–100.

Newton-Smith, W. (1982) 'Relativism and the Possibility of Interpretation', in M. Hollis and S. Lukes (eds) *Rationality and Relativism*, Oxford: Blackwell: 106–22.

Nietzsche, F. ([1878] 1984) *Human all too Human*, trans. R. J. Hollingdale, Cambridge: Cambridge University Press.

—— ([1882, 1887] 1974) *The Gay Science*, trans. W. Kaufmann, New York: Vintage.

—— ([1886] 1996) *Beyond Good and Evil*, trans. W. Kaufmann, New York: Vintage.

—— ([1888] 1967) *Ecce Homo*, trans. W. Kaufmann, New York: Vintage.

—— (1968) *The Will to Power*, trans. W. Kaufmann and R. J. Hollingdale, New York: Vintage.

—— (1994) *On the Genealogy of Morals*, ed. K. Ansell-Pearson, Cambridge: Cambridge University Press.

—— (1999) 'On Truth and Lies in an Extra-Moral Sense', trans. R. Speirs, in R. Guess and R. Speirs (eds) *The Birth of Tragedy and Other Writings*, Cambridge: Cambridge University Press: 139–53.

Nisbett, R. and Ross, L. (1980) *Human Inference: Strategies and Shortcomings of Social Judgment*, Englewood Cliffs, NJ: Prentice-Hall.

Norman Smith, D. (2001) 'The Stigma of Reason: Irrationalism as a Problem for Social Theory', in K. M. Ashman and P. S. Baringer (eds) *After the Science Wars*, London: Routledge: 151–82.

Norris, C. (1985) *The Contest of Faculties*, New York: Methuen.

—— (1991) *Deconstruction: Theory and Practice*, London: Routledge.

—— (1993) *The Truth about Postmodernism*, Oxford: Blackwell.

—— (1996) *Reclaiming Truth: Contribution to a Critique of Cultural Relativism*, London: Lawrence and Wishart.

—— (1997a) *Against Relativism: Philosophy of Science, Deconstruction and Critical Theory*, Oxford: Blackwell.

—— (1997b) *New Idols of the Cave: On the Limits of Anti-realism*, Manchester: Manchester University Press.

Nozick, R. (1993) *The Nature of Rationality* Princeton, NJ: Princeton University Press.

—— (2001) *Invariances: The Structure of the Objective World*, Cambridge, MA: Harvard University Press.

Nussbaum, M. C. (2000) 'Women and Cultural Universals', in M. Baghramian and A. Ingram (eds) *Pluralism: Essays on the Philosophy and Politics of Diversity*, London: Routledge: 197–227.

Nussbaum, M. C. and Sen, A. (eds) (1993) *The Quality of Life*, Oxford: Oxford University Press.

Nye, A. (1990) *Words of Power: A Feminist Reading of the History of Logic*, London: Routledge.

O'Grady, P. (2002) *Relativism*, Chesham: Acumen Press.

O'Shea, J. (2000) 'Sources of Pluralism in William James', in M. Baghramian and A. Ingram (eds) *Pluralism: Essays on the Philosophy and Politics of Diversity*, London: Routledge: 17–43.

Papineau, D. (1978) *For Science in the Social Sciences*, London: Macmillan.

—— (1987) *Reality and Representation*, Oxford: Blackwell.

—— (2000) 'The Evolution of Knowledge', in P. Carruthers and A. Chamberlain (eds) *Evolution and the Human Mind*, Cambridge: Cambridge University Press: 73–95.

Patterson, O. (1973–4) 'Guilt, Relativism, and Black–White Relations', *The American Scholar*, 43(1): 122–32.

Peacocke, C. (1986) *Thoughts: An Essay on Content*, Oxford: Blackwell.

Phillips, D. Z. (1995a) 'Where Are the Gods Now?' in *Relativism and Religion*, ed. C. M. Lewis, London: Macmillan: 1–15.

—— (1995b) 'Philosophers' Clothes', in *Relativism and Religion*, ed. C. M. Lewis, London: Macmillan: 135–53.

Piatelli-Palmarini, M. (1989) 'Evolution, Selection and Cognition', *Cognition*, 31: 1–44.

Pinker, S. (1994) *The Language Instinct*, London: Penguin.

—— (1997) *How the Mind Works*, New York: W. W. Norton.

Plato (1997a) *Plato: Complete Works*, ed. John M. Cooper and D. S. Hutchinson, Cambridge: Hackett Publishing Co.

—— (1997b) *Cratylus*, trans. C. D. C. Reeve, in Plato (1997a): 101–56.

—— (1997c) *Euthydemus*, trans. R. K. Sprague, in Plato (1997a): 708–45.

—— (1997d) *Meno*, trans. G. M. A. Grube, in Plato (1997a): 870–97.

—— (1997e) *Protagoras*, trans. S. Lombardo and K. Bell, in Plato (1997a): 746–90.

—— (1997f) *The Sophist*, trans. N. P. Whine, in Plato (1997a): 235–93.

—— (1997g) *Theaetetus*, trans. M. J. Levett, rev. Myles Burnyeat, in Plato (1997a): 157–234.

Plumwood, V. (1993) *Feminism and the Mastery of Nature*, New York: Routledge.

Politis, V. (forthcoming, 2004) *Routledge Philosophy Guidebook to Aristotle and the Metaphysics*, London: Routledge.

Pompa, L. (1990) *Vico: A Study of the 'New Science'*, 2nd edn, Cambridge: Cambridge University Press.

Popkin, R. (2003) *The History of Scepticism*, new revised edn, Oxford: Oxford University Press.

Popper, K. R. (1963) *Conjectures and Refutations*, New York: Basic Books.

—— (1994) *The Myth of the Framework: In Defence of Science and Rationality*, London: Routledge.

Potter, E. (1993) 'Gender and Epistemic Negotiation' in L. Alcoff and E. Potter (eds) *Feminist Epistemologies*, London: Routledge: 161–86.

Preston, J. (1997) *Feyerabend: Philosophy, Science and Society*, Cambridge: Polity Press.

Price, H. (1992) 'Metaphysical Pluralism', *Journal of Philosophy*, 89(8): 387–409.

Priest, G. (1979) 'The Logic of Paradox', *Journal of Philosophical Logic*, 8: 219–41.

—— (1987) *In Contradiction: A Study of the Transconsistent*, Dordrecht: Kluwer.

Priest, G., Routley, R. and Norman, J. (eds) (1986) *Paraconsistent Logic*, Dordrecht: Kluwer.

Putnam, H. (1978) *Meaning and the Moral Sciences*, London: Routledge.

—— (1979a) 'The Analytic and the Synthetic', in *Mind, Language and Reality: Philosophical Papers*, vol. 2, Cambridge: Cambridge University Press: 33–69.

—— (1979b) 'Language and Reality', in *Mind, Language and Reality: Philosophical Papers*, vol. 2, Cambridge: Cambridge University Press: 272–90.

—— (1979c) *Mathematics, Matter and Method: Philosophical Papers*, vol. 1, 2nd edn, Cambridge: Cambridge University Press.

—— (1979d) 'The Meaning of "Meaning"', in *Mind, Language and Reality:*

Philosophical Papers, vol. 2, Cambridge: Cambridge University Press: 215–71.

—— (1981) *Reason, Truth and History*, Cambridge: Cambridge University Press.

—— (1983a) *Realism and Reason: Philosophical Papers*, vol. 3, Cambridge: Cambridge University Press.

—— (1983b) 'Why Reason Can't Be Naturalised', in H. Putnam (1983a): 229–47.

—— (1987) *The Many Faces of Realism*, La Salle, IL: Open Court.

—— (1989) 'Truth and Convention: On Davidson's Refutation of Conceptual Relativism', in M. Krausz (ed.) *Relativism: Interpretation and Confrontation*, Notre Dame, IL: University of Notre Dame Press: 173–81.

—— (1990) *Realism with a Human Face*, ed. and intro. J. Conant, Cambridge, MA: Harvard University Press.

—— (1992a) *Renewing Philosophy*, Cambridge, MA: Harvard University Press.

—— (1992b) 'Replies', *Philosophical Topics*, 20(1): 347–65.

—— (1994) *Words and Life*, ed. J. Conant, Cambridge, MA: Harvard University Press.

—— (2000) *The Threefold Cord: Mind, Body, and World*, Cambridge, MA: Harvard University Press.

—— (2002) *The Collapse of the Fact/Value Dichotomy*, Cambridge, MA: Harvard University Press.

Quine, W. V. O. (1953) *From a Logical Point of View*, Cambridge, MA: Harvard University Press.

—— ([1959] 1974) *Methods of Logic*, 3rd edn, London: Routledge.

—— (1960) *Word and Object*, Cambridge, MA: MIT Press.

—— (1969) 'Speaking of Objects', in *Ontological Relativity and Other Essays*, New York: Columbia University Press: 1–25.

—— (1970) *Philosophy of Logic*, Englewood Cliffs, NJ: Prentice Hall.

—— (1974) *The Roots of Reference*, La Salle, IL: Open Court.

—— (1975) 'On Empirically Equivalent Systems of the World', *Erkenntnis*, 9: 313–28.

—— (1976) *The Ways of Paradox and Other Essays*, Cambridge, MA: Harvard University Press.

—— (1981a) 'On the Very Idea of a Third Dogma', in *Theories and Things*, Cambridge, MA: Harvard University Press: 38–42.

—— (1981b) *Theories and Things*, Cambridge, MA: Harvard University Press.

—— (1984) 'Relativism and Absolutism', *Monist*, 67, 293–6.

—— (1992) *The Pursuit of Truth*, revised edn, Cambridge, MA: Harvard University Press.

—— (1993) 'Three Indeterminacies', in R. Barrett and R. Gibson (eds) *Perspectives on Quine*, Oxford: Blackwell: 1–15.

Quinn, P. L. (1995a) 'Comments', in C. M. Lewis (ed.) *Relativism and Religion*, London: Macmillan: 111–18.

—— (1995b) 'Religious Pluralism and Religious Relativism', in C. M. Lewis (ed.) *Relativism and Religion*, London: Macmillan: 35–51.

Ramberg, Bjorn T. (1989) *Donald Davidson's Philosophy of Language*, Oxford: Blackwell.

Reichenbach, H. (1957) *The Philosophy of Space and Time*, New York: Dover.

Rescher, N. and Brandom, R. B. (1980) *The Logic of Inconsistency*, Oxford: Blackwell.

Rorty, R. (1979) *Philosophy and the Mirror of Nature*, Princeton, NJ: Princeton University Press.

—— (1982) *Consequences of Pragmatism*, Minneapolis: University of Minnesota Press.

—— (1985) 'Solidarity or Objectivity?' in J. Rajchman and C. West (eds) *Post-Analytic Philosophy*, New York: Columbia University Press: 3–20.

—— (1990) *Contingency, Irony and Solidarity*, Cambridge: Cambridge University Press.

—— (1991a) *Objectivity, Relativism, and Truth: Philosophical Papers*, vol. 1, Cambridge: Cambridge University Press.

—— (1991b) *Essays on Heidegger and Others: Philosophical Papers*, vol. 2, Cambridge: Cambridge University Press.

—— (1998) *Truth and Progress: Philosophical Papers*, vol 3, Cambridge: Cambridge University Press.

—— (2000) 'Universality of Truth', in R. B. Brandom (ed.) *Rorty and his Critics*, Oxford: Blackwell: 1–30.

Routley, F. R. and Meyer, R. K. (1972) 'The Semantics of Entailment', *Journal of Philosophical Logic*, 1: 205–23.

Russell, B. and Whitehead, A. N. (1913) *Principia Mathematica*, Cambridge: Cambridge University Press.

Ryan, A. (ed.) (1973) *The Philosophy of Social Explanation*, Oxford: Oxford University Press.

Ryle, G. (1954) *Dilemmas*, Cambridge: Cambridge University Press.

—— (1979) *On Thinking*, ed. K. Kolenda, Oxford: Blackwell.

Sale, K. (1990) *The Conquest of Paradise*, London: Macmillan.

Samuels, R., Stich, S. and Bishop, M. (2002) 'Ending the Rationality Wars: How to Make Disputes about Human Rationality Disappear', in R. Elio (ed.) *Common Sense, Reasoning and Rationality*, Vancouver Studies in Cognitive Science, vol. 11, New York: Oxford University Press: 236–68.

Samuels, R., Stich, S. and Faucher, L. (forthcoming, 2004) 'Reason and Rationality', in I. Niiniluoto, M. Sintonen and J. Wolenski (eds) *Handbook of Epistemology*, Dordrecht: Kluwer: 1–50.

Samuels, R., Stich, S. and Tremoulet, P. (1999) 'Rethinking Rationality: From Bleak Implications to Darwinian Modules', in E. LePore and Z. Pylyshyn (eds) *Rutgers University Invitation to Cognitive Science*, Oxford: Blackwell: 74–120.

Sandel, M. (ed.) (1984) *Liberalism and its Critics*, Oxford: Blackwell.

—— (1996) *Democracy's Discontent*, Cambridge, MA: Harvard University Press.

Sapir, E. ([1949] 1985) *Selected Writings in Language, Culture, and Personality*, ed. D. G. Mandelbaum, Berkeley: University of California Press.

Saussure, F. de (1974) *Course in General Linguistics*, London: Fontana.

Sayre-McCord, G. (ed.) (1988) *Essays on Moral Realism*, Ithaca, NY: Cornell University Press.

Scanlon, T. M. ([1976] 2001) 'Fear of Relativism', in P. Moser and T. Carson (eds) *Moral Relativism: A Reader*, New York: Oxford University Press: 142–63.

Schrift, A. D. (1995) *Nietzsche's French Legacy*, London: Routledge.

Searle, J. (1995) *The Construction of Reality*, London: Penguin.

Sextus Empiricus (1994) *Outlines of Pyrrhonism*, trans. J. Annas and J. Barnes, Cambridge: Cambridge University Press.

Shapere, D. ([1966] 1981) 'Meaning and Scientific Change', in I. Hacking (ed.) *Scientific Revolutions*, Oxford: Oxford University Press: 28–59.

Sharrock, W. and Read, R. (2002) *Kuhn: Philosopher of Scientific Revolution*, Cambridge: Polity Press.

Sheffler, I. (1967) *Science and Subjectivity*, Indianapolis, IN: Bobbs-Merrill.

Shklar, J. N. (1987) *Montesquieu*, Oxford: Oxford University Press.

Shweder, R. A. (1989) 'Post-Nietzschean Anthropology: The Idea of Multiple Objective Worlds', in M. Krausz (ed.) *Relativism: Interpretation and Confrontation*, Notre Dame, IL: University of Notre Dame Press: 99–139.

—— (1991) *Thinking through Cultures*, Cambridge, MA: Harvard University Press.

Siegel, H. (1987) *Relativism Refuted: A Critique of Contemporary Epistemological Relativism*, Dordrecht: Reidel.

—— (1992) 'Relativism', in J. Dancy and E. Sosa (eds) *A Companion to Epistemology*, Oxford: Blackwell: 428–30.

—— (1996) 'Reason and Rationality' in J. J. Chambliss (ed.) *Philosophy of Education: An Encyclopedia*, New York: Garland Publishing: 536–9.

—— (forthcoming, 2004) 'Relativism', in I. Niiniluoto, M. Sintonen and J. Wolenski (eds) *Handbook of Epistemology*, Dordrecht: Kluwer.

Smith, B. H. (1997) *Belief and Resistance: Dynamics of Contemporary Intellectual Controversy*, Cambridge, MA: Harvard University Press.

Sokal, A. ([1996] 1998) 'Transgressing the Boundaries: Toward a Transformative Hermeneutics of Quantum Gravity', in A. Sokal and J. Bricmont (1998) *Intellectual Impostures*, London: Profile Books: 199–240.

Sokal, A. and Bricmont, J. (1998) *Intellectual Impostures*, London: Profile Books.

Sperber, D. (1982) 'Apparently Irrational Beliefs', in M. Hollis and S. Lukes (eds) *Rationality and Relativism*, Oxford: Blackwell: 149–80.

Stein, E. (1996) *Without Good Reason*, Oxford: Oxford University Press.

Stich, S. (1990) *The Fragmentation of Reason*, Cambridge, MA: MIT Press.

—— (1998) 'Epistemic Relativism', *Routledge Encyclopaedia of Philosophy*, London: Routledge.

Sumner, W. G. (1906) *Folkways*, New York: Dover.

Sutherland, S. (1994) *The Enemy Within*, London: Penguin.

Swoyer, C. (1982) 'True *For*', in M. Krausz and J. Meiland (eds) *Relativism: Cognitive and Moral*, Notre Dame, IL: University of Notre Dame Press: 84–108.

—— (1988) 'Relativism and Representation', *Philosophy and Phenomenological Research*, 49(1): 151–5.

Tarski, A. (1969) 'Truth and Proof', *Scientific American*, 194: 63–77.

—— (1983) *Logic, Semantics and Mathematics: Papers from 1923 to 1938*, ed. and trans. J. H. Woodger, Indianapolis, IN: Hackett Publishing Company.

Ten, C. L. (ed.) (1994) *The Nineteenth Century*, Routledge History of Philosophy, vol. 7, London: Routledge.

Throop, W. M. (1989) 'Relativism and Error: Putnam's Lessons for the Relativist', *Philosophy and Phenomenological Research*, 49(4): 675–86.

Thugard, P. and Nisbett, R. E. (1983) 'Rationality and Charity', *Philosophy of Science*, 50: 250–67.

Todorov, T. (1993) *On Human Diversity*, trans. C. Porter, Cambridge, MA: Harvard University Press.

Tooby, J. and Cosmides, L. (1992) 'The Psychological Foundations of Culture', in J. Barkow, L. Cosmides and J. Tooby (eds) *The Adapted Mind: Evolutionary Psychology and the Generation of Culture*, Oxford: Oxford University Press: 19–136.

Trevor-Roper, H. (1969) *The European Witch-Craze of the Sixteenth and Seventeenth Centuries*, London: Penguin Books.

Trigg, R. (1991) 'Wittgenstein and Social Science', in A. Phillips Griffiths (ed.) *Wittgenstein Centenary Essays*, Cambridge: Cambridge University Press: 209–22.

—— (1993) *Rationality and Science: Can Science Explain Everything?* Oxford: Blackwell.

Turner, T. (1997) 'Human Rights, Human Difference: Anthropology's Contribution to an Emancipatory Cultural Politics', *Journal of Anthropological Research*, 53: 273–92.

Tversky, A. and Kahneman, D. (1986) 'Rational Choice and the Framing Decision', *Journal of Business*, 59(4): 251–78.

Tylor, E. B. (1871) *Primitive Culture*, London: John Murray.

Unwin, N. (1985) 'Relativism and Moral Complacency', *Philosophy*, 60: 205–14.

Vico, G. ([1774] 1984) *New Science*, trans. T. G. Bergin and M. H. Fisch, Ithaca, NY: Cornell University Press.

Voltaire, F.-M. ([1771] 1994) 'Man', in *Voltaire: Political Writings*, trans. and ed. D. Williams, Cambridge: Cambridge University Press.

Warnock, M. (1978) 'Nietzsche's Conception of Truth', in M. Pasley (ed.) *Nietzsche: Imagery and Thought*, Berkeley: University of California Press: 33–63.

Wason, P. (1968) 'Reasoning about a Rule', *Quarterly Journal of Experimental Psychology*, 20: 273–81.

Weber, M. (1964) *The Theory of Social and Economic Organization*, Glencoe, IL: Free Press.

Weinberg, J., Nichols, S. and Stich, S. (2001) 'Normativity and Epistemic Intuitions', *Philosophical Topics*, 29: 429–60.

Wellman, C. (1963) 'The Ethical Implications of Cultural Relativity', *The Journal of Philosophy*, 60(7): 169–84.

Wellmer, A. (1998) 'Truth, Contingency and Modernity', in A. Wellmer, *Endgames*, Cambridge, MA: MIT Press: 137–54.

Westermarck, E. (1912) *The Origin and Development of Moral Ideas*, London: Macmillan.

—— (1932) *Ethical Relativity*, New York: Harcourt.

White, H. (1977) 'Historical Emplotment and the Problem of Truth', in K. Jenkins (ed.) *The Postmodern History Reader*, London: Routledge: 392–6.

Whorf, B. L. (1956) *Language, Thought and Reality*, Cambridge, MA: MIT Press.

Wiggins, D. (1991) 'Moral Cognitivism, Moral Relativism and Motivating Moral Beliefs', *Proceedings of the Aristotelian Society*, 91: 61–85.

Williams, B. (1972) *Morality: An Introduction to Ethics*, Cambridge: Cambridge University Press.

—— (1982) *Moral Luck*, Cambridge: Cambridge University Press.

—— (1985) *Ethics and the Limits of Philosophy*, London: Fontana Press/ Collins.

Wilson, B. R. (ed.) (1979) *Rationality*, Oxford: Blackwell.

Wilson, J. Q. (1993) *The Moral Sense*, New York: The Free Press.

Wilson, N. L. (1959) 'Substances without Substrata', *Review of Metaphysics*, 12: 521–39.

Winch, P. (1958) *The Idea of a Social Science and its Relation to Philosophy*, London: Routledge.

—— (1964) 'Understanding a Primitive Society', *American Philosophical Quarterly* 1: 307–24 (reprinted in Winch 1970).

—— (1970) *Ethics and Action*, London: Routledge.

Wittgenstein, L. (1922) *Tractatus Logico-Philosophicus*, London: Routledge and Kegan Paul.

—— (1958) *Philosophical Investigations*, Oxford: Blackwell.

—— (1967) *Zettle*, Oxford: Blackwell.

—— (1968) *On Certainty*, Oxford: Blackwell.

—— (1971) *Philosophical Grammar*, Oxford: Blackwell.

—— (1975) *Philosophical Remarks*, Oxford: Blackwell.

—— (1976) *Wittgenstein's Lectures on the Foundation of Mathematics*, Hassocks: Harvester Press.

—— (1978) *Remarks on the Foundations of Mathematics*, Oxford: Oxford University Press.

—— (1980) *Culture and Value*, Oxford: Blackwell.

—— (1993) 'Remarks on Frazer's *Golden Bough*', in J. Klagge and A. Nordmann (eds) *Ludwig Wittgenstein: Philosophical Occasions 1912–1951*, Indianapolis, IN: Hackett.

Wolterstorff, N. (1995a) 'Will Narrativity Work as a Linchpin? Reflections on the Hermeneutic of Hans Frei', in C. M. Lewis (ed.) *Relativism and Religion*, London: Macmillan: 119–24.

—— (1995b) 'Response', in C. M. Lewis (ed.) *Relativism and Religion*, London: Macmillan: 71–107.

Wong, D. (1984) *Moral Relativity*, Berkeley: University of California Press.

Wright, C. (1980) *Wittgenstein on the Foundations of Mathematics*, London: Duckworth.

—— (2001) 'On Being in a Quandary: Relativism, Vagueness, Logical Revisionism', *Mind* (N.S.) 110(437): 45–98.

Zadeh, L. A. (1975) 'Fuzzy Logic and Approximate Reasoning', *Synthese*, 30: 407–28.

Zammito, J. H. (2002) *Kant, Herder, and the Birth of Anthropology*, Chicago: University of Chicago Press.

Index